Faith, Love, Hope

A History of the Unitas Fratrum

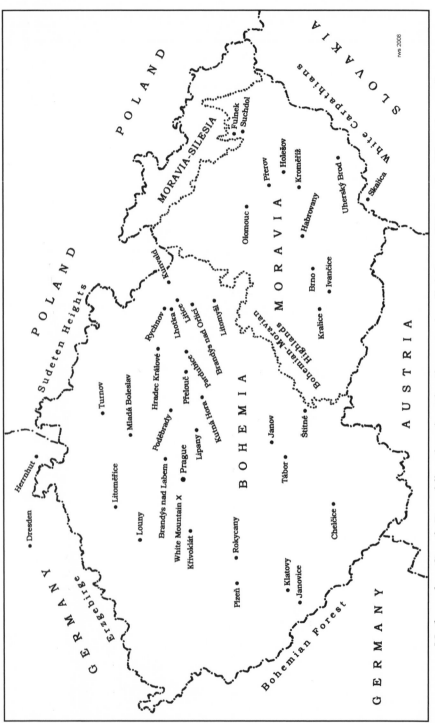

Modern-day Czech Republic, showing the three major divisions of Bohemia, Moravia, and Moravia-Silesia, with main sites connected with the history of the Unitas Fratrum.

Faith, Love, Hope

A History of the Unitas Fratrum

C. Daniel Crews

Moravian Archives
457 S. Church Street
Winston-Salem, North Carolina
www.MoravianArchives.org

Library of Congress Control Number 2008927022

ISBN 0-9719411-3-0

Moravian Archives
457 S. Church Street
Winston-Salem, North Carolina
www.MoravianArchives.org

Dedication

To all those members of the Unity in all its years whose faith, love, and hope have provided inspiring witness to the gracious will of God the Father for our salvation, the saving work of Christ, and the gifts of the Holy Spirit. In these essentials we are united.

C. Daniel Crews, Archivist

Contents

Chapters

Appendices

Maps, Pictures, & Designs

Maps

Pictures

Picture Sources

C. Daniel Crews: pages 31, 97.

Internet: pages 294 (Vok), 333.

Moravian Archives, Winston-Salem, North Carolina: pages 46, 66, 236, 357, 375.

Moravian Music Foundation: pages 247, 303.

Joseph Th. Müller, *Geschichte der Böhmischen Brüder* 3 vols. (Herrnhut: Missionsbuchhandlung, 1922, 1931): pages 181, 207, 261, 305.

A. H. Mumford, *Our Church's Story* (London: Wightman & Co., 1911): 40, 70, 71, 81, 91, 223, 249, 343, 345, 351, 382. The drawings in Mumford were done by John Carey, son of a Moravian minister and a noted illustrator of the late 19th and early 20th centuries.

Edmund de Schweinitz, *History of the Church Known as the Unitas Fratrum,* 2nd (reprint) ed. (Bethlehem, Pa.: Moravian Publication Concern, 1901): pages 38, 178, 294 (Budova), 349.

Unitas Fratrum Moravian Church in Pictures. (Prague: 1957). This beautiful and informative 500th anniversary picture book, published by the Czech Province of the renewed Unity, cites the following sources: E. M. Haejčl: page 101. Ministry of Education and Culture, Prague: pages 61, 88, 104, 119, 123, 151, 187, 201, 212, 277. National Gallery, Prague: page 365. University Library, Prague: 135, 138, 148, 155, 165, 171, 194, 229, 267, 273, 282, 284, 294 (Žerotín), 311, 314, 318, 321, 326, 328, 370.

Designs

The designs throughout this book are taken from the 1954 Czech Moravian hymnal and are based on designs in the 1618 hymnal, the last Unity hymnal before the Thirty Years War.

Preface

The purpose of this book is to provide a coherent, readable, and reliable history of the Unitas Fratrum (Unity of Brethren) in Bohemia, Moravia, and Poland from the 15th to the 17th centuries. Coming out of the Middle Ages, the Unity built on its Czech Hussite heritage. Persecuted and banished throughout almost all its history, the Unity nevertheless developed a rich theological literature and disciplined devotional life of its own amidst the changing world in which it grew up. This is a great story, and it deserves to be more widely known and enjoyed today.

The year 2007, celebrated by the modern Moravian Church as its 550th anniversary, seemed a good year to start this project. March 1, the traditional day of the Unity's founding, seemed an appropriate day on which to begin. Our Renewed Moravian Church is not the only heir of the Unity's heritage, and we gladly share its legacy with other "Hussites" in the Czech Republic and elsewhere. Some of this book stems from our "Herrnhuter" background, but it is intended for all who value or simply want to know more about the Unity in the lands of its birth and initial development.

A glance at the table of contents will reveal that we do not get to the founding of the Unity until chapter six. There are sound reasons for this. The Unity did not rise out of nothing. It cannot be understood aside from its Hussite roots. It seemed wise then to include chapters on John Hus and the Hussites before reaching the establishing of the Unity itself. And Hus and the Hussites make no sense unless we have some appreciation of their background in Czech history, and that background is grounded on the development of the Western Christian Church and the early Christian Church from the time of the apostles through the Middle Ages. This is why the first chapters are in a sense "from Jesus to John Hus." Readers may, of course, plunge in wherever they feel comfortable.

I have tried to keep the writing style light enough to be enjoyable as a "good read." At the same, time I have worked to provide accurate and reasonably complete details for people with more academic interests. This explains why the book has both footnotes and endnotes. The footnotes contain additional or amusing information that does not fit into the narrative itself. The endnotes provide more academic citations for readers who need to know where the information comes from, or other sources where they can go for more details. Readers who are not so concerned with that can simply skip the endnote pages and continue with the story itself.

Main sources for this history are Rudolf Říčan's *The History of the Unity of Brethren* and Joseph Theo. Müller's *Geschichte der Böhmischen Brüder*. Říčan taught at the University of Prague, and wrote his history in 1957 as *Dějiny jednoty bratrské*. It is still the standard history of the Unity in Czech. I translated it into English in 1992. Müller served as archivist of the Renewed Moravian Church. His monumental three-volume work of some 1,600 pages appeared from 1922 to 1931. It has not been translated into English. Both Říčan and Müller made great use of primary sources composed by the Unity itself. These are what the Unity called its *Akty* and *Dekrety*, which we know as the Lissa Folios, from the place of their discovery in the 1800s (see chapter 21 below). Müller made a complete translation of these into German, and for his account generally summarized (and often quoted *verbatim*) these documents directly. Around 1970 Dr. Andrew Slaby translated a considerable block of these documents into English for the Moravian Archives in Bethlehem, Pennsylvania. I have been able to consult those materials as well. From time to time, Bishop Edmund de Schweinitz's delightful but dated *History of the Church Known as the Unitas Fratrum* (1885; 2nd ed. (reprinting) 1901) provides colorful insights as well.

Other scholarly writings on aspects of the Unity's background and development have been consulted. Articles in *Church History* and the University of Prague's *Communio Viatorum* were helpful, as were other books and articles by "non-Moravians." Particular mention should be made of Zdeněk David's book-length study *Finding the Middle Way*, which provides unique insights from the perspective of the Utraquists, who were often Hussite competitors with the Unity. Students looking for scholarly sources to pursue further will find the bibliography helpful.

Special thanks are due to Dr. Craig D. Atwood, Moravian minister and professor at Wake Forest University. Craig has written a scholarly study of the Unity's theological heritage, which will soon be published by a major university press. At his invitation, I was able to offer him bits of advice as his work was in preparation. He has more than repaid that by a careful reading of the first draft of these chapters. Not only has he saved me a few embarrassing factual errors, but his other suggestions have helped the flow and understandability of my work. (All errors remain mine, of course.) Craig and I consider our works as complementary to one another.

Thanks are also due to many others: To my colleague Richard Starbuck, assistant archivist of the Moravian Archives, Southern Province, for his painstaking and meticulous editing, indexing, and formatting; to Dr. Paul Peucker and Lanie Williamson of the Moravian Archives in Bethlehem; and to the Archives Board of the Moravian Church in America, Southern Province, who encouraged the writing of this work and allowed me the time to do it. The list goes on — you and God know who you are.

Finally, many thanks are due to the readers of our previous works on Moravian history and theology. Without your enthusiasm and questions of "What's coming out next?" there would have been little reason to write. May these pages provide enjoyable reading, useful information, and fuel to the fire to know more.

C. Daniel Crews, Archivist
Moravian Church in America, Southern Province
Winston-Salem, North Carolina
April 2008

How to Pronounce Czech

Czech has some sounds that are difficult for English speakers, though only a couple will cause much trouble. On the other hand, it is consistent and has no silent letters, so once you learn to pronounce the letters, you can pronounce them wherever you meet them. The stress in Czech words is always on the first syllable, and that helps too. That is, the first syllable is always pronounced more strongly than the others.

Czech has several accent marks, developed by John Hus, to assist in pronunciation. These let you know which vowels are long, and avoids strings of consonants to get one sound, as is the case with some other Slavic languages. The first of these is the ´ (accent), which marks a long vowel. The uniquely Czech one is the ˘ (haček), which generally indicates a softening of the sound. For details on these and a couple more, see below.

Vowels

Czech vowels are generally pronounced like those of the Latin or Romance languages (French, Italian, Spanish, etc.).

Long "a" (á) is "ah" like the "a" in father
Short "a" is "uh" like the "u" in put
Long "e" (é) is "ay" like the "a" in cake
Short "e" is "eh" like the "e" in met
Long "i" (í) is "ee" like the e's in meet
Short "i" is "ih" like the "i" in mitt
Long "o" (ó) (often "ou") is "oh" like the "o" in note
Short "o" is " o" like the "o" in offal

Long "u" (ú or ů[1]) is "ooh" like the "oo" in tool

Short "u" is a shorter "ooh" like the "ui" in fruit

In addition:

"y" (or "ý") is sometimes used as a vowel, and is pronounced like "i" and "í"

"r" also sometimes functions as a vowel, pronounced "ur" like the "ur" in furl

"e" with the "haček" (ě) acquires a "y" lilt, pronounced "yeh"

Consonants

Czech consonants are generally pronounced as in English.

An exception is "c," which is never like a "k" as sometimes in English. Neither is it another way of spelling "s." Instead it is always a "ts," as in "Tsar."

Another exception is "ch," which is considered one letter in Czech. It is pronounced like the German "ch," sort of a cross between a gutteral "k" and a cat hissing.

"j" is pronounced like "y" in "yes" or "yawn."

"w" is not a native Czech letter. When it occurs in foreign names, etc., it is pronounced "v."

If consonants have special accents, or come before certain vowels, there are a few changes:

"d," "n," and "t" acquire a "y" sound after them when they come before "i" or "í." So "dí" is pronounced "duh-yee" closely run together, and "ni" is pronounced "nuh-yih"

"n" with the "haček" (ň) also acquires the "y" lilt before other vowels and consonants, pronounced "nuh-yeh"

---

[1] The "°" is used instead of "˙" with "u" in some cases. You only need to recognize it when you see it.

"d" and "t" may do the same, but because of the shape of the letters, the " ˇ " is not used, and they are followed by a " ' " instead (ď and ť)

"č" is pronounced "ch" as in "church"

"š" is pronounced "sh" as in "shush"

"ž" is pronounced like the "z " in azure" or the "s" in "pleasure"

"ř" is the tricky one. The closest we can get is "urzh" or "ursh." Don't worry. Even Czech children have trouble learning this one.

A few examples:

pátek = **pah**-tek

matko = **Muht**-koh

milé = **mill-**ay

beranek = **be**-ran-ek

milost = **mill**-ost

bílý = **bee**-lee

opět = **o**-puhyet

doufam = **Doe**-fam

čísti = **chees**-tyee

tiše = **tuhyi-** sheh

ženy = **zheh**-nee

bratři = **bruht**-ursh-ih

jednota = **yed**-noh-tuh

dětinsky = **duhyet**-in-skee

ulice = **uh**-lih-tse

půl = **pool**

Faith, Love, Hope

A History of the Unitas Fratrum

Chapter 1

The Broad Stream

*The Rise and Development of the Medieval Church
and Western Feudal Society* 1
A.D. 33-1415

> When the day of Pentecost had come, they were all
> together in one place. And suddenly from heaven
> there came a sound like the rush of a violent wind,
> and it filled the entire house where they were sitting.
> Divided tongues, as of fire, appeared among them,
> and a tongue rested on each of them. All of them were
> filled with the Holy Spirit and began to speak in other
> languages, as the Spirit gave them ability.
>
> Acts 2:1-4 (NRSV)

From this beginning on the day of Pentecost, fifty days
after Easter, the Christian church began its mission of
proclaiming the word of the resurrected Christ throughout the world. As related in the New Testament, the church
spread from Jerusalem, first into the surrounding countries,
and then farther into the lands around the Mediterranean Sea.
This spread was helped by the "Pax Romana," the condition of
relative peace, prosperity, and stability imposed by the Roman
Empire, which stretched from the Atlantic Ocean to the
Euphrates River and the German border to northern Africa.

The spread of Christianity even in its earliest days was met
with controversy and difficulty, both inside and outside the
church. In a council held in Jerusalem (Acts 11), the followers
of Christ had to decide whether it would remain a Jewish sect,

devoutly observant of the dietary laws and other restrictions of the Old Testament, or whether it would reach out to all humanity as a truly world religion. Paul, the convert apostle, championed the wider view, while James of Jerusalem maintained the centrality of the Law. The apostle Peter and presumably many other Christians wavered between the two. Ultimately the Pauline view won out, and Christian communities, each with its own emphases and interests, began to proliferate throughout the Roman Empire, encompassing many races, wealthy and poor, slave and free.

Rome's tolerant religious pluralism worked in Christianity's favor, though even in New Testament times Christians' insistence on one God and Lord to the exclusion of all others brought opposition from many. The silversmiths associated with the temple of Diana in Ephesus (Acts 19:23-24) provide one example. Rome itself, which in the earlier writings of the New Testament was seen as a benevolent force for order in the world, came to pose a threat to the church as Christians grew in number and resolved not to show "proper" reverence to the emperor as divine. The story is still told that Emperor Nero blamed Christians for the fire that destroyed Rome in A.D. 64, and that as a result Peter and Paul, along with many faithful, were martyred. By the time the book of Revelation was written near the end of the first century, Rome was portrayed as evil and oppressive.

Throughout the second century Christianity remained an illegal religion, and sporadic persecutions broke out, mostly local in nature. Apologists for the new religion, such as Aristides and Justin Martyr, wrote reasoned defenses for it, and while they had little effect on opponents of Christianity, they did serve for further development of the church's understanding of itself.

The church met challenges from within as well. Gnosticism, which saw the material world as evil and which claimed a special "knowledge" given only to the privileged few, was a serious threat in the middle of the second century, as were the claims of a man named Montanus, who purported to be a new vessel of revelation from the Holy Spirit superior to Christ. The result of such divisive challenges was a unifying spirit. The power of bishops who presided over various areas was strengthened. The term "catholic," meaning "universal," came to distinguish the "true" and "orthodox" church from "heretics." And a move toward greater uniformity spread among the scattered Christian communities. By the year 200 the formation of an authoritative canon of New Testament scripture was well under way (though the final list was not settled for another two centuries).

In addition, the importance of the bishop of Rome was on the rise. This trend was aided by Rome's prominence as the empire's capital, and the destruction of Jerusalem again in 135. While strong bishops were active in Rome, Christian leaders in the East failed to rise to prominence. Moreover, the Roman Church's position, particularly in the western part of the empire, was enhanced by the fact that it alone among the western cities could claim direct founding by the apostles. Then too, Rome had provided firm and authoritative leadership in the Gnostic and Montanist controversies, and its baptismal creed was soon adopted as the Apostles' Creed. By the end of the second century, the Roman Church's practice of always celebrating Easter on a Sunday rather than on a fixed calendar date predominated over the customs of several "older" Christian centers in the East. Theologians such as Irenaeus (d. 200?) and Cyprian (d. 258) expanded and helped standardize the church's theological expression. Tertullian (d. 225?) began writing theology in Latin rather than Greek, which up to that point had been used even in Rome.* Ultimately, the prominence of the Roman Church was strengthened by its developing definite views of the Trinity and Christ, views that were later recognized by most Christians, while opinions in the East were much more fluid.

---

* Tertullian is often called the "Father of Latin theology," and besides making important theological contributions on the nature of the Trinity, laid great stress on moral living as essential for believers.

Throughout the third century the church continued to expand in the West, particularly in Spain, Gaul (modern France), and Latin-speaking North Africa, though it was still officially illegal and subject to occasional short-lived persecutions. It was not until the last half of the century that persecutions became universal and systematic. This was in part connected with the 1000th anniversary of Rome's founding, which was celebrated in 248. By this time the empire was feeling strains of internal dispute and external threats, and a general response was to look back to the "good old times" and gods of antiquity. Christians again provided a convenient scapegoat for all that was wrong in "modern" times, and their strong internal organization and loyalties could easily be perceived as a threat to the state. Persecutions led by the emperors Decius and Diocletian beginning in 250 and 303 were by far the worst the church as a whole had known, but though many died for their faith, the church emerged stronger than before.

Other political developments continued to shape the fortunes of the church. To provide more efficient administration and defense of the empire, Emperor Diocletian devised a system that redrew the boundaries of the old Roman provinces into larger administrative units called "dioceses."* To govern the empire two co-emperors (Agustusti) were named, one in the East and one in the West, and two "vice-emperors" (Caesars). This worked while Diocletian himself kept a firm hand on all, but after his retirement in 305, it was not long before his successors and their sons were involved in a life-and-death struggle for supremacy.

Civil war broke out in the once united empire. One of the claimants for supreme authority was Constantine, a son of Constantius Chlorus, one of Diocletian's "Caesars." Tradition says that faced with overwhelming odds from the forces of his rival Maxentius, the night before the battle Constantine saw in a dream the "Chi Rho" (☧) monogram of Christ, with the words

---

* This term, which means "administrative district," was adopted by the church for the area administered by a bishop.

"By this sign, you will conquer." The next morning Constantine hurriedly painted the monogram on his helmet and ordered his soldiers to paint it on their shields. Thus, with his victory on 28 October 312 at the Milvian Bridge over the Tiber River, Constantine became ruler in the West and a "Christian." In gratitude for his victory, he drew up a document known as the Edict of Milan, extending the limited toleration of Christianity already given in 311.

Constantine consolidated his power over the whole empire in 323. Soon he moved the empire's capital to the east, and on the site of the ancient city of Byzantium built a splendid new capital named after himself, Constantinople. The bishops of this new city naturally assumed a leading role in the church, and in the next century Constantinople joined Jerusalem, Antioch, Alexandria, and Rome as one of the great "patriarchates" of the church.*

Whether Constantine himself was a genuine convert or whether his ends were far more political is a matter for debate, but his mother Helena (d. 330?) enthusiastically embraced the new faith and led an expedition to the Holy Land to find the sites of Christ's birth and death and the true cross. Whatever Constantine's personal faith may have been, the fact remains that in a few short years the Christian church had moved from being severely persecuted to becoming, if not yet the "official" church of the empire, the victorious emperor's favorite. There was good and bad for the church in this. Church historian Williston Walker observes:

> The church was everywhere free from persecution. Its steadfastness, its faith, and its organization had carried it through its perils. But, in winning its freedom from its enemies, it had come largely under the control of the occupant of the Roman imperial throne. A fateful union with the state had begun.[2]

---

* Originally, the patriarchal cities were Antioch, Alexandria, and Rome. Constantinople and Jerusalem were recognized as patriarchates at the Council of Chalcedon in 451, though the title itself was not used until the 500s. A patriarch had jurisdiction and right of consecration over other bishops in the region.

Constantine now had a unified empire, and he was determined to have a unified church as well. Even before gaining complete supremacy, he called a synod at Arles in Gaul to settle a dispute in northern Africa. When a priest named Arius threatened a split in the church by asserting that the Son was not equal in divinity to the Father, Constantine called for a synod of the whole church to meet in Nicea (Nicaea) in 325 to settle the issue. This was the first General Council of the church since the "council of Jerusalem" had decided that Gentiles could become Christians without becoming Jews first. Most of the bishops present at Nicea were from the East, though a few Western bishops were in attendance. Constantine himself was present in a highly visible way, though he had not yet been baptized. Most historians agree that he did not care about theological niceties but demanded a formula that would be widely accepted, whatever it might be.

The Council of Nicea declared that the Son was "begotten, not made," and was "of one substance" ('ομοουύσιος, homoousios) with the Father. A creedal formulation incorporating these ideas was adopted. Controversy over the precise terminology persisted for another half century, and at times the Arians gained the ascendancy, but with the vocal support of such leaders as Athanasius of Alexandria (d. 373) the basic Nicean decisions eventually came to be accepted as orthodox.

The work of the three great Cappadocian fathers, Basil (d. 379), his brother Gregory of Nyssa (d. after 394), and his friend Gregory of Nazianzus (d. 389?) combined gifts of administration, mysticism, and oratory to further develop the Nicean, or "New-Nicean" interpretation of the faith. It was from these continuing discussions that the great creed used most often in the liturgies of the church was developed. This came to be known as the Nicene Creed, though this creed as we know it is not exactly the one adopted at Nicea, but was reconsidered at the second* General Council of the church, at Constantinople

---

* The Roman Catholic Church numbers General Councils beginning with the first one, at Nicea in 325, following the council of Jeru-

in 381, and underwent various additions and refinements later. In this era church doctrine became part of imperial secular law. In the new ways of the imperial church, the weapon of state persecution that had formerly been used against the church was now aimed by Christians against other Christians officially regarded as "heretics."

As the fifth century opened, it appeared that the church had attained a pinnacle of earthly and spiritual success. It was the recognized church of the Roman Empire, and Constantine's move of the capital from Rome to Constantinople had left a power vacuum in the West which the bishop of Rome filled in many respects. In addition, Ambrose, bishop of Milan (d. 397), had done much to stabilize the Western church's thinking and expression, and Augustine of Hippo (d. 430), after his mother Monica's (d. 387) prayers for his conversion had finally been answered, was in the wings to carry on the legacy. Jerome (d. 420) had given the Latin Church a fine translation of scripture in its own language, and in the East John Chrysostom (d. 407), despite difficulties as bishop of Constantinople, had left a wealth of beautiful sermons which earned him a place with Basil and the two Gregorys as one of the four great fathers of the Eastern church.

Yet, earthly success and security are fleeting at best. For many years, Germanic tribes had been moving around the boundaries of the Roman Empire. There had been occasional battles and incursions, but the empire had so far held. Now in the fifth century, however, its political unity was weakened by a series of partitions of areas of authority among the emperors' sons, and its army was not the fierce machine it had once been. Thus, when the Germanic Visigoths were themselves threatened in 376 by the Huns invading from central Asia, they sought shelter in Roman lands on the Danube. They rebelled against what they felt was mistreatment by Roman officials, and a few years later almost captured Constantinople. In 410,

---

salem as related in Acts 11. The second Vatican Council, 1962-65, was the 21st General Council.

under their King Alaric, they captured Rome itself. This was a shock of unimaginable proportions. Rome, the "master of the world," had fallen to the barbarians! Other tribes — Vandals, Avars, Franks, Burgundians, and Saxons, Angles, and Jutes — began carving out kingdoms of their own in empire territory. In 452 the Huns under Attila also approached the walls of Rome, but their attack was averted, supposedly through the efforts of the Roman bishop Leo I (the Great, d. 461). The empire continued to exist in the East and in theory also in the West. However, though emperors were named for a while longer, when Romulus Augustulus (great in name but not in power) was deposed in 476, no one bothered to replace him. The Roman Empire in the West was no more.

But did this mean that the church in the West was no more as well? It might have, if our popular view of "pagan hordes" sweeping in to burn and pillage were true. But most of the tribes settling in the former Roman lands had already been Christianized. They were mostly Arians, but that could be dealt with in time. Neither were they for the most part intent on destroying all that had gone on before. True, some, such as the Vandals, whose name has come to mean wanton destruction, were an exception. Many, though, adapted much of classical civilization to their own needs and understandings.

The bishops of Rome, or popes* as we may now call them, were a stabilizing force and were able to exercise much of the prestige of the emperors of old. Pope Innocent I (d. 417) and Leo I laid a solid groundwork of papal authority and supremacy upon which their successors could build. However, papal power was not absolute. Within the emerging nations local bishops often assumed positions of secular as well as religious power. Particularly among the Franks and later among the Germans, these church officials often united with their rulers to keep the papacy from having everything its own way. Sometimes this actually increased the influence of

---

* The word "pope" comes to us from the ancient Latin and Greek and means quite literally "papa," as in father.

the church in those areas. Everywhere, as the most learned and literate members of society, the clergy assumed positions of importance. Many lower clergy, imitating the bishops, served in political as well as religious positions.

Doctrinal disputes faded to a minimum, especially in the West, after the Council of Chalcedon (451) decided questions of the relation of the divine and human in Christ. The Council of Nicea (325) had concluded that the Son was truly and fully God, but had not determined how the divine and human natures were related in Jesus. A bewildering array of opinions proliferated, under such names as Apollinarianism, Nestorianism, and Eutychianism, as to whether Christ's human will was replaced by a divine one, or whether human and divine natures were totally separate, or whether somehow they were combined into a special nature that was neither fully human nor fully divine. Chalcedon effectively settled the matter, giving us the Christian understanding as is generally accepted today, that Christ is fully human, fully divine, very God from eternity, yet complete in his humanity as we are, except for sin.[3]

Though this "Definition" of Chalcedon was not accepted in all the Eastern churches (notably Alexandria and Antioch), the principle of Christ as fully divine and fully human in one person was accepted in Constantinople and Rome. Indeed, Leo I of Rome had been a major proponent of what was deemed the orthodox interpretation. This too enhanced papal prestige.

The emergence of monasticism also strengthened the church in the West beginning in the sixth century. The idea that some Christians were called to a "higher" life of devotion than others had been around for many years. Anthony of Egypt (d. 356?) had popularized the practice of withdrawing from society to live as a hermit totally devoted to God. Inspiration for this came from the ideals of the Sermon on the Mount (Matt. 5-7). The most famous example of this sort of monasticism is Simeon Stylites (d. 459), who lived atop a pillar for 30 years. Pachomius (d. 346), also in Egypt, developed the idea that monks should live together in closely organized communities, and this form of monasticism was encouraged by the great theologian Basil, which enhanced the Eastern church's prestige. Monastic practice had spread into the West from the East well before the fall of the empire, but it was the work of Benedict of Nursia (d. 547?), which gave Western monasticism its classic organization and rule. Similar houses for women also sprang up, and the nuns played an important role in the life of the church. A more mystical and free-wheeling asceticism grew up among the Celts in Ireland and Britain, but gradually the structured communities of the Benedictine Rule predominated in the western lands. These monasteries provided a pillar of emerging medieval society. Not only did they offer refuge for souls seeking assurance and peace, but they also served as storehouses of knowledge and education, provided missionaries to still un-christianized areas, and attracted some of the best minds of the time.

Similar to the ascetic ideals of monasticism was the idea that all priests should be celibate. This, it was felt, would evidence a higher moral standard for the clergy and a further withdrawal from the things of the world. The Eastern churches required that bishops be unmarried, but allowed marriage for priests and deacons before ordination. In the West the idea for celibacy for all clergy in "major orders" (bishops, priests, deacons, and sometimes sub-deacons) had been around since the early fourth century. There was resistance to the idea, however, and decrees to enforce it were repeated over the centuries.*

In the seventh century the church as a whole faced its greatest external threat since the persecutions and the fall of Rome. This was the rise of Islam, whose prophet Mohammed (d. 632) had raised the standard of another monotheistic religion alongside Judaism and Christianity. Not only did the new religion call for persons to embrace the new faith, but its followers embarked on military conquests as well. The

---

* The Lateran Council of 1179 finally declared all clerical marriages invalid, and this was reiterated by the Council of Trent (1545-63). Celibacy remains the rule in the Latin Rite of the Roman Catholic Church.

patriarchal cities of Antioch and Jerusalem fell in short order, and all of Syria, Egypt, and North Africa soon followed. In the West, Spain was mostly lost, but the tide was stopped at Tours in France in 732 by the Frankish army under Charles Martel (d. 741). Constantinople itself still held out, but much of the Eastern Empire's population and territory were now under Islamic rule, and while conversions were at first generally not forced, the majority of people in those areas were eventually lost to the church. This naturally led to an enhancement of the Roman papacy at the expense of Constantinople and the other ancient patriarchates.

A complete and lasting break between East and West did not come for another three centuries (1054), but rivalries (with politics often masquerading as theology) between eastern and western Christianity festered and at times exploded. The Eastern church, however, later did much to make up its losses to Islam by converting the Slavic peoples to the north and farther east, most notably the Ukrainians and Russians.

In the last years of the eighth century the partnership of church and state in Western Europe took a new turn. In France, Pepin (d. 768), the son of Charles Martel, wanted to be king of the Franks, and Pope Zacharias (d. 752) helped secure this dignity for him. In turn, Pepin defeated the Lombards, who were threatening Rome, and in 756 granted the territory around Ravenna to Pope Stephen II. The pope had actually ruled in Rome for some time, but was now officially, as well as in fact, a temporal sovereign. This was the beginning of the Papal States, which lasted until 1870 (and the "mini-state" of the Vatican City, which continues today). Around this time also a document called the "Donation of Constantine" began to circulate, which purported to record a giving of lands by Emperor Constantine to the pope. The document was a forgery, but for many centuries it was widely believed to be genuine.

Pepin's son Charles, known as Charlemagne or "Charles the Great," carried things further. In Aachen Cathedral on Christmas Day 800 Pope Leo III (d. 816) crowned Charlemagne emperor, thus establishing the Holy Roman Empire. Cynics in later times observed that it was neither holy nor Roman nor an empire, but at the time the event was hailed as the restoration of the Roman Empire in the West. Charlemagne's empire was real, and included France and the Low Countries, and northern and central Italy. Charlemagne went on to conquer the Saxons, and brought Germany and parts of Austria and lands farther east under his sway.

This expansion led to greater tension between East and West in the church. Both Rome and Constantinople sought to expand their jurisdiction into the lands bordering these areas. As we shall see in the next chapter, the bringing of Byzantine Christianity to the Balkans and then into Bohemia and Moravia by Saints Cyril and Methodius had political as well as religious ramifications.

Charlemagne himself was no scholar, but he encouraged the educational work of Alcuin (d. 804), whom he named as head of the monastery of St. Martin of Tours, to lift the intellectual level of his new realm, which was lagging behind the Byzantine Christians and the followers of Islam as well.

Thus church and state became partners in what formed the basis of medieval society for hundreds of years. Such a partnership was not always equal or amicable. Kings tried to control the church, and popes and bishops tried to control kings. The best known of these disputes is perhaps that of Pope Gregory VII (d. 1085)* with Holy Roman Emperor Henry IV (d. 1106). Gregory asserted the papacy's ultimate authority over all things, political as well as religious. As God's representative on earth, the pope should have the final say not only in the appointment of bishops, but also in the crowning and deposition of emperors and kings. Henry, on the other hand, claimed that his own office also had divine sanction, and that he should have the right of "investiture"† of bishops and abbots in his realm, especially since many of them were as

---

* Sometimes known as Hildebrand, his name before he became pope.

† This meant specifically that the emperor had the right to "invest" a bishop or abbot with his ring and staff of office before consecration. In practice it meant the right to appoint bishops and abbots.

much political as they were religious offices. In the midst of the argument, Henry got a number of German bishops to declare Gregory deposed. The pope excommunicated Henry and declared his subjects no longer bound to obey him. Henry on his part called the pope some unkind names, among which "false monk" was perhaps one of the milder ones. In the end, Henry did not have the full support of his nobles, who in 1076 declared that if he was not absolved from his excommunication within a year, they would no longer recognize him as emperor. Thus in a classic moment of Western history, Emperor Henry stood in the snow before the Castle of Canossa in 1077 begging Pope Gregory inside to absolve him. This total papal victory did not last long, for since he got to keep his throne Henry could rebuild his opposition to Gregory, once again causing the pope much trouble. This "love-hate" relationship of ecclesiastical and secular power grew through the centuries.

By the close of the first millennium, Western European society was thoroughly feudal in organization. That is, all the land was seen as belonging to the king or emperor in the various countries which had formed out of Charlemagne's great empire. The king or emperor granted portions of land to great nobles in exchange for military service and the payment of certain fees and revenues. These nobles in turn granted portions of their lands to lesser nobles on similar conditions, and these nobles did the same to other lesser nobles and knights. At the bottom of the scale were the peasants, who were obliged to work for their immediate overlord and were often bound to the land they farmed but could never own. This sounds like a well-oiled self-perpetuating machine, but in fact it depended much on the forcefulness of the personalities involved. Kings struggled with other kings, and their nobles often vied with the king and each other for additional rights, privileges, and more land. Particularly in times of civil unrest, loyalties might switch to another feudal overlord. Marriages in noble families were often used to consolidate or aggrandize holdings.

A similar organization prevailed in the church. The popes claimed absolute jurisdiction, and granted authority in local areas (dioceses) to bishops, who in turn granted parishes to priests, with loyalty and financial contributions expected in return. Here again the theoretical system did not always work so simply, and various "livings" were at the disposal of secular lords, monasteries, or other religious institutions.

The increasing wealth of the church made all these church-state relationships more crucial and contentious. We have seen the popes become temporal sovereigns beyond direct royal control. Many of the great prelates also became secular landlords. Even many of the monasteries, which had been founded on ideals of poverty, became wealthy landholders. Of course, it was argued, these institutions needed their holdings in order to support themselves.

As time went on, however, donations to the church accumulated. The seven sacraments — baptism, confirmation, holy communion, penance, marriage, and final anointing, along with ordination to provide priests to administer the others — provided means of grace and salvation for all. In gratitude, many pious souls left gifts of money and property to the church. In addition, many property holders who had perhaps not been all that they should be in life thought it wise to "hedge their bets" with a final gift to the church in hopes of a little more mercy in eternity. In many places this had led to great wealth and land holdings for the church, and this further blurred the distinction between spiritual and secular overlords. Commendable efforts were made to reject worldly wealth and to embrace a simple life strictly regulated by the commands of Christ. Such orders were founded by Francis of Assisi (d. 1226) and his devoted friend Clare (d. 1253), and Dominic (d. 1221). In their success, though, they themselves were soon led to ownership of great property and wealth.

The followers of Peter Waldo (Valdes) also returned to a simple life of extreme poverty (c. 1176). These Waldensians combined the poverty of Francis of Assisi with doctrinal simplifications that anticipated many later Protestant ideas.

Their insistence on lay preaching led to their condemnation by the Roman clergy, and they were driven into remote areas.

Theologically, the church provided firm doctrinal teaching for spiritual security. Peter Lombard (d. 1160) in his *Four Books of Sentences* gave a balanced exposition of Christian teaching, which served as a standard of theological education for more than three centuries. Thomas Aquinas (d. 1274) wrote an intellectually satisfying philosophical exposition of Christian doctrine in his *Summa Theologica*. Aquinas taught that human reason needs to be supplemented by divine revelation. Reason and revelation are not at odds with one another, since both come from God. The Scriptures are God's word and are authoritatively interpreted by the fathers, councils, and current prelates of the church. Philosophically, Aquinas managed to adapt newly rediscovered ideas of Aristotle into a system not too much at odds with popular concepts derived from Plato.* His *Summa* treats of so many questions that its subtitle might have been "Inquire Within about Everything."

For most Western Christians in the Middle Ages, such lofty theological compositions were not of much practical everyday use. The cathedrals and churches, however, which were beginning to rise in the modern "Gothic" style, with their soaring ceilings and stained glass, paintings, and statues, were visible proclamations of church teaching, just as the sacraments were visible means of receiving invisible grace.

The seven sacraments were seen as essentials for grace. Failure to participate in them led to damnation.† The doctrine of transubstantiation said that the bread and wine were

---

* Plato's followers were called "realists." That is, collective ideas such as the concept of "chair" are "real" and exist in the mind of God. It is from this ideal of "chair" that all individual chairs come into being. Aristotelians, on the other hand, were "nominalists." That is, it is the individual chairs that really exist. The collective idea of "chair" is merely a name (Latin "nomen, nominis") derived by us from all the individual chairs. These distinctions may seem obtuse to modern minds, but they were the cause of much controversy in the medieval and following eras.

† The sacraments of marriage and ordination were not for everybody.

replaced by the true body and blood of Christ at the time of consecration. This led to adoration of the elements. People bowed to them as if the transformed bread and wine were Christ Himself (which according to this doctrine they are). Both elements continued to be served to the laity in the Eastern churches. In the West, fear of spilling the Lord's blood led to the laity's receiving the sacramental bread alone. The chalice and its contents were reserved for the clergy.[*]

Devotion to the saints played an important role in popular Christianity. The church had honored the saints in its early years, and at least since the end of the fourth century they were seen as accessible intercessors before the divine majesty. The Virgin Mary as the mother of Jesus, indeed as the Theotokos (God bearer) or Mother of God, received special devotion. Relics of other saints, either small portions of the saints' bodies or objects used by them, also provided a tangible form for devotion and the reception of grace. Many of these were mistakenly attributed or were out-and-out fakes, but that did not hinder the devotion of those who bowed before them.

Pilgrimages to various shrines of the saints also provided an outlet for devotion, not to mention a chance to travel. The popularity of pilgrimages also played a large role in one of the Middle Ages' most famous (or infamous) undertakings — the Crusades. If a local saint was worth a pilgrimage, the land where Jesus himself had trod was surely an even more worthwhile destination.

Palestine had been in Moslem control since 638, but access had been given to Christian pilgrims. That changed when the Turks took control in 1071. A call went out in Western Europe from Pope Urban II (d. 1099) for liberation of the Holy Land, and after some fits and starts the flower of Western chivalry set out for the East in 1096. Motives may have varied from true piety to hope of prestige and financial gain to a simple lust for

---

[*] Apparently the idea of withholding the chalice from the laity arose first among the lay people themselves (possibly in the 12th century) and was not imposed on them by the clergy.

adventure, but the crusade did succeed in capturing Jerusalem in 1099. This First Crusade was the only one that had much military success. A Latin kingdom was now established in the Holy Land, ignoring the rights of the Eastern patriarchs. Additional crusades to meet further threats continued to the end of the 13th century, but most were disasters. Indeed, the Fourth Crusade (1202-04) ended up not fighting Islamic forces but sacking Christian Constantinople, as if this venerable center of Eastern Christianity were no better than "heathen." This further weakened the Byzantine Empire and fanned bad feelings between the Eastern and Western churches. Other ventures followed, but in 1291 the Crusader kingdom was lost forever.

Despite the ultimate failure of the Crusades, the 1200s are usually regarded as the high point of the Middle Ages under such extraordinary popes as Innocent III (d. 1216). In addition to accomplishments listed above, Spain was being wrested from Moslem control. Universities were founded, growing out of older cathedral schools. Bologna, Paris, and Oxford quickly became beacons for intellectual thought and activity. On the other hand, frustrated by the failure of gentler methods to win the Cathars (or Albigensians) back to church obedience, the synod of Toulouse in 1229 systematized the Inquisition as a means of rooting out heresy. The Cathars, who like the Gnostics of ancient times held the material world to be evil, were virtually exterminated. The church, with the might of the state, was determined to keep a firm hand on belief and practice.

In the 1300s, however, the grand Western medieval edifice was developing deep cracks. Theologically, Aquinas's lovely rational system was challenged by such writers as William of Occam (d. 1349?), a proponent of Aristotelian "nominalism."* Henceforth Western philosophers divided more sharply into "realists" and "nominalists." Occam finally concluded that ultimately theology cannot be rationally proven at all. In this

---

* See footnote above.

he was in sympathy with Duns Scotus (d. 1308), who had already opposed some of the ideas of Aquinas. Occam was willing to accept things on "authority," but it was not long before others questioned: "What is the authority for this authority?"

Another challenge to traditional church teaching and authority was provided by John Wycliffe (d. 1384) in England. Philosophically, Wycliffe was a "realist," and this led him to assert that the true church was the ideal heavenly church, not the earthly institution. He also contradicted the doctrine of transubstantiation in the holy communion, and labeled the institution of the papacy as scripturally "dubious." He called for church reform in general and demanded that the church give up its secular authority. Most tempting to the secular lords was his statement of "dominion," that governments could seize the property of clergy who did not exercise their offices "in a state of grace."*

Beginning in 1347 the horrible plague of the "Black Death" decimated European populations and disrupted society. On the other hand, horizons had been widened by the Crusades, trade had been increased, a money economy was emerging, and the importance of cities not strictly in the feudal system was on the rise. Nationalism and dissatisfaction with the wealth of the church also increased. For the papacy, this was the time of the "Babylonian Captivity."† From 1309 to 1377 the papal residence was not Rome, but Avignon. Technically at the time it was not French territory, but it was close enough for the rest of Europe to complain that the pope was "in captivity" under the French king's thumb.

After much urging by such persons as Catharine of Sienna (d. 1380), Pope Gregory XI finally returned to Rome, partly to quench criticism and partly to look after his neglected interests in the old imperial city. He died only a year later in 1378, and

---

* Much more will be said about Wycliffe in later chapters.
† The term derives from the 70-year captivity of the Jews in Babylon in scripture.

while the cardinals who would elect a successor were mostly French, the Roman populace would have no more "French popes" and threatened mayhem if the electors did not choose an Italian who would stay in Rome. The cardinals elected Bartolomeo Prignano, who took the name Urban VI (d. 1389). Urban, however, was notably lacking in "people skills" and managed in a few short months to offend the cardinals so much that they declared him deposed and elected Clement VII (d. 1394), who set up headquarters in Avignon. Urban in Rome continued to maintain that he was the legitimate pope. Thus began the Great Western Schism.

There had been "antipopes" before, chosen by disaffected factions. This time, however, it was the legitimate electors who deposed the one they themselves had elected, and then chose another. This, to put it mildly, was a huge problem. There cannot be two Supreme Vicars of Christ on earth. Western and Central Europe divided as to which pope to follow. This gave impetus to the ideas of such thinkers as Marsilius of Padua (d. 1342?), who even before the crisis had said that ultimate authority in the church lay not in the pope but in a general council of bishops and others representing the whole church. The supporters of Urban and Clement continued to elect successors even after those two died, so there were still two popes, each claiming to be the only legitimate successor to St. Peter. A council was called at Pisa (1409) to settle the issue, but it only compounded the problem by electing yet another pope who could not get universal acceptance. Now there were three.

So it was when the Council of Constance met in 1415. Though its leaders were generally moderates in favor of some basic reform, their prime objective was to resolve the Great Schism once and for all, so that as far as possible things could go back to the good old ways. A new age was dawning, however, and the clock could not be put back.

Notes

[1] A longtime standard work on general church history is Williston Walker, *A History of the Christian Church*, 4th ed. revised by Richard A. Norris, David W. Lotz, and Robert T. Handy (New York: Charles Scribner's Sons, 1985). Walker is the source for this chapter. Another good general church history for the later portion of this period is Francis Oakley *The Western Church in the Later Middle Ages* (Ithaca and London: Cornell University Press, 1979). Another from a less Western oriented perspective is Dale T. Irvin and Scott W. Sunquist, *History of the World Christian Movement*, vol. 1 (Maryknoll, N.Y.: Orbis Books, 2001).

[2] Williston Walker, *A History of the Christian Church*, 3rd ed. revised by Cyril C. Richardson, Wilhelm Pauck, and Robert T. Handy (New York: Charles Scribner's Sons, 1959), 102.

[3] Numerous sources can be cited for the "Definition" of Chalcedon, yet we like the translation given by Justo L. González, *The Story of Christianity* (San Francisco: HarperSanFrancisco, 1984), 1:257.

Chapter 2

The Direct Stream

The Czechs and Their History before Hus

Now that we have followed the broad stream of the development of the church and medieval society to a point just before our main story begins, we need to go back upstream a bit and follow one of that stream's lesser known tributaries to bring us even closer to our starting point. With that in mind, let us have a look at the land, people, and history of the Czechs.

In the heart of central Europe, southwest of Poland, southeast of Germany, north of Austria, and west of Slovakia, lie Bohemia and Moravia, the homelands of the Czech people. Bohemia consists of a fertile lowland plateau with natural boundaries of four mountain ranges: the heights of the Bohemian Forest, the Erzgebirge, the Sudeten Heights, and Bohemian-Moravian Highlands. Moravia lies to the east, extending toward the White Carpathian mountains. In Bohemia the main rivers are the Moldau (Vltava) and the Elbe (Labe), and in Moravia the Morava flows through a fertile valley. Both lands produce abundant crops: grains, sugar beets, fruit, flax, and hops. Coal, silver, copper, and lead deposits are rich, and natural spas and springs abound. Bohemia and Moravia together total around 30,000 square miles, about the same as Scotland or South Carolina. The natural frontier barriers of these lands should have provided protection from invasion but over the centuries have proved remarkably unsuccessful in doing so.

A few archaeological remains indicate that people lived in these lands in the Paleolithic age, but other than that they were hunters and fishers, we do not know who they were or what they were like.[1] From Roman sources we learn that a Celtic people called the Boii (pronounced "boy-ee" or by some "bow-hee") moved into the area sometime in the second century before the Christian era, and it is from them that the name Bohemia comes. The Boii were eventually displaced by the Germanic Quadi tribe. In turn, these Germanic peoples were apparently themselves displaced by Attila the Hun in the course of his rampages across Europe in the mid 400s.[2]

Bohemia and Moravia still stood relatively empty when the first Slavic peoples came into the area sometime around the early 500s. These were the Czechs, and legend has it that they took their name from their leader Czech (Čech). The root meaning of "Czech" is not certain, but it appears that "Czech men" was originally a title referring to the ruler's bodyguard, and was only later applied to the nation. The mythical founder was probably invented by a medieval chronicler to explain his people's origin, just as another writer in the Middle Ages, never having heard of the long-departed Boii, invented a great warrior named Bohemus to explain Bohemia.[3] Strictly true or not, the legends about the Czechs' pre-history are charming and deserve to be remembered. We may not know much about their early mythology, but their deities with such names as Perun, Radihost, Lada, and Morana resound with a melody of their own. Or who would want to lose historian Edmund de Schweinitz's[*] enchanting rhapsody on the Czechs, which

---

[*] This introduces the first of three major historians of the Ancient Unity, on whom this volume relies. Edmund de Schweinitz, 1825-87, was president of Moravian Theological Seminary, 1867-85, and was author of numerous historical sketches about Moravians. His great devotion, his memoir states, was "the study of the history of the Ancient Unitas Fratrum." The result was *The History of the Church Known as the Unitas Fratrum or the Unity of the Brethren*, first published in 1885 and reprinted in 1901. De Schweinitz wrote a rollicking story, but did not have available more recently discovered facts.

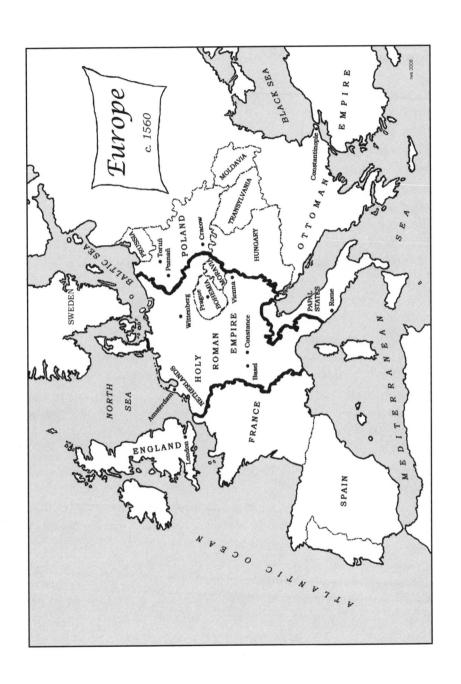

Europe
c. 1560

BLACK SEA

OTTOMAN EMPIRE

Constantinople

MOLDAVIA

TRANSYLVANIA

POLAND

PRUSSIA
Toruń
Poznań
Cracow

HUNGARY

BALTIC SEA

SWEDEN

MORAVIA
BOHEMIA
Prague
Wittenberg

Vienna

HOLY ROMAN EMPIRE
Constance

PAPAL STATES
Rome

MEDITERRANEAN SEA

NORTH SEA

NETHERLANDS
Amsterdam

Basel

FRANCE

ENGLAND
London

SPAIN

ATLANTIC OCEAN

rwk 2008

concludes: "The country was full of sacred hills and fountains and rivers, where the Czech brought his offering in the twilight hour, smiting upon his forehead and singing a hymn of praise."[4]

The stories continue about Krok, successor of Czech, who died without a male heir. The people chose the wisest of his daughters, Libuše, to lead them, but they insisted she take a husband. Offended by the suggestion that she needed a man to make the real decisions, she married not one of the nobles, but a simple cowherd named Přemysl.[5] Legend or not, the later chief dukes and kings of Bohemia until the direct line finally died out in 1306 proudly proclaimed themselves to be of the Přemyslid dynasty.*

By the beginning of the ninth century we are on more solid if not absolutely stable historical ground. Charlemagne's empire expanded close to the borders of Bohemia and Moravia, and his Frankish state had an interest in expanding even farther to the east. Indeed, the Franks asserted some claim on these lands, though they were not strictly speaking within the empire. The emperor in Constantinople also had designs on gaining influence in these lands to his north.[6] Here the tributary that is the story of the Czechs begins to flow more directly into the main stream of history.

At this time Moravia outshone its neighbor Bohemia. Indeed, its rulers had achieved such prominence and territorial gain that the emperor in Constantinople gave the title "Great Moravian Empire" to this realm, which included Silesia, Slovakia, southern Poland, and northern Hungary.[7] Moravia also at times claimed rights to Bohemia. The Moravian Prince Mojmir was reported to have accepted Christianity through the Franks, and it is definitely recorded that in 845 fourteen Bohemian noblemen were baptized in the German town of Regensburg. We must question the sincerity of this conversion, however, for it appears this step was taken in hope of

---

* Legend also records that Přemysl's peasant shoes and bag were for generations part of the coronation regalia of the lords of Bohemia.

preventing a Frankish invasion. When the Franks invaded anyway, the nobles renounced their Christianity.[8] Among the common people, the new religion made few inroads. A few German and Italian missionaries attempted to evangelize in the Czech lands, but as they did not learn the local language, their efforts met with little or no success.[9] The Latin Church and the Germans, though, based claims for ecclesiastical or political sovereignty in the Czech lands on these early "conversions" and missions.

The Great Moravian Empire did not long endure and totally disintegrated in the early 900s, but as one modern historian writes: "Great Moravia's most significant historical legacy was the introduction of Christianity, and with it a written Slavonic liturgical language, to the region."[10] Given the intrigues of the age, politics as well as religion played a large role even in this.

The German (Holy Roman or Frankish) emperor, feeling that Great Moravia was becoming too much a rival, managed to depose Prince Mojmir in 846, and replace him by Mojmir's nephew Rastislav (846-70). Rastislav, however, did not fancy being merely a puppet ruler and some time later moved to obtain friendship and backing from the "other emperor," the Eastern one in Constantinople, requesting him to send missionaries to bring his people to the "true faith." Perhaps Rastislav was moved by genuine religious motives, but if so, they fit well with his political ambitions. The Eastern (Byzantine) emperor, Michael III, was quick to see advantages in putting a spoke in the wheel of the Holy Roman Empire and the Latin Church, and in 863 dispatched two missionaries to evangelize the Czechs.[11]

These were brothers, Cyril* (d. 869) and Methodius (d. 885), born in Thessalonica in Greece to a well-to-do senatorial family. The story of their early years contains many legends, but few facts. Both, however, were extremely capable, and

---

* Cyril's name was actually Constantine. He took the name Cyril only late in life when he entered a monastery in Rome, and that is the name everyone knows him by.

turned their backs on promising secular careers to live in a monastery on the Bosporus in Constantinople. One account has Cyril serving as librarian for the great cathedral of Santa Sophia.[12] They learned the Southern Slavic language (which was close enough to the dialect of the Czechs to be understood),* then emerged from monastic life to do missionary work among the South Slavs in the Balkans. According to tradition, Cyril also began work on an alphabet to give the Slavic tongue a written form. Scholars differ over whether Cyril invented the alphabet which bears his name, or whether it was the Glagolithic script which he invented, or whether he drew from earlier Glagolithic to develop his own. In any case, he and Methodius arrived in Moravia equipped with means to provide service books and Scriptures in the Slavonic language of the people among whom they were to work. Talking, praying, and preaching in the language of the people proved far more productive than yelling at them in Latin or German, and before long Christian churches were being planted throughout Moravia. Opinions differ as to whether the brothers made it into Bohemia, but their disciples soon did, and Methodius about 880[13] baptized the Bohemian Duke Bořivoj and his wife Ludmilla while they were on a visit to the Moravian Prince Svatopluk (871-94), who had replaced Rastislav.

Such success aroused the opposition of German bishops, and they complained to Rome about the "Byzantine" mission.[14] Pope Nicholas I (d. 867) was the more concerned about these charges since he and the Patriarch of Constantinople, Photius (d. 892?), had recently quarreled and traded excommunications with each other. Nicholas summoned Cyril and Methodius to Rome in 867, and they complied. Nicholas himself died before they arrived, but they met with the new Pope, Adrian II (d. 872), and satisfied him with their orthodoxy and recognition of his authority. Adrian appointed Cyril and

---

* The language used is known as "Old Church Slavonic." The modern Slavic languages (Czech, Polish, Russian, etc.) developed from a common source close to this.

Methodius as bishops, but Cyril, perhaps because of ill health, declined the honor, and entered a monastery in Rome, where he died in 869.

Adrian also sanctioned the use of the Slavonic liturgy in Bohemia and Moravia. It may seem strange that a pope would grant this dispensation when the Roman Church was so insistent on Latin elsewhere. Still, Christianizing the Czechs would be an advantage, and previous attempts had failed. It was enough that his jurisdiction was clearly acknowledged, and concessions could always be withdrawn later (as indeed they were). It has also been suggested that the papacy hoped to use this mission as a springboard to resuscitate the old Diocese of Pannonia (in Austria, Hungary, etc.) to keep yet another area out of the control of Constantinople. At the same time, an independent Roman Church hierarchy in these lands would restrict the influence of the Germans, with whom the pope also had occasional difficulties.

Methodius returned to Moravia and continued his efforts with marked success. It was at this point that he baptized the Bohemian Duke Bořivoj and his wife Ludmilla. The German authorities were no more pleased than before, however, and succeeded in having Methodius summoned back to Rome. Pope John VIII (d. 882) was then attempting reconciliation with the Patriarch in Constantinople, and so reconfirmed the work of Methodius, made him an archbishop, and again sanctioned the Slavonic liturgy.[15] This time it came with a few conditions, namely that in the services the Gospel should be read in Latin before the Slavonic version, and that Methodius should have a German assistant bishop. This German bishop, Wiching by name, continued to cause problems until Methodius died in 885.[16]

After this, the Latinization of the church in the Czech lands moved forward. Pope Stephen V* (d. 891) withdrew sanction for

---

* Some sources say Stephen VI. A Pope Stephen was elected in 752 who died before consecration. The Vatican in 1961 decided he was not a real pope and renumbered the subsequent Pope Stephens.

the Slavonic liturgy, though it continued in places until after the death of Duke Wenceslas in 935. At this time too, the Great Moravian Empire was disintegrating, and Slovakia was lost to the Magyars (Hungarians). Among the Czechs, the impetus now passed to Bohemia, where the Přemyslids were gaining the ascendancy. Bořivoj, after his baptism by Methodius, increased in influence until his death c. 894.[17]

Internal intrigues weakened the ducal house. Drahomira, daughter-in-law of Bořivoj had her mother-in-law Ludmilla killed in 921, and Drahomira's son Wenceslas (Václav) was assassinated by friends of his younger brother Boleslav I in 935. These murders may have been the result of a pagan reaction[18] in Bohemia, but politics certainly also played a role. In any event, the piety of Ludmilla and Wenceslas was emphasized in Czech accounts and both were hailed as martyrs. Historically, Wenceslas built the first church on the Hradčany height above Prague,[19] but he is best known as "Good King Wenceslas" from the old English carol.

The next few centuries were full of ups and downs for the Czechs, with all of the usual political and ecclesiastical machinations.[20] For our purposes, the main political developments to note were the continuing rise of the Přemyslid dukes in Bohemia and Moravia, the definite incorporation of those lands into the Holy Roman Empire in 950, and the granting of the title "King of Bohemia" to the Přemyslid ducal house about 1200. In the 13th and 14th centuries increased silver mining helped spur the development of cities, and with imperial support more and more Germans continued to move into them, forming a wealthy and sizable minority in the Czech lands. Ecclesiastically, the Slavonic liturgy was but a memory, and the Bohemian and Moravian churches were overseen by the bishop of Regensburg in Germany. Prague was important enough to get its own bishop about 973, but remained under the supervision of the archbishop of Mainz (again in Germany). Efforts of the Bohemian rulers to get their own archbishopric were frustrated by the maze of imperial and ecclesiastical politics. From the introduction of the first Benedictine nunnery in Prague in the 970s, Western monasticism spread, and eventually perhaps a third and possibly more of the total land in Bohemia and Moravia belonged to the church.[21]

When Wenceslas III was murdered in 1306, the Přemyslid dynasty, which had ruled in Bohemia for half a millennium, came to an end. The barons and important city dwellers then had to decide who should be king. After a couple of false starts, they settled in 1310 on John of Luxembourg (1310-46), son of Holy Roman Emperor Henry VII (d. 1313). This was a triumph for Henry's political ambitions, but the Bohemians agreed to accept John only if he married Elizabeth, a daughter of Wenceslas II, thus keeping the old bloodline alive. John, however, imported so many foreign advisors that he angered the Czechs, and when his father the emperor died in 1313 they demanded the foreigners be dismissed. Eventually the Czech nobles told John in effect that he could keep the title of king as long as he went away and left them alone. Actual rule of the country then fell into the hands of the barons, the large towns, and the monasteries for 30 years.

Failing as a sovereign, John of Luxembourg spent most of his life going around Europe as what we today would call a "playboy," but he did die nobly in 1346 at Crécy fighting for his friend and relative Charles of France against the English King Edward III. That left John's son Charles (d. 1378), who had fought alongside his father at Crécy, as heir presumptive to the Czech throne.

Charles was quite different from his father as far as kingship went.[22] True, he used his confirmation name Charles (after his uncle Charles IV of France) instead of his Czech birth name Wenceslas (Václav), and he had been brought up in Paris at the French court. However, his mother was the daughter of a Bohemian king (Wenceslas II), so the old Czech royal blood flowed through his veins, and he had been born in Prague, facts that made him more acceptable to the Czech people. Those advantages were given to him, but he had also taken the trouble to learn the Czech language. He had come to Bohemia in 1333, assumed the position of Margrave of Moravia in 1334, and had taken a hand in governing. Moreover, he was a sound judge of people and had a talent for selecting the right advisers for the job at hand. He also had a fine political sense of when to act and when not to. More than that, people simply liked him.[23]

In addition to his election as Bohemian king, he was also elected Holy Roman emperor in 1347 and crowned in 1355, taking the name Charles IV (Karl, Karel), by which he is generally known today.[24] Given the tensions that had existed between the empire and Bohemia this could have caused trouble, but Charles proceeded to balance Czech and German interests to an exceptional degree. He saw that he needed to base his power as emperor on a solid hereditary throne, so he delighted the Czechs by making Prague his official residence. On his seal he displayed the Czech lion beside the imperial eagle. He initiated huge building projects in Prague, large buildings in a "New Town" quarter, additions to the Hradčany castle and St. Vitus Cathedral, impressive walls around the city, and the bridge that still bears his name. With a nod to Czech memories of Cyril and Methodius, he sanctioned the establishment of a Slavonic monastery (Na Slovanech) in Prague. The local populace benefited economically from all this building activity, and artists and jewelers began flocking to Prague for royal and imperial patronage. In 1348 Charles also established the University of Prague (Charles University), the first in Eastern Europe. Prague came to be called the "Second Rome."[25]

This was also an age when the need for ecclesiastical reform was becoming obvious, even to high church dignitaries. The increasing wealth and secular involvement of the church, and the worldly morals of too many of its clergy caused protest. The "secularized Avignon" papacy had scandalized many, and the time was ripe to do something about it. Even before becoming king, Charles IV had been instrumental in freeing the Czech church from the control of the German archbishopric of Mainz with the elevation of Prague to an archbishopric in 1344. The first archbishop, Arnošt of Pardubice, favored reform, and

A 1606 view of Prague. St. Vitus Cathedral (upper left) rises above the extensive Hradčany castle. The Charles Bridge with its towers spans the Vltava (Moldau) River.

Charles was quick to see that the outward splendor of his new capital and archdiocese was tainted by the moral decay of his lay and clerical subjects.

To forestall the problem, Charles, with the archbishop's approval, in the early 1360s summoned the popular Augustinian preacher Konrad Waldhauser (d. 1369) from Vienna to hold a series of sermons in the spirit of what we today might call "revival meetings." Waldhauser "warmed up" in Litoměřice, then tackled Prague itself.[26] He preached in German, which was not the best method of gaining Czech popular approval, but many of the citizens of Prague were German, and the Czechs understood him enough to realize he was denouncing the people they wanted denounced: worldly church officials, greedy noblemen and wealthy merchants, even some corrupt court officials. Attendance at his sermons was huge, and Konrad was appointed rector of the central Týn Church in Prague.

Prague at this time also found itself a center for "devotio moderna," popular in the Netherlands and elsewhere, which urged Christians to go beyond a minimum keeping of church law. "Individual religious experience was to be attained by prayer and contemplation of suitable texts."[27] As a consequence, a large body of Latin and German devotional literature was translated into Czech. Charles IV himself commissioned Czech and later German translations of the Scriptures. The Czech layman Tomáš Štítné (d. before 1409) produced Czech theological writings which circulated widely.

The ministry of Waldhauser was continued by Milíč of Kroměříž. Milíč was born in Moravia and had attained lucrative positions both in the church and in the imperial chancellery.[28] To the amazement of the archbishop, he resigned all these positions to join in the reform work of Waldhauser. He preached in Czech, though his strong Moravian accent sounded to the sophisticated citizens of Prague about like a preacher from rural Alabama speaking to New Yorkers. His message surmounted that difficulty, and he later learned German to preach in that language also. Milíč continued the strictures of Waldhauser against corruption in church and society in general. He added a mystical turn to them, however, and in apocalyptic images (like the biblical Book of Revelation) predicted the coming of Antichrist and the end of the world. Such speculative oratory was not as popular as the rest of his message, and those he offended were able to use his excesses to get him suspended. A visit to Rome, to which Pope Urban V (d. 1370) had briefly returned from Avignon, persuaded Milíč to tone down that part of his message, but he still sounded the themes of general church reform, a return to apostolic origins and Scripture, and the discarding of whatever did not conform to those ideals. His enemies again lodged various charges against him, and Milíč again went to defend himself before the pope, now back in Avignon. He might have fared worse before the papal court, had not Charles IV interceded,[29] but before a final decision was handed down Milíč died in Avignon in 1374.

For all his speculative apocalyptic fervor and his own program of "personal renewal" which had affinity with the contemplative "devotio moderna," Milíč was well in line with what became a prime characteristic of the later Czech Reformation. This is the principle that theology and faith must find practical expression and application in life. Milíč undertook a ministry to rescue the prostitutes of Prague, and since most of them had nowhere to go and no means of supporting themselves otherwise, he persuaded wealthy disciples to contribute toward the establishment of a large and well-funded house for them, which was named "Jerusalem." His wealthy followers also joined in 1391 to build the Bethlehem Chapel in Prague for the free preaching of the Gospel in the language of the people.[30] Lest the term confuse the reader, "chapel" did not refer to the size of the edifice, but meant it was a private institution and not a parish church. Bethlehem Chapel could hold 1,100 persons, and it quickly became a center for the emerging reform movement.

Matthias (Matěj) of Janov (d. 1393) expressed reforming ideas similar to those of Milíč, though in a more academic fashion. He had been influenced by Milíč in his youth, and this perhaps explains his concentration on Scripture when he studied at the University of Paris. He was not so influenced to neglect his own chances for advancement, however, and on his way home from Paris he stopped by the papal court to secure the position of canon in St. Vitus Cathedral. Any lingering illusions he had about the ecclesiastical system of his day were dispelled when upon arriving in Prague he discovered that not only did the position he had been granted still have a living incumbent, but that five others had been promised it ahead of him.[31] Janov worked more in treatises than in sermons: "He was a writer and not a preacher."[32] His work *De regulis veteris et novi testamenti* (On the regulations of the Old and New Testament) was widely circulated and respected. One of his major themes was "faith formed by love," that is, faith put into living practice. Janov also advocated frequent reception of holy communion as a means of grace, and while he did not make such use of apocalyptic visions as Milíč did, he did observe that Antichrist was already on earth in the form of a corrupt hierarchy.

The academic side of the emerging Czech reform movement was represented on the faculty of the University of Prague by such people as Stephen of Kolín.[33] Stephen turned more to theological subjects during the 1390s, and in 1396 he was appointed preacher of Bethlehem Chapel. His few surviving sermons continue the work of the earlier reformers by stressing the authority of the Scriptures and the necessity for clerical reform. He also urged the laity to live their faith and not rely on prayers to the saints to get them into heaven.

It was not only the Czech faculty who favored the emerging reform movement at the University of Prague. The Czech students quickly got on board as well, and their discussions rang with issues of reform. No doubt a great deal of this sprang from sincere motives, but the fact that most of the German teachers and students at the university opposed the movement did not hurt its popularity among the young Czechs.

It is now a long way from the mythical migrations of the first Czechs, and their story is definitely flowing along within the broad stream of church and political history. The stage is now set for the emergence of the distinctly Hussite reform movement, which quickly became the Czech Revolution.

Notes

1 Jiří Sláma, "Boiohaemum-Čechy," in *Bohemia in History*, ed. Mikuláš Teich (Cambridge: Cambridge University Press, 1998), 23.

2 "Bohemia," in Internet version of *The Catholic Encyclopedia* (New York: Robert Appleton Co., 1908).

3 Sláma, 37.

4 Edmund de Schweinitz, *History of the Church Known as the Unitas Fratrum*, 2nd (reprint) ed. (Bethlehem, Pa.: Moravian Publication Concern, 1901), 7. De Schweinitz made great use of the 19th century nationalistic Czech writer Franz Palacky, who recorded his people's beloved stories in such works as *Geschichte von Böhmen, Grösstentheils nach Urkunden und Handschriften*, whose volumes were published 1844-67. See also Alois Jirásek, *Old Czech Legends*, trans. Marie K. Holoček (Boston: Forest Books, 1992).

5 Derek Sayer, *The Coasts of Bohemia: a Czech History* (Princeton: Princeton University Press, 1998), 30.

6 Zdeněk Měřínský and Jaroslav Mezník, "The Making of the Czech State: Bohemia and Moravia from the tenth to the fourteenth centuries," in Teich, 38-40.

7 Ján Dekan, *Moravia Magna: The Great Moravian Empire, Its Art and Times*, trans. Heather Trebatická (Minneapolis: Control Data Publishing, 1981).

8 Sayer, 32.

9 "Moravia" in *Catholic Encyclopedia*.

10 Sayer, 30.

11 Marvin Kantor, *The Origins of Christianity in Bohemia: Sources and Commentary* (Evanston: Northwestern University Press, 1990), provides translations of a number of early chronicles and devotional works of the early church in Bohemia.

12 *Oxford Dictionary of the Christian Church*, 2nd ed. with revisions, eds. F. L. Cross and E. A. Livingstone (Oxford: Oxford University Press, 1983), 370.

13 Sláma, 33.

14 De Schweinitz, 10-12. *Oxford Dictionary*, 370.

15 Sayer, 30.

16 De Schweinitz, 12. *Catholic Encyclopedia*, "Cyril and Methodius."

17 Sayer, 30.

18 De Schweinitz, 13-14.

19 Sayer, 30.

20 Those who want the gory details will find them in Zdeněk Měřínský and Jaroslav Mezník "The Making of the Czech State: Bohemia and Moravia from the tenth to the fourteenth centuries," in Teich, 38-58.

21 Frederick G. Heymann, *John Žižka and the Hussite Revolution* (Princeton: Princeton University Press, 1955) 39.

22 For more details see František Kavka, "Politics and Culture under Charles IV," in Teich, 59-78.

23 Měřínský and Mezník, 55.

24 De Schweinitz, 19.

25 Kavka, 73.

26 De Schweinitz, 20.

27 Kavka, 68.

28 De Schweinitz, 22-25. Kavka, 69-70. Amedeo Molnár, "L'Évolution de la théologie Hussite," *Revue d'Histoire et de Philosophie Religieuses* 43 (1963): 136.

29 Kavka, 70.

30 Thomas Fudge, "Ancellus Dei and Bethlehem Chapel," *Communio Viatorum* 35 (1993): 127-61. Fudge, 128, notes that the chapel was dedicated to the Holy Innocents and that John (Jan) Protiva was the first preacher to 1396, when he resigned and Stephen of Kolín took over until 1402. John Hus followed him.

31 S. H. Wrastislaw, *John Hus* (London: Society for Promoting Christian Knowledge, 1882), 61-74.

32 De Schweinitz, 25.

33 Matthew Spinka, *John Hus' Concept of the Church* (Princeton: Princeton University Press, 1966), 37-39.

Chapter 3

John Hus [1]

And the Czech Reform Movement, 1372-1414

John (Jan) Hus, the leader of the Czech reform movement, was born in the little Bohemian town of Husinec about 1372. We know little of his childhood.[2] His parents, though not wealthy, had enough to send him to school. His teachers and the local clergy were impressed with his abilities and about 1390 arranged for him to enter the University of Prague. Charles IV's newly expanded and beautified city must have been a new setting for the boy from rural Bohemia. The welter of ideas circulating among the faculty and students at the university in the lectures, questions, responses, and debates, both formal and informal, must have opened a fascinating if sometimes confusing new world.[3]

His student life seems to have been fairly typical of many another poor but promising country boy whose only chance for success was to gain enough education to secure ordination to the priesthood. He had little money and occasionally had to beg in the streets. He did, however, have a fine singing voice and sang in paid church choirs to supplement his begging receipts. In later years he recalled his time as "a hungry little student" who made a spoon out of bread to eat his peas, and when they were gone he ate his spoon as well.[4]

Hus later lamented that his motives for entering the priesthood in those early years flowed mostly from a desire for prestige, secure shelter, decent clothing, and a full stomach.

He confessed too that he had taken part in student pranks. His conscience must have bothered him, so he scraped together a few coins to buy an indulgence to reduce his time in purgatory.

During his stay at the university his thinking and dedication changed, more it seems from a gradual deepening of mind and soul than from any spectacular conversion event. He came to accept many of the ideas of Waldhauser, Milič, and Janov as

John Hus

his own, particularly since Stephen of Kolín was one of his principal teachers. Hus also made friends at the university, in particular one young man of similar background named Jerome, who would soon loom large in his march toward destiny.

John Hus attained his Bachelor of Arts degree in 1393 and probably also received ordination to the minor orders (preparatory to full ordination) of the church. But bright young men with minor orders were a dime (or kopeck) a dozen in medieval Europe, so more education for ordination as a priest was required. Even then, it usually took money (which Hus didn't have) to secure a parish even as a priest, so he took the one course remaining to him and decided on an academic career in the church. He therefore continued at the university until 1396, receiving his Master of Arts degree in philosophy. For the next two years he lectured there on Aristotle and in 1398 secured an appointment to the full-time faculty. With this new dignity, he began signing himself "Master Jan Hus" instead of "Jan of Husinec." He was ordained a deacon in June 1400.*

His first foray into the public forum was a series of protests in 1401 against atrocities inflicted on Czech peasants during an invasion by German forces of Ruprecht of the Palatinate, who was trying to wrest the Holy Roman Empire from Bohemia's King Wenceslas IV (d. 1419). Wenceslas had been duly elected emperor to succeed his father, Charles IV (d. 1378), but he exhibited none of his father's abilities. He quickly lost support and was never crowned. Hus's protests gained him notice among the common people of Bohemia, who saw him as one of their own.

Hus's ordination to the priesthood probably also came in 1401 after the usual year service as a deacon.† He did not secure a parish, but the pastor of St. Michael's Church in Prague occasionally let him preach from its pulpit. This may have brought him some remuneration, but more importantly it allowed him to hone his preaching skills and become better known to the citizens of Prague.

His academic career was prospering, and he was appointed in 1401 dean of the philosophical faculty for the coming winter semester. This position rotated among all the faculty in turn, so his appointment was more a result of administrative procedure rather than of academic excellence, but it did give him considerable prominence and power (at least temporarily). These responsibilities did not occupy all his time. He still managed to spend more than a few evenings at the home of

---

* This meant that he could preach and distribute the sacrament, but could not yet consecrate the elements.
† The precise date is not known since he was ordained not in Prague, but at the archbishop's palace at Roudnice, whose registers have been lost.

Wenceslas the Cupmaker, a favorite haunt of the young Bohemian intelligentsia.[5]

The year 1401 also provided unhappy consequences for Hus, which were unforeseen at the time. His friend Jerome returned from his studies at Oxford in far off England. Since Princess Anne of Bohemia had become the queen of England's Richard II in 1382, travel, especially student travel, between the two realms had increased. History might have remained much quieter, however, if this particular young Bohemian had never set foot off his native soil. Tucked in among Jerome's other belongings as he entered Prague that day in 1401 were several treatises by one John Wycliffe,[6] an Englishman of

Jerome of Prague

some fame and notoriety alike. Wycliffe's philosophical works had been known in Bohemia for some time, and Hus himself had used several of them in his own undergraduate study and had lectured on four of them in classes he himself taught. For the most part, however, the Englishman's radical theological opinions were little known in Bohemia until Jerome re-

turned to Prague. Had Hus known all the trouble those few new volumes would stir up, his greetings to his friend might have been more subdued.

All that was in the future, however. In March 1402 Hus was installed as preacher of Bethlehem Chapel, succeeding his teacher Stephen of Kolín. Since Stephen handpicked Hus, that means he saw in him a spirit sympathetic to the tides of reform. Hus's reputation as a preacher grew by leaps and bounds. Vernacular preaching, while not unheard of, was something of a novelty. Though Hus preached three times a Sunday and several more times during the week, he usually spoke to a full house. Singing was also an important part of worship in Bethlehem Chapel, and Hus himself wrote several hymns. People came, returned, and more kept coming. Even the queen was among his hearers, and referred to him as "our chaplain."[7]

As of 1402, then, Hus at about the age of 30 had reached the pinnacle of his earthly success. He had all the things he had dreamed of as a poor hungry student, and more besides. Still more honor would come his way, but 1402 marked the last year of peace he ever knew.

The Wycliffe theological treatises brought back by Jerome were circulated, copies multiplied, and discussion spread. Among Wycliffe's ideas[8] was the doctrine of "remanence," which stated that the essence of bread and wine remained in holy communion after the consecration and were not totally replaced by the essence of the body and blood of Christ, as the orthodox doctrine of transubstantiation held. In late medieval Europe (as we shall see) such issues stirred up more excitement than they would today. Of more immediate concern (to secular authorities at least) was Wycliffe's idea of "dominion." This began with the medieval idea that all power, authority, and dominion belong to God, who like a feudal sovereign parcels them out to others below him. Wycliffe's radical application of this idea was to say that any church official who did not use this authority properly in fact lost it. That still was not a new idea, but what pricked the interest of secular powers in Wycliffe's concept was his assertion that secular rulers could (and perhaps should) divest erring church officials of their property. For the church to have too much property was itself an error, which might mean that kings and barons had a free hand to seize it. In Bohemia and Moravia, where the church held as much as one-third of the land,[9] Wycliffe's concept of "dominion" provided great danger or opportunity, depending on your point of view.

Already, in 1382, a church panel under the archbishop of Canterbury in England had declared 24 of Wycliffe's statements heretical. A German faculty member at the University of Prague pointed this out and added an additional 21 articles he himself considered heretical. In May 1403 the

University of Prague convened a meeting to consider the issue. The rector of the university that year was a German, as was the majority of the faculty. Most of these were of the nominalist school of philosophy.* Most of Czech faculty members were solidly "realist" school. Wycliffe himself was a realist, and so the Czechs were inclined to support him. The Germans were minded to reject him out of hand, both philosophically and theologically.

In addition, the Czech faculty was generally in favor of reform, and much of what Wycliffe wrote concerning corrupt clerics, return to Scripture, moral reform for all, etc., seemed in harmony with their native reform movement. Also they resented the Germans' dominance in the Czechs' "own" university. The Germans, who benefited from the status quo, were generally anti-reform. The senior Czech reform leaders, Stanislav of Znojmo and Stephen Páleč, vigorously defended Wycliffe. As for Hus, he was a rising star, and his influence was not yet supreme. He both agreed and disagreed with different points of Wycliffe. In any event, neither side paid attention to his measured speech requesting no rash action be taken. Numbers ruled, and, in an action that led to future trouble, the Wycliffe articles, all 45 of them, stood condemned by the faculty of the University of Prague.

The year 1403 also saw the accession of Zbyněk von Hasenburg as archbishop of Prague. He had little or no theological training. Soldiering had been his profession, and his appointment was political. Surprisingly, though, he took his new responsibilities seriously. Offended by the poor morals of many of the clergy, the "old soldier" turned to Hus for assistance in remedying the problem, and appointed him preacher of the provincial synod. Zbyněk asked Hus to address clerical morals head on, and also to report to him any abuses, irregularities, or other laxness he might see. Hus delivered his first synodal sermon in February 1404. Apparently it was just what the archbishop had in mind, for he renewed Hus's

---

* See chapter 1 for an explanation of nominalism and realism.

appointment. Priests whose toes Hus had stepped on were not happy with him, but in 1405 the relation of Hus and Zbyněk became even closer.

When three communion wafers were discovered soaked in "blood" in a ruined church, "miracles" started happening, pilgrims thronged, and the local clergy raked in the funds. Fearing that this was a scam to profit from false relics, Archbishop Zbyněk asked Hus to serve on a commission, which investigated and exposed the forgery. As the number of Hus's enemies increased, Hus's attitude toward corrupt clerics hardened.[10]

At this point the Wycliffe question came up again. The dispute of 1403 was painful at the time, but seemed relatively minor with the passing of a year or so. In 1405, though, Stanislav of Znojmo, leading the Czech reform party, reiterated his unqualified defense of Wycliffe, particularly of the doctrine of remanence in opposition to transubstantiation. Another faculty member promptly charged Znojmo with heresy of the gravest order. Archbishop Zbyněk, having insufficient theological training to settle the issue himself, appointed a commission. At this point Znojmo changed his tune, and claimed he meant his statements only for academic debate. Moreover he hadn't meant anything radical, much less heretical. His longwinded explanation saved him this time, but the archbishop was very concerned about rumors of heresy running rampant in his diocese.

The next year, 1406, Zbyněk issued a decree prohibiting the teaching of remanence in any form. He even forbade use of the word "bread" in referring to the sacrament after its consecration. Upset at Znojmo's cowardly conduct and partly to redeem the tarnished image of the Czech party, Hus wrote *De Corpore Christi* (On the Body of Christ). In it he expounded the orthodox doctrine of transubstantiation, though he did object to a few of Archbishop Zbyněk's statements, which he thought went too far in the other direction. Nevertheless, Hus was in basic agreement with the archbishop.[11]

Hus quietly continued to work on his doctorate, and in another year or two of uninterrupted study he would have earned the degree. However, in his sermon to the provincial synod on 18 October 1407, he issued an extremely scathing attack on clerical corruption. He was so harsh, in fact, that Archbishop Zbyněk thought he had gone too far and did not renew his appointment as synod preacher.[12]

This seemed a small matter, and Hus and the archbishop remained on reasonably good terms. After all, Hus had merely gone a little too far in a task the archbishop himself had assigned him, to preach against immorality in the clergy. The German faculty and wealthy clerics, though, were looking to discredit the Czechs and the voices of reform, and were eager to drive a wedge between them and the archbishop. They arranged to have Stanislav of Znojmo, the weak-kneed Czech reformer, charged again with Wycliffite heresies, but this time before the Curia* in Rome. This was serious, for having largely eliminated Wycliffism in its native England, papal officials were not about to allow it to take fresh root in Bohemia.

In Prague another Czech faculty member was charged with similar heresies before the archbishop's court. The archbishop was horrified that heresy might seem to be tolerated in his archdiocese and ordered the teacher to recant without more ado. The other Czech masters saw this as an attack on them all, but they promised not to teach the condemned articles "in their heretical, erroneous, and objectionable sense." That was a phrase obviously open to wide interpretation, and the archbishop suspected they were prevaricating. The rift between Zbyněk and the Czech reform movement had begun.

In the meantime, Stanislav of Znojmo and Stephen Páleč, by now implicated with his fellow reformer, set out for Rome to answer the charges against them. Along the way they were imprisoned, and while they were shortly released, their brief experience of the horrors of the medieval prison system turned

---

* The Roman Church's administrative department, which in the 21st century still rules on matters of faith and orthodoxy.

them into extremely cautious men. They realized that further dabbling in Wycliffism could get them a longer stint in the dungeons or worse. In terror both precipitously turned from arch-reformers into arch-conservatives. Henceforth none levied more scathing denunciations at Hus and the other reformers than did these former friends.

The most important immediate consequence of these events was that John Hus, of necessity, was now chief leader of the Czech reform movement. The former leaders, Znojmo and Páleč, had defected, and Stephen of Kolín had died. The abuse formerly divided among four leaders now fell on Hus alone.[13] It proved a heavy burden.

Relations between Archbishop Zbyněk and the reform movement were strained, but when he ordered all copies of Wycliffe's books submitted for review Hus complied, and the possibility for reconciliation remained. But then repercussions of the Great Western Schism described in chapter 1 intervened.

In the wider world, many thought that having two popes was appalling and division in the Western church simply had to end. A council was called to meet in Pisa, and its advocates scampered over Europe to drum up support. Through all this, Bohemia had been loyal to the Roman and not the Avignon pope. Now, however, emissaries promised weak-willed King Wenceslas IV of Bohemia that if he supported the council they would help him regain his title as Holy Roman emperor, from which he had been deposed. Wenceslas was already inclined toward the council idea, so the offer was too good to refuse. He declared for the council.

Then he discovered a complication. Archbishop Zbyněk remained loyal to the Roman Pope Gregory XII. No amount of argument would change his mind, so the king turned to the University of Prague for support. In December 1408 the Czech faculty declared its "neutrality" on which was the real pope. This was in effect an endorsement of the council.

With the university behind him, Wenceslas would have the clout he needed to overrule the archbishop. To his dismay, he

The Bethlehem Chapel in Prague.

found that while the Czech faculty supported the council, the German faculty did not. Wenceslas therefore decided the time had come for a long overdue reform of the university. "Is it right," he asked, "for the Czechs to be a minority in their own university?" Issuing the Edict of Kutná Hora in January 1409, he gave the Czech faculty a three-to-one vote over the German faculties in determining university policy, an exact reversal of the former ratio. Needless to say, support from the newly reorganized university for the king's papal policy was quickly forthcoming.

The Council of Pisa convened on 25 March 1409 with the support of Bohemia minus its archbishop. Two months later, the German faculty of the University of Prague, realizing their power was gone forever, resigned to found a new university of their own in Leipzig, Germany. In Bohemia, Archbishop Zbyněk was left practically alone in his support of Pope Gregory. Finally, royal, academic, and popular leverage broke his resolution. He agreed in September 1409 to recognize Pope Alexander V (d. 1410), who had been elected in Pisa that June, even though the Roman and Avignon popes refused to resign.

In October 1409 John Hus became the first rector of the newly reorganized University of Prague. The Czechs took great pride in their newly reformed university, and Hus received most of the credit for persuading the king to give them the ruling voice in university affairs. Hus, of course, was in favor of the changes, but as we have seen, the king's decision was based more on hopes of political gain than on sensitivity to nationalist sentiments.

Archbishop Zbyněk assumed Hus was to blame for recent events and also worried over Wycliffite heresy in his diocese. In 1410 he published a degree he had obtained from the pope (the Pisan one) restricting preaching to parish churches only. Since most of the parish clergy were anti-reform, this was aimed at the university and at Hus, whose Bethlehem Chapel was a special, not a parish, church.

Hus's reaction was quick and furious. He appealed to Pope John XXIII,* who had succeeded Alexander V in the Pisan line of popes. Hus and others also refused to obey Zbyněk's decree pending the outcome of the appeal. They declared that Christ's command to preach the Gospel had more authority than the

---

* The Council of Constance later decided this John XXIII was not a true pope, and so the name and number were used again by the beloved Pope John XXIII of Vatican II fame in the 20th century.

archbishop's prohibition. For the first time, Hus was in open rebellion against church authorities.

Archbishop Zbyněk was enraged. He ordered all Wycliffe's books burned, the philosophical along with the religious ones. Hus angrily retorted, which infuriated the archbishop even more. He pronounced a decree of excommunication against Hus. Hus again appealed to John XXIII, and a papal commission agreed with Hus that burning *all* Wycliffe's works was unjustified.

John XXIII, however, was not about to risk losing the support of the archdiocese of Prague by censuring its archbishop. He had gone to too much trouble to gain it. He turned the case over to Cardinal Odo de Colonna, who summoned Hus in harsh terms to appear before him in Bologna. Up to this point, Hus's case was a priest in dispute with his bishop, not a heretic summoned before an inquisitor. At least that is how Hus and his supporters viewed it.

Perhaps Hus remembered the tales Znojmo and Páleč had told of their treatment by a papal official (in fact this same Colonna) two years before. In any case, he refused to appear before Colonna, but offered to send representatives. More threats followed, but Hus ignored them and continued preaching. The king chose to support Hus, and so his enemies could do little.

In February 1411 a cardinal condemned Hus, not for heresy but for failure to appear. Hundreds in Prague cheered as the document was tossed on a bonfire. Hus's case bounced around in the Curia, and another cardinal reversed the original condemnation. Again the charge was for preaching without permission, not what he preached in itself. The case finally landed on the desk of a cardinal who chose to do nothing at all about it, and there for months it lay in ambiguous deadlock.

Archbishop Zbyněk and King Wenceslas remained at odds. After the archbishop left Prague for the safety of his country estate, the king seized church property on the grounds that the clergy were negligent in performing their functions. That act exuded Wycliffe's theory of "dominion" and only confirmed the opinion of those who feared the Czech reform was a new species of Wycliffism. Wenceslas's action also confirmed one objection to Wycliffe's ideas: unscrupulous secular rulers will gladly seize the slightest opportunity to confiscate church property if they have the notion of "dominion" to justify their actions.

The archbishop responded in the harshest terms available to him. He placed Prague under interdict, which closed all churches and suspended all sacraments. To medieval minds this was the most awesome of weapons, for the means of grace and salvation were thus denied them. The king, however, forbade the clergy to obey the interdict, and for whatever reasons the clergy this time sided with the king. Practically speaking, Archbishop Zbyněk had suffered defeat.

He salvaged what he could. A royal commission offered the following terms: the archbishop must submit to the king, annul Hus's excommunication, lift the interdict, and request all papal proceedings against the reformers be dropped because "there was no heresy in Bohemia." In return, Hus would write a testimonial attesting his orthodoxy to the pope, and the king would return the seized property to the church. Zbyněk felt all this was monstrous blackmail just to get back what was his by right in the first place. It seemed he would have to agree anyway, but then the "old soldier" in him showed his true mettle. In September 1411 he told the king that his conscience would not let him accept the conditions and that he would go into exile in Hungary rather than be humiliated in Prague. He indeed set out, but became ill as he reached Bratislava on 28 September. Worn out by all the disputes and the rigors of the journey, he died the same day.

Thus ended the dispute of Hus and Archbishop Zbyněk, and so perished an excellent man who, but for fate, might have been one of Hus's greatest champions. He was not particularly suited for high religious office, but once he assumed his position he tried to perform his obligations to the best of his abilities. Works favorable to Hus have tended to judge Zbyněk harshly. This is unfortunate, for it must be remembered that he had been a firm friend of church reform. He cooled toward the movement only when several of its proponents turned to extremism. Zbyněk honestly wanted to protect the Catholic faith of Bohemia against what he feared were dangerous Wycliffite innovations. Circumstances drove him to rash acts, but only after he had attempted a more measured approach without success. Opponents of church reform were able to use Hus's leanings toward some of Wycliffe's ideas to estrange the archbishop from him. Nationalism and the politics of the Great Western Schism combined in a tragic manner to widen this separation. Zbyněk and Hus had the misfortune to be dedicated to many of the same goals, but to see them from different viewpoints. Both were too uncompromising in their ideals to reach honest reconciliation. Both suffered exile for their conscience and convictions, so near and yet so far apart.

The death of Archbishop Zbyněk might have stopped the progress of events that led Hus to the fires of Constance. The case against him at Rome had ground to a halt, and without the archbishop to push it, it might have remained that way or been dismissed. But events in the wider world conspired to stir things up again. Ladislas of Naples, a supporter of Pope Gregory, drove John XXIII from Rome in the very month in which Archbishop Zbyněk died, and John promptly proclaimed a crusade against Ladislas. To finance this war, John hit upon the idea of a wide-scale sale of indulgences.

Accordingly, on 22 May 1412 Wenceslas Tiem and Pax de Bologna arrived in Prague, having procured the indulgence franchise for the kingdom of Bohemia (with the right to sublet). Soon, hawkers roamed the streets, and large chests were set up in the principal churches to receive the proceeds.

Such chests were conspicuously absent in Bethlehem Chapel. Hus himself had forbidden them, and in a sermon delivered to a large congregation he sternly denounced the sale of indulgences. He was very careful not to deny the validity of indulgences as such. He was willing to admit that the surplus merit of Christ and the saints might be applied to other people to reduce their time in purgatory. It was the present commercialization that he opposed as well as the many misunderstandings the sales caused. Repentance for sins was included as a condition for receiving an indulgence; but in actual practice this essential condition was being ignored, and a monetary contribution was the only condition mentioned. Hus also objected that the indulgence sellers implied that the granting of forgiveness did not depend on God's grace, but on their own wills and mercy — and these had to be bought.

As usual, the university held a disputation to consider the issue. Hus made a mild statement; his friend Jerome used more forceful language; and their former friends Znojmo and Páleč defended anything the pope's officials wanted to do. Having narrowly escaped imprisonment, those two had learned well the dangers of radicalism and had renounced opposition to church policy forever.

One other change of heart had dire consequences for Hus. King Wenceslas, who had defended him against the archbishop, suddenly came out in favor of Hus's opponents. Perhaps he feared that further disturbances might threaten the stability of the country. Perhaps he thought that support for John XXIII's crusade might gain him the title of emperor again. Then again perhaps he was guaranteed a percentage of the indulgence profits, and that is what swayed him.[14]

Others took up Hus's opposition to the sale of indulgences. Students at the university rioted, and on Sunday 10 July 1412 three young apprentices jumped up in the cathedral and two other churches and called the indulgence sellers frauds and liars even as they stood in the pulpits. The apprentices were arrested, and Hus rushed to the town hall to offer himself in exchange for them. Their actions, rash as they were, he said, were stirred up by his preaching, and he accepted responsibility for their deeds. The officials refused the exchange, perhaps fearing that the angry crowd that accompanied Hus would tear them apart if they imprisoned Hus. They assured Hus that no serious action would be taken against the offenders, and Hus persuaded the mob to go home. Then no sooner than the crowd dispersed, the magistrates led the three young men into the public square and executed them.

Faced with this *fait accompli* and a strongly barricaded town hall, the youths' friends could only carry their lifeless bodies in procession to Bethlehem Chapel, singing a hymn in honor of martyrs. There on the next day Hus buried them, again using the psalms and prayers appropriate to martyrs of the faith.

This further angered the king, and on 29 July the wealthy clergy of Prague urged John XXIII to take action against Hus and his anti-establishment supporters. John appointed a more active cardinal to take over the case, and this cardinal summoned Hus to appear in person before him in Rome under pain of excommunication. Previous threats had not caused Hus to comply, but this time to the excommunication was added the condition that if Hus did not obey, the city of Prague or any place that gave him shelter would be placed under interdict as long as he remained there. The decree was published in Prague on 18 October 1412.

Seeing that all human means had been exhausted, Hus took an unprecedented step. He appealed from the judgment of the church directly to the judgment of Christ.[15] This was a shocking action, since to the medieval world the church was the instrument *sine quā non*, chosen by Christ to rule his flock and govern its affairs. In seeking help beyond the church, Hus shattered the established order and squelched all real hope of reconciliation.

Archbishop Zbyněk had tried to use the interdict before, but that time the king had opposed it, and the clergy had not enforced it. This time when the dread decree arrived and Hus refused to submit, the king refused to interfere. The interdict would strike Prague with full force — no one could receive the sacraments, so crucial to salvation.

Hus now faced a hard decision. He had no intention of backing down himself, but was it right, he wondered, to make the whole city, the flock to which he had pastoral responsibility, suffer for his action, even if many were willing to do so? On the other hand, shouldn't he stand valiantly against what he considered unjust and arbitrary use of ecclesiastical power?

At length he decided on a mid course. He could make his stand just as forcefully away from Prague, thus relieving his fellow citizens of heavy burdens. So in October 1412 he left Prague and early in 1413 sought refuge at Kozí Hrádek, the estate of a nobleman friend in southern Bohemia.

Various commissions studied the issue, and one even ruled in Hus's favor. Tiring of all the charges and counter-charges, King Wenceslas now turned his anger upon Znojmo and Páleč for their "obstinate" refusal to compromise with Hus in the slightest degree. These gentlemen deemed it safer for their health to take an extended vacation in foreign parts.[16] Rome, however, remained firm in its opposition to Hus, who had to remain in exile, since the king was again unwilling to give him full support.

During these months of exile Hus compiled a collection of his sermons and brought forth several Czech works, using accent marks such as "š" instead of the older combinations of letters such as "sz" or "sch." Thus Hus standardized the written Czech language as Calvin later standardized French. In addition, Hus wrote several Latin treatises, of which the foremost was his *De Ecclesia* (On the Church), which set forth his basic understandings of the "true" church in its heavenly and earthly aspects. He also completed his *De Simonia* (On Simony), which condemned buying and selling church offices and further infuriated, if possible, Hus's wealthy clerical enemies.

While Hus labored on his theological works in exile and occasionally preached to the people in south Bohemia, affairs in the wider world moved on. After years of infighting and disputed elections which for a time produced three "emperors" to match the three "popes," Sigismund (d. 1437) was finally declared Holy Roman emperor in 1411, replacing his brother Wenceslas, who retained his crown as king of Bohemia. As emperor, Sigismund* pressured John XXIII to call a truly General Council to settle the Great Western Schism once and for all. Fearing the outcome, John postponed action as long as he could until finally it became obvious even to him that something had to be done, and if he did not take the initiative, others would seize it for their own benefit. Accordingly, John solemnly proclaimed a General Council, to open on the Feast of All Saints, 1 November 1414, in the imperial German city of Constance near the Swiss border. John preferred less neutral ground, but the general mood demanded a location where supporters of all three popes could meet in relative safety. At last it seemed as if the terrible schism that had divided the Western church since 1378 might be brought to an end.

This council gave promise to benefit the kingdom of Bohemia as well. The land of the Czechs had been getting too much of a reputation as a seedbed of Wycliffite heresy. Now King Wenceslas hoped that the council, besides healing the schism, would provide a chance to clear the name of his realm. Emperor Sigismund was also anxious to remove the suspicion of heresy from his part of the world.

To accomplish these ends, the sovereigns had to deal with John Hus in some way. Sigismund dispatched two messengers, Wenceslas of Dubá and John of Chlum, to persuade Hus to appear before the council to defend himself and vindicate his nation's name. As an added enticement, Sigismund offered Hus a safe conduct to and from Constance. What this "safe conduct" meant has raged in debate for centuries, but obviously to Hus it guaranteed his safety, no matter what happened at Constance, despite the fact that no details of the assurance were written down.[17]

It is not clear what Hus expected to accomplish in this venture. Having spent the last years in exile and disfavor, any

---

* Though Sigismund was elected emperor in 1410, succeeding Wenceslas and Rupert (Wittelsbach), he was not crowned emperor until 1433. Historians, however, simplify matters by calling him emperor from 1410 on.

chance of vindication must have seemed attractive. He had never given up on the church as such, and reform was part of the council's agenda. He was also under pressure from the king to go. Most of all, Hus absolutely and passionately believed in his total innocence of all charges brought against him, and he clearly thought his innocence would be plain to all once he had a fair hearing. Hus certainly realized he was exposing himself to danger, but he made the decision to appear in Constance with some hope of success.[18]

Notes

[1] The basis for this and the next chapter is my doctoral thesis, "The Theology of John Hus" (University of Manchester, 1975).

[2] Details of Hus's life are mostly from Matthew Spinka, *John Hus: A Biography* (Princeton: Princeton University Press, 1968). A helpful earlier work is David Schaff, *John Hus: His Life, Teachings, and Death after Five Hundred Years* (New York: Charles Scribner's Sons, 1915). Edmund de Schweinitz, *History of the Church Known as the Unitas Fratrum*, 2nd (reprint) ed. (Bethlehem, Pa.: Moravian Publication Concern, 1901), is also a good read.

[3] For more details on the universities in general, see Hastings Rashdall, *The Universities of Europe in the Middle Ages,* ed. F. M. Powicke and A. B. Emden, 2 vols (Oxford: Clarendon Press, 1936). Also, for curriculum, see David Knowles, *The Evolution of Medieval Thought* (London: Longmans, Green, and Co., 1962).

[4] Schaff, 21.

[5] A. H. Wrastislaw, *John Hus* (London: Society for Promoting Christian Knowledge, 1882), 79.

[6] Variously spelled as Wyclif, Wiclif, Wickliffe, etc.

[7] "Letter of Queen Sophia to John XXIII," F. Palacky, ed. *Documenta Mag. Joannis Hus* (Prague: F. Tempsky, 1869), 423.

[8] Gordon Leff, *Heresy in the Later Middle Ages: The Relation of Heterodoxy to Dissent c. 1215- c. 1450,* 2 vols. (Manchester: Manchester University Press, 1967). See also Amedeo Molnár, "Recent Literature on Wiclif's Theology" *Communio Viatorum* 8 (1964): 186-92. Also Herbert B. Workman, *John Wyclif: A Study of the English Medieval Church,* 2 vols. (Hamden, Conn.: Archon Books, 1966, unaltered reprint of Clarendon Press edition, 1926).

[9] Some scholars, such as Frederick G. Heymann, *John Žižka and the Hussite Revolution* (Princeton: Princeton University Press, 1955, reissued by Russell and Russell, 1969), 39, estimate that the church owned at least half of the land in Bohemia.

10 Matthew Spinka, *John Hus at the Council of Constance* (New York: Columbia University Press, 1965), 33.

11 Catholic theologian Dom Paul de Vooght states unequivocally that Hus was completely orthodox in his exposition. See "Huss a-t-il enseigné la remanentia substantia panis post consecrationem?" in *Hussiana* (Louvain: Publications Universitaires de Louvain, 1960), 263-91.

12 Count Lützow, *The Life and Times of Master John Hus* (London: J. M. Dent and Co., 1909), 86.

13 Spinka, *John Hus at the Council of Constance*, 30.

14 Spinka, *John Hus at the Council of Constance*, 41.

15 Schaff, 138. See Amedeo Molnár, "Hus et son appel à Jésus Christ," *Communio Viatorum* 8 (1965): 95-104.

16 Shaff, 154.

17 Henry Charles Lea, *A History of the Inquisition of the Middle Ages* (New York: Macmillan Co., 1922 reprint of the 1887 ed.), 2:462.

18 Spinka, *John Hus' Concept of the Church* (Princeton: Princeton University Press, 1966), 334.

Chapter 4

Hus at Constance

'I Am Willing Gladly to Die Today,' 1414-1415

Once he decided to go to Constance, John Hus applied himself to preparations for his journey and defense. In this he enjoyed the assistance of John of Jesenice, a remarkably astute canon lawyer who was completely devoted to Hus and had served as his advocate before. Jesenice himself had been exiled because of his defense of Hus, and so could not accompany Hus to Constance. He had a clear idea, though, of what would be required there, and did his best to prepare Hus for the ordeal to come.

Jesenice knew that for Hus to appear before the council as one already condemned for Wycliffism by curial or episcopal courts would be certain doom. If he could show that Hus's previous condemnations and excommunication were for administrative and not doctrinal issues, then some hope of success remained. He therefore arranged for Hus in August 1414 to have public notices posted throughout Prague challenging anyone knowing of any heresy in him to make formal charges against him and debate with him before the diocesan synod. The new archbishop of Prague, Conrad of Vechta, was persuaded to write a certificate attesting to Hus's orthodoxy. Jesenice even got a similar affidavit from the papal inquisitor in Prague. With all this, Jesenice believed he had assured Hus's appearance at Constance would not be as a heretic before the Inquisition. This was extremely important, for as a free person coming to share his views, Hus would be entitled to due process of law. As one charged with heresy, particularly as one holding views already condemned, he would have no rights at all.

Jesenice's preparations went even further. He knew Hus must refute erroneous allegations concerning his previous trials and hearings, so he composed a detailed chronological summary of events entitled *Ordo procedendi* (Order of proceedings), to which Hus could refer for specific dates, wording, and the like.[1] Jesenice also arranged to give what advice he could by letter as affairs progressed in Constance.

Hus too prepared for Constance, but his own efforts were less calculating and more naïve than those of his lawyer friend. He composed a sermon, *De pace* (On peace), which he expected to be allowed to deliver to the entire council, and also a short treatise, *De sufficientia legis Christi* (On the sufficiency of the law of Christ). Just in case things went badly, however, he left behind his "last will and testament" and several letters to his friends. Hope, if not extreme optimism, was the order of the day as the time for departure drew near.

And so on 11 October 1414 Hus set out for Constance accompanied by Wenceslas Dubá and John of Chlum, the royal messengers who had become his friends, and several other persons and wagons.[2] They went through Germany, where Hus was encouraged by the friendly reception he received from most people. The writ guaranteeing Hus's safe conduct had been promised but not delivered, and it was thought wise to have it in hand before Hus appeared before the council, so Dubá went to find Emperor Sigismund, who was also on the road, to secure the document.

The Czechs arrived in Constance on 3 November 1414, and Hus took lodgings in the house of the widow Fida in St. Paul's Street.* Hus's friends went to announce his arrival to John XXIII, who declared "even if he had murdered the pope's

---

* The house is still there, with a plaque noting its most famous lodger. The street is now called the "Hussenstrasse" (Hus Street).

own brother, he should be safe in Constance." Hus's ex-communication and the interdict that followed him were suspended.* He was given the free run of the city, and he continued to say Mass and the Divine Office daily, though in private. The opening of the council was delayed because most of the delegates, including the emperor, had not arrived. Dubá came bringing the safe conduct on 5 November.

During this time, however, Hus's enemies were not idle. Michael de Causis, official representative for the vested inter-ests of wealthy Bohemian clerics, had been working behind the scenes to secure Hus's condemnation. Wenceslas Tiem, the indulgence seller whom Hus had opposed, also lent a hand. On 15 November the anti-Hus forces were bolstered by the arrival of Stephen Páleč and Bishop John the Iron of Litomyšl, who brought with them copies of Hus's latest writings. All of them, as Hus's friend Peter of Mladoňovice wrote, "scurried around" daily, lobbying the arriving bishops to place Hus under formal arrest. They also posted signs charging him with deception, and they spread a rumor that he had tried to escape the city hidden in a farmer's wagon.

All this conniving against him didn't seem to faze Hus. He composed a work on giving the chalice to the laity,† and in letters to friends back home he reported political gossip, complained about high prices, and boasted about his horse Rabštyn's performance on the journey to Constance.

Hus should have worried more about his enemies. They persuaded the pope and others that he would embarrass the

---

* Lifting the interdict was necessary, otherwise the council itself could not hold services while Hus was in the city.

† Hus did not initiate giving the chalice to the laity in Bethlehem Chapel, but his friend Jakoubek of Stříbro learned that the cup had been given to the laity in the Latin Church until only a couple of hundred years before. Based on that and Christ's mandate ("Drink from it, all of you," Matt. 26:27), Jakoubek initiated the practice after Hus's departure for Constance. Hus approved when he heard about it. See Matthew Spinka, trans. and ed., *The Letters of John Hus*, 181-82 and notes 2 and 7. See also Spinka, *John Hus: A Biography*, 255-57.

council if he were allowed to preach a sermon denouncing clerical morals (John XXIII's in particular couldn't stand too much scrutiny), calling for radical reforms, and spreading Wycliffite poison. The emperor's "safe conduct" was voided in two ways. First, it promised Hus's safety going to and from Constance but did not apply in Constance itself. Second, Hus was obviously a heretic, and promises made to heretics did not have to be kept. The council leaders therefore decided to treat Hus as one "accused of heresy and awaiting trial."[3]

John Hus now fell subject to the full rigors of the papal Inquisition, a system designed to prevent the least mistake in favor of the accused. The charges need not be revealed. Once formally accused, a defendant was immediately imprisoned to prevent flight. Accusers reporting heresies did not have to agree on details, since judges could assume the defendant was guilty by applying the principle "where there is smoke there must be fire." The defendant's writings (if any) were examined for the most minuscule theological error. Confession was the goal, and torture was an accepted means to that end. When a defendant was finally brought before the judges, guilt was normally assumed proven from what had gone before, and recantation, not proof of innocence, was the aim. If a defendant did not recant at once, the judges could order imprisonment, sometimes for years, until the accused was ready to confess.

In such a system defense was difficult, and acquittals rare. If the defendants were not told what they were accused of, asserting innocence of the charges was hard to do. Defendants had no right to confront their accusers. A defendant could have the testimony of a personal enemy excluded, but since even the accusers' names were often withheld, naming a lot of personal enemies in hope of hitting on the right ones was dangerous. After all, heretics were by nature "hateful people," and having a long list of enemies could be taken as further proof that one was a heretic.

Ignorance also provided a very limited defense. One might have unwittingly denied an accepted dogma or asserted an erroneous one and thus be guilty only of "material heresy."

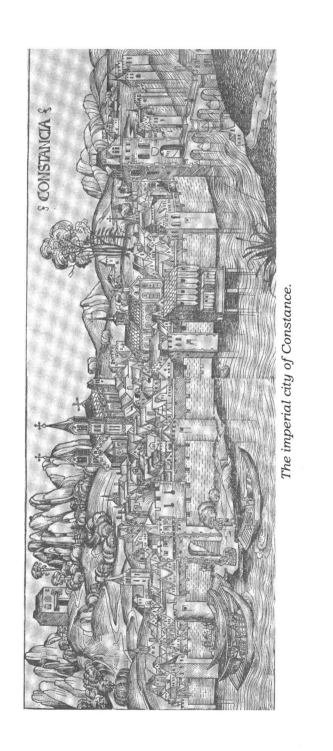

The imperial city of Constance.

Once the teaching of the church was explained, however, persisting in former opinions made the accused guilty of the more serious crime of "formal heresy." Either way, the verdict was guilty, and punishment followed. "Invincible ignorance" was about the only way to be let off entirely. That is, if defendants could convince the judges that they were too stupid to understand the charges, the judge might let them go. Such a defense was viewed with extreme skepticism (as the insanity plea is sometimes questioned today), since nothing but lies and deceptions could be expected from heretics.

When the accused recanted or when the inquisitor was convinced the prisoner was hopelessly obstinate, the final sentence was handed down. Only at this point did the Inquisition break the secrecy that characterized the rest of its procedures. A public ceremony, or *auto-da-fé*, was held. After the preaching of a solemn sermon, the heretics' names were read, together with their crimes, recantations, and sentences.

Punishment could be major or minor. For "material heresy" it might include public penance, pilgrimages, confiscation of property, etc. Major punishment for "formal heresy" included imprisonment, torture, and death. The church itself did not deign to shed blood, but left it to secular governments to actually carry out executions. One might save oneself from the death penalty even at the last moment by recanting, but life imprisonment, not freedom, was the result. Such was the Inquisition to which the council now committed the case of Master John Hus.

On 28 November 1414 two bishops, a knight, and the mayor of Constance came to Hus's lodgings just as Hus and his friends were taking their midday meal. The bishops said they had been sent by John XXIII to invite Hus to a "private conference." John of Chlum suspected something was up and protested "such treachery." Hus said he had come to Constance to express his views publicly but that he would also talk in private, and rose to accompany the delegation. This was just as well, for the house had meanwhile been surrounded by soldiers.

Hus was taken to the pope's quarters, where he spoke with a few cardinals, and then was left to cool his heels. A curial theologian disguised as a simple friar entered and in "casual" conversation tried to catch Hus saying something incriminating. Hus frustrated him by resolutely denying belief in remanence, etc. While this was going on, Páleč and Michael de Causis were in another room urging the cardinals to keep Hus under strict arrest. Around 4 o'clock in the afternoon the cardinals did just that.

As darkness fell, the master of the papal court told Chlum he could go, but Hus must remain. Chlum angrily burst in on John XXIII crying treachery. The pope denied knowledge of what was going on, but neither did he order Hus's release. John was apparently trying to bolster his own tenuous position with the council leaders.[4] Chlum left the palace in bitter disgust; Hus remained a prisoner.

Around 9 o'clock that night Hus was taken to the house of the precentor (choir leader) of the cathedral. Perhaps worried over Emperor Sigismund's reaction to the arrest, John XXIII wanted Hus out of his immediate custody as soon as possible.[5] Chlum continued to rave, but Hus's friend Peter of Mladoňovice was more practical and brought Hus his fur coat and a breviary to comfort the prisoner's body and soul.

Hus remained at the precentor's house for eight days while workmen prepared a cell for him in the Dominican monastery on a small island in Lake Constance.* It lay below ground and was exceedingly damp. To make matters worse, a latrine outlet ran right next to it, and the noxious vapors quickly made Hus critically ill. John XXIII sent his own physician to treat him, though clearly a change in location was what was most needed. John acted probably not out of generosity, but because he wanted Hus to live to recant rather than die as a "martyr" in prison.[6]

---

* The monastery is now the famous Insel Hotel, which provides luxurious accommodations to tourists who come to see the "Hus sites."

As one accused of heresy, Hus lost all normal rights to have his accusers sworn in his presence. Nevertheless, the council was aware of the Czech nobles' anger at Hus's seizure, and as a gesture of conciliation had the witnesses brought before Hus to take their oaths, an "unusual condescension."[7]

In December Hus was given a hearing at which he was accused of propounding Wycliffite heresies, remanence in particular. When Hus denied this, the attempt to convict him on the simple grounds of defending Wycliffe failed, but Páleč was commissioned to draw up a list of charges drawn from Hus's writings.

Emperor Sigismund finally arrived in Constance on 24 December 14. He went through the motions of protesting Hus's arrest, but a subtle hint that a council that had met to depose popes might also depose emperors was enough to damp his anger.[8]

Hus was finally moved to a better cell in the monastery on 9 January 1415. His health improved, and he was allowed to correspond with his friends. His letters from Constance provide a poignant view of his mood and thoughts during his imprisonment.[9] John of Chlum arranged for Hus to have pen and paper by the simple expedient of bribing Hus's jailers.

On the official side, however, Hus's case was progressing inexorably, and he was denied the right to have a lawyer. In spite of all of John of Jesenice's careful preparations, it was now clear that Hus was being treated as an already condemned heretic. As such he was lost from the start.

In the months that followed, the Council of Constance was too busy proclaiming itself the supreme authority in Christendom to give much thought to John Hus of Bohemia. On 21 March 1415 John XXIII saw all hope was gone of his being declared the true pope and he fled the city. Hus's jailers were under John's jurisdiction, and once their employer had fled they handed the keys to Hus's cell over to Sigismund. This presented the emperor with a perfect opportunity to redeem his pledge to Hus and order his release before matters went any further. Such a desire does not seem to have crossed his imperial mind. He quickly handed the keys over to the bishop of Constance.

On Palm Sunday night, 24 March 1415, Hus was transferred from the Dominican monastery to the bishop of Constance's castle at Gottlieben. It was a windy open tower, the opposite of his first cell, and Hus suffered from constant exposure. He was chained day and night, though by day he had a longer chain to move around somewhat. Since he could not escape from the lofty tower, the chains were unnecessary, but this was the closest the council came to imposing the accepted Inquisition practice of torture to produce a confession.

At first Hus's supporters did not know where he had been taken. Once they found him, they again bribed his jailers to give him better treatment and to allow him to write and receive letters. This was common practice at the time; jailers relied on bribes to supplement their inadequate salaries,* except that the inquisitorial nature of Hus's case made it riskier than usual.

In the weeks that followed, Hus was left to correspond with his friends, for the council was occupied with formally deposing John XXIII (29 May), thus eliminating one of the three claimants to the papal throne. It did find time on 4 May to condemn the 45 Wycliffite articles again. This did not bode well for Hus, but the council did not deal directly with him — for now.

Hus's friends tried to get him released on bail, which shows that they did not fully understand the inquisitorial process.[10] They kept up pressure, which may actually have hastened his death.[11] They finally received word from Sigismund that Hus would be given a public hearing on 5 June.[12] Since Hus's guilt was already "legally proven" the council did not have to talk any more with him. All that remained was to formally condemn him and hand him over for execution. Nevertheless, Sigismund apparently persuaded the judges that the Czechs did not understand the process, and if Hus were not given a hearing it

---

* This has been compared to the modern practice of tipping.

John Hus before the Council of Constance. In this painting by Wenceslas Brožík, the bishop of Concordia pronounces the sentence upon Hus. Emperor Sigismund sits upon the throne.

might look as if the council was afraid to face him. That could cause trouble later. So the council agreed to alter the standard rules and grant an open session. It was, however, a public relations ploy and little more.[13]

On 3 June Hus was moved to the Franciscan monastery in Constance, and a new commission of four cardinals was appointed to replace the one appointed by John XXIII, which had lost its authority with John's deposition. On 5 June 1415, as promised, the formal trial began.

Contrary to a promise made to Emperor Sigismund for a public hearing, the proceedings began without Hus present. Dubá and Chlum learned of this and rushed to Sigismund, who angrily demanded that Hus be present and that he himself be informed before anything was done. Thus Hus was able to attend his own trial and to introduce copies of his works for whose authenticity he could vouch. When Hus tried to explain his views he was shouted down and ordered to give only "yes" and "no" answers. For a time he lapsed into silence, which was hailed as an admission of guilt. The presiding judges soon completely lost control of the session, for inquisitors were not used to "discussing" charges with the accused. The session dissolved into such a hubbub that the proceedings had to be adjourned until 7 June.

Following an almost total eclipse of the sun, the second session of the trial opened. Sigismund was present, and again made no move to defend Hus, but urged him to throw himself on the mercy of the council. In reality, that was all Hus could have done, for he had already been condemned by an archbishop and a cardinal, with many of the clergy speaking against him, and he had indeed used many of Wycliffe's ideas, which also had already been condemned. He did, however, continue to deny holding to remanence, the notion that the essence of the bread and wine of holy communion remained even after consecration into the body and blood of Christ, but the judges assumed he was lying.

The session continued the next day with the reading of formal charges against Hus. Cardinal d'Ailly intoned:

> Master John! Behold, two ways are placed before you,
> of which, choose one! Either you throw yourself
> entirely and totally on the grace and into the hands of
> the Council, that whatever the Council shall dictate to
> you, therewith you shall be content. And the Council
> . . . will deal kindly and humanely with you. Or, if
> you still wish to hold and defend some articles of
> the aforementioned, and if you desire still another
> hearing, it shall be granted to you.[14]

The implication was clear. If Hus chose the second course the
council would not deal "kindly and humanely."

Almost stubbornly now, Hus asked for another hearing,
another chance to explain his views. It was never given. The
final charges were drawn up on 18 June, and were 30 in
number. He was accused of holding extreme views of predestination that made the church and pope superfluous, and
claiming that sinful ecclesiastical or secular officials had no
authority. He was also accused of defending the 45 Wycliffite
articles[15] and urging the faithful to ignore church authority.
Most of those charges were drawn from his *De Ecclesia*.
Another 17 were taken from witnesses' statements, which
claimed that he defended the heresies of Wycliffe, particularly
remanence and the seizing of church property. He also supposedly called the Roman Church the "Synagogue of Satan,"
and denied indulgences, the authority of the papacy and canon
law, and ultimately the sacramental system.[16]

How would Hus have answered these accusations? A copy
of the charges has been preserved with his replies written in
his own hand.[17] In defining the church as the predestinate, he
wrote, he was referring only to the Eternal Church which
would join Christ in heaven. The church on earth naturally
contained both predestinate and "foreknown." He also qualified
the charges made against him concerning the authority of
the pope, clerics, and secular rulers, saying that when they
followed Christ they exercised their authority "worthily." He
protested that statements from his own works had been taken
out of context or were given the most radical interpretation
possible. As to Wycliffe, he again denied holding to remanence

and said others had twisted his statements to make it appear that he accepted all of Wycliffe. He explained his position on other charges in a similar manner. For example, he did not reject the idea of indulgences, only the corrupt sale of them to finance military campaigns.

All Hus's explanations fell on deaf ears, for the Council of Constance saw only a heretic standing before it. From 18 June to the early days of July officials of both church and empire urged him to recant. Hus refused, saying he would not perjure himself by confessing to things he had never said.

The council condemned serving the chalice to the laity in holy communion, stating that the practice, newly restored in Prague with Hus's blessing, was now "against the custom of the church."* In impotent fury Hus remarked: "Alas! Now malice condemns Christ's institution as an error!"[18]

Desperately wanting a submissive penitent rather than a revered martyr on their hands, Hus's judges went far beyond normal procedure. They could not set him free, for his name was too closely associated with that known heretic Wycliffe, and the council could not afford to seem soft on heresy. Still, in an "almost incredible" gesture, a confessor gave him absolution even though he refused to abjure his "heresies."[19] Hus did offer to swear that he had never held, nor would he ever hold, the errors imputed to him. This novel suggestion momentarily threw his judges into a quandary. They fashioned a formula whereby Hus would acknowledge that he had been accused of some things he never said, but he would still "revoke, recant, and abjure" them. Digging in his heels, Hus refused, saying this still implied an acknowledgement that he had held *some* heresies. He scorned the suggestion made by a council official known only as "Pater" (the father) that any guilt for a false confession would be the council's, not his.[20]

A final attempt to reach an agreement was made 5 July 1415. The cardinals offered to set aside the witnesses' charges

---

* It remained "against the custom of the church" until the 1960s when Vatican II reversed this decree of the Council of Constance.

and have him "abjure" only the extracts from his books. Hus said those extracts were twisted and made him appear to say things he never meant. Neither was Hus won over by the suggestion that to "abjure" meant simply to repudiate, not to acknowledge one's own guilt. His judges could only conclude that he was "obstinate," and death was the only course left.

In another age Hus might have fared better. The Council of Constance, however, was faced with chaos in the church, which desperately needed restoration of authority and order under a single pope. It was clear to the council fathers that the individual conscience, to which Hus appealed, must bow to the general will, or even worse chaos would result. This was no time to allow "free and open" discussion of heretical opinions. Three popes at once was bad enough and could not be tolerated; thousands of free thinking "heretics" roaming about was a nightmare beyond imagination. In short, Hus was rocking the boat when everyone was already seasick. The council could not quibble over fine points with a single Bohemian.[21]

Hus arrayed for the stake.

The council now dealt with Hus once and for all. On the morning of 6 July Hus was led into the cathedral, where the council was assembled. As he entered the church he fell on his knees and prayed silently "for a long time." The bishop of Lodi, following the time-honored procedure of the Inquisition, preached a sermon on the necessity of uprooting heretics. Then the formal charges were read once again. Hus attempted to answer these, but was told to be quiet, for the time for

John Hus at the stake, 6 July 1415.

speaking was past. Hus attempted to explain himself again as the formal condemnation was read. His words were ignored.

Hus was then ordered to put on the priestly vestments for Mass so that he might be formally defrocked. When he had done this, each vestment was stripped from him in turn with an appropriate curse. Finally a tall paper hat with three devils drawn on it was placed on his head, and he was led to the place of execution outside the city walls of Constance.* There Hus was bound to the stake, and wood and straw were piled up to his chin. The imperial marshal asked him one last time if he wished to recant. To this, Hus replied in a loud voice:

> God is my witness that those things that are falsely ascribed to me and of which the false witnesses accuse me, I have never taught or preached. But that the principal intention of my preaching and of all my other acts or writings was solely that I might turn men from sin. And in that truth of the Gospel that I wrote, taught, and preached in accordance with the sayings and expositions of the holy doctors, I am willing gladly to die today.[22]

At these words the officials gave the signal, and the torch was applied to the pyre. Hus's friend Peter of Mladoňovice carefully recorded the last moments of his beloved master:

> When the executioners at once lit [the fire], the Master immediately began to sing in a loud voice, at first "Christ, Thou Son of the living God, have mercy upon us." And secondly, "Christ, Thou Son of the living God, have mercy upon me," and in the third place, "Thou who art born of Mary the Virgin." And when he began to sing the third time, the wind blew the flame into his face. And thus praying within himself and moving his lips and the head, he expired in the Lord. While he was silent, he seemed to move before he actually died for about the time one can quickly recite "Our Father" two or at most three times.[23]

And so died Master John Hus of Bohemia, whom an intricate series of events had brought to this violent end. When the fire had burned down, the executioners took special care that his head and heart were thoroughly consumed. Then loading the ashes into a cart, lest the Czechs preserve them as relics, they bore them away and flung them into the quiet waters of the Rhine River, which flowed nearby. At last the turbulent life of John Hus had ended in rest.

---

* This area is now inside the city surrounded by apartment buildings. A large stone called the "Hussenstein" marks the spot where Hus was burned at the stake.

Notes

1 This invaluable document is published in V. Novotny, ed., *M. Jana Husi Korespondence a dokumenty* (Prague: Komise pro vydávání pramenu náboženského hnutí českého, 1920), 225-34.

2 The details of Hus's experiences in Constance, unless otherwise noted, are drawn from an eyewitness account left by Hus's friend and companion Peter of Mladoňovice, translated in Matthew Spinka, *John Hus at the Council of Constance* (New York: Columbia University Press, 1965), 89-234.

3 For more on this and inquisitorial procedures, see Henry Charles Lea, *A History of the Inquisition of the Middle Ages* (New York: Macmillan Co., 1922 reprint of the 1887 ed.), vol. 2, and G. G. Coulton, *Inquisition and Liberty* (Boston: Beacon Press, 1938).

4 John Holland Smith, *The Great Schism, 1378* (New York: Weybright and Talley, 1970), 183.

5 Louise R. Loomis, trans., *The Council of Constance: The Unification of the Church*, ed. John H. Mundy and Kennerly M. Woody (New York: Columbia University Press, 1961), 469, translating the journal of Cerietano, a papal notary.

6 Lea, 2:461.

7 Lea, 2:477.

8 David Schaff, *John Hus: His Life, Teachings, and Death after Five Hundred Years* (New York: Charles Scribner's Sons, 1915), 186.

9 Matthew Spinka, trans. and ed., *The Letters of John Hus* (Manchester: Manchester University Press, 1972), passim.

10 Lea, 2:427-31, 447.

11 Lea, 2:478, 482-83.

12 Matthew Spinka, *John Hus: A Biography* (Princeton: Princeton University Press, 1968), 239-40.

13 Lea, 2:484.

14 Spinka, *John Hus: A Biography*, 271-72.

15 Hus's use of Wycliffe has remained controversial. Hus indeed copied passages of Wycliffe into his own writings, but this was common practice at the time, and was seen as a compliment to the original author, not plagiarism. However, Hus used so much of Wycliffe that some later scholars asserted he had few if any original ideas of his own but merely parroted the Englishman. (See Johann Loserth, *Huss und Wiclif: Zur Genesis der husitischem Lehre*, 2nd ed. (Munich: R. Oldenbourg, 1925). An English translation of the first (1884) edition is *Wiclif and Hus*, trans. M. J. Evans (London: Hodder and Stoughton, 1884.) Other scholars have disagreed and have insisted that Hus modified many of the Wycliffe passages he used to give them a different meaning of his own. (Jan Sedlák, Vaclav Novotný, F. M. Bartoš, and Vaclav Flajšans, for example. For a

consideration of many of these see Lea, 2:656, and Amedeo Molnár, "Recent Literature on Wiclif's Theology" *Communio Viatorum*, 8 (1964).) Hus's adding "worthily," as mentioned in chapter 4, for instance, changed a heretical statement into a perfectly orthodox one. Matthew Spinka presented this viewpoint but concluded that Hus might have been wiser to have openly disagreed with Wycliffe rather than merely inserting orthodox modifiers: "At least, it should be clear that he differed from Wyclif to an essential degree and that even those articles he chose to defend he interpreted in a sense not only divergent from that ascribed to them by his enemies, but even inconsistent with Wyclif's own intention." (Spinka, *Biography*, 160.) Belgian Catholic scholar Dom Paul de Vooght also did a thorough study of this issue and concluded that the parts Hus copied from Wycliffe were largely "pure Catholic doctrine," at least as they were modified and used by Hus. (L'hérésie de Jean Huss (Louvain: Publications Universitaires de Louvain, 1960), 81-84 et passim.)

[16] Spinka, *John Hus: A Biography*, 265-71, discusses the individual charges at length.

[17] Spinka, *John Hus at the Council of Constance*, 260-70.

[18] Spinka, *John Hus: A Biography*, 257.

[19] Lea, 2:488.

[20] Spinka, *John Hus: A Biography*, 278-80.

[21] Vilém Herold in his "Jan Hus — A Heretic, a Saint, or a Reformer," *Communio Viatorum* 45 (2003): 5-23, notes on 21 that Pope John Paul II in 2003 appointed a commission to reinvestigate the Hus case and expressed "deep sorrow" over Hus's "cruel death."

[22] Spinka, *John Hus at the Council of Constance*, 233.

[23] Spinka, *John Hus at the Council of Constance*, 233.

Chapter 5

Hussite Wars

Divisions within Divisions, 1415-1452

𝕴f the Council of Constance thought it had solved the John Hus/Czech problem, it was sadly mistaken. Making Hus a martyr had all the bad consequences some of the council leaders had feared. The flames that consumed him touched off a wildfire that would not easily be put out, and whose aftermath continues through the centuries.[1]

As soon as news of Hus's death reached Prague the whole city was stirred from top to bottom.* Even some who had not supported Hus and the Czech reform movement were roused to protest the "insult" to the Czech national honor. In the weeks following, angry crowds plundered houses of priests known to have had a hand in Hus's death, Archbishop Conrad of Vechta fled the city, and most churches were placed in the hands of priests sympathetic to the reform movement.

Letters from the Council of Constance to the Czech people justifying its actions and threatening "severest discipline" on those who still defended Hus only made the anger seethe hotter. On 2 September 1415 Bohemia's national assembly (Diet) passed a defiant answer to the council, and a large

---

* The report of Hus's death is supposedly the source of the expression "his goose is cooked." Hus's name in Czech sounds like "husa" the word for goose, and legend has it that the message, "The goose is cooked," was a code devised to let the folks in Prague know that the worst had happened.

number of barons and knights signed the document, which was "full of reproaches and counter menaces." On 5 September, 452 nobles and knights formed the "Hussite League" and covenanted that for six years they would defend the cause of reform and acknowledge the University of Prague, not any pope, as having the last word in theological matters.[2] Hus's friend Jakoubek of Stříbro, who had introduced the giving of the chalice to the laity and was to succeed Hus as preacher of Bethlehem Chapel, assumed leadership of the reform movement. Popular support for their leaders was high, though even in Prague not everyone had suddenly become a Hussite.

The treatment by the Council of Constance of another friend of Hus, Jerome of Prague, did nothing to calm the storm.[3] Jerome had been seized just before he reached the Bohemian border on his way home to Prague, and was returned to Constance in chains. He was charged with holding the "heresies of Wycliffe and Hus" and was tortured by being hung by his feet. The council did not want another martyr and was determined to force a recantation from Jerome at all costs. Stephen Páleč was again one of the main accusers. Jerome, by his own admission, thought to win release by agreeing with whatever the council demanded, and then, when he was at a safe distance, take back his recantation. To his horror he found that, in accordance with standard inquisitorial practice, even after he had denounced his great friend Hus as a heretic, the council would not set him free, but ordered his continued imprisonment. Jerome then repudiated his earlier recantation and demanded another hearing. After nearly a year of imprisonment, this was granted on 23 May 1416, and the sessions were as chaotic as those of Hus's trial. Finally, the council concluded that Jerome was hopelessly obdurate, and on 30 May condemned him to death. He was led to the same spot where Hus was burned and tied to a stake of his own. In a final burst of defiance, when the executioner was about to light the fire behind his back, Jerome called to him to come around front to do it, "for if I feared it, I would not have come here!"[4] Jerome's name is placed alongside Hus's on the rock that marks the spot.

Pope Martin V, almost as soon as he was elected at Constance in November 1417 as the one pope recognized by all, called for a crusade against the recalcitrant Czech supporters of Hus. That did not materialize, thanks to the assurances of Emperor Sigismund and King Wenceslas that they would take steps to cool the situation. However, their own inaction to prevent Hus's death had totally discredited them with a large portion of the population.

By the time the Council of Constance was ready to adjourn on 22 April 1418, Bohemia and Moravia were ready to erupt in revolt. The council had indeed united around one pope, Martin V, but the reforms promised as part of the agenda were postponed until a future council. Of course, the condemnation of Hus and Jerome remained a raw sore. No wonder Stephen Páleč, who had done so much to secure the deaths of both, was afraid to return home. He spent the rest of his life in Poland.

Not all Czechs supported the reform movement, and to counter the "Hussite League," a "Catholic League" was formed. Several nobles and cities remained solidly loyal to Rome, and certainly many of the "common people" clung to the Catholic Church as they had known it. It would take only a small spark, though, to ignite violent civil war.

Within the reform movement, leadership was provided at the university by Hus's longtime friends. John of Jesenice and Peter of Mladoňovice took a conservative approach, insisting only on clearing Hus's name and the giving of the chalice to the laity. Jakoubek of Stříbro agreed with that, but wanted more general reform of the church.[5] Many of the nobility and wealthier citizens of Prague associated themselves with these leaders. There was also a "left wing" element in Prague led by John Želivský, a former monk who had originally followed Jakoubek, but soon turned to more radical ideas.

The "common people's" more radical strand of the reform movement came to be known as the "Taborites" from their main center, the town of Tábor, which in turn got its name from a hill in southern Bohemia called Mount Tábor after the biblical Mount Tabor (*e.g.*, Psalm 89:12), where they would gather for open-air rallies. Wenceslas Koranda* and later Nicholas (Mikuláš) of Pelhřimov provided clerical leadership to this group. A squire, Nicholas of Hus,† provided early political leadership.

Not all Taborites were rural peasants, though generally they came from the more "marginalized" strata of society. Most had less to lose than the wealthier conservative citizens of Prague, hence they called for a more widespread transformation and leveling of society. Moral reform was a cornerstone of the whole Czech reform movement, but the Taborites developed an emphasis on this like the later Puritans, even to wearing "sober" dress. They were also more radical theologically than the university Hussites. With other Hussites they held to the centrality of Scripture, but the Taborites rejected anything not expressly warranted in the Bible. Thus they discarded transubstantiation in their understanding of holy communion, and Nicholas of Pelhřimov actively opposed adoration of the elements of the sacrament, calling it "idolatry." The Taborites also opposed praying to the saints and constructing ornate churches. The more radical among them, the Chiliasts, later believed that destroying such churches and citadels of worldly wealth was their task assigned them by God, and they fought for an egalitarian society on earth.[6]

A slightly more theologically and politically moderate group was called the Orebites, after their own hill of gathering. Particularly in matters of defense they worked closely with the Taborites.

The large open-air rallies quickly became a characteristic of the Hussite movement. One, held on 22 July 1419, brought

---

* Not to be confused with the later Utraquist archbishop-elect of the same name.
† Nicholas was not, as some have thought, the hereditary nobleman of John Hus's hometown, but had been the garrison head of a royal castle by that name.

together thousands* for preaching, partaking of communion in both kinds, and mutual encouragement. By this point, the chalice had become the symbol of the Hussites, since giving communion in both kinds was one thing agreed on by all.[7] From this came the name by which Hus's followers were known: *Utraquists*, from the Latin phrase *sub utraque*, meaning "in both kinds."† Particularly at these large rallies a Hussite banner featuring a blood red chalice on a black field served as a rallying point.

By the summer of 1419 King Wenceslas and the Catholic officials and nobles had managed to regain control of most of the churches again, especially in Prague. They did this through a careful blend of diplomacy and executive power. In addition several of the leading Hussite nobles had died, which temporarily weakened the movement's political power. The Catholic Czechs took advantage of this temporary Hussite power vacuum to initiate maneuvers calculated to regain control. After the king earlier in the year had restricted the serving of communion in both kinds to only three churches in Prague, many Hussite priests and followers withdrew to the countryside to join the Taborites.‡ Not all radical Hussites left Prague, however, and Wenceslas's moves to return churches to Catholic control, turn schools into anti-Hussite institutions, and install a city council against reform caused their growing frustration to erupt into armed conflict.

The radical Hussite leader in Prague, John Želivský, decided to force a showdown.[8] On 30 July 1419 in his church

---

* De Schweinitz, 81, drawing on contemporary chronicles, says 42,000 attended, but this should be taken with a grain of salt. Sources of that time tended to exaggerate such numbers, sometimes tenfold or more.

† Later, "Utraquist" came to refer more to the conservative Prague party and the national church they led as opposed to the radical Taborites. All the Hussites were sometimes also called Calixtines, from the Latin word for chalice, *calix*. Calixtines were not a separate party of Hussites.

‡ Strictly speaking, they were not generally called Taborites until after the town of Tábor was founded.

of St. Mary of the Snow he preached a fiery sermon[9] to rouse the people. A procession, probably led by Želivský, formed, and moving through the city streets it broke open and seized St. Stephen's Church, which had been taken from the Hussites by the Catholic party. A priest holding consecrated communion bread in a monstrance then led the mob to the New Town Hall, where they demanded release of prisoners who had been arrested for Hussite beliefs. The royal councilors refused. A shout went up that one of the councilors had thrown a rock at the priest with the monstrance. Thus infuriated, the crowd broke into the town hall. Some of the councilors escaped through a back door, but others were caught and thrown from the windows to the street below. Those who survived the fall were killed by the mob, who had come armed for just such a purpose. This event is known as the "First Defenestration* of Prague," to distinguish it from the second one which started the Thirty Years War 200 years later.

Whether Želivský had intended such violence or not, he had prepared for the inevitable reprisal by recruiting the services of John (Jan) Žižka. A small landholder of the lesser nobility, Žižka† (b. 1354?)[10] up to this time had been a soldier in service to the king, and had already lost his sight in one eye. His military experience seems to have been well regarded by King Wenceslas. Žižka had some trouble of conscience in renouncing his loyalty, but ultimately felt compelled to follow the "Law of God." Having cast his lot with the Hussites, Žižka set to work organizing the occupation of the town hall and the formation of militia companies.[11]

---

* Literally: "out the window." Defenestration is a peculiar means of settling a dispute: failing to reach agreement, one party summarily tosses the other out a second-story window. De Schweinitz, 82, has the councilors cast down and impaled on the uplifted spears of the crowd. Spinka, 302, and Kaminsky, 294, do not mention "impaling"; but Heymann, 63, says at least some of the crowd were armed. All agree that the "defenestrated" councilors were killed.

† Žižka provides another example that not all radical Hussites were "marginalized."

When King Wenceslas heard of the defenestration he fell into an "attack of apoplexy." His councilors calmed him down, but on 16 August 1419 he suffered a severe stroke and died within hours.[12] Wenceslas IV was childless, but an agreement had been reached in 1411 that his brother Sigismund, the Holy Roman emperor, would succeed him as king of Bohemia. That, of course, was before Sigismund had angered a large portion of the Czechs by "conniving" in the deaths of Hus and Jerome. He wisely did not rush to Prague to claim his throne.

As rioting continued, Želivský and Žižka feared that Sigismund would try to stifle the reform movement. The archbishop again imposed an interdict on Prague, but that old song was wearing thin, and the decree was ignored. More constructively, Bohemia's national assembly drew up conditions on which the country would accept Sigismund as king. These included free preaching of the Word of God, communion in both kinds, refraining from referring to Hus and Jerome as heretics,

John Žižka

and getting the papacy to agree to these conditions. Sigismund did not accept, only giving a non-committal answer. Wenceslas's widow, Queen Sophia, was appointed temporary regent.

Sigismund's troops controlled some areas of the city, and the moderate Utraquists of the higher nobility, hoping to avoid bloodshed, persuaded the people of Prague to hand over the Vyšehrad castle to the royal forces. Žižka and Nicholas of Hus left the city in disgust to recruit forces in the countryside for the onslaught they knew was coming.

Breaking off his expedition against the Turks, Sigismund began gathering his own forces in Saxony. He appointed Čeněk of Vartenberg as Bohemia's new regent, oddly enough with Wenceslas of Dubá, a friend of Hus, as one of his assistants. Sigismund arranged for the pope in March 1420 to proclaim a real crusade against the "Hussite heretics," then armed with that support formally declared war on the Hussites. He went first to Brno in Moravia, where he conferred with Queen Sophia and members of the nobility.[13] Then with a large army he crossed the Bohemian frontier in April 1420. A number of Catholic Czechs rallied to his standard. The people of Prague appealed to Žižka for help, and he arrived in the city with 9,000 men on 20 May.

As a means to work together, the various factions of Hussites drew up the famous "Four Articles of Prague," which demanded:

> (1) that the Word of God be freely preached by Christian priests in the Bohemian kingdom; (2) that the sacrament of the body and blood of Christ be freely ministered in both kinds of bread and wine to all Christians; (3) that priests and monks be deprived of secular power and that they live exemplary lives in accordance with the Scriptures; (4) that all mortal sins be prohibited and punished in each estate* by those in authority.[14]

The Hussites still differed among themselves on many points, but on these Four Articles and the defense of their country and religious liberty they could unite. Amazingly, the archbishop of Prague, Conrad of Vechta, accepted the Four Articles and agreed to ordain priests for the Hussites. Had he gone on to consecrate other bishops, this could have been the beginning of a truly independent Utraquist Church. But the time was not right for such a radical step.

---

* The three "estates" of medieval times consisted of (1) the nobility and knights, (2) the clergy, and (3) the commoners, later called bourgeois. Peasants or serfs were not considered.

Sigismund reached Prague with a huge army and occupied the castles. Facing him were the combined forces of Žižka, other units from the countryside, and any troops the people of Prague could muster. To strengthen their fortifications, particularly in the direction of the hostile castles, the Hussites of Prague, both women and men, had pitched in to dig ditches at strategic points.[15] Žižka fortified the Vítkov* hill to the east, and there on 14 July 1420 the imperial forces attacked him. Sigismund's troops were soundly defeated, and the Hussites' reputation as invincible warriors was begun.

It is often wondered how the Hussite "peasants" were able to defeat all the well-armored armies that came against them. In the first place, not all the Hussites were peasants. They also had some mounted knights. Most were of the lower classes, however, but by taking farm wagons, stoutly covering them, and leaving only slits to shoot through, they succeeded in neutralizing the advantages of the knights of the Catholic forces. In effect, the Hussites had invented the tank. They also developed small, easily manufactured, portable handguns called *pištal*, from which we get the English word "pistol." Most of all, John Žižka was an inspiring leader and brilliant strategist who knew how to make the most of what resources he had.

With his army defeated and suffering from epidemic and lack of supplies, Emperor Sigismund withdrew, but not before having himself hastily crowned king of Bohemia on 28 July 1420. Thus, for the Catholic forces, the "First Crusade" against the Hussites was a stunning defeat.

The victorious Utraquists took control of Prague, and John Žižka returned in triumph to the newly established city of Tábor, which the Taborites built that year as a center of defense where their social ideas could be given expression in a new settlement uncluttered by the "depravity" of the old

---

* This hill was thereafter often called "Žižka Hill," and a statue of the great commander in battle armor sits at its top.

"Babylon."[16] The Hussite reformation/revolution was at a high point.

However, the Hussites remained divided among themselves, and this division widened over the years. The Utraquists in Prague, while they also had more moderate and conservative parties, still hoped for reconciliation with a "reformed" Roman Church on the basis of the Four Articles of Prague. For the rest they were content to retain most of the usages of the medieval church.[17]

The Taborites, on the other hand, had given up on the Roman Church, and soon after the victory over Sigismund had established their own priesthood by electing Nicholas (Mikuláš) of Pelhřimov as bishop. He was consecrated by their priests without consideration of "apostolic succession" from St. Peter. Moderate Taborites were led by John of Jičín, John Žižka, and Prokop the Great. These could still work with some of the less conservative Utraquists who favored more distance between themselves and Rome, and more moral and liturgical reform.[18] However, more Taborites were coming to share the revolutionary and militant views of such leaders as John Němec or the frankly left wing opinions of John Čapek. This meant that the Taborites could often be as much a threat to the Utraquists as crusading Catholic armies were. One group called the "Picards"* became so radical that Žižka expelled them from Tábor. Portions of this splinter group developed into the ultimate extremist group called the "Adamites" because they wore no clothes and believed they were sinless like their "first parents" (Adam and Eve). Žižka dealt with them severely, and finally exterminated them.[19]

Another option between Prague and Tábor was provided by Peter (Petr) of Chelčický.[20] Born about 1380, Chelčický read Wycliffe and Štítné, and not only used Hus's writings but heard him preach. He favored reform but was horrified that the

---

* Or Pikarts. So called from their affinity to some French and Belgian radicals of the same name who had been expelled from Picardy and elsewhere and sought refuge in Bohemia in 1418.

Hussites would use military force even in their own defense. After the Catholics' "First Crusade" against the Hussites he withdrew to his native Chelčický, where he spent the rest of his life. In *O boji duchovním* (On spiritual combat) he wrote in no uncertain terms that spiritual warfare is the only one permitted to Christians. Not just military might, but all political power is wrong, because it too uses force to compel its will. In *Sít' víry* (The net of faith) he declared that the medieval partnership between church and state, which traced to the "Donation of Constantine," should be dissolved, and indeed in *O trojím lidu* (On the three sorts of people) he advocated abandonment of the whole medieval social order of nobles, clerics, and peasants. In his doctrinal writings as well Chelčický took a middle way between the Utraquists and more extreme Taborites. For example, in speaking of the presence of Christ in the holy communion, he did not hold with transubstantiation, but neither did he reject the real presence and consider it merely a symbol. Instead, he preferred to keep to the statements of Scripture itself, and acknowledge Christ's presence, but not attempt to define exactly how that presence is constituted. Neither should theological disputes get in the way of a Christian's main duty: living life in accord with the Law of God, especially as expressed in the Sermon on the Mount (Matt. 5-7). Peter attracted a group of like-minded people around him, but it was a loose fellowship and not a rigidly organized community.

Events in the wider world prevented the Czechs from working out their religious systems in peace. In June 1421 Bohemia's national assembly officially adopted the Four Articles in Latin, German, and Czech. It also repudiated all allegiance to Sigismund and appointed 20 regents to administer the kingdom. After negotiations with the rulers of Poland and Lithuania, the national assembly elected the nephew of the Polish king as king of Bohemia. His name was Sigismund Korybut (not to confuse him with the deposed Sigismund). He promised to observe the Four Articles, but was interested in making peace with Rome and became so involved in plots to eliminate Hussite, particularly Taborite, leaders that six years later he was seized and invited to leave the country never to return.[21]

Additional crusades against the Hussites followed. A mostly German army attacked from the north and won a partial victory at Žatec. Žižka was not there, having lost the sight of his remaining eye at the siege of Rábí. When in December 1421 Emperor Sigismund joined the attack through Moravia, Žižka assumed command of all the Hussite forces and completely put to flight the imperial forces on 6 January 1422.

Despite the victory, all was not well among the Hussites. John Želivský, leader of a more radical group in Prague, was assassinated in March 1422 by agents of a newly chosen town council. Žižka left Tábor to lead the Orebite party. He was still in the field, though totally blind, but died of the plague at Přibyslav in October 1424. After Žižka's death the Orebites called themselves "the Orphans." The regular Taborites were now led by Prokop the "Hairless" (or "Beardless"), who was called "the Great." The less numerous "Orphans" were led, appropriately enough, by Prokop "the Less."

The Hussites under Prokop the Great took the offensive in 1426 and invaded Germany, where they spread terror among the populace. In 1428 another crusade against Bohemia, led by Henry Beaufort,* the English cardinal of Winchester, was also soundly defeated at Tachov. Hussite incursions into Germany increased, including one toward Magdeburg that was so successful and rich in spoils it was called *Spanilá Jízda*, "the Magnificent Ride."[22]

Thoroughly annoyed, the German princes and Pope Martin V organized yet another crusade in 1431.[23] Immense resources were devoted to this venture to stamp out the "heretics" once and for all. However, this great army, commanded by Cardinal Julian Cesarini, fared no better than the others. In fact, it was the worst defeat yet, for when the Catholic forces heard the

---

* Ironically, he was the legitimized son of John of Gaunt, Wycliffe's protector.

rumble of the Hussite battlewagons and the loud tones of the Hussite "Battle Hymn" ("Ye who God's warriors are") coming toward them, they turned and fled without a fight. The Hussites pursued and killed a great number of them and seized many vehicles to convert into more battlewagons.

By now, even the most fervent Catholics, Czechs and non-Czechs alike, realized their military option was not working. Pope Martin V called for another General Council to meet in Basel but died in 1431 before it convened. Emperor Sigismund and Cardinal Cesarini, who had led the last anti-Hussite crusade, convinced the new pope, Eugene IV (d. 1447), to invite the Hussites to attend the council for negotiations. Given what had happened at Constance, the Hussites were naturally suspicious of this invitation. Still, many of them were also weary of war and desired reconciliation. They therefore agreed to meet a deputation from the Council of Basel in the Czech city of Cheb on 9 May 1432. John (Jan) Rokycana, Martin Lupáč, Nicholas of Pelhřimov, and Prokop the Great were among the Czech representatives. Also with them was Peter Payne, an English Wycliffite who was living in Prague and had joined the Hussites. It was stipulated by all parties in a document called the Agreement of Cheb (*Soudce chebský*) that Scripture and the early fathers of the church would be the basis for pronouncements. This reassured the Hussites that the council would function within these limits to give them a fair hearing. The Hussites decided to go to Basel.

On 4 January 1433, 15 delegates representing all three major Hussite factions — Utraquists, Taborites, and Orebites — arrived in Basel and were welcomed by the council.[24] Negotiations went on for three months. In April they were continued in Prague, and at length an agreement called the *Compacta* of Basel* was reached. This was a watered down version of the Four Articles of Prague. It agreed to the Czechs' *sine quā non* demand for communion in both kinds, but only in the Czech lands for those who would obey the church in all else. The

---

* Often referred to as the *Compacta* of Prague.

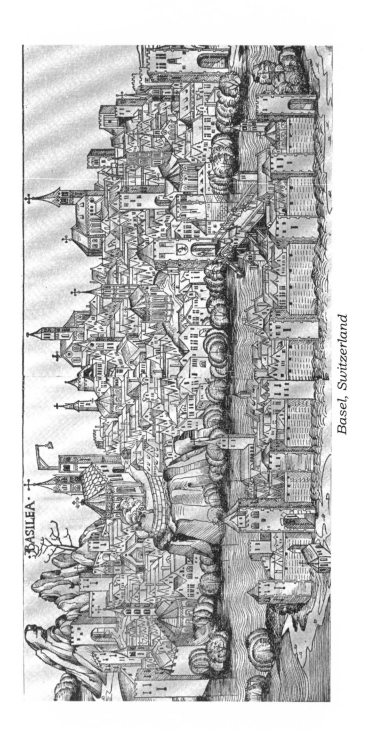

Basel, Switzerland

Compacta was grudgingly agreed to by the Council of Basel in August 1433 and ratified by Bohemia's national assembly on 30 November 1433.

The conservative Utraquists hailed this as a triumph, but others were not so pleased. The extreme Catholics, of course, still wanted the "heretic" Hussites to submit to pope and council in all things and do hard penance besides. The Taborites and other more radical Hussite "brotherhoods" felt the agreement gave away much and gained little. They saw the *Compacta* merely as a first step and as a basis for further negotiations. Having the right to the chalice in the Czech lands alone did not fit their wider vision of a thoroughgoing reform of the whole church and society in every land.[25] Still, it was something.

The long negotiations, however, had allowed the Catholics to see just how divided the Hussites really were. Emperor Sigismund had argued that only Czechs could defeat the Czechs. Even before agreement on the *Compacta* was reached, and more after, Catholic representatives had secret meetings with Czech Catholic and Utraquist noblemen aimed at further splitting the Hussites and eliminating the Taborites entirely. The Czech Catholics naturally supported this move, and many Utraquists did also. The Utraquists continued to hold basic Catholic doctrines and retained the Catholic liturgy. In fact, they considered themselves good Catholics and hoped that cooperation in eliminating the Hussite radicals would help prove their orthodoxy to Rome.

Money from Basel helped equip a Czech anti-Taborite army, and the attack was launched on Hussite strongholds in Prague. An urgent call for help went out, and the Taborite and Orphan (Orebite) armies turned from their siege of the Catholic stronghold in Plzeň (the *Compacta* had not ended all fighting) to rescue their allies.

On 30 May 1434 the two armies met at Lipany near Kolín. The anti-Taborite army was larger, but at first the Taborites seemed to be winning. The Catholic-Utraquist forces fell back, and the Taborites left their defensive perimeter of armored wagons to pursue them. The retreat was only a ruse, and more forces appeared to catch the Taborites between two pincers of hostile troops. By the end of the day Prokop the Great and 13,000 of his men lay dead on the field. A few escaped, but another 1,000 who were captured were locked in barns and burned to death. Historian Matthew Spinka sums up the result with a heart-wrenching expression of Czech national pride and sorrow: "Thus ended the hitherto invincible power of the brotherhoods; those who remained were relatively powerless to offer further effective resistance. It took Czechs to defeat other Czechs in a fratricidal combat."[26]

After Lipany the radical Hussites could only come to terms and a truce. Emperor Sigismund promised to have the Council of Basel reaffirm the *Compacta* if the Czechs would at last accept him as king. Although the council had previously accepted the *Compacta*, with victory in hand it was reluctant to agree again until Sigismund assured council fathers he would revoke the *Compacta* after he assumed power. Sigismund re-ascended the Czech throne in April 1436.

The leadership of the Utraquist Church now fell to John Rokycana.[27] Archbishop Conrad of Vechta had died before the negotiations with Basel, and Rokycana was elected as his successor by Bohemia's national assembly in October 1435 while negotiations with Sigismund were still under way. Rokycana's election was not confirmed by the pope or council, however, and he was never consecrated.* Nevertheless, within the Utraquist Church he functioned as administrative head and was accorded the courtesy title of "archbishop."

Rokycana was born in Rokycany near Plzeň to poor parents, but won a charity scholarship to the University of Prague. He received his master's degree there and in 1425 was appointed

---

* The Utraquists did not see themselves as having left the Roman Catholic Church. They insisted on serving the chalice to the laity, and many genuinely wanted moral reform in the church. In theology and worship they remained mostly Roman Catholic, and had all their clergy ordained by bishops with apostolic succession in communion with Rome.

to Prague's prestigious Týn Church, where his eloquence brought him fame as a preacher. He was one of the main negotiators with the Council of Basel, and was thus a major agent

in getting limited recognition for the Utraquist Church from the Roman Church. He spent the rest of his life trying to secure recognized consecration as archbishop while walking a delicate line between the various factions and interests around him.

As soon as Sigismund entered Prague in 1436 he began to undermine the Utra-

John Rokycana

quists, forcing Rokycana to flee the city. Administration of the Czech church was given into the hands of two legates appointed by the Council of Basel. This provoked yet another revolt against the king, who was once again forced to leave the city. Sigismund was saved from doing more harm when he died on 9 December 1437.

Religious matters were put on hold until Bohemia's national assembly elected a new king, Sigismund's son-in-law Albrecht II of Austria. Albrecht reigned for only a year and died in 1439 while on a campaign against the Turks. He did, however, leave an unborn son, who after his birth was duly elected king

George Poděbrady

and was known as Ladislas "the Posthumous." It appeared at first that anarchy might reign, but a regent was in time appointed for the infant king in the person of George (Jiří) Poděbrady.[28]

Born in 1420, George was from a noble, but not royal, Czech Utraquist family. He was extremely gifted and politically wise, and was only 24 when he became political leader of the Utraquists in 1444. By 1448 he was able to get the Utraquist Church administration reinstated. That brought Rokycana back to Prague, though he still was not recognized by the papacy as archbishop. Ladislas was formally crowned king in 1453, but George Poděbrady was retained as regent, ably running the country.

Frustrated by the lack of papal recognition, Rokycana in 1452 considered seeking consecration from the Greek Church and appointed a delegation to go to Constantinople to begin negotiations.* This would certainly have been an interesting development, but the fall of Constantinople to the Turks in 1453 put an end to the negotiations. The continuing hostility of Pope Nicholas V (d. 1455) to the *Compacta* also angered Rokycana.†

Rokycana was also disturbed by what he saw as a decline in moral standards since the earlier days of the Czech reformation. Religious discussion was plentiful, but dedicated Christian living was rare. Rokycana addressed this problem forcefully in his sermons, but still tried to keep lines of communication open with the various parties at home and abroad.

Since their defeat at Lipany in 1434, the Taborites had been finished as a political force. Some joined the Utraquists, but many were in a nebulous quandary not knowing where to turn. When the last Taborite stronghold, Tábor itself, submitted to George Poděbrady in 1452, its adherents dispersed through the land. Numerous informal societies made

---

* The Greek (or Byzantine) Church was not in communion with Rome, but its patriarch and bishops had valid apostolic succession.

† Nicholas's opposition to the *Compacta* was understandable since the Council of Basel, which had agreed to it, also tried to depose him and even elected an antipope, Felix V. The Western church had had enough of schism, however, and the Council of Basel was thoroughly disgraced by the time it finally adjourned (or petered out) in 1443.

up of former Taborites and others sprang up seeking spiritual nourishment, comfort, and guidance. For them, Rome was not the answer; the Utraquist Church went only part way toward real reform; and Tábor was no more. Surely, people thought, there must be something better.

Notes

1 Standard sources for this period are Howard Kaminsky, *A History of the Hussite Revolution* (Berkeley: University of California Press, 1967), and Frederick G. Heymann, *John Žižka and the Hussite Revolution* (Princeton: Princeton University Press, 1955, reissued by Russell and Russell, 1969). F. M. Bartoš in his *The Hussite Revolution 1424-1437*, English ed. prepared by John M. Klassen (New York: Columbia University Press, 1986) picks up the story where these leave off. Matthew Spinka in his *John Hus: A Biography* (Princeton: Princeton University Press, 1968) provides a very helpful 30-page epilogue covering this topic. As always, the relevant chapters of Edmund de Schweinitz, *History of the Church Known as the Unitas Fratrum*, 2nd (reprint) ed. (Bethlehem, Pa.: Moravian Publication Concern, 1901), provide a good read. Another charming, if dated, account is Count Lützow, *The Hussite Wars* (New York: E. P. Dutton and Co., 1913).

2 De Schweinitz, 80. Spinka, 298.

3 For details see Spinka, 291-97.

4 Spinka, 296.

5 Kaminsky, 180-82.

6 For a brief summary of Taborite principles see Heymann, 75-79.

7 See chapter 4 above. See also Helena Krmíčková, "The Janovite Theory and the Renewal of the Lay Chalice," in *The Bohemian Reformation and Religious Practice* 3 (2000): 63-68.

8 Details from Heymann, 61-64.

9 Excerpt printed in Josef Macek, *The Hussite Movement in Bohemia*, 2nd ed. (Prague: Orbis, 1958), 121-22.

10 Heymann spends several pages, 18-23, discussing various possibilities for the year of Žižka's birth. De Schweinitz, 83, n. 7, gives a more convenient biographical summary.

11 Kaminsky, 295.

12 Spinka, 302, gives the date as 13 August, but de Schweinitz, 82, Heymann, 66, and Kaminsky, 296, all agree on 16 August.

13 Lützow, 35.

14 Quoted from Spinka, 305. He also refers to Heymann, 148-57, for a fuller discussion of these. The full text of the articles is given in

Jaroslav Pelikan and Valerie Hotchkiss, eds., *Creeds and Confessions of Faith in the Christian Tradition* (New Haven: Yale University Press, 2003), 1:793-95.

[15] Lützow, 45. For more on the role of women in the Hussite movement, who could resist a title like John M. Klassen's *Warring Maidens, Captive Wives, and Hussite Queens: Women and Men at War and Peace in Fifteenth Century Bohemia* (New York: Columbia University Press, 1999).

[16] Kaminsky, 335.

[17] For the Utraquists' attempts to reconcile with Rome, see Zdeněk V. David, *Finding the Middle Way: The Utraquists' Liberal Challenge to Rome and Luther* (Washington, D.C.: Woodrow Wilson Center Press, 2003).

[18] Kaminsky, 183.

[19] Kaminsky, 418-20, 428-31.

[20] For the fullest account of Chelčický's life and social and theological views see Murray L. Wagner's book length study, *Petr Chelčický: A Radical Separatist in Hussite Bohemia* (Scottdale, Pa.: Herald Press, 1983). A shorter account by Wagner is "Petr Chelčický: A Free Church Separatist," *Transactions of the Moravian Historical Society* 24 (1986): 63-70. See also Matthew Spinka, "Peter of Chelčický, the Spiritual Father of the Unitas Fratrum," in *Church History* (1943), 271-91. Peter Brock in *The Political and Social Doctrines of the Unity of Czech Brethren in the Fifteenth and Early Sixteenth Centuries* (The Hague: Mouton and Co., 1957), 25-69 provides a lengthy discussion of Chelčický's views.

[21] Bartoš, 13-24, esp. 23.

[22] Thomas Fudge, *The Magnificent Ride: The First Reformation in Hussite Bohemia* (Aldershot and Brookfield: Ashgate, 1998), uses this phrase to characterize the entire Hussite movement.

[23] Bartoš, 60-72.

[24] Bartoš, 86-88.

[25] See Macek, 75-76, for a discussion of the distribution of Hussite manifestos throughout Europe.

[26] Spinka, *John Hus: A Biography*, 318.

[27] See Frederick G. Heymann, "John Rokycana: Church Reformer Between Hus and Luther," *Church History* 28 (1959): 240-80.

[28] For details see Otakar Odložilík, *The Hussite King: Bohemia in European Affairs, 1440-1471* (New Brunswick: Rutgers University Press, 1965).

Chapter 6

The Birth of the Unity

An Answer in the Storm, 1453-1467

*A*mong the many small groups seeking spiritual guidance in the 1450s in Bohemia was one consisting of members of the Týn Church in Prague.[1] We do not know the names of most of these persons.[2] Their leader, however, was definitely Gregory (Řehoř), later called "the Patriarch."[*] We do not know the year of his birth, but he was the son of one of Utraquist Archbishop Rokycana's sisters, who had married a country squire of "moderate means." Gregory had previously served as a business manager for lords and wealthy merchants, and since around 1446 had occupied a similar position at the Slavonic monastery (Na Slovanech) in Prague, which had allied itself with the Hussites. Gregory knew some Latin, and occasionally gave talks at the monastery, but did not become a monk.

Gregory and his group had been attending his uncle's sermons at the Týn Church since George Poděbrady had secured Rokycana's return to Prague in 1448. Rokycana was not an innovative thinker, but was an effective preacher. As described by one historian: "His eloquence captivated their minds and his earnestness touched their hearts."[3] In the course of time

---

[*] He was also called "the Tailor," but this may have been a profession he adopted after the founding of the Unity. It was a title used in contempt by his enemies to sneer at his lack of formal theological training.

Rokycana preached through almost all of the New Testament, holding on to basic Catholic dogma but urging people to put their faith into living practice.[4]

Gregory's group listened to these sermons with attention, took notes on them for future study and discussion, and at times conferred with Rokycana himself on issues he raised. The archbishop particularly lamented the loss of zeal in the Hussite church, saying that in those days "a genuine Christian was as rare as a stag with golden antlers," and condemning immoral priests as "counterfeit money."[5] This ministry of unworthy priests was dangerous, for while their sacraments might be valid, the people might be led astray by false assurances, thus threatening the salvation of their souls.[6] With the coronation in 1453 of the 13-year-old King Ladislas, who had been brought up a staunch Catholic opposed to Hussite reform, Rokycana's preaching took on a more strident note, as he foresaw only a small number of faithful and persecuted Christians persevering to the end.

"What shall we do?" wailed Gregory and his friends. "How can we be sure of the salvation of our souls?" They looked at other groups in the country and found only confusion. In particular they investigated a monastery at Vilémov, which had also gone over to the Hussites, but even there they found lax discipline, particularly in regard to dispensing holy communion.[7] In desperation they again turned to Rokycana for advice, and he in turn sent them to Peter Chelčický, probably in 1455. Having read some of Chelčický's works, Gregory and his group took Rokycana's advice.

By now Gregory and company were sure that they needed to separate themselves from corrupt society if they were to live the fullness of the Christian life and be secure in salvation. Rokycana still maintained an attitude of compromise with the Catholic institutional church, and felt an obligation to provide spiritual leadership to the whole Czech people. He had had contact with Chelčický in the past, and felt that this might be a good place for his zealous nephew and companions. At this

The Týn Church (upper right) anchors the square in the Old Town of Prague.
Left: the Charles Bridge with its eastern tower.

point the archbishop still saw these young people as a means of "leavening" within the broader Utraquist Church.

For their part, the "Gregory group" was fascinated by Chelčický's teaching, particularly the emphasis on Scripture, simple and holy living, and avoidance of violence. They came to Rokycana and asked for help in securing a place where they could live away from the world as a peaceful and "righteous remnant" in the dangers of "the last age."

Why did they not simply join with the Chelčický group? It may have been there was no room for a sizable influx of new-comers into his community, but Chelčický himself died around this time. His followers, never well organized, could not match the rigid standards of discipline and pastoral care that Gregory expected. Also Gregory's fellowship had expanded, and he was in contact with men and women throughout the land who were looking for him to take the lead.[8]

Rokycana first advised them to settle in various villages wherever small groups of them could find the ministry of a "good priest" among the Utraquists. Gregory disagreed. Unlike Chelčický, he *was* a good organizer and felt that his scattered friends still needed a focal point where some could settle, and others could come from time to time for spiritual nourishment.

During his travels, Gregory heard of an ideal place in Kunvald on the manor of Litice near Žamberk, about 100 miles east of Prague. Historian de Schweinitz characterizes it as "a retreat, amidst lonely hills and mountains, where they could worship God in fellowship and peace, and a centre around which their associates from the country could gather."[9] Besides the natural surroundings, the area was served by a particu-larly "good priest," Michael (Michal) Bradacius, a Utraquist who had received Roman ordination in Italy.[*] Michael was born possibly around 1425, since when he died in 1501 he was called "an old man."[10]

---

[*] All Utraquist priests received ordination from sympathetic Catholic bishops, either in Bohemia and Moravia or abroad.

This estate happened to belong to George Poděbrady, the regent of Bohemia. Gregory asked his uncle Rokycana to secure permission for them to settle there. Poděbrady had dismantled the last Taborite stronghold at Tábor in 1452, and was still moving to uproot other suspected "heretics," but though Gregory and his friends were zealous in their faith, they were still in the Utraquist Church and were not accused of heresy. Besides, Rokycana's request could be seen as vouching for them, and Poděbrady was glad to get hardworking pious settlers for this remote possession.* He gave his assent.[11]

Gregory invited Rokycana to make a resolute break from the current corrupt society and join the new community. Rokycana declined. He was still willing to offer his advice, though, and for the moment relations between uncle and nephew remained cordial.[12] Work began on building cottages and other necessary buildings, and others joined Gregory and the first settlers.

Gregory and Michael Bradacius drew up the new society's regulations which were grounded in Scripture, the Four Articles of Prague, moral living, and peacefulness. The reception of the Lord's Supper was very important to them. Besides members of Gregory's original group, some displaced Taborites, several Waldensians, and even some repentant Adamites were attracted to the community. All sincere and repentant applicants were welcomed. But when did this happen, and what did they call themselves?

The traditional date observed for the founding of this new society is 1 March 1457. Historians Rudolf Říčan and Joseph Th. Müller† speculate the year was actually 1458, since re-

---

* The author has been to Kunvald; it is still in the middle of nowhere.
† Chapter two introduced Edmund de Schweinitz, the first of three major historians of the Ancient Unity. Rudolf Říčan and Joseph Th. Müller round out the trio. A Czech native, Říčan was on the Comenius faculty of the University of Prague when his *Dějiny Jednoty bratrská* was published for the 500th anniversary of the Unity in 1957. It was translated into English by the author of this volume and published in 1992 as *The History of the Unity of Brethren*. In his 34 years as Unity Archivist at Herrnhut, 1905-1939, Müller was

ference was later made to George Poděbrady as "king" in giving them permission to settle, and he did not ascend the throne until that year.[13] That may be so, but it is not absolutely conclusive, since we might say "Queen Elizabeth drove an ambulance in the last months of World War II," even though she was not "queen" until 1952. Neither is there hard evidence for the specific day of 1 March, but historian de Schweinitz has a sensible answer:

> While there is no authority for celebrating the first of March as the day of the founding of the Unitas Fratrum, as is done throughout the Church, it is proper to commemorate the event, and this may as well be done on that day as any other.[14]

Without conclusive evidence that the traditional day and year are both wrong, we may agree with de Schweinitz that for general purposes, they will do.[*]

The name for this new group is also problematical. Again, tradition holds that they first called themselves "Brethren of the Law of Christ," but since that sounded like a new monastic institution, they often named themselves simply "the Brethren," and when their group was fully organized they later adopted the title "Jednota bratrská" in Czech, and "Unitas Fratrum" (Unity of Brethren[†]) in Latin.[15] Once again, the precise dates these titles came into use are not known, and

---

able to glean the manuscript Unity volumes known as the Lissa Folios (see chapter 21), to write his three-volume *Geschichte der Böhmischen Brüder*, published in 1922 and 1931. Accurate and thorough as this work is, it has not yet been translated into English, a task we leave to a rising generation.

[*] The modern Moravian Church, at least through its 550th anniversary in 2007, has celebrated the birth of the worldwide Unity on 1 March.

[†] We usually translate Unitas Fratrum properly as Unity of Brethren, but in Czech "Jednota" is a noun and "bratrská" is an adjective, so a translation of that is properly "Brotherly" or "Fraternal" Unity. The title of "United Brethren," oft used by the church in 18th- and 19th-century English-speaking countries, exactly reverses the original noun and adjective but still got the basic idea across. Historian Říčan, 35, Czech edition, 45, gives the original name as "Brothers *and Sisters* of the Law of Christ" ("se Bratří jmenují Bratry a Sestramy zákona Kristova"), which other scholars have not noted.

By tradition, this is the scene of the birth of the Unitas Fratrum in Kunvald in 1457.

may be a few years after the founding. This study will generally use the term "the Unity" and occasionally in context (with apologies to the Sisters) "the Brethren."

Initially the Unity objected to being called "Waldensians," and especially "Picards," a name which at the time was applied to any notorious heretics, particularly those who rejected the real presence of Christ in the sacrament, which the Brethren did not, though they spoke of this presence differently from transubstantiation. In later times, however, after the name lost much of its pejorative connotation, the Brethren gave in and for external purposes sometimes also referred to themselves as "Picards."

It appears that at this time the Unity thought of itself not as a new church, but rather as a voluntary association within the existing state church to fulfill the reform that Hus had begun, but which the Utraquists did not have the courage to put into practice. They hoped to be an example to the rest of the church for thoroughgoing renewal, and were content to be served by "good priests" wherever they could find them. They remained in correspondence with Rokycana, and their number increased.[16]

Considering the widely divergent backgrounds of those who formed the Unity, it is not surprising that differences arose. In 1459 tension grew between those of Utraquist background and those who were influenced by Tábor concerning their understandings of the holy communion. The leaders of the Unity were deeply concerned, and called for an emergency "synod" or meeting of members to resolve the issue. They quickly decided to stick simply to the words of Scripture and receive the sacrament "according to the mind of Christ," without trying to explain exactly how Christ was present in the elements.[17] They held that the sacrament was more than a symbol: Christ was truly present in the sacrament, but not physically. They also agreed to avoid speculative sectarian tracts, Taborite or Picard or otherwise, and all writings that only complicated issues, inflamed debate, and confused the faithful.[18]

About this time too, Michael Bradacius began to simplify the Utraquist ritual for celebrating communion, and in their scattered communities the Brethren held the sacrament not just in churches, which were not always open to them, but also in homes, mills, etc.[19] Following earlier Taborite practice, vestments began to be omitted, ordinary vessels, not gold chalices and patens, were used, and ordinary bread replaced special "hosts." Such practices scandalized the Brethren's more traditional neighbors. On the other hand, they were attracting others outside their immediate fellowship. In 1460 a sizable group of former Taborites from Moravia affiliated with them. Also in 1460 relations warmed so with German Waldensians living around Žatek, that the Brethren were in talks with the Waldensian Elder Stephen (Štěpán) about uniting with them. Suspicious Utraquist priests who were also talking with the Waldensians frustrated this effort.[20]

But then, as with so many Czechs before them, members of the Unity were caught up in the web of world politics. To the east in 1460 the Turks were a real threat, and Holy Roman Emperor Frederick III, like his predecessor Wenceslas IV in the time of Hus, was proving incompetent to rectify the situation. The regent of Bohemia, George Poděbrady, had assumed the throne in 1458 after the death of young King Ladislas in 1457. King George fulfilled his office so capably that he was often compared with Charles IV. His competence and accomplishments led several German princes to suggest that he should replace Frederick as Holy Roman emperor. That would certainly end the Czechs' isolation and "disgrace" with the rest of Europe.

Of course, before Poděbrady could ascend to the imperial throne he had to have rapprochement with Rome.[21] Since he was a Utraquist, much of Europe considered him the "heretic king." In Bohemia, many feared he would give away too much, and this would lead to sad consequences for the Hussites in general. So the "George for emperor" campaign quickly fizzled, but he still sought closer relations with the papacy on the basis of the *Compacta* of Basel. These efforts too fell short when Pope

Pius II answered by revoking the *Compacta* on the grounds that it was meant for only one generation, which had long passed. Poděbrady tried to keep negotiations alive by reassuring Rome that with the *Compacta* in place Bohemia and Moravia were not breeding grounds for heresy.[22] At the same time, he could not afford to alienate his Utraquist subjects.

And then there were the Brethren. For Poděbrady's purposes they had several strikes against them. First, they had among them such "disreputables" as Taborites, Waldensians, and even some former Adamites. Secondly, they had simplified rituals and did not speak of communion in traditional transubstantiation language, so they must be Picards. And third, they

The Litice (Lititz) castle of King George Poděbrady.

were proliferating not just in a forgotten corner of the country (on his own estate, no less), but throughout the kingdom. In addition, several Utraquist priests were already complaining about them, and allegations were made that they were plotting armed revolt. Not only could Podĕbrady not ignore the Unity; he must be seen to take steps to suppress it or risk charges of harboring heresy in his kingdom.

King George Podĕbrady, therefore, in 1460 had the priest Michael Bradacius banned from Litice and imprisoned for a time until he escaped. Then in 1461 the king revived an old law of Charles IV against heresy.[23] Gregory and others went to Rokycana to assure him that they had no violent intentions and asked the archbishop to intercede with the king for them. Rokycana did not fulfill their expectations, and henceforth Rokycana and the Unity were more at odds.

In March 1461 Gregory was in Prague to hold a meeting that included some university students. Tipped off that the meeting would be raided, he advised the students to flee. Tradition has it that they declared: "The torture shall be our breakfast, and the stake our dinner!" Gregory then felt obliged to remain with them, and all were imprisoned. The students were indeed tortured, and for several days the executioner visited their cell, apparently hoping to increase their terror. Three of the students promptly recanted, and it has been said: "After having tasted of their breakfast, they had no appetite for their dinner."[24] The recanting students were released, but two others remained in prison for up to two years.

Historians differ on whether Gregory was also tortured. Older sources state that he was, and while on the rack he had a vision of the future ministers of the Unity.[25] Later historians, however, generally agree that since this was not a formal inquisitorial proceeding, his status as a member of the knightly class probably protected him from physical torture. It appears that he was released after his uncle Rokycana promised to give him a good talking to.[26]

The persecution gradually eased, but its effects were the opposite of those intended. The pope remained unimpressed with King George Poděbrady as an opponent of heresy and still worked for his removal. Moreover, instead of suppressing the Unity, the persecution attracted sympathy for it. The Unity emerged with greater inner cohesion, resolve, and self-awareness, and with a sharpened willingness to go its own way independent of any national church.

The Unity's leaders called for a gathering (or synod) to meet in the mountains of Rychnov in 1464. There they agreed on a series of "Statutes" that form the oldest existing expression of the Unity's faith and order.[27*] Throughout the Unity's existence, even into the 21st century, we hear echoes of this document in our many confessions and statements of faith and simple living. It opens with an expression of faith, love, and hope as the crucial human response to God's grace, saving work, and gifts. The Statutes then outline how this fundamental theological relationship is to be lived with practical instruction for the various members.

The clergy are exhorted to faithfulness, simple living, and accountability. In addition to their spiritual obligations, they are to work for their own support, and if they earn more than they need, they are to give the surplus to the poor. Conversely, if the clergy are in need, the congregations will collect alms for them. To avoid even the appearance of scandal, the clergy are to be accompanied by a reliable witness on their rounds, and receipts are to be kept for all financial transactions.

Similar practical direction is given to lay members: masters and mistresses in relation to servants, and servants to those over them. Trades people are to provide fair value with their goods. All are to practice generosity to the poor and be ready to accept friendly correction when necessary. Efforts are to be made to reimburse members who lose property in persecutions, and penitents are to be helped back to a proper relation with God and the Unity. All are to pray for secular authorities and peaceably obey them in so far as Scripture will allow.

---

[*] The Statutes of 1464 are published as an e-book on the Internet at www.MoravianArchives.org.

Again, the emphasis is on simple, practical Christian living and not on intricacies of speculative theology.*

Around the time of the Unity's Statutes of 1464 there also arose lay elders (also at times called helpers or judges) to assist and supervise the clergy in individual congregations.[28] The Unity was finding its way to a more definite organization and identity.

The question of "good priests" persisted. Members of the Unity wondered how much longer they could depend on the services of godly and sympathetic Utraquist priests as their clergy in the congregations. The Catholic Church was resolute in efforts for their destruction. Now the Utraquist Church was turning oppressor as well. Besides, the Utraquists were themselves dependent on what the Unity considered a corrupt papal system for the ordination of their clergy. Had the time come for a clean break, for the Unity to establish its own ministry independent of Prague and Rome?

Even the Utraquists had pondered taking this step, especially after 1453 when the fall of Constantinople made securing consecration from the Greek Church impossible. Some, such as Martin Lupáč, the elected but never consecrated assistant bishop to Rokycana, urged the Utraquist clergy to simply consecrate a bishop for themselves. There is no real difference in "order" between priests and bishops, he argued, only one of administrative jurisdiction. Rokycana himself toyed with the idea but again lacked resolution to carry it through.

As the Unity's Gregory saw it, all Christians are priests in the universal priesthood of believers.† God indeed calls some for the ministry of word and sacrament, and they are indicated by their gifts for the office. Ultimately, it is Christ who consecrates these ministers. True, the church should have a bishop to formally inaugurate such persons into their ministry, but "papal ordination or consecration was worth nothing," and

---

* Modern Moravians may identify this as a combination of *The Ground of the Unity* and the Moravian Covenant for Christian Living.
† A foreshadowing of the later Protestant doctrine of the priesthood of all believers (John 20:21; 1 Pet. 2:5-9).

the whole Roman idea of priesthood was "erroneous." Gregory believed it was time for "a new priestly order."[29]

Gregory's thinking, however, was ahead of most members of the Unity. They hesitated to take such a radical step. Surely, they thought, somewhere on earth were devout Christians who had preserved the faith and order of the primitive church and had a priesthood that was not corrupt. They determined to find them. Peter Payne, the English Wycliffite who had settled in Prague, arranged a meeting for them with representatives of the Greek Orthodox Church, but they were as little impressed by that "imperial church" as they were by Rome. The Armenians had a bishop in Lvov in Poland, but this church did not meet their standards either. Br. Tůma Písař ("the Writer") visited a group called the Bogomiles in Hungary. They turned out to be "Paulicians," similar in beliefs to the ancient Gnostics and later Cathars who declared all physical existence evil. Though impressed by their morality, Br. Tůma considered their theology beyond the pale.

Back home, a few Taborite priests were still around, but they had relied on warfare to accomplish their ends. Waldensians were better, but had lost their earlier dedication, and some of their elders were reportedly diverting alms to their own selfish use. The Unity stood alone. Yet breaking with both Rome and the Utraquists by establishing an independent ministry was still too big a step to take.

Then in 1467 the pope pronounced a ban on King George Poděbrady, Catholic nobles in Bohemia began a civil war, and all illusions of harmony vanished.[30] The final straw came when the Catholic bishop of Olomouc ordered a member of the Unity burned at the stake. Br. Jacob (Jakub) Chulava of Vyškov thus became the first member of the Unity to die a martyr's death. The time for a final break with the state church was at hand.

Strengthened by his vision* of a priesthood for the Unity, Gregory and other leaders sent out a call for fasting and

---

* This was the vision earlier writers reported him having on the rack during the first persecution of the Unity, which later historians have

prayer. True to their principle of following Scripture, they relied on the lot* to ask if this was the time to consider establishing a ministry of their own. The answer was "yes."

Accordingly, about 60 Brethren gathered in Lhotka near Rychnov in the house of a man whose name was Duček, a friend but not a member of the Unity.[31] The traditional date for this "synod of Lhotka" is Holy Thursday, 26 March 1467. First, about 20 were elected as elders† to provide leadership and supervision for the entire Unity. Then they proceeded to the selection of ministers.

They first chose nine Brethren who they agreed had gifts suitable for the work of the ministry. True to the scriptural example of the apostles' using the lot in selecting Matthias to replace Judas (Acts 1:21-26), they took 12 slips of paper, on three of which were written "Jest" ("it is he"). This would still leave the actual selection of priests up to the Lord. It was possible that only one or two positive lots might be drawn. In fact, none of the positives might be drawn, and this would be taken as a sign from God to postpone the action. The lots were put into a container and distributed to the candidates by a young boy whose name tradition gives as Prokop.[32] All three "Jests" were drawn. The fact that all three were drawn, and not just one or two, was taken as an additional sign that the Lord *truly* approved of the institution of the Unity's ministry.

The three selected were Matthias (Matěj) of Kunvald, a farmer's son, Tůma (Thomas) Přeloučský, "a tailor who knew Latin," and Elias (Eliáš) of Chřenovice in Moravia, a miller. According to later sources, the hymn "Come let us all with gladness raise" (*Radujme společně*) was composed and sung for the selection of these first ministers of the Unity.‡

---

discounted. Nonetheless, Gregory acted with the definite conviction that at some point he had had a vision.

* The lot in both the Ancient and Renewed Unity was a prayerful calling upon the Savior for guidance when human reasoning had been exhausted.

† The "elders," or "judges," mentioned earlier appear to have had responsibility for a specific district, not for the Unity as a whole.

‡ It is still used in Moravian ordinations and consecrations today.

Some sources say that those present then had themselves rebaptized as a symbol of their rejection of Roman sacraments. Other sources do not mention this, but it is a fact that for a number of years the Unity did rebaptize those entering it from the Catholic and Utraquist Churches.[33]

Though the synod of Lhotka had not selected him as a candidate for the ministry, Gregory continued his unique leadership role. He suggested that Matthias (who at 25 was the youngest of the three) be accorded first place among the Unity's priests, for Gregory now revealed that it was Matthias's face he had seen in his vision as leading the clergy of the Unity. That may have been enough for Gregory, but the synod wanted something more concrete than a "vision." It again turned to the lot to ask who should be "senior" priest (or bishop), and the lot indeed fell to Matthias.

For Gregory and some of the Brethren, God's selection through the lot was all the ordination the new priests needed. However, since the three had been laymen with no sort of ordination from Catholic or other churches, others felt some sort of formal setting apart was needed. Those who agreed with Gregory argued that none of those already "ordained" had been selected through the lot, so human ordination was not necessary. That still left many in the Unity uneasy, and it was also pointed out that having laymen suddenly proclaimed as priests with no sort of consecration would be a scandal to the Utraquists, not to mention the Catholics.

Some now suggested that the "good priest" Michael Bradacius should ordain them. Others were bothered by his Roman ordination. Some suggested that the new priests be sent to a Waldensian bishop or "elder priest" for ordination since the Waldensian priesthood was believed to extend back to the uncorrupted pre-Constantinian times of the apostles.[34] But that might offend Michael's supporters.

Finally a compromise where everyone gave a little was reached. Michael was sent to the "eldest" Waldensian priest in Bohemia, and this priest's willingness to consecrate him as a bishop of the Unity was taken as an additional sign of divine approval.

For many years it was assumed that this unnamed Waldensian was Bishop Stephen, who had had conversations earlier with the Unity, but more recent research has indicated that Stephen was either imprisoned or already dead when the Unity's ministry was established.[35]

Having been consecrated by this unnamed Waldensian, Michael then returned and consecrated Matthias as bishop. Michael's job was only to convey the blessing of ordination, and so he immediately resigned his Roman and Waldensian ordinations and (again with the approval of the lot) was himself ordained as a priest of the Unity by Matthias, "the one he himself had ordained."[*]

This circuitous sequence of events makes more sense if it is viewed more as pastoral care and relationship rather than theology. Hardly anyone seriously expected recognition of this ordination by the Catholics or most Utraquists.[36] Within the Unity, however, the situation was different. Many members were not as able as Gregory to accept the new ministry without some sort of human validation. The Waldensians, who were thought to have a ministry from "untainted" apostolic times, were in the best position to give this, which would satisfy many. Having Michael be the intermediary would mollify his personal supporters and any who still thought the priesthood of the "old church" should play a role. On the other hand, since he was only a "carrier" his Roman priesthood was really irrelevant to those who were offended by it. His resignation and ordination by Matthias made it clear that this was a new ministerial order. Thus a convoluted procedure to satisfy all gave birth to the ministry of the young Unity.

The all-too-human process of consecration should not divert our attention from the true significance of the Unity's

---

[*] History is not clear whether it was Michael or Matthias who ordained Tůma and Elias, the other two selected by the lot as senior priests of the Unity.

step in establishing its ministry. Its members consciously established for themselves their own priestly order with the assurance that the origin of the Unity was undeniably founded on the pattern of the apostolic church and the revelation of the will of God.[37] It would be a shame if obsession with a bishop's "pedigree" is allowed to overshadow the Unity's conviction that ultimately it is Christ who ordains and consecrates, and that this is manifested by the spiritual and other gifts that Christ bestows on the individual. It is no accident that the Unity generally spoke not of "ordination" or "consecration," but rather of "confirmation" to the ministry.

In any event, the Unity now had its own church, independent of either Rome or Prague. What would it — or God — do with it?

Notes

[1] A standard source for this period is Rudolf Říčan, *The History of the Unity of Brethren*, trans. C. Daniel Crews (Bethlehem, Pa.: Department of Publications and Communications, Moravian Church, Northern Province, 1992), 1-41. This work was first published in Czech in 1957 by Kalich in Prague with the title *Dějiny Jednoty bratrská*. An abridged German edition was published in 1961 by Union Verlag in Berlin with the title *Geschichte der Böhmischen Brüder: Ihr Ursprung und ihre Geschichte*. Also important is Joseph Th. Müller, *Geschichte der Böhmischen Brüder* 3 vols. (Herrnhut: Missionsbuchhandlung, 1922, 1931), 1:46-149. These are the two principal sources for general information in this chapter.

[2] Peter Brock in *The Political and Social Doctrines of the Unity of Czech Brethren in the Fifteenth and Early Sixteenth Centuries* (The Hague: Mouton and Co., 1957), 72, says that Martin of Krčín, who had a role in the early years of the Unity and then disappeared, was one of them.

[3] Edmund de Schweinitz, *History of the Church Known as the Unitas Fratrum*, 2nd (reprint) ed. (Bethlehem, Pa.: Moravian Publication Concern, 1901), 98.

[4] For his theology see Říčan, 14-17; and for an analysis of his sermons see Müller, 1:50-61.

[5] Říčan, 16-17.

[6] Říčan, 17. Müller, 1:53.

[7] Müller, 1:65.

[8] Říčan, 27, and Müller, 1:72.

9 De Schweinitz, 106. See also Říčan, 28.

10 Müller, 1:70.

11 Říčan, 28.

12 Říčan, 28.

13 Říčan, 28. Müller, 1:70.

14 De Schweinitz, 109.

15 Říčan, 35. Müller, 1:109. De Schweinitz, 107-8.

16 De Schweinitz, 108-11.

17 Říčan, 30-31. For more details on this and later statements of the Unity on communion see Erhard Peschke, *Die Theologie der Böhmischen Brüder in ihrer Frühzeit. Vol 1: Das Abendmahl, Untersuchungen* (Stuttgart, 1935).

18 Říčan, 30. De Schweinitz, 111-12.

19 Müller, 1:78.

20 Říčan, 29-31. A leader of these German Waldensians was Frederick Reiser, who presumably was made a bishop by the Taborite bishop Nicholas. Reiser was killed in Strasbourg in 1458.

21 Otakar Odložilík, *The Hussite King: Bohemia in European Affairs, 1440-1471* (New Brunswick: Rutgers University Press, 1965), 127-28.

22 Říčan, 30-31. For more details see Odložilík, 130-60.

23 Müller 1:69.

24 Both de Schweinitz, 117, and Müller, 1:81, note that these colorful details come from Luke of Prague much later, and that Luke was a fine theologian but not as reliable as an historian. Both, however, and Říčan, 31, as well, agree that the basic facts are correct.

25 De Schweinitz, 117-18. See below for more on Gregory's "vision."

26 Müller 1:85.

27 De Schweinitz, 122-26, quotes a translation of the document, which is published on the web site www.MoravianArchives.org. See Miloš Štrupl, "The Confessional Theology of the Unitas Fratrum," *Church History* 33 (1964): 279-93.

28 Říčan, 34.

29 Říčan, 36-37.

30 Říčan, 38.

31 Müller, 1:126-48, gives the best and most likely description of the selection and later "confirmation" of the first ministers of the Unity, including the question of apostolic succession. His booklet *Das Bischoftum der Brüder-Unität* (Herrnhut: 1889) gives the same basic account. The account given here follows his, supplemented by others as indicated. The 15th and 16th century accounts themselves are remarkably complex and seemingly contradictory. Amedeo Molnár lists and gives a good description of them in his "Bratrský Synod u Rychova," originally published in *Bratrský sborník* (Prague: Komenského evangelické fakulta bohoslovecká, 1967), 15-37. This is available in an English translation (possibly by Molnár himself) in a mimeographed article entitled "The Synod of the Unity of Brethren at Lhotka near Rychnov, 1467-1967" at Moravian Archives,

Winston-Salem, N.C. Citations are from the English version. De Schweinitz, 142-46, lists the documents also.

[32] Molnár, "Bratrský Synod u Rychova," 8, says Luke of Prague is the source for the boy's name.

[33] De Schweinitz, 137, citing Anton Gindely, *Geschichte der Böhmischen Brüder*, 2 vols. (Prague, 1857, 1858), 1:36. De Schweinitz rightly points out that this was not done for the same reasons as the Anabaptists later had. Říčan, 42, also alludes to the possibility of rebaptism at Lhotka. The Unity officially abandoned the practice of rebaptism in 1534. See page 189.

[34] See Jean Gonnet and Amedeo Molnár, *Les Vaudois au Moyen Age* (Turin: Claudiana Press, 1974). For the perspective of a more recent Moravian on this see Edwin Sawyer, "The Waldensian Influence on the Moravian Church," *Transactions of the Moravian Historical Society* 25 (1988): 47-61. Documents relating to the apostolic succession in relation to the recent "Full Communion" dialog of the Episcopal Church and the Moravian Church in America (Northern and Southern Provinces) include Thomas Ferguson, "The Moravian Episcopate and the Episcopal Church," *Anglican and Episcopal History* 71, no. 4 (2002): 498-518; Colin Podmore, "The Moravian Episcopate and the Episcopal Church: A Personal Response," *Anglican and Episcopal History* 72, no. 3 (2003): 351-84; and Thomas Ferguson, "A Reply to Colin Podmore," *Anglican and Episcopal History* 72, no. 3 (2003): 385-90. Podmore depends on Müller's *Das Bischoftum*. For an earlier Moravian perspective on talks with the Anglicans see the report "Die anglicanische Kirche und der brüderische Bischofsweihe" in *Zeitschrift für Brüder Geschichte* 2, no. 1 (1908): 89-101.

[35] Müller, 1:136. Říčan, 40. De Schweinitz in naming the consecrator as Stephen did not have this information.

[36] De Schweinitz's idea, 147-48, of a friendly Catholic bishop giving a Waldensian unauthorized but valid episcopal consecration in the apostolic succession in hopes of getting the Bohemians to agree to the *Compacta* is a little hard to swallow. If the Waldensian who consecrated Michael had any sort of episcopal consecration himself, it was likely from the line of the radical Taborite Bishop Nicholas of Pelhřimov, which is hardly the validation de Schweinitz was looking for. In any case, neither a succession derived from the papal episcopal system nor from the warlike radical Taborites was what the Unity was looking for in 1467.

[37] Říčan, 41.

Chapter 7

The Old Brethren

Faith and Order in the First Generation,
1467-1490

It would be nice if we could report that, after the establishment of its own ministry, the Unity had time to refine its beliefs and work out details of its church order in peace. That is not the way the world usually works, and it certainly was not the case here. The Unity did in fact give clearer expression to its faith and establish a basic pattern for its church life in the quarter century after 1467, but it did so in the face of severe challenges from the wider world.

Persecution had died down by 1467, but the 1461 ban on heresy was still in force. The Brothers and Sisters were still subject to violence, particularly if the local noble was hostile. Establishing their own ministry was a provocative act and did not go unnoticed. In addition, the Unity itself now opposed the Utraquist priests more openly. Those priests complained, and Archbishop Rokycana could not ignore their accusations. By now Gregory and the others were at odds with Rokycana. They had not consulted him in their decision to establish their own ministry. Indeed, the Unity now looked for counsel more to Rokycana's assistant, Martin Lupáč, who was more of "an old school Hussite" than the politically sensitive archbishop.[1]

Unity members did not inform Rokycana of their new ministry until May 1468 after he had heard the news from others. In a series of six letters, probably penned by Gregory himself, they explained their actions and urged Rokycana to "return" to his former reforming zeal. The fourth of these letters gives the most information about the Unity's beliefs and order at this time.[2] The Unity also sent out public manifestos to the Prague University masters and to the Czech people in general. With King George Poděbrady under papal pressure to suppress all the Hussites, the Unity may have hoped that the Utraquists would join it in abandoning Rome entirely. But even with the pope's stirring up Hungarians to attack Czech lands from the east, Poděbrady and Rokycana clung to hope of compromise with Rome.

Rokycana sent a letter to be read in all pulpits in Bohemia and Moravia denouncing the Unity. He called the Unity sectarian and said it refused to bow before the sacrament, and that it rebaptized converts, claimed to turn lay persons into priests, and misused the words he had spoken in the past in the Týn Church. The Unity was indignant, though it was guilty of several of Rokycana's charges. The difference was that the Unity saw these things not as heresy but as faithful obedience to the Law of Christ and the pattern of the apostolic church.[3]

Much public attention was diverted by the war with Hungary, but in some places the Unity again suffered persecution, and some were martyred. The places where this happened were scattered throughout the country, which indicates how widespread the Unity had already become. Its members did not back down, but gave what relief they could to families of those who had been killed and dispossessed. The persecutions only confirmed their agreement with Chelčický that force, whether ecclesiastical or secular, was evil. George Poděbrady was now seen as an enemy, and the war as God's punishment on him. They charged Rokycana with taking "the broad way" rather than the "narrow way of Christ," and urged him to repent and come to their defense.[4]

Rokycana indeed sympathized with much of what the Unity was doing, but political considerations won out. He was afraid of being branded a heretic himself, and so he remained silent.

Historian Říčan observes: "The Brethren were too straight-forward to be able to understand his diplomatic ambiguity."[5] There remained some mutual affection between Rokycana and his former disciples, though, so when the archbishop fell gravely ill in early 1471 they sent him a final letter expressing genuine concern for his salvation. Rokycana responded in equal good spirit and issued a pastoral letter that spoke of the Unity in more moderate terms, which secured a lessening in the persecutions.[6]

Rokycana died on 22 February 1471, and King George Poděbrady exactly a month later on 22 March. Though the dowager Queen Johanna publicly denounced the Unity, the deaths of the king and archbishop effectively put an end to violence against it.

On its part, the Unity made use of the opportunity given by this respite to recruit members not only in the countryside but also in the cities where king and archbishop had prevented it before. Membership in the Unity showed a marked increase.[7]

Politically, Bohemia now concerned itself with crowning a new king. None of George Poděbrady's sons shared their father's political or personal gifts, and they were not serious contenders for the throne. In fact, Poděbrady himself had ar-ranged that he would be succeeded by Vladislav II Jagellonský, a son of the king of Poland. Poděbrady may have taken this step in hopes of recruiting another Slavic nation as an ally against the hostile powers surrounding Bohemia and Moravia.[8]

Vladislav, who was only 15, was a devout Catholic, but he did promise to observe the *Compacta* allowing the chalice to the laity, and pledged to try to get Rome to approve. The new king also declared an amnesty, and several members of the Unity, including the priest Michael Bradacius, were released from prison. However, for all his likable characteristics, Vladis-lav suffered from "innate passivity" and was far weaker than the Hungarian King Matthias, who kept up sporadic warfare trying to gain control of all the Bohemian crown lands.[9]

With a weak monarch on the throne, the lords and barons quickly filled the power vacuum in the land. In fact, they became virtual despots on their own estates, reducing the peasants to serfdom, taking rights away from the formerly largely independent cities, and obeying royal decrees only when it suited them.

This was bad for the country but had positive results for the Unity. Some nobles welcomed its members as hard workers on their estates, protected them, and gave them freedom to practice their faith openly. Among these was John (Jan) Kostka,* whose estates in eastern Bohemia included Brandýs nad Orlicí and Litomyšl, both of which became centers for the Unity. In addition, John Tovačovský allowed them to settle in Mladá Boleslav† northeast of Prague, and Ctibor Tovačovský, who was the wealthiest lord in Moravia, welcomed them to Hranice and Přerov.[10]

Br. Gregory remained in Rychnov near Kunvald to supervise Unity members around there. Br. Tůma Přeloučský moved to Přerov to administer the Moravian congregations in that area, and Br. Elias of Chřenovice settled in Lenešice near Louny to administer the Unity members scattered in northwest Bohemia. Prague itself was counted in this district since the Unity was still not allowed to have an official congregation within the city.

Growth continued as several Utraquists, now agreeing that Utraquism's attempt to get acceptance from Rome was futile, joined the Unity. Some educated persons (of whom more later) also joined and assisted Br. Gregory in literary work. Finally, it is also recorded that the Sisters of the Unity engaged in effective missionary work of their own.[11]

Utraquist priests, at whose expense most of these new members were gained, spread salacious stories about the Unity, and the more fantastic they were, the more the populace

---

* John Kostka's brother had tortured some of the Brethren, and John, in sorrow, vowed to Br. Gregory on his brother's coffin that he would be good to the Unity. He was true to his word.

† Mladá Boleslav in time became such an important center that the Unity was often referred to as the "Brethren of Boleslav" (Boleslavstí Bratří).

Litomyšl, a center of the Unity until a fire burned the church and most of the town in 1546.

lapped them up. One man, John of Teplitz, called Ležka,* claimed to have been a member of the Unity and to have participated in orgies and other depravities. He tried to turn the Tovačovskýs against the Unity, but was finally discredited.

In 1473 Bohemia's national assembly moved to condemn the Unity, but a friend urged it not to act without a hearing.[12] It was arranged that representatives of the Unity meet with Wenceslas Koranda,† Rokycana's elected but likewise never consecrated successor. They were also to meet with the masters of the University of Prague, who with the new archbishop now formed the Utraquist consistory (or administrative body). By now the Prague masters were accustomed to decreeing theological positions, not negotiating with "country bumpkins." Koranda also did not understand the Unity as Rokycana did, and tried to impress its delegates with longwinded allegorical interpretations of Scripture, a method so beloved of medieval scholastic theologians. The meeting did not go well. The Brethren explained their stand on the priesthood, baptism, and the Lord's Supper. The consistory decided their "moral earnestness" was "a cloak for heresy."[13]

Shortly afterward, Br. Gregory, whom the Unity's *Memorial Book*‡ calls its "patron and patriarch," died on 12 August 1474. It is said he was buried in a lovely and peaceful spot surrounded by beehives near Brandýs nad Orlicí, and his last words warned his followers not to let leadership of the church fall into the hands of "learned men."[14] He had put his personal stamp on the Unity, and his organization and drive had given it courage and character, while his writings defined its positions for those inside as well as outside the Unity.[15] He had no official position, but everyone knew who the leader of the Unity was. No one else could fill that place. Leadership passed to

---

* Müller, 1:167-68, suggests the name Ležka was given him by the Brethren, for "lež" means "lie" or "falsehood" in Czech, and Ležka would therefore mean something like "the little liar."
† Not to be confused with the earlier Taborite cleric of the same name.
‡ A register of brief biographies of bishops and ministers of the Unity spanning the years 1467 to 1606.

Br. Matthias of Kunvald, who as senior minister or bishop was the logical choice.

Another hearing before the Prague consistory was arranged in 1478 for the Unity by its noble friends. This had scarcely better results than the one in 1473. The consistory found the Brethren's "essentials" of faith, love, and hope acceptable, but did not like their views on the sacraments. They did not understand the Unity's insistence that agreement on the essentials, and not on details of the "ministrative" sacraments, was what mattered. Another letter went out from the consistory warning people to beware the Brethren.

For their part, members of the Unity did not see themselves as unbending except in the essentials. In fact, following discussions with the consistory in 1478 they did agree to baptize children born into the Unity.[16] It may be that their abandoning infant baptism was not the universal practice in the Unity even in its first decades.[17]

Also in 1478 warfare that had dragged on as Matthias of Hungary tried to gain the Bohemian crown for himself finally came to an end. For Bohemia it was a hollow victory, for Vladislav got to keep only Bohemia. Of the original Bohemian "crown lands," Slovakia had long been lost to Hungary, and now Silesia, Lusatia, and even Moravia passed to Matthias.[18] There was peace, but at what a price!*

About this time the Unity attracted unfavorable attention when its members gave shelter to a group of Waldensians who had been driven by persecution from Brandenburg in Germany. These Waldensians had had dealings with various Hussite groups in the past and had maintained contact with the Unity in the 1470s. The Unity felt some responsibility for these people since one of its own manifestos sent to Germany had fallen into the hands of a Catholic priest, and this had caused the Waldensians' persecution in the first place. Arrangements were made for them to settle around Lanškroun

---

* Ironically, when King Matthias was killed in 1490, who was elected his successor but Vladislav!

in eastern Bohemia and for others to settle on the Fulnek estate of Lord John Žerotín in northeast Moravia.[19] These settlements developed into the German-speaking branch of the Unity.

This good deed caused trouble for the Unity, since the Catholics in Moravia did not welcome the influx of several hundred Germans, particularly "heretical" Germans. Complaints were lodged before Hungary's King Matthias, who now controlled Moravia, and in 1481 he ordered all the Brethren to leave Moravia.[20] Thus the "First Exile of the Brethren."

The exiles fled to Moldavia, whose ruler who was glad to get thrifty, hard working inhabitants for his domain. Their religion did not bother him, for there had been some Hungarians associated with the Hussites living there since the 1450s. A second group of Brethren arrived and was welcomed, and thought was given for all the Brethren to emigrate there to find a more secure home. But while they did not have to worry about being persecuted by other Christians in Moldavia, the Turks continued to threaten from the east, so "secure" was a relative term.

Back in Moravia, several noblemen pointed out to King Matthias that his banishing the Unity had lost him (and them) hundreds of hard workers, and the economic impact was considerable. Matthias saw the validity of this, and rescinded his decree of banishment, and members of the Unity returned to Moravia, where prospects for them were more promising than in Bohemia, where restrictions remained.[21] Their return meant that centuries later members of the Unity would be called Moravians, not Moldavians.

In Bohemia the Catholic party had grown stronger, and King Vladislav began oppressing all Hussites, Utraquists included. One Utraquist priest, Michael the Pole, had been so zealous in his defense of the *Compacta* of Basel and in castigating the moral laxity of the clergy that he sounded like the young Rokycana. That got him burned at the stake in 1480. The Utraquists were strengthened in 1482 when an Italian bishop, Augustine Luciana,[22] settled in Prague and

*Fulnek in northeastern Moravia had a German-speaking congregation.
John Amos Comenius served part of his ministry at Fulnek.*

agreed to perform ordinations and confirmations for them.* Otherwise, Catholics continued to pressure the Utraquists, and the Utraquists returned the pressure. To avoid civil war, the Catholics and Utraquists in 1485 agreed that both their churches would be recognized as legal in Bohemia, and that people could belong to either as their conscience directed them. This became the basis for co-existence of the two groups for the next hundred years.23

That left the Unity out in the cold. This was a pact solely between Catholics and Utraquists, not a decree of universal "religious freedom." It meant that Catholics and Utraquists now had a reasonable expectation of not being persecuted in their own country. Everyone else, however, remained fair game.24

For its part, the Unity felt more estranged from the Utra-quists than ever. Leaders warned its members to keep as far away from the Utraquists as they could. Formerly the Brethren had made use of their "good priests," and the Utraquists still indeed had some moral and devout clergy, but now that the Unity had its own ministers, it was safer to rely on them. Against the claims of both Catholics and Utraquists, the Unity declared that no single church is the universal church. Whether they were Romans, Utraquists, or Brethren, they were all part of the one church of Christ.25 Neither did the Unity jump at the chance when the Czech national assembly ordered its members as "Picards" to appear before the Catholic and Utraquist faculty at the university to defend themselves.26 The Unity felt it did not need the approval of anyone but Christ. Protected on the estates of several friendly and powerful nobles, the Unity was now determined to go its separate way administratively and theologically.

---

* Only a bishop could administer confirmation. Until his death in 1493 Luciana performed these services for the Utraquists, but he was not their administrative head, nor did he consecrate bishops for them. They were still waiting for approval from Rome.

Now that it had its own clergy, the Unity in the 1480s was able to maintain in more developed form the basic church order established by the Lhotka synod in the Statutes of 1464. Matthias of Kunvald stood as the church's administrative head as "Senior" or bishop.* To assist him in guiding the church was an Inner Council (Úzká Rada) composed of clergy and lay members. Synods, or assemblies of clergy and lay delegates, could be called as needed to deal with larger issues either on a district level or for the Unity as a whole.[27]

In the congregations the priest was "spiritual administrator"† and was assisted in decision-making by local lay elders, sometimes referred to as helpers or judges. Women elders had particular responsibility for other women.[28] Almoners, always lay people, saw to dispensing funds as needed to the poor. Deacons served as assistants to the priests preparatory to their own ordination to the priesthood, and accompanied the priests on their travels as witnesses of proper conduct. Married men could be ordained, but unmarried priests could not marry after ordination.‡ There also appear to have been "teachers" or lay preachers in some places.[29]

Worship services were held on Sundays and major saints' feast days (which were societal holidays the Unity retained so as not to further scandalize the neighbors). Services might be held on weekdays also. These were held in homes, since the churches were closed to them, and the Unity had not yet begun to build its own chapels. Crucifixes, statues, and "holy pictures" were considered unnecessary.[30] Free prayer and the reading and explanation of Scripture characterized the services, which were in Czech, not Latin. The New Testament was preferred over the "incomplete" Old Testament,[31] and since printed and manuscript books were rare and prohibitively expensive, members and priests memorized large blocks

---

* The Unity preferred the term "Senior" rather than "bishop" because of the latter's unfortunate connotations in its "Roman" sense.
† The Unity also preferred that term over "pastor," which also had bad Catholic associations.
‡ This is still true in the Orthodox Church today.

of Scripture.* Also, historian Říčan writes: "The singing of spiritual songs undoubtedly belonged through Hussite example to the Brethren's worship from the beginning."[32] These too were learned by heart.

The theology underpinning the Unity's organization and practice is simple and crucial. Faith, love, and hope form the "essentials" of our response to God's saving will, the saving work in Christ, and the gifts of the Holy Spirit.[33] With these essentials the Unity faithfully shared in the purity of the apostolic church and the church universal. And in its many writings the Unity distinguished itself from other churches by making a careful distinction between the essentials and "ministrative things."

Ministrative things are given to lead people to the essentials, that is, to our proper relationship with God and each other. While there is the one true heavenly church to which all the saved belong, no earthly church can claim to be that church. Within the earthly "mixed" churches, the Scriptures, sacraments, etc., are used by God to call and maintain people in the universal church. Even the sacraments alone are not enough; they certainly do not have the "magical" power attributed to them by much of medieval piety. Using all the gifts of God's grace, including the sacraments, the earthly church can be a means used by God to call and feed true believers. No earthly church is perfect, but the Unity's aim was to see that it got as close to that ideal as possible in belief, practice, and consecrated living.

The Unity at this time retained the seven sacraments of the Western church, namely baptism, confirmation, the eucharist, penance, orders (which we have discussed with the Unity establishing its ministry), matrimony, and extreme unction. Accounts of the way the sacraments were administered are

---

* At this time the Unity accepted the "Apocryphal Books" as the Catholics did, since scholarship of the time did not know they were an addition to the Hebrew Scriptures.

rare, but we have seen that from its early years the Unity greatly simplified Catholic rites.

Baptism was the sacramental means of entry into the church. In accord with Romans 6:3, baptism was spoken of as being "into the death of Jesus,"[34] though so far as we know that phrase was not added to the baptismal formula itself at this time. Adult candidates were first given basic instruction in Christian faith, then allowed to attend preaching services, and when they were deemed ready, were baptized. When it was said to them that baptism was unrepeatable, the Brethren agreed and claimed they did not "rebaptize." They insisted on baptizing converts (as the Catholics also did), because they were not sure those persons' baptisms were valid. Children also were baptized after 1478, but the Catholic practice of immediate emergency baptism for children in danger of death was rejected. In any case, baptism was administered with plain water by pouring, not immersion.[35]

Confirmation was administered to children who had been baptized in infancy and could now make their own profession of faith. Confirmation was seen as a sort of completion of baptism. One interesting rite of the Catholic Church which the Unity did retain in confirmation was that after prayer and the laying on of hands, the confirmands received a light slap on the cheek from the minister to remind them that they must be ready to suffer for Christ. Given the frequent persecutions the Unity had to endure, that was one medieval practice the Unity felt had real meaning.

Concerning holy communion or eucharist, the Unity maintained its decision of 1459 that it is not merely a symbol, but how Christ is truly present in the sacrament is beyond human knowledge. Simply accepting Christ's words of institution and intending to do what Christ did is sufficient. Besides prayer and the words of institution, the Lord's Prayer formed an important part of the communion service. No doubt hymn singing did also. Plain bread could replace the special unleavened "host." Of course, both the consecrated bread and wine were always given to the lay people as well as to the clergy. It was not considered proper to bow to or adore the sacrament, as if it were the actual physical body of Christ (which is seated at the right hand of the Father in heaven). The consecrated bread could be received in the mouth (as the Catholics and Utraquists did) or in the hand as desired. Few if any vestments were used, and precious metal chalices and patens were not needed. Communion was not celebrated on a fixed liturgical schedule, but whenever it was deemed appropriate or needed.*

The sacrament of penance was administered following confession to the priest, and if the sin was a public one it also had to be confessed to the congregation. Verbal confession to the priest was not necessary before every communion, but was done when a person was conscious of a grave sin. The penance given for one's sins did not consist of "ascetic actions" (so many prayers or pilgrimages, etc.), but was a real making good of the harm caused, so far as possible. However, in a holdover from medieval asceticism, fasting, self-scourging, and a hard bed were thought to help against "carnality."[36] Fasts were declared for the entire Unity in times of persecution and before major decisions. It appears that the Brethren even in this period considered the idea of purgatory unscriptural.[37]

The Unity viewed the sacrament of marriage much as medieval asceticism did. Romance was not emphasized, but the Unity recalled the scriptural admonition "it is better to marry than to burn" (1 Cor. 7:9). Divorce was permitted for unfaithfulness or difference in religion.[38]

---

* Both the Confession of 1535 and the *Ratio Disciplinæ* or church constitution of the 1600s strongly imply that the mechanics of serving holy communion were remarkably similar to the Moravian Church today. The Confession states that while the priests "distribute" (*distribuunt*) the elements, "the people make expressions of gratitude ... in hymns and spiritual songs." The *Ratio* states that "our ancestors in the year 1494 had introduced the communion standing but were compelled to give it up by the fierce persecution which was excited on that account." Both documents can be found as e-books on the web site, www.MoravianArchives.org. The Confession quote is on the e-book page 29, and the *Ratio*'s is on page 37.

Extreme unction, or the last anointing, was retained as the seventh sacrament, though the Unity again gave it a solid pastoral and not a magical interpretation. Many in the medieval church thought of extreme unction as a last minute "get out of hell free card." The Unity used it as a time of re-assurance of God's grace and love, which they already had through faith. Historian Říčan states:

> . . . we hear that the Brethren performed "the seventh sacrament" by anointing the sick in the presence of many friends, "and the talk concerning hope and heavenly joy was often so lovely that the people wept." This pastoral consolation was clearly the main purpose of the act.[39]

Life in the early Unity was hard, not just because of frequent persecutions but also because its members were expected to seek the "higher righteousness" of Matt. 5:20 and be guided by the "six small commandments" of the Sermon on the Mount (Matt. 5-7). These commandments formed an important part of Waldensian and Hussite literature and spirituality in general. These were (1) do not be angry with your brother without a cause; (2) do not look upon a woman with lust; (3) do not divorce your wife except for cause of adultery; (4) do not take an oath; (5) do not repay evil for evil; and (6) love your enemies. Gaining admission to the Unity was difficult, for it wanted only members with true commitment.

The original founders' idea of withdrawing from the world to avoid contamination and for the assurance of salvation was still very much alive. That generally meant that living among the "temptations" of cities was frowned upon.[40] City dwellers recruited by the Unity were urged to move to the country. Once admitted to the Unity, members were expected to observe rigid ethical and moral standards. Faith was necessary for salvation, but this meant total commitment, not just agreement to certain doctrines, for the "fruits" of faith as expressed in how one lived in righteousness were absolutely required.

This applied to one's trade, where not only good value but also usefulness was a factor. Thus such pastoral occupations as farming, shepherding, garment making, shoemaking, and the like were permitted, while urban activities like tavern-keeping were not. Even in permitted occupations, simplicity was expected. For instance, tailors should make good plain clothing, not fancy embroidered gowns for the rich. Profit was not a motive. Historian Říčan notes: "The easier the gain promised by a business, the more anxiously they asked if by it they would be living off the hard work of strangers to the detriment of their fellows." [41]

All this was in line with Peter Chelčický's radical thinking, as was their avoidance of public affairs, which involved the taking of oaths and the use of power to punish offenders.[42] Brothers and Sisters should not take one another to court (the Unity had its own helpers and judges to arbitrate), and military service was to be avoided. Lords and knights who applied for admission had to renounce their feudal rights over their subjects, which helps explain why there were so few of them in the early Unity.[43]

Indeed, one may marvel that the Unity, while never a wildly popular institution, attracted the numbers that it did, a couple thousand or so at this point.[44] Not only were standards within it strict, but the Unity itself warned its members to expect nothing but persecution and scorn. Still, for those sincerely concerned for the salvation of their souls it offered a spiritual haven with far more security than the fallen society around them. And yet as the 15th century neared its close, even some members in the Unity were wondering if the "narrow way of Christ" needed to be quite as narrow as they had made it.

Notes

1 Joseph Th. Müller, *Geschichte der Böhmischen Brüder* 3 vols. (Herrnhut: Missionsbuchhandlung, 1922, 1931), 1:149-50.

2 Rudolf Říčan, *The History of the Unity of Brethren*, trans. C. Daniel Crews (Bethlehem, Pa.: Department of Publications and Communications, Moravian Church, Northern Province, 1992), 42. Müller, 1:152-57.

3 Peter Brock, *The Political and Social Doctrines of the Unity of Czech Brethren in the Fifteenth and Early Sixteenth Centuries* (The Hague: Mouton and Co., 1957), 87.

4 Říčan, 43. Müller, 1:158-61.

5 Říčan, 43.

6 Brock, 82-83.

7 Müller, 1:163.

8 Otakar Odložilík, *The Hussite King: Bohemia in European Affairs, 1440-1471* (New Brunswick: Rutgers University Press, 1965), 276-79, notes that some of George's sons did get positions in Silesia for a time, and a grandson, Bartholomew, evidenced great potential but drowned in a boat accident before that potential could be realized. See also Müller, 1:164.

9 Brock, 97. Říčan, 44.

10 Müller, 1:165.

11 Říčan, 45.

12 Muller, 1:167.

13 Müller, 1:167. Říčan, 46.

14 Edmund de Schweinitz, *History of the Church Known as the Unitas Fratrum*, 2nd (reprint) ed. (Bethlehem, Pa.: Moravian Publication Concern, 1901), 165-66.

15 Brock, 84.

16 Říčan, 46.

17 Müller, 1:206.

18 Müller, 1:177. Říčan, 44.

19 Říčan, 47.

20 Müller, 1:180-81.

21 Müller, 1:185. For a letter of encouragement to the exiles in Moldavia, see Lissa Folio 5 (film 365-66), Andrew Slaby translation, notebook 12, 89-96, in Moravian Archives, Bethlehem, Pa.

22 Říčan, 51.

23 Říčan, 48.

24 Müller, 1:190.

25 Müller, 1:191-92.

26 Říčan, 48.

27 Organizational information from Říčan, 51-52.

28 Říčan, 77.
29 Müller 1:203.
30 Müller, 1:216.
31 Brock, 86.
32 Říčan, 54.
33 Müller, 1:198-216, is the basis for this discussion of the Unity's theology at this time.
34 Müller, 1:204.
35 Müller, 1:206-7.
36 Říčan, 53.
37 Müller, 1:215.
38 Říčan, 53.
39 Říčan, 54.
40 Brock, 98.
41 Říčan, 56.
42 Brock, 90.
43 Brock, 97.
44 Říčan, 45.

## Chapter 8

A Time of Transition

Reorganizing the Unity, 1490-1501

*A*s long as Gregory (d. 1474) was alive, no one questioned the Unity's rigorous regulations concerning good works, restricted trades, etc.[1] In 1479, when several nobles applied for admission, they were required to divest themselves of their worldly authority. Some of these nobles did so, but others withdrew their application. This and similar instances led to discussion within the Unity about the severity of requirements, not just for nobles but for all members. In addition, questions were raised not only about the regulations but also about the theology that lay behind them.

Among the Unity's leaders, Bishop Matthias and many of the older clergy were content with the way things were. Other members of long standing were gravely concerned for the church and its members, and wondered if they were on the right path to attain the "higher righteousness." Among these were John Klenovský, John Táborský, and Br. Prokop of Neuhaus, all of whom had university training.[2]

Among the members who joined in the 1480s were several younger university students who had formed a circle around the noted preacher Michael the Pole, much as Gregory and his group had gathered around Rokycana.[3] These students had heard popular tales against the Unity and were suspicious of it, but the question, "How may I save my soul?" was as momentous for them as it had been for Gregory and the other founders of the Unity.

One of these students was Luke (Lukáš), who was born in Prague about 1458, around the time of the Unity's founding.[4] He grew up in Prague, but details of his pre-university years are lacking. Ironically, though he became one of the Unity's greatest scholars, he was not an outstanding undergraduate student, finishing eighth in a class of eleven.[5] While in college, Luke read Chelčický's works given him by his friend Adalbert (Vojtěch), who had already had positive contact with the Unity but was not yet a member. In response to Luke's expressed desires to find a "real" Christian community, Adalbert told him about the Brethren in Litomyšl, and Luke typically said: "I'm going to go and check it out."[6]

Luke and Adalbert joined the Unity shortly after Luke's graduation in 1481, and Luke also brought in his older brother John (Jan) Černý, who became a noted physician. Both played a valuable role in the Unity's development.

Another university-trained member also joined the Unity around this time. This was Lawrence (Vavřinec) Krasonický, who had graduated in 1479 and had been ordained to the Utraquist priesthood.* Krasonický had long been fascinated by the works of Chelčický, and after hearing from some teachers at the university that the Unity valued his writings, he had sought out the Brethren in Litomyšl. Krasonický was impressed and later became a leader and historian of the Unity. Several others of similar background came into the Unity in these years also.

Tension was rising in the Unity over maintaining the old strict standards. "Where is the easy yoke (Matt. 11:30) of Christ?" some were asking. Does our salvation, then, depend only on works, particularly if they are done "in an attitude

---

* He was ordained by the Italian bishop Augustine Luciana, mentioned in the previous chapter, who had settled in Prague to conduct ordinations and confirmations (but not the consecration of bishops) for the Utraquists.

Among intellectuals joining the Unity was Luke of Prague's brother, John Černý, a physician who wrote this medical manual.

of renunciation of the world?" What about grace and the redemption won by Christ, received in faith? Others feared that any change would open wide the floodgates of depravity. Even within the Inner Council opinion was divided.[7] That was serious, for members had joined the Unity for security of salvation, and relied on its leaders to guide them. Was God telling some one thing, and others another? Where is the security in that?[8] Some recalled with sighs how Br. Gregory's last words had warned about the "educated Brethren."

Discussions continued, harmoniously for the most part. Some, such as John Klenovský and Luke of Prague tried to present the two viewpoints as complementary to one another, each position keeping the other from going to extremes. A synod of the time, however, acknowledged the necessity of God's grace for salvation, but warned the priests to talk "judiciously" about it and not to forget to urge the people to more faithful living.[9]

More nobles and city dwellers were seeking admission to the Unity, and in the face of urgings to move to the country, these latter particularly reminded the leaders that in New Testament times (to which the Unity looked for guidance) the country was where the "pagans" lived, and the apostles went from city to city.[10] In addition, some members' only means of livelihood were geared to city life. Filip the Soapmaker, who did not see much market for his product in a sparsely populated rural setting, crossly complained to Br. Matthias: "Cows don't want soap to eat!"[11]

A practical matter brought things to a head for clergy and laity alike. In 1490 Lord Bohuš Kostka* was building a new town quarter to enlarge the city of Litomyšl, and he invited members of the Unity to settle there. That would gain Kostka sober, hard-working citizens, and would provide members of the Unity with a protected place to live and earn a livelihood. But the opportunity also tempted Unity members to engage in

---

* Son of John Kostka, who had proved to be a friend of the Unity (see previous chapter).

less essential but more profitable trades. In addition Kostka made it clear that he expected the Brethren to fulfill their civic duty to serve on town councils, juries, etc.

The people asked Br. Matthias for advice. He grumbled that they should have stayed in the farms and villages in the first place, but since several of them had already moved to the city, they would just have to do the best they could and hope it did not lead to damnation.[12] This was hardly reassuring or conclusive. Was there no way to take advantage of this opportunity without condemning their souls?

A synod was called to meet in Brandýs nad Orlicí in 1490 to consider the issue of the Unity's relation to worldly power. Br. Prokop had prepared a sermon on Matthew 5 for the occasion, and Br. Klenovský, in Br. Matthias's name, welcomed the delegates and asked for their help, since "we simply do not know how to settle this."[13] Br. John Táborský's careful words proved most effective: Theologically, Christians are called to moral living, but works alone are not what save us. God's grace and forgiveness play an essential role, so Christians do not have to be perfect, without any hope of forgiveness for some accommodation to living in a fallen world. If one has a "good will" and does one's best, God for the sake of Christ will be understanding.[14] In practical terms, this meant that nobles no longer would have to renounce all their feudal rights to become members of the Unity, though the dangers of their position were to be pointed out to them. Similarly, members might with caution live in cities, and even take an oath in court if compelled to do so. Some trades that are not absolutely necessary, but are not actually harmful, were permitted.[15]

This was the consensus the Brandýs synod arrived at in 1490. Delegates were given opportunity to object, but none did. At the close of synod delegates were cautioned that if members objected to the decision, they should speak to their priest or write Br. Matthias directly, but should not stir up trouble.

Though synod closed without a murmur, almost immediately there arose discussion aplenty.* Two priests, Jacob (Jakub) and Amos, objected vehemently and persuaded others to do so also. When word of opposition reached Br. Matthias, he took it as an occasion to do what he had probably wanted to do all along: he arbitrarily and unilaterally annulled the decisions of the Brandýs synod.

Members of the Inner Council who favored the synod's decision did not provoke the constitutional crisis they certainly could have over Matthias's defiance of synod and acting like a Roman bishop or pope. For the sake of peace in the church they quietly resigned from the council and were replaced by old-line thinkers.

There things stood, but Matthias's action did not make the problems go away or ease the conscience of many. The Unity was submissive, but still divided in spirit. The idea arose that although the Unity had not been able to find an

Members of the Unity in search of a pure apostolic church.

uncorrupted "apostolic" church to give it guidance before the establishment of its own ministry, surely somewhere in the world there was a Christian community that could show the way now. All the Unity had to do was find it.

A group of four, representative of various backgrounds, was assigned to travel east to make the search: Luke of Prague

---

* This may be the first recorded instance of the famous Moravian "parking lot meetings" following official meetings.

from among the "younger" clergy; Mareš Kokovec, a knight; Martin Kabátník, a city dweller; and Caspar of Brandenburg, formerly a German Waldensian. Even Luke and his "forward looking" allies shared older members' concerns that rich members might corrupt the Unity,[16] but they and the "hard liners" as well were willing for Lord Bohuš Kostka to secure passports and letters of introduction for them, and to supply money for the trip.

They went first through Moravia to Cracow, and then down the Danube to Constantinople. Br. Caspar remained in Constantinople to consult the Greek Orthodox there, and Luke traveled through the Balkans. Kokovec went to Russia, and Kabátník went through Turkey and the ancient Christian patriarchal cities of Antioch and Jerusalem as well as Damascus and Cairo. After a year they reassembled once again in Constantinople with disappointing results. Nowhere had they found a Christian community fully keeping and living the apostolic faith.[17] Once again, the Unity was on its own.

Discussions continued in the congregations, and Luke wrote theological works such as *The Ship (Bárka)* to try to understand and explain the nature of the church.* He laid stress "on the grace of God and on the merits of Christ."[18] Gradually, more members concluded that complete rejection of worldly society was impossible. Finally in 1494 Bishop Matthias summoned a synod to meet in Rychnov.[19] There he confessed that his annulling the Brandýs synod was a mistake, and he tendered his resignation along with those of his supporters on the Inner Council.

With Bishop Matthias sufficiently chastened for his attempt to veto the Brandýs synod, the Rychnov synod proceeded very gingerly. Refraining from specific mention of Brandýs, since the very name had become a battle cry for both sides, the Rychnov synod declared the 1490 decrees were "vyzdvihnúti," a Czech verb meaning "re-established" or the opposite, "abolished."[20]

---

* The ship was an allegory for the church, sailing on the troubled seas of the world.

Why so ambiguous? Historian Müller suggests the most likely scenario, that, determined to live up to the name of its church, the *Unity*, the Rychnov synod carefully avoided a definitive ruling that would irrevocably antagonize either party. Yet by leaving a vacuum of indecision it permitted a natural turn of events, a filling of the vacuum with the "majority party" of progressives superseding the "minority party" of conservatives. And that is exactly what happened. In short order, the new Inner Council declared Br. Gregory's writings and opinions, while not totally rejected, no longer binding.[21]

Choosing not to be vindictive, and to insure that the new direction would be seen as the "manifestation of the common inclination to a better-known truth,"[22] the "majority party" begged Br. Matthias not to resign entirely. The senior priest of the Unity next to Matthias was Tůma Přeloučský, but he could not be persuaded to assume overall leadership. Matthias and the other members of the new Inner Council followed him to his home at Přerov and persuaded him to remain on the council. They agreed that Br. Matthias would retain his authority to ordain (whom the council instructed him to). His administrative authority, however, was assumed by Br. Prokop, who became the effective leader of the Inner Council and judge of the Unity. New members, one of whom was Luke of Prague, were named to replace the old-line members who had resigned from the council. Br. Krasonický was assigned as "special adviser" (minder) to Br. Matthias, and the other administrative duties were split among the members of the Inner Council.[23] Within this new administrative arrangement, Luke quickly rose to be the most influential member of the Unity. He shouldered even more responsibility on the death of Br. Táborský right after the synod at Rychnov, and Br. Klenovský in 1498.

Most members of the Unity breathed a sigh of relief after Rychnov, but "old order" priests Jacob and Amos refused to agree and tried to stir up revolt among the congregations. Br. Matthias and Luke tried to meet with them to resolve differences, but reconciliation was impossible. Amos attracted a small band of followers called the Amosites, and they later elected their own priests and had them ordained by laymen. This group claimed to be the "true" Unity which kept to the ways of its founders, but their reason for existence came more and more to consist only of hurling recriminations at the "apostate" Unity of Luke. They apparently died out a half century later or joined the Anabaptists.

Having accepted that we live in a sin-filled world, the Unity now sought to live as pure a life as possible within Christ's grace. Though the Unity was now open to new, more cosmopolitan ideas, the new Inner Council did not throw open the door to lax behavior. It explicitly reaffirmed the Statutes of 1464.[24] Since total withdrawal from the world was no longer required, there was more theological emphasis on grace and redemption, but plain and sober living was still expected. Even when some prohibitions were relaxed, they were not relaxed very far. One could take an oath, for example, but only when compelled to. Likewise it was acknowledged that noblemen might summon Brethren for military service. If that happened, the Brother was to keep to the rear of battle.[25]*

The Unity had set a new course, but was it the right one? What is its true identity, and should it continue to exist? Again the Unity sought other like-minded Christian communities. Having had little success in finding answers in the East, Luke on behalf of the Unity visited the West in 1498. He went directly to the self-proclaimed seat of western Christendom in Rome, and was appalled by much of what he saw: "pagan" humanism, opulent palaces, and imperious bejeweled clerics. He wrote he "found nothing but the stools and tables of the moneychangers, and sellers of doves, sheep and so forth, sellers of fodder, prebends, pardons, and, in short, every-thing."[26] His thoughts of the cleansing of the temple were not improved when he happened to be present at the execution of the extremist reformer Girolamo Savonarola in Florence, where Luke had gone for medical help.[27] Luke was the more strength-

---

* This was not to foster cowardice, but to save a Brother from breaking the Commandment against killing (Exod. 20:13).

ened in the Unity's conviction that faith cannot be compelled by either spiritual or secular authorities.

Luke next visited the Waldensians in Italy. The "minority party" had cited the Waldensians as examples of "proper apostolic poverty," but Luke concluded that they too were caught up in earthly pursuits,* and that "it is not for others to go to them, but rather it would be better for them to come to others."[28] These experiences did not, however, destroy Luke's faith in the universal church.[29] Indeed, correspondence between the Unity and the Waldensians of Italy continued.

One surprising fruit of Luke's Italian trip was his deepening respect for the Virgin Mary. He denounced the excesses of Roman Mariology, which he had observed, but in no sense did this imply disrespect for the Mother of Jesus. His work on her, written soon after his return in 1498, is lost, but in a 1505 writing on the incarnation, he speaks very highly of Mary.[30]

After Luke's return from Italy, the Unity decided that a more definitive arrangement of its organization was needed. Br. Matthias had given up his administrative responsibilities, but was still the only one with a bishop's authority to ordain. It was decided that this should be entrusted to more than one man. In 1499, therefore, Tůma Přeloučský and Elias of Chřenovice were commissioned by Br. Matthias for this. In actual fact, it had been agreed for years that if Matthias should die, that Tůma and Elias, as the other first priests of the Unity would themselves assume his task of ordaining, or that they would consecrate whomever the Unity chose as bishop.[31] In line with the Unity's thinking of priest and bishop as essentially the same "order," this commissioning was done through a "handshake" rather than the "laying on of hands" of a customary "episcopal" consecration.† Tůma and Elias were

---

* Another example of how the "majority party" had no intention of loosening its standards too much.

† Müller, 1:280, reports this event and says Tůma and Elias were commissioned "durch Handschlag," and that in the Czech sources the words "dáním rukou" (by giving the hand) rather than "rukou

thus consecrated as bishops of the Unity, and an orderly and continuous passing on of the ministry was accomplished.

The Unity was fortunate to have newly authorized bishops when it did, for Bishop Matthias, though still only 58 years old, died in 1500 while on his way to a synod at Přerov. He was not a gifted administrator, and himself admitted he had made mistakes. That fact alone evidences his basic humility, and he did the best he knew to serve the Unity and the Lord.

In an emergency synod at Rychnov before the end of that year, it was decided that henceforth four bishops would stand at the head of the Unity. In addition to Tůma and Elias, Luke of Prague and Ambrose (Ambrož) of Skuteč were chosen and consecrated.* Tůma ranked first, and he became president of the Inner Council with administrative duties restored to the bishop in that position.† Elias, Luke, and Ambrose came next to Tůma in seniority and were assigned an area of specific responsibility, two bishops for Bohemia and two for Moravia, a further development in the "diocesan" system of the Unity.[32]

Otherwise, the administration and organization of the Unity remained much as it had been before. One other addition around this time was the assigning of some members of the Inner Council to be "co-seniors" or assistant bishops to aid the bishops in their administrative duties. These "co-seniors" were not considered to be full bishops, but could represent a bishop in visitations of congregations, etc. Also while up to this time a good number of lay delegates had taken part in synods, in the future the clergy dominated. This was a matter not of priests arrogantly seizing control but of practicality. Now that nobles were entering the Unity, they became the "lay" delegates to

---

vzkládáním" (through the laying on of hands as in ordination) were used. This point is visited again in chapter 14.
* Here Müller, 1:294, says that Tůma and Elias consecrated Luke and Ambrose through the laying on of hands to be bishops ("weihten diese die Brüder Lukas und Ambros durch Handauflegung zu Bischöfen"). See also Müller's *Das Bischoftum*, 20.
† Though Br. Prokop retained the title of "judge," actual authority passed more to the bishops.

synods. The clergy, who came from the middle and lower classes, were seen as better representatives of the common people than the lords were.[33]

With his new authority Luke began to make innovations with insights gained from his experience in Rome. He introduced certain features of Roman liturgy to enrich the austere worship of the Brethren. He prepared new liturgical forms (for ordination and the sacraments in particular), fostered greater emphasis on the church year seasons and festivals, and encouraged the use of the traditional lectionary of assigned Scripture readings.[34] As he saw it, the Unity should depart only from what was bad in the Roman Church, but should hold on to what was good.[35] He even cited Thomas Aquinas as a Catholic theologian who could quote from the Scriptures "sensibly."[36] He stated as much in a letter to Master Havel at Auste, who Luke had heard had been ignoring the pericopes and the church year: "For you know that our separation is from the bad, and not from that which may be used for good purpose honestly."[37] Luke went on that if something does not lead to misunderstanding or evil, then the church should make use of it. To emphasize his point, Luke dated his letter "the Saturday after the Virgin Lucy['s Day], 1502."* Talk about keeping the days of the church year!

Evidently Master Havel was not the only one unhappy with Luke's innovations. In a letter to one concerned person at Brandýs, Luke explained that he was not introducing fancy vestments or gold chalices and embroidered altar cloths everywhere, but had only sent such a cup from an old abandoned Catholic or Utraquist Church to replace the vessels lost by a congregation to fire.[38]

In spite of complaints of this sort, Luke's influence continued to increase as the 16th century dawned, and for the next quarter century his theology and the Unity's were virtually one and the same.[39]

---

* The feast day of St. Lucy the Virgin is 13 December.

Notes

1 Marianka Foušek, "The Perfectionism of the Early Unitas Fratrum," *Church History* 30 (1961): 396-413.

2 Joseph Th. Müller, *Geschichte der Böhmischen Brüder* 3 vols. (Herrnhut: Missionsbuchhandlung, 1922, 1931), 1:234-36.

3 Rudolf Říčan, *The History of the Unity of Brethren*, trans. C. Daniel Crews (Bethlehem, Pa.: Department of Publications and Communications, Moravian Church, Northern Province, 1992), gives the most complete account of these developments and personalities, 58-89. Biographies of these students are given, 49-51.

4 Scholars are divided on the date. Müller, 1:238, says "around 1460." Peter Brock, *The Political and Social Doctrines of the Unity of Czech Brethren in the Fifteenth and Early Sixteenth Centuries* (The Hague: Mouton and Co., 1957), 105, says "shortly before 1460." Říčan, 49, has "perhaps in 1458." My "Luke of Prague: Theologian of the Unity," originally presented at the 1997 Moses Lectures at Moravian Theological Seminary and printed in *The Hinge* 13, no. 3 (autumn 2005): 21-54, provides an extensive account of Luke's life and theology. *The Hinge* did not print most of the Czech accent marks.

5 Brock, 106. Amedeo Molnár, "Études et conversion de Luc de Prague," *Communio Viatorum* 3 (1960): 255, 257.

6 Müller, 1:238: "Ich gehe hin, und prüfe es." See also Brock, 107.

7 Říčan, 58.

8 Müller, 1:237.

9 Říčan, 59.

10 Říčan, 61.

11 Říčan, 62.

12 Müller, 1:242.

13 Lissa Folio 5 (film 331), Andrew Slaby translation, notebook 11, 15-34, in Moravian Archives, Bethlehem, Pa.

14 Müller, 1:244. Říčan, 62-63. See Lissa Folio 5 (film 352), Andrew Slaby translation, notebook 11, 202.

15 See Edmund de Schweinitz, *History of the Church Known as the Unitas Fratrum*, 2nd (reprint) ed. (Bethlehem, Pa.: Moravian Publication Concern, 1901), 174-75.

16 Brock, 229.

17 Říčan, 63-64.

18 Říčan, 64.

19 Müller, 1:254.

20 Brock, 146. Müller, 1:256. Brock, 147, n. 42, and Molnár in his "Luc de Prague devant la crise de l'Unité des années 1490," *Communio Viatorum* 4 (1961): 323, n. 11, explicitly disagree over the action taken by the Rychnov synod, thanks to the Czech word "vyzdvihnúti."

[21] Řičan, 67.

[22] Řičan, 65. Brock takes a sympathetic view throughout of the "minority party" as the true upholders of the original principles of the Unity. That is undeniably true; the question is whether those principles needed modification.

[23] Řičan, 65.

[24] Řičan, 70.

[25] Řičan, 88.

[26] Řičan, 70. Müller, 1:273-74. Řičan, 71.

[27] Řičan, 70 (Czech version (*Dějiny Jednoty bratrská*. Prague: Kalich, 1957), 80), says Savonarola was burned, but other sources say he was hanged. Still others say Savonarola was hanged, and then his body was burned. In any case it was traumatic for Luke.

[28] Řičan, 70.

[29] Amedeo Molnár, *Bratr Lukáš: Bohoslovec Jednoty* (Prague: Husova Fakulta, 1948), 12.

[30] Müller, 1:277-78.

[31] Řičan, 74. See Joseph Th. Müller, *Das Bischoftum der Brüder-Unität* (Herrnhut: self printed, 1889), 19.

[32] Řičan, 75.

[33] Řičan, 72-73.

[34] Řičan, 75.

[35] Müller, *Geschichte der Böhmischen Brüder,* 1:295, 298-99. Molnár, *Bratr Lukáš: Bohoslovec Jednoty,* 16.

[36] Lissa Folio 5 (film 352), Andrew Slaby translation, notebook 11, 207.

[37] Lissa Folio 5 (film 354), Andrew Slaby translation, notebook 12, 3.

[38] Lissa Folio 5 (film 351), Andrew Slaby translation, notebook 11, 196.

[39] Müller, 1:271. Miloš Štrupl, "The Confessional Theology of the Unitas Fratrum," *Church History* 33 (1964): 283.

Chapter 9

Life as 'Heretics'

Persecution and the Mandate of St. James,
1501-1517

The first couple years of the new century went well for the Unity, as it experienced significant growth both in numbers and in its internal development. Bishop Matthias had died in 1500, and Michael Bradacius, the "good priest" who had cared for the Unity in its infant years and had played a crucial role in establishing its own ministry, had likewise been "called home" in 1501, but the new administration was in place and functioning. Luke of Prague continued his work of enriching the worship and instructional materials available to the church. He produced a catechism for children in the faith, *Questions for Children* (*Dětinské Otazky*).* He also in 1501 brought forth a new *Agenda*, or liturgical instructions for ministers, to replace earlier versions.

As a "lover of fairly fashioned temples," Luke continued to enrich and embellish the Unity's worship, though by Catholic standards it remained plain. A hymnal was produced in Prague in 1501, containing several Hussite hymns and compositions by Luke and other members of the Unity. This "first Protestant hymnal" was not an official Unity publication, but apparently

---

* The complexity of the answers implies that instructors were to put them into their own words to help the children understand as appropriate.

was sponsored by private sources. In 1505, however, the Unity did bring out its first official hymnal, containing many old Latin hymns translated into Czech and others by Luke and other Brethren. No copies of this hymnal have survived, but from the descriptions, Luke's hand in it is obvious.[1]

With a weak and mostly absent king, Vladislav II, on the throne, the nobles continued to run their estates as they pleased, and the Unity continued to benefit, for several of these powerful lords still gave them shelter and a chance to make the advances mentioned above. The peace negotiated in 1485 between Catholics and Utraquists was holding, and while the Unity was not included in that agreement, lack of religious strife in the land was to their advantage.

Unity children and parents attend catechism classes together.

Among the Utraquists, though the Italian bishop Luciana, who had been doing ordinations for them, had died in 1493, they had found a temporary replacement in Philip de Villa Nova. They still had hopes of receiving papal recognition of the *Compacta* of Basel and an archbishop of their own.

Trouble for the Unity was just over the horizon. As it continued to gain in popularity, and as the dedicated pastoral care shown by its ministers reflected badly on many of the Catholic and Utraquist clergy, complaints about the Brethren increased. Its enemies claimed that it numbered 100,000 members, which is surely an exaggeration, perhaps by ten times. These inflated totals given out by its opponents do, however, show what a challenge they felt from the Unity, and they were trying to make sure Rome understood just how big a threat it was.[2]

The Utraquist consistory hoped that if it could play a part in eliminating the Unity its own case for recognition by Rome would be helped. For their part, many of the Catholics simply wanted the "heretics" wiped out. To Catholic humanists influenced from Italy, the Unity added insult to injury. These humanists valued the reclamation of "classical" culture and learning, and their influence was spreading into Bohemia through such advocates as Bohuslav Hassenstein. Yet the Unity cared little for such things. The humanists wondered how such uncouth and unlettered persons as the Brethren could dare claim to be legitimate Christians, much less priests and bishops! The Unity's use of "rough" Czech instead of "refined" Latin in reading, preaching, and even singing was proof of their boorish nature. King Vladislav's new queen, Anna de Foix-Candale, whom he married in 1502, also had no use for these "primitive" Wycliffites and Picards.[3]

Pope Alexander VI (d. 1503) took note of the complaints and dissatisfaction and appointed Dr. Henry Institoris to undertake the conversion of the Brethren, using secular force if necessary. Institoris was a learned Dominican who had written a book with the ominous name of *Malleus Maleficarum*, (*Hammer of the evil doers*). Supporting his efforts in Bohemia were the Catholic bishop John Filipec and another scholar, Dr. Augustine Käsenbrod.* Albrecht of Kolovrat, who became head of the Bohemian national assembly in 1503, also wanted to clear the country of heretics.

Käsenbrod opened the attack with a series of letters against the Brethren.† Institoris followed by inviting the Unity's leaders

---

* Yes, his last name is German for "cheese bread" or "cheese sandwich," which may explain why he and his friends referred to him simply as "Dr. Augustine of Moravia," or "Dr. Augustine from Olomouc." Müller simply calls him "Dr. Augustine."

† Käsenbrod had been treated by Luke's physician brother John Černý without realizing he was a member of the Unity. He was astounded that such a well-educated and intelligent man could

to a colloquy in Olomouc. He tried to dazzle the Brethren with stories of Italian saints and miracles to prove the truth of the Catholic position. Historian Říčan wryly observes: "Of course, he did not convince them." Indeed, simple Bishop Tůma said that if the Catholics have all these saints with all those powers, why don't they use them against the Turks?[4]

Failing with colloquy, Institoris and others spread absurd charges against the Unity hoping to weaken it in the eyes of the Czechs in general. An example of these accusations is that the Brethren worshipped God (or some said the devil) in the form of a fly, whom they would receive in "communion" in their mouths.[5] The propaganda had little effect.

The Unity's opponents then asked King Vladislav to take active steps against the "heretics." To encourage him in this, charges made by the Amosites against the Unity were reported to the king, the most serious of these being that the Brethren were becoming complete Taborites and were plotting an armed insurrection. This enraged Vladislav, who said in effect: "So they want to play Žižka, do they? We'll show them!"[6]

On 5 July 1503 (the day before John Hus Day) the king decreed that "heretics are more noxious than Turks,"[7] and forbade the Unity to hold public services. Its priests were to be arrested, and its lay members were to join either the Catholic or Utraquist parishes. The decree was binding on all territories under the king's direct control, but had to be passed by the national assembly before it was the law of the land throughout Bohemia, on the estates and towns controlled by the powerful nobles. The king even tried to get the nobles in neighboring Moravia to adopt similar measures.[8]

In Bohemia's assembly, however, Chancellor Kolovrat and other enemies of the Unity were in the minority. Several Utraquist nobles were aware that the Catholics held little good will for the Utraquists either and feared they would be next for persecution. These plus nobles friendly to the Unity persuaded

---

belong to such an ignorant sect (Müller, 1:308-10), but this did not make him think better of the Unity.

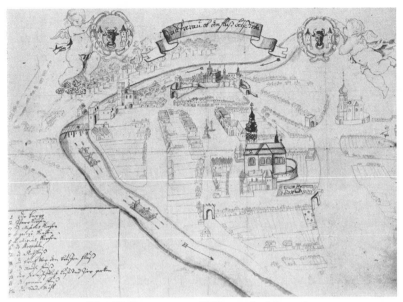

The Unity center of Přerov in Moravia.

the assembly not to condemn the Brethren without giving them a hearing in another colloquy, which was set for January 1504. In the meantime, public services of the Unity were forbidden. As yet there was no general persecution.[9]

As persecution loomed, Bishop Elias died in September 1503. The Unity's *Memorial Book* said of him: "He was a tender and loving and very friendly man, who suffered much." It also remarked that he had accompanied the Brethren on their first exile to Moldavia.[10] In such threatening circumstances it was not feasible to call a synod to elect another bishop, so his responsibilities were temporarily assigned to the other bishops.

Some nobles repressed the Unity at this time. In November 1503 six Brethren were burned at the stake in Bor. One of them was offered time to consider and recant, but he replied he did not wish his Brethren to go on to heaven without him. The Unity's main centers in Rychnov, Litomyšl, Mladá Boleslav, Brandýs, and Přerov were on the estates of nobles who favored and protected the Unity. In west Bohemia, though, the Unity did not fare as well. Dr. Käsenbrod wrote letters against it, and the queen tried to influence King Vladislav to take sterner measures. On the other hand, the noble ladies Johanna (Jana) of Pernštejn and Johanna of Šelnberk (of the Krajíř family) used their influence for more favorable treatment of the Unity.[11] On their part, the elders of the Unity wrote to strengthen and encourage their members, called for fasting and prayer, and urged them to hold fast whatever might come. Members were to profess and not try to hide their membership in the Unity.[12]

In preparation for the assembly-mandated colloquy, the Unity in late 1503 brought out a new confession of faith to explain its positions. This short statement was based on the Apostles' Creed and dealt also with the sacraments. Other Unity documents of the time defended its separation from the Catholic and Utraquist Churches, stressed the crucial distinction of essential and ministrative things, and called for the release of those who had been imprisoned for their faith. King Vladislav and other authorities took little notice.[13]

After Christmas 1503 as the time for the big colloquy approached, representatives of the Unity including Bishop Luke, Lawrence Krasonický, and Filip the Soapmaker* traveled to Prague, where they were lodged in various homes. The wife of the house where Luke was staying was so upset at having a "heretic" under her roof that she packed up and left. Luke arranged for different lodging so she could return home.[14]

Before going to the colloquy, Luke wrote a long letter to the members in Mladá Boleslav containing his last will and testament.[15] He had sound reasons for his apprehension.

Excitement in Prague was running at fever pitch.[16] Mobs roamed the streets hoping for a glimpse of the "infidels." Some accounts reported it was as if the king or a circus was parading through town. This worried Prague's city council, which had guaranteed the safety of the Unity delegates to their powerful noble overlords. There was fear that the crowds might lynch them, and rumors that the king might arrest them. To forestall

---

* This is the same Filip who a decade earlier had defended members of the Unity's living in cities on the grounds that "cows don't want soap to eat!"

any unpleasantness or embarrassment, the city council had the delegates brought quietly before it on 1 January 1504, announced they had fulfilled their obligations by merely showing up, and told them they were free to go. In fact, they were told to get out of town as quickly and quietly as they could, and by 2 o'clock the next morning they were all safely out of Prague. It was lucky they left when they did, for a letter from the king did indeed arrive ordering them to be seized and tried as heretics.[17]

Thus the grand colloquy fizzled, but it only postponed rather than settled matters. In the meantime the royal prohibition against the Unity was still in force in places. Unity elders encouraged members to hold private services and instruct their children in their homes. Heads of households were to read or repeat from memory passages of Scripture, and to pray and join in singing where they could. Where it was considered safe and a minister could come quietly, small groups gathered for communion.

During this time Bishop Luke continued to write defenses of the Unity and letters of encouragement to its members. He also prepared commentaries on various portions of Scripture and a paraphrase of the Psalms. These writings contained practical advice on Christian living in difficult times rather than launching into speculative theology. It was also at this time (1505 as noted above) that the Unity brought out its first official hymnal, *Hymns for the praise of God* (*Písně chval božských*). Perhaps this was seen as another instructional work now that the congregations could not come together to learn and sing hymns in the services.

Queen Anna died in childbirth in 1506, and while this removed an enemy, it did not ease the pressure on the Unity. The Unity suffered a personal loss in 1507 when Br. Prokop, who had been "judge" of the Unity since 1494, died in Brandýs.* He was not a gifted administrator and was never elected a

---

* Br. Prokop had the nickname "Rufus," which means "Red," presumably because of his hair color (Müller, 1:338).

bishop, but he had a gift for mediation and personal relations which served the Unity well. Br. Tůma Přeloučský, the senior bishop, succeeded him as judge and was the official head of the Unity. He and the two other remaining bishops, Luke and Ambrose, directed the Inner Council, but as before, Luke was the real leader.

More trouble descended on the Unity. Chancellor Kolovrat, who was viceroy in Bohemia while King Vladislav was occupied in his Hungarian domains, in December 1507 issued another decree with royal assent which continued the former prohibitions against the Unity and now summoned its bishops for an "examination." It also threatened dire consequences for any noble who gave shelter to Unity members. This last provision backfired, for the nobles saw it as an infringement of their rights on their estates. Even nobles who did not care if the Unity was persecuted considered this an insult and joined in an angry protest to the king, reminding him that former kings who had crossed the nobles had been forced to leave the country.

Noble women friends of the Unity also came to its defense. Among these were Lady Krescencia of Orlík and Lady Marta of Boskovice in Moravia. Lady Marta was particularly outspoken and sent the king not only a defense prepared by the Brethren, but also a cover letter of her own saying that by persecuting the Unity the king was bringing God's judgment on himself. "You should be our protector so that we can live peaceful and quiet lives," she wrote.[18] This scandalized Dr. Käsenbrod, who was offended that women would venture into the public forum in defense of heretics who were "so vile that they would pollute the very fire used to burn them." True, the queen had opposed the Unity, but she had had the decency to do so properly by talking to her husband in private. Lady Marta, however, had dared rebuke the king publicly. The fact that the Unity had allowed women to speak on its behalf could be seen as further evidence of its "depravity." Käsenbrod called Lady Marta "the Devil's barmaid," and said she should stick to her flax and spinning like a "proper" lady.[19]

The enemies of the Unity now saw the time had come to deal with it once and for all with a nationwide law properly passed by Bohemia's national assembly. They counted and found that this time they had the numbers to do it, since many of the nobles who had protested in 1507 had done so only in defense of their ancestral rights.[20] It would be different if the king and viceroy, rather than demanding, politely asked them to pass a law outlawing the Unity throughout the land. Accordingly, the assembly met on St. James Day (July 25) 1508 to do just

The coat of arms of Lady Marta of Boskovice.

that. The Unity's noble protectors protested, but did not have the votes to defeat the measure.

This "Mandate of St. James" contained the following main points: (1) the Unity's religious services, public or private, are forbidden; (2) all its publications are banned and must be destroyed; (3) its priests may not administer the sacraments (including marriage); (4) its priests must recant or be punished; (5) all nobles (men or women) are to enforce this decree or be penalized; (6) any who harbor these "Picards" will be fined; (7) lay Unity members must join either the Catholic or Utraquist Church and be instructed by their priests.[21]

The edict was published on 10 August 1508, and nobles and others were given until Christmas to fully implement it. The Unity was now illegal throughout Bohemia according to the law of the land. It remained so for the next hundred years.

One bit of good news was that Chancellor Kolovrat, presumably because of his mishandling of the matter the year before, was dismissed. His successor, though, Leo of Rožmitál, was little better. The Unity was still an illegal "sect" not to be tolerated but to be uprooted wherever it was found.

Unity elders sent out another call for fasting and prayer.[22] Leaders of the Unity also observed that "the king should leave us alone and see and do something about the oppression of the poor."[23]

A limited version of this decree was adopted by neighboring Moravia's national assembly on 24 August 1508, but Lord Žerotín, who was a friend if not already a member of the Unity, managed to pull most of its teeth. For example, harboring a member of the Unity brought only a lengthy series of warnings and moderate fines. In fact, even that was not enforced, and nobles continued to abide by the decree on their estates only if they wanted to, and no action was taken if they did not.[24]

Even in Bohemia the letter of the law was not always followed. Enforcement was largely limited to the prohibition of public services. For the rest, though the Unity had to be careful, many aspects of church life could go on. This was certainly true on most of the estates of the Unity's friends, but as was true in the first exile of the Brethren in 1481, even several Catholic or Utraquist lords were reluctant to bother "such industrious and peaceable subjects."[25] Little effort was devoted to searching out and turning in the Unity's priests. At the end of 1509 five lords did bring in 11 Brethren and turn them over to the Utraquist consistory as required. These were possibly local elders, not priests, and their interrogation was a formality since, again, the Prague faculty was not sure how to deal directly with "ignorant laypersons."[26]

A few members did suffer martyrdom. Br. Andrew (Ondřej) Polívka, a lay member of Kutná Hora, allowed himself to be persuaded by his non-Unity wife to conform to the edict and attend the Utraquist Church. He did so for a while, and joined in the adoration of the host. But his conscience rebuked him for this, and in the middle of Mass one day he stood up and denounced those who worship "idols of bread." He was burned at the stake in 1511. A priest, Jiřík Volyňský, was thrown into prison and threatened with starvation if he did not repudiate the Unity. After several days, his captors gave up when it became obvious that he would indeed die before renouncing his faith.[27] Such instances of violence were rare, but the threat was always there, and the descendants of nobles friendly to the Unity did not always share their predecessors' views.[28]

In the first years after the 1508 Mandate of St. James, for safety's sake the Inner Council removed to Moravia, where the prohibitions against the Unity were not as severe as in Bohemia. Luke of Prague, though, stayed in hiding in the Mladá Boleslav area and provided what pastoral care he could to his flock. He also drew up an important confession of faith, the *Apologia sacrae scripturae*, and a few years later (1511) the Unity had 100 copies printed in Nürnberg. Historian Říčan characterizes it as "a comprehensive defense of the whole of their doctrine" and "the first (and very effective) confession of faith of the Brethren directed at a foreign public."[29]

Luke continued to send out pastoral letters to the scattered members urging them to penance and dedication. It was felt that God had allowed these persecutions to fall on the Unity to recall its members to renewed dedication.[30] Luke also warned them not to return to worldly ways as soon as the persecution let up. Considering how dependent the Unity was on the good will of its noble protectors, it took courage for him to chastise these lords also. Warning them against pride and luxury, he compared them to birds that have their nests on lofty rocks above the commoners. He also criticized those who take away the people's meadows to make ponds for themselves.[31]

The Unity reserved at least some blame for its persecutors. Several enemies died in short order, which the Unity saw as God's judgment on the evildoers. Queen Anna had already died at the birth of her son Ludvík in 1506. The Catholic bishop John Filipec in 1509 wounded his stomach on a sharp nail while getting out of his vehicle and succumbed to infection. Chancellor Kolovrat had a lengthy illness and died in 1510

from a festering boil.* Finally, in 1513 Dr. Augustine Käsenbrod suddenly fell dead from his chair at the dinner table.[32]
Historian Říčan observes: "The Brethren's historiography lingered with pleasure over these events, embellishing them with
many an edifying legend."[33]

The Unity was strengthened in 1512 when the noble lady
Johanna of Šelnberk publicly joined its ranks. Her wealth
and influence were valuable, and in 1513 she paid for the
publication of a confession of faith and defense of the Unity's
teaching. Even Lady Johanna, though, was not above the
Unity's admonitions. It cautioned her not only to lead a pious
and sober life herself, but also to treat her subjects fairly and
humanely.[34] So much for the charges of the Amosites that the
Unity under Luke was lax on morals.

Luke himself ran into personal danger again while making
a pastoral visit to Janovice in western Bohemia.[35] The unscrupulous local nobleman, Peter (Petr) Suda, learned of Luke's
presence and, feigning friendship, invited him to the castle and
fed him a fish dinner. He even promised to attend Luke's
service the next day. During the night Luke suffered an attack
of "stone"† and was incapacitated. Suda then made excuses to
keep Luke around and ultimately imprisoned him. It appears
that Suda acted not out of religious convictions but for the
ransom he thought the Unity would pay for Luke's release.
Failing that, he might have thought the king or Utraquist
consistory would pay him a reward for turning Luke over. Here
he was disappointed, for the Utraquists told him he could burn
Luke at the stake, for all they cared. Ultimately the people of
Janovice raised a ransom, and Luke's overlord, Kunrát of
Krajek, had him freed on bail. The threat remained, though,

---

* De Schweinitz, 197, with his typical gift for memorable words calls it
more spectacularly a "malignant carbuncle."

† The precise medical condition of "stone" is unclear. In this case,
after a rich dinner, it might be gallstones, but that is far from
certain. Luke suffered from this condition throughout his life.
Seeking specialist medical attention for it may have been another
reason for his earlier trip to Italy.

that the king could order Krajek to produce Luke for trial.*

Fortunately for the Unity, King Vladislav died in 1516. His son and successor Ludvík, only 10 years old, was preoccupied with his Hungarian domain, and so in Bohemia and Moravia the independence of the nobles greatly increased again. Enforcement of the Mandate of St. James fell into abeyance for the next 20 years or so,[36] and in these brighter circumstances the Unity began holding services in public once more.[37]

Within the Unity's administration, Bishop Tůma Přeloučský, who had been the official head of the Unity, died in February 1517.[†] He was the last of the three original priests of the Unity, and was known as a good writer with a sense of humor[38] (a trait not often noted in leaders of the early Unity). He was not always comfortable with the new ways imported by Luke, but was resigned to the will of the church and had often prayed: "Lord, if I am in the way of your work, take me hence."[39]

Luke of Prague now became the leader of the Unity in title as well as in fact. Associated with him were Bishop Ambrose of Skuteč and Bishop Martin Škoda, who was elected bishop later in 1517.[‡]

The administration of the Unity from the synod of Rychnov in 1494 to Luke's ascendancy in 1517 is admittedly confusing. Perhaps a recap will help: Matthias of Kunvald was originally bishop, president of the Inner Council and "judge" (which seems in most cases to be another word for president of the

---

* Amedeo Molnár, in his "Pasteur dans le tormente," *Communio Viatorum* 6 (1963): 282-83, gives a slightly more positive view of Suda's actions. There may be merit in this, but the fact remains that just five years later the surrounding cities became so disgusted with him that they stormed his castle and tore it to the ground (Říčan, 101).

† Müller, 1:390, and Říčan, 102, place Tůma's death in 1518, but de Schweinitz, 228, states their source, the *Memorial Book*, is wrong, that Tůma died in 1517. The sequence of events gives the edge to de Schweinitz.

‡ De Schweinitz, 228-29, gives this sequence, that the synod that elected Škoda was held in 1517 after the death of Tůma earlier in the year. Müller, 1:389, n. 273, says the synod was held in 1516 or maybe in 1517, but nonetheless before Tůma's death in 1518.

council). After 1494, Matthias remained as ordaining bishop, but Br. Prokop assumed his administrative duties as judge and was in effect president of the Inner Council. After the death of Matthias in 1500, Br. Prokop retained the title of judge, but real administrative powers passed to the four bishops (Tůma, Elias, Luke, and Ambrose of Skuteč), with Tůma as the official senior bishop and effective head of the Inner Council (though he and the others actually followed the lead of Luke). Only in 1517 did Luke become senior bishop, president of the Inner Council and judge, thus reuniting the functions originally held by Matthias (though the authority to ordain was now shared by Bishops Luke, Ambrose, and Martin Škoda).

Other members of the Inner Council who had died could now be replaced, and so in 1517 the Unity had a respite from persecution and a renewed administration firmly in place. This was fortunate, for news of the German Reformation was about to break upon them, and how to respond to it would be a critical issue.

Notes

1 Rudolf Říčan, *The History of the Unity of Brethren*, trans. C. Daniel Crews (Bethlehem, Pa.: Department of Publications and Communications, Moravian Church, Northern Province, 1992), 103-4.

2 Říčan, 90. Joseph Th. Müller, *Geschichte der Böhmischen Brüder* 3 vols. (Herrnhut: Missionsbuchhandlung, 1922, 1931), 1:311.

3 Říčan, 90. Müller, 1:306-8.

4 Říčan, 91.

5 Müller, 1:312.

6 Müller, 1:314.

7 Lissa Folio 6, Andrew Slaby translation, notebook 12, 115, 122, in Moravian Archives, Bethlehem, Pa.

8 Říčan, 92. Müller, 1:315-16. See Lissa Folio 6, Andrew Slaby translation, notebook 12, 133-136.

9 Indeed, the king in letters to the Utraquist administrator and to the citizens of Prague in 1503 bemoaned the people's lack of enthusiasm in persecuting the "Pikarts." These are given in Lissa Folio 6, Andrew Slaby translation, notebook 12, 137-142.

10 Müller, 1:316.

11 Müller, 1:321.

12 Říčan, 93.

13 Müller, 1:321-24.

14 Müller, 1:326.

15 Lissa Folios 6 and 14 (films 31-33), Andrew Slaby translation, notebooks 13, 196-208, and notebook 14, 1-17. Additional letters relating to this "trial" are in notebook 14, 18-96.

16 The Unity's account of these events is in Lissa Folio 6, Andrew Slaby translation, notebook 12, 203-7, and notebook 13, 3-57.

17 For details see Müller, 1:326-31.

18 This letter is in Lissa Folio 6, Andrew Slaby translation, notebook 13, 186-91. The king's answer follows on 192-94.

19 Říčan, 95. Müller, 1:342-44.

20 Jindřich Halama in "The Crisis of the Union of Czech Brethren in the Years before the Thirty Years War, or On the Usefulness of Persecution," *Communio Viatorum* 44 (2002): 51-68, says the Unity was persecuted because it simply would not fit in with the world and its society. See 53 especially.

21 Říčan, 95. Müller, 1:346-50, quotes most of the official text.

22 Several examples of such letters from various times are found in Lissa Folio 5. These are translated in Andrew Slaby's notebook 11, 55-130. One from this time particularly is in Lissa Folio 6, Andrew Slaby translation, notebook 12, 150-59.

23 Lissa Folio 6 (film 45-46), Andrew Slaby translation, notebook 14, 162.

24 Müller, 1:352-53.

25 Říčan, 96.

26 Říčan, 96.

27 Říčan, 100-101.

28 Müller, 1:371-77.

29 Říčan, 100.

30 Müller, 1:365.

31 Říčan, 98-99.

32 Müller, 1:366-67.

33 Říčan, 100.

34 Říčan, 101.

35 Details are given in Müller, 1:383-86.

36 Peter Brock, *The Political and Social Doctrines of the Unity of Czech Brethren in the Fifteenth and Early Sixteenth Centuries* (The Hague: Mouton and Co., 1957), 207.

37 Luke's letter announcing this is in Lissa Folio 5. See Slaby translation, notebook 11, 180-84. Luke says: "You know this handwriting" as a means of authenticating the message.

38 Müller, 1:390.

39 Müller, 1:390-91.

Chapter 10

To the Death of Luke

First Contacts with the German and Swiss
Reformations, 1518-1528

The Unity made good use of the lapsed enforcement of the Mandate of St. James. Particularly on the sheltered estates of friendly nobles the Unity not only resumed holding public services, but under Luke's guidance it brought out a new hymnal in 1519* and a supplemental book of funeral hymns in 1521.[1] The Unity fostered education by opening schools for its young people. And it operated a new invention, the printing press, both in Litomyšl and Mladá Boleslav, publishing not only its own theological works, but also some by leading scholars of the day.[2]

One of these scholars was the well-known Dutch Catholic humanist Desiderius Erasmus (1466?-1536). As we saw in the last chapter, the Unity had not fared well with Italian-influenced humanists, but Erasmus was of a different stripe, famous for his moderation and fairness. In addition to his classical publications, he sought a reform of abuses in the church. He conducted a lively correspondence with scholars throughout Europe including the Czech humanist John Šlechta of Všehrd. In one of his letters Šlechta told Erasmus

---

* The 1519 hymnal has not survived, but it is mentioned in the preface of the hymnal of 1561.

of the religious situation in Bohemia and Moravia, with its Catholic, Utraquist, and Unity parties. He went into some detail about the beliefs and church order of the Unity, though in a less than positive light. Surprisingly, in response Erasmus expressed guarded approval of several of the Unity's positions. Moreover, this correspondence was printed and distributed to the public.

The Unity, which for years had been yearning for an impartial hearing, was bowled over by such an even-handed evaluation — and by the famous Doctor Erasmus himself. If he endorsed its teachings and practices, it might make a great difference in the way the Unity was regarded in the Czech lands and the rest of Europe. It might even be the beginning of reform elsewhere. So the Unity elders, eager to get more of their true opinions into his hands, in 1520[3] sent Erasmus a copy of the Confession printed in Nürnberg in 1511 by way of two messengers, Nicholas Klaudian and Lawrence Votík, to provide further information. The Unity asked Erasmus to review the document and give a public opinion.

Erasmus blinked. The Confession looked all right at a glance, he said, but he was too busy to go into it in detail, and besides, an endorsement from him probably wouldn't do much good anyway. In the end he admitted that agreeing with the Brethren too much might land him in trouble with his Catholic Church.[4] Erasmus's reforming zeal did not extend to enduring charges of heresy. The Brethren were understandably disillusioned by his temerity, and did not pursue further contact with him, though later he did pass on some of their writings to Martin Bucer (1491-1551), a leader of the Reformed movement in Switzerland and south Germany.[5]*

In spite of their disappointment with Erasmus, the Unity elders hoped for better results from Martin Luther when they heard of his reforms taking place in Germany. Luther (1483-1546) started out as a Catholic monk frantically seeking the

---

* Bucer and the Unity had much in common and had closer contact later in the 1540s.

salvation of his soul,[6] but came to a realization of justification by faith apart from works of the Law. Angered as well by the church's sale of indulgences,* he posted his famous "Ninety-Five Theses" on the cathedral door at Wittenberg on 31 October 1517, thus sparking what is commonly regarded as the start of the Protestant Reformation. Like most Germans, Luther had originally seen Hus and all the Hussites as abominable heretics, but by the time of his famous disputation with Dr. Johann Eck at Leipzig in 1519, at which Luther openly broke with certain Catholic dogmas, he was inclined to speak favorably of Hus. In fact, when Eck accused Luther of holding views on indulgences similar to those of the condemned heretics Wycliffe and Hus, Luther asked for time to consult the records. He then surprised everyone by declaring that the Council of Constance had done wrong in condemning Hus.[7] Tradition has Luther exclaiming: "I am a Hussite!" A Czech who was at the disputation arranged for him to get a copy of Hus's *De Ecclesia*, and Luther was amazed at how much of Hus's thinking paralleled his own. Luther sent some of his and his associate Philip Melancthon's (1497-1560) works to Utraquists in Bohemia.[8]

News of Luther's actions spread through Europe like wildfire with printing presses turning out numerous copies of his "Ninety-Five Theses." By 1519 a preacher named Matthias the Hermit was attracting large crowds in Prague. He was not allowed in the churches, but preached in the squares and streets and on the banks of the river. Like most Czech reformers, his message was mostly about moral living, but he also praised the teaching of Luther.[9] Matthias also gained respect for his message by his selfless caring for victims of an outbreak of pestilence in the city. In addition, Thomas Münzer (1490-1525) was active in Prague in 1521, attacking the Utraquist establishment and praising some of the opinions of Luther.

All of this caused a stir in Prague, and some of the Utraquist clergy were ready to embrace the new reformation. Others, however, were far more wary.[10] When in August 1523

---

* Like Hus.

Unity presses were the first to print works of John Hus.

a student of Luther, Havel Cahera, was elected head of the Utraquist consistory it appeared that the Utraquists might proceed in a thoroughly Lutheran direction. A year later, however, Cahera found that most of his constituents were not ready for Protestant ideas. He switched sides and became an arch anti-Lutheran conservative.[11] It is reported that Luther was bitterly disappointed in his former student.

Many Utraquists, as we shall see, remained influenced by Luther,[12] but historian Říčan cautions:

> It was, however, clear from the beginning that Luther's influence on Bohemia did not primarily concern winning over the Hussites to his basic proclamation of the Gospel of grace alone. It was, rather, his courageous conduct which was for them a **strengthening of their old Hussite program**. It stimulated them to a more determined turning away from Rome even in matters in which Luther himself remained more conservative, for example, in religious ceremonies.[13]

The leaders of the Unity were also interested in Luther and his reforms, but they remained cautious. They were glad to see someone else courageously proclaiming many of the truths they had long championed. Perhaps they were not alone after all! On the other hand, the Unity had been in existence for more than 60 years and had proven itself by resisting persecution. It had developed a rich and disciplined church life. Besides, although Luke and the "liberal" party in the Unity had argued for grace and a lessening of reliance on good works and abstaining from the things of the world, by no stretch of the imagination could they be called morally lax or indifferent.* So Luther's loud proclaiming of "justification by faith apart from works of the Law" seemed dangerous to the Unity as promoting a notion that faith did not have to produce works as its fruits. The fact that some of the newly "Lutheranized" Utraquist clergy went overboard in this direction increased the Unity's reservations.

---

* The Amosites did, of course, but that was unjustified.

Indeed, so far as Bishop Luke was concerned, Luther was the "new kid on the block," and having come through years of persecution he was in no mood for anyone to suggest that the Unity should jettison its own ways and embrace the new movement. True, even before 1500 the official decrees (*Dekrety*) of the Unity had said that if a group with "better teaching and church order" should someday arise, the Brethren might join them.[14] But that was theory. "The elders of the Unity certainly did not consider that such a case had now occurred,"[15] historian Říčan observes. And de Schweinitz probably has the right of it: "Bishop Luke watched these developments with an eagle eye."[16]

Contact with Martin Luther arose after three monks who had accepted his teaching were forced to seek sanctuary in Bohemia in 1518. The three, Michael Weisse, John Zeising (called Čížek which means finch or "little bird"), and John the Monk,* were received into the Unity in Litomyšl by the pastor, Lawrence Krasonický. The Unity could use educated German speakers, and Krasonický and his deacon, John Roh,† were interested in the Lutheran ideas reported by these converts. One who remained unimpressed was Bishop Luke, who warned of their "German methods," saying, "It would be better to leave the Germans to God as before."[17] Events ultimately proved Luke right, but for now Roh was particularly intrigued. When he was transferred to a congregation near the German border he decided in 1522 to pay Luther a visit, and he took Weisse with him. This first contact between the Unity and Luther was therefore personal rather than official.[18]‡

Luther already knew of the Unity, though his friend Paul Speratus had sent him some documents that implied the Unity

---

* We shall meet these again, not as Lutherans, but as Zwinglians.
† Roh means "horn," and his name is sometimes given as that in German or English. In Latin he called himself Cornu, *i.e.*, "horn."
‡ As usual in history, complications arise over use of words like "first." When Roh and Weisse arrived in Wittenberg they found a deacon of the Unity, Beneš Bavoryňský, but he was a student there and not a quasi-official "spokesman" for the Unity.

held a symbolic rather than a "real presence" view of holy communion. Roh was able to explain the Unity's true position on this and other matters, and the visit ended cordially.[19]

Roh reported the results of his visit to the Unity's Inner Council, and more official contacts with Luther followed including five separate personal visits by Unity representatives as well as a frequent exchange of written documents in the early 1520s.[20] Luther differed with the Unity's view on some details of the holy communion and on its retention of seven sacraments and celibacy for its clergy. The Unity's practice of rebaptism was also an issue, as was its great emphasis on works in salvation. Still, historian Říčan observes: "His former mistrust of the heretical Brethren disappeared under the influence of a closer acquaintance with them."[21] He wrote to the Brethren, calling them "my dear sirs and friends," and Luke answered Luther's reservations in detail. Luther took these disagreements with surprising good grace, and Luke was generally firm but not antagonistic. Říčan says of Luke:

> His response and critique was carried on with the calm self-assurance of the old teacher who was able to deliver superior teachings and church orders, which had been tested in adversity, to a young comrade who had only recently begun to make his way out of the Roman Babylon to a better knowledge of the truth.[22]

After 1524 contact with Luther was discontinued for the rest of Luke's life. This may have been partly for personal reasons on the part of Luke, but in addition to differences of theological interpretation, the Brethren were concerned with "the free way of living at Wittenberg."[23] The Unity's messengers had reported that the morals in Lutheran Wittenberg were far too liberal for the Unity's taste. Moreover, Luther supported the nobles' suppression of rebels in the German Peasants' War in 1525, and that did not increase his appeal to the Unity.[24]

Luke's attention was not absorbed with Luther alone. In 1525 the three former monks, Michael Weisse, John Zeising (Čížek), and John the Monk, who had entered the Unity in 1518, abandoned their earlier fascination with Luther and began teaching the ideas of Ulrich Zwingli (1484-1531), the

Swiss reformer of Zürich. Zwingli went beyond Luther in abolishing the ways of the medieval church. Luther said the body and blood of Christ were present in the sacrament "in, with, and under" the bread and wine. Zwingli declared the holy communion was simply a symbolic meal with no "real presence" of Christ in the elements. If Luke had problems with details of Luther's positions, which spoke of Christ's presence in a more physical way than the Unity did, he had real trouble with Zwingli's. Luke was even more upset when Čížek prepared a treatise advocating Zwinglian ideas on communion and circulated it within the Unity hoping to win it over. Luke reiterated the Unity's tried and true position derived from the Taborites that Christ was present in the sacrament "spiritually, powerfully, and truly," and Čížek was expelled from the Unity. For a time Čížek was with the Anabaptist camp, and in 1528 was burned at the stake (not by the Unity!). John the Monk disappeared, but Michael Weisse stayed with the Unity, though he still held Zwinglian tendencies.

In 1527 or 1528,[25] a nobleman named John Dubčanský in Moravia formed a Zwinglian "unity" called the Brethren of Habrovany or the Brethren of Líleč. He tried to get the Unity to join him, but Luke would have none of that. Although some German members of the Unity in southern Moravia were swayed by Dubčanský, the Unity as a whole remained aloof.[26]

Around this time also the Amosites had a sort of revival under John Kalenec, who had succeeded Amos as leader of the party. Kalenec bitterly reproached Luke for having abandoned the original principles of the Unity and claimed that only the Amosites were the real Unity. Luke replied that while the Unity had indeed changed some of its views, this was according to the will of God. Luke reproached Kalenec also for his lack of Christian love in the way he expressed his opinions.[27]

By now the Unity also disagreed with the Anabaptists, who rejected infant baptism and insisted only on "believers' baptism."* People who joined them, even if they had been

---

* "Ana-" means "again," so Anabaptist is "one who baptizes again."

baptized as infants, had to be baptized as adults. The Unity had taken some of these into membership when they fled persecution.[28] After dealing with them and their demands for the rebaptism of practically everyone including infants baptized in the Unity, Luke came to agree that Luther's rejection of rebaptism was well founded. "In a letter to a friend he said, that he no longer considered it essential and that it would be well to abolish this practice in course of time."[29] The Unity did indeed give up rebaptizing converts shortly after this.[30]

It is sad that in his last years Luke of Prague was mired in disputes with other groups, but these quarrels do have a value today. They caused historical and doctrinal works to be produced that provide much information about the early years and beliefs of the Unity. One example is Luke's answer to a charge of the Amosites that the Unity's ministry was tainted by Roman origins. He retorted that the Unity's ministry does not depend on either Roman or Waldensian sources, but that God and the congregation had empowered Michael Bradacius to *confirm* their first ministers.[31]

Here and elsewhere Luke built upon and refined the theological heritage of the Unity. He did not invent the distinction of essential and ministrative things in theology, but he expressed it in a systematic way for the age in which he lived. At times his writing style matched the most convoluted medieval writers, and he sometimes let the system get in the way, as when he tried to force all his points into series of threes whether they fit or not.* Still, whether it was in theological treatises, pastoral letters, catechisms, or in the many hymn texts he wrote throughout his life,† he devoted all his efforts to the service of the Unity and the Lord. Luke traveled perhaps more than any other leader of the Unity before Comenius. Through his reading he traveled intellectually

---

* More than a century later another Unity bishop, John Amos Comenius, also habitually expressed himself in trinitarian series.

† He was a much better hymn writer than elegant prose theologian. His hymns are not flowery, but express their message in simple clarity, which is an elegance of its own.

On his deathbed, Luke of Prague made provision in his will for printer George Štyrsa, who published many works for the Unity including Luke's O Původu církve svaté (On the origin of the holy church).

further still. Yet his far-ranging experience (physical, mental, and spiritual) always led him home to the Unity, bringing what good he could find from abroad and cherishing and enriching the good he knew at home. The faith that he and members of the Unity shared was tested by years of persecution and internal examination. We should bear these facts in mind when we stand amazed that he valued but still dared to disagree with such a giant as Martin Luther on theology and discipline.

During this time of doctrinal discussion with the newly emerging Protestants, other events concerned the Unity. Bishop Ambrose of Skuteč died in 1520 while on a trip to Mladá Boleslav and was buried there. Though his death left the Unity with only two bishops, Luke and Martin Škoda, more were not elected during Luke's lifetime, though during the respite from persecution there was at least one synod (1521) at which such an election could have taken place.[32] This almost certainly means that Bishop Luke was not in favor of electing more bishops to share authority with them.

The Turks under Suleiman the Magnificent (1494-1566) made fresh conquests in the Balkans and advances into Hungary. Ludvík, the youthful king of Bohemia and Hungary, moved to oppose him, but in 1526 at Moháč in southern Hungary the small and unprepared Hungarian army was slaughtered. King Ludvík himself fell from his horse while fleeing in a marshy area and was drowned. Most of Hungary was lost to the Turkish Ottoman Empire for the next 150 years.

With the death of Ludvík, once again Bohemia needed a new king. Given the threat to the east, political considerations meant that he should be someone who could provide powerful alliances with other western countries. Ferdinand of Hapsburg (b. 1503) was the logical candidate. He was the younger brother of Charles V, the reigning Holy Roman emperor whose personal empire included Spain and the Netherlands. In addition, in 1515 Charles's predecessor, Holy Roman Emperor Maximilian, and Bohemia's King Vladislav had arranged for Ferdinand to marry Ludvík's sister Anna. Upon Ludvík's death,

Ferdinand tried to claim the Bohemian throne, which was an elective office, by right of succession, but the national assembly refused to accept him until he agreed to honor the *Compacta* of Basel, among other conditions. The assembly then proceeded to elect him king in October 1526.[33] Having gained control of Bohemia and Moravia, the Hapsburgs did not let go of the Czech lands for the next 400 years.

Ferdinand was brought up in Spain and was a very devout Catholic who was inclined to oppose the Unity and the Utraquists and Lutherans as well. In addition, he held a high opinion of royal power, and like his brother Charles V, he took every opportunity to extend it.[34] Bringing Bohemia solidly back into the orbit of the Holy Roman Empire was one goal.[35] Moreover, he was personally very astute and was excellent at playing opponents off against one another.[36] Since Ferdinand needed all the help he could get in holding off the Turks and could not afford to offend the Czechs at the start of his reign, he did not immediately move to extend royal and Catholic power, though he did begin to quietly bring in royal officials from outside who shared his ideas. Trouble would come later, but for now peace within the kingdom prevailed.

In the relative peace of the late 1520s, Luke's last official act was appropriate: he ordained six deacons as priests. In the past, ordinations in the Unity had to be done secretly, but this was performed in a public service. Říčan speculates this was either "a significant demonstration of the confidence of the Brethren's senior [Luke] in the unhampered development of its work, or rather an intentional display of intrepidity for facing new trials."[37]

Historian Říčan continues:

> He [Luke] took leave of the Inner Council through a letter in which, after recalling his work for the Unity, he bequeathed to its elders his writings that they should treat them well as the property of the Unity and amend them according to need. He advised that again four seniors [bishops] be elected and bequeathed to [these] custodians in the Lord the diligent care of the flock to the end. He willed his money to care

for the poor and exiled and to reimburse the printer
Štyrsa, who had suffered loss in the service of the
Brethren.[38]

Luke died in Carmel, the Unity's center in Mladá Boleslav
at 3 in the morning on 11 December 1528 with only his faithful disciple, Br. Martin Michalec, by his side. The nature of his
last illness is not recorded, but it may have been the "stone"
from which he suffered throughout his life. He was buried at
Carmel, where he had labored so long and faithfully.[39]*

It is difficult to overestimate the importance of Luke of
Prague to the Unity. He played a major role in its development
from the 1490s, and gave it steady guidance for more than a
quarter century through troubled political and theological
times. His writings gave expression to its doctrine and self-
understanding, and his talents as a hymn writer continued the
enrichment of its worship which he had introduced. Indeed,
Luke was working on a new edition of the hymnal at the time
of his death.[40] Amedeo Molnár calls him simply "the theologian
of the Unity,"[41] and F. M. Bartoš says that in his theological
work Luke was the "second founder of the Unity."[42]

Perhaps the best statement concerning him was by John
Blahoslav in the Unity's *Memorial Book*: "There has never been
such a man in the Unity. May the Lord God give us and to his
flock many such faithful and diligent, learned and unyielding
men."[43] Despite this prayer, and despite the worth, courage,
and dedication of those who came after Br. Luke, the Unity has
not yet seen his like again.

---

* Local Mladá Boleslav legend (as told to me by Br. Jindřich Halama,
Sr., on a visit there in 1978) has it that Luke was buried on the
grounds in an unmarked grave. Thus enemies would never be able
to find and desecrate it.

Notes

1 Rudolf Říčan, *The History of the Unity of Brethren*, trans. C. Daniel Crews (Bethlehem, Pa.: Department of Publications and Communications, Moravian Church, Northern Province, 1992), 160.

2 Říčan, 106.

3 See Joseph Th. Müller, *Geschichte der Böhmischen Brüder* 3 vols. (Herrnhut: Missionsbuchhandlung, 1922, 1931), 1:395, n. 285, for his explanation of his dating this trip then.

4 Říčan, 106-7.

5 Amadeo Molnár, "The Brethren's Theology," in Říčan, 417.

6 Perhaps the best known biography of Luther is Roland Bainton's *Here I Stand: A Life of Martin Luther*, rev. ed. (Nashville: Abingdon Press, 1978). Another is Heiko Oberman, *Luther: Man Between God and the Devil*, trans. Eileen Walliser-Schwarzbart (New Haven: Yale University Press, 1989).

7 Craig Atwood, *Always Reforming: A History of Christianity since 1300* (Macon, Ga.: Mercer University Press, 2001), 85-86.

8 Müller, 1:396-97.

9 Müller, 1:397.

10 Müller, 1:400.

11 Říčan, 109, 117. Müller, 1:419-20.

12 Müller, 1:422.

13 Říčan, 109. See also 110-11 for a discussion of the basic differences in the core of the Hussite and Lutheran reformations.

14 Říčan, 57. See Josef Smolík, "Martin Luther and Luke of Prague," *Communio Viatorum* 27 (1984) and F. M. Bartoš, "L'Unité des Frères Tschèques," *Communio Viatorum* 21 (1978). The latter was actually written in 1956.

15 Říčan, 111.

16 Edmund de Schweinitz, *History of the Church Known as the Unitas Fratrum*, 2nd (reprint) ed. (Bethlehem, Pa.: Moravian Publication Concern, 1901), 233.

17 Lissa Folio 5 (film 349-50), Slaby translation, notebook 11, 185-95, in Moravian Archives, Bethlehem, Pa. The letter is undated, but whether it applies to Weisse's and his friends' Lutheran or Zwinglian phase, it still warns against "wrong ideas which the Unity never held."

18 Müller, 1:400-401. Říčan, 111-12.

19 A helpful source for Luther's thoughts on the church, sacraments, etc., remains Hugh T. Kerr, ed., *A Compend of Luther's Theology*, 2nd ed. (Philadelphia: Westminster Press, 1966).

20 See Müller, 1:402-17, for all the details.

[21] Říčan, 113.

[22] Říčan, 114.

[23] De Schweinitz, 236. Říčan, 116, supports this.

[24] Říčan, 116.

[25] Říčan, 119, says 1528. Müller, 1:449, says 1527.

[26] Müller, 1:442-45. Říčan, 118-19.

[27] Říčan, 116-17.

[28] Říčan, 120. For more details see Lissa Folio 5 (film 334), Andrew Slaby translation, notebook 11, 36-50.

[29] De Schweinitz, 239.

[30] For a detailed account see Jarold Zeman, *The Anabaptists and the Czech Moravian Brethren in Moravia, 1526-1628* (The Hague: Mouton, 1969), 207-10.

[31] Müller, 1:437-39.

[32] Müller, 1:391 and n. 279.

[33] Hugh LeCaine Agnew, *The Czechs and the Lands of the Bohemian Crown* (Stanford: Hoover Institution Press of Stanford University, 2004), 59.

[34] Müller, 1:433.

[35] S. Harrison Thompson, *Czechoslovakia in European History*, 2nd. ed. (Princeton: Princeton University Press, 1953), 39-40.

[36] Kenneth J. Dillon, *King and Estates in the Bohemian Lands, 1526-1564* (Brussels: Les Éditions de la Librairie Encyclopédique, 1976), 111.

[37] Říčan, 120.

[38] Říčan, 120-21.

[39] Müller, 1:453.

[40] Říčan, 160.

[41] Molnár, *Bratr Lukáš: Bohoslovec Jednoty*, the title of his 1948 book.

[42] Bartoš, "L'Unité des Frères Tschèques," *Communio Viatorum* 21 (1978): 31. See also Peter Brock, *The Political and Social Doctrines of the Unity of Czech Brethren in the Fifteenth and Early Sixteenth Centuries* (The Hague: Mouton and Co., 1957), 206.

[43] Říčan, 121. A "Letter Read to the Boleslav Synod after the Death of Br. Luke," looks for grim times ahead and laments a decline in moral standards among young and old. See Lissa Folio 5 (film 330), Slaby translation, notebook 11, 3.

Chapter 11

New Directions

Leadership, Politics, Confessions of Faith,
1529-1540

With the death of Br. Luke in 1528, Martin Škoda remained as the only bishop of the Unity, and was the natural choice to take over as president of the Inner Council and judge. He had lived and worked in Přerov in Moravia for the past several years, and the headquarters of the Unity now moved there. Škoda was an "admirer of plainness," who wanted to maintain things in the Unity as they had been in the time of Luke. He was not, however, a strong leader, and new ideas were stirring that he could not keep out of his beloved Unity.[1]

A synod in 1529 decided to return to the custom of having four bishops in the Unity. Luke himself had suggested that but only for after he was gone. The choice for the three additional bishops fell upon John Roh, Wenceslas Bílý, and Andrew (Ondřej) Ciklovský. Br. Roh received the highest number of votes, which everyone assumed entitled him to second place among the bishops after Br. Škoda, until Br. Škoda arbitrarily announced: "Br. Bílý." The shocked synod dutifully went along with the senior bishop's decree. This did not please Br. Lawrence Krasonický, who, although he was now one of the older ministers,* was open to fresh ideas. It was obvious to all

---

* He entered the Unity about the same time as Luke of Prague and may have been a bit older.

that Br. Škoda had picked conservative Br. Bílý over Br. Roh because Br. Roh advocated new directions in the Unity.[2]

Br. Roh, who was born c. 1487 and was a linen weaver,[*] was fond of scholarship, although he did not have an academic

degree. He had read widely, including new works that were being produced by the Reformation in Germany. Other members, though, feared that if too many new ideas were introduced, particularly if ministerial students started going to foreign universities instead of being apprenticed and working in the "Brethren's houses" as before, the Unity would lose its cherished simplicity. This was similar

John Roh (Horn)

to the "educated Brethren" controversy of the 1490s when more ascetic opinions had clashed with a broader world view. This time, though, the division was not so sharp.[3]

Tradition-loving Bishop Škoda could not halt the new direction for long, and his closest allies were soon taken from him. Bishop Ciklovský died only a few weeks after his election (1529), and a couple of years later, Bishop Bílý was deprived of his office by the Inner Council for an unspecified "moral offense." He is the only bishop in the history of the Unity to be thus removed from office. He later repented and was eventually allowed to function as a priest but never again as a bishop.[4] So only Škoda and Roh remained as bishops, and Roh was the "progressive." Signaling his increasing influence, he was assigned to take up residence in Bishop Luke's headquarters in Mladá Boleslav.[5] There he had direct supervision of one

---

[*] At this time, remember, every Unity priest was expected to have a trade and earn his support, as ministerial duties allowed.

of the Unity's main schools plus the printing press, which gave him influence over the Unity's rising generation and publications.[6]

In the face of this, Bishop Škoda remained in office but gave up trying to hold back change. In 1530 the Unity began sending some of its ministerial students to the Lutheran university at Wittenberg.[*] It was acknowledged that in these changed times the Unity's ministers would need higher education and should know more Latin to be able to converse with theologians and produce theological works aimed at people outside the Unity. The first experiments were not overly successful, for the freer lifestyle in Wittenberg appealed to some of the students. One of them, Wenceslas Mitmánek, wrote home ridiculing the Unity's "stuffiness" and criticizing its discipline.[7] Despite that, the Unity continued sending students to Wittenberg, though perhaps more carefully selecting and cautioning them before they went.

Another event of 1530 also heralded new times ahead. Twelve powerful nobles were baptized and received into the Unity in a festal celebration in Mladá Boleslav. The membership had contained a few nobles before, but they were mostly of the knightly class of lesser nobility. Greater nobles had been friends of the Unity, but had rarely joined, and when they did, it was done quietly. These 12 great nobles came in with fanfare. Inspired by the example of the nobility in Lutheran Germany, they saw themselves as advocates for the Unity and its representatives in political life. They did not go so far as their German fellows who founded the Schmalkald League in 1531 to fight for Lutheran security and expansion, but their openly joining the Unity worried Catholic and Utraquist authorities nonetheless. It harked back to the Hussite League of the previous century, with all the horror that evoked in their minds. Within the Unity, the elders had to figure how not to

---

[*] Recall that the Unity's first messengers to Luther had found Beneš Bavoryňský studying at Wittenberg. He was already ordained but was not an "official ministerial student."

offend these nobles, who were their protectors and now fellow members, but keep them in check enough to avoid the church's being controlled by political figures.[8]

A very significant synod met in 1531, which changed the orientation of the Unity. It was decreed that as they sought to minister and find answers for the present, priests were not to be bound by the thoughts and writings of their predecessors. While former statements "did not have to be blamed or rejected, neither were they to be extolled to the harm of truth."[9] While it was not explicitly stated, it was obvious that this referred to the statements of Luke of Prague.

Thus the Unity now turned away from Luke's expressions as it had turned away from the writings of Br. Gregory when Luke and his "majority party" gained ascendancy in the 1490s. The synod quietly set aside Luke's *Instructions for Priests* (*Zprávy kněžké*), and a new catechism and ritual were authorized. Beneš Bavoryňský, the first Unity Wittenberg student, was a major author of such new productions. The synod also decided it was no longer necessary to celebrate many of the saints' days as had been done before, but that the major festivals of Christ's life and doctrines would be sufficient.* It is significant that the new catechism was titled *Catechism* (like the Lutherans') while the Unity's catechisms to this point had always been called *Questions* (*Otázky*). In such subtle and not so subtle ways, the Unity evidenced the influence of the larger Reformation going on around it. Finally, as it looked to the future, the synod of 1531 ordained 10 new priests and five new deacons.[10]†

Publication of the Unity's first German language hymnal

---

* The Unity had retained these minor festivals not because it liked saints' days, but to avoid further offending Catholic and Utraquist neighbors. Now that whole nations of Protestants were jettisoning such rituals, the Unity apparently felt it could do so without undue danger to itself.

† It did not, however, elect new bishops, though Bishop Ciklovský had died in 1529. It appears that Bishop Bílý did not fall from grace until after the synod of 1531, and that the synod considered three bishops enough for the present. That changed at the next synod.

Michael Weisse's hymnal, Ein New Gesengbuchlen, *was published in 1531.*

also took place in 1531. German-speaking congregations had long desired a hymnal of their own, and this was provided them through the work of Michael Weisse. It was entitled *Ein new Gesengbuchlen* (*A New Little Songbook*) and contained 157 hymns. Only 16 were translations of Czech Unity hymns. The rest were from German Lutheran, Waldensian, and even Anabaptist sources, with several written by Weisse himself.[11] Some of these hymns were picked up and used by various groups in Germany, which gained recognition for the Unity, but also created a problem. Unnoticed by the Unity's elders, Weisse had introduced into some of the hymns his own Zwinglian inclinations, particularly in regard to the Lord's Supper. For example, in places he spoke of the bread and wine as signs or "testaments" of the body and blood of Christ, rather than as the sacramental presence. It took the elders several years to correct that, but first they had to deal with more pressing issues.

Another synod met in April 1532 in Brandýs nad Orlicí to fill vacancies in the church administration. The Inner Council had experienced several deaths, among them Br. Krasonický, who died in January 1532. With the death of Bishop Ciklovský and the removal of Bílý, only two bishops, Škoda and Roh, remained. Younger priests took a dominant role in the synod with John Augusta, who had been ordained only the year before, as their main spokesman. They reproached the past and current administrations for "weakness" and inability to provide guidance to meet current needs. The clergy who wanted changes nominated themselves and others who agreed with them for seats on an enlarged Inner Council. They were elected. They were Martin Michalec, Mach Sionský, John Tejnský, and Michael Weisse, and Augusta himself.[12]

Synod then proceeded to elect bishops. Bishop Škoda resigned the presidency of the Inner Council "because of his age"* and went into retirement, which meant that three addi-

---

* And perhaps because of his dissatisfaction with all the changes. He died later that year.

tional bishops would be needed to join Br. Roh and bring the number up to the requisite four. Chosen were Beneš Bavoryňský, Vít Michalec, and John Augusta. Speaking of Augusta's rapid elevation, someone, presumably of the older generation, supposedly griped: "A year ago ordained a priest; a few hours ago elected to the Inner Council; and now a bishop of the Unity!"[13] Bishop Roh was elected president of the Inner Council, and the Unity headquarters moved back to Mladá Boleslav from its sojourn in Moravia to accommodate Br. Škoda.

Of these new members of the Inner Council, we have met Michael Weisse as a German exile. He was originally Lutheran and was a companion of John Roh on his visits to Luther. Weisse soon developed Zwinglian sentiments. Martin Michalec (b. 1484) was a tailor by profession and a student of Luke of Prague. He had worked mostly in Moravia and became known for his shepherding of apprentices and deacons. Mach Sionský was born c. 1501 near Mladá Boleslav, and took his name from a cloister called Zion (Sion) near his birthplace. He was a draper or cloth maker by profession. Little is known of Br. Tejnský.

Of the newly elected bishops, Vít Michalec was a brother of Martin, who had been elected with Augusta to the Inner Council. Vít received his bachelor of arts from the University of Prague, and lived as a hermit for a time before entering the Unity. He was ordained a priest c. 1526.

Beneš Bavoryňský was one of the few Unity priests of knightly origin. We first met him in 1522 when he was already ordained and studying in Wittenberg, where he attended lectures by Luther and Melancthon. He later worked with Br. Roh in Mladá Boleslav, and was one of the main writers authorized by the synod of 1531 to prepare new worship and doctrinal texts. His writing style was called "eloquent and clear, but plain."[14]

Of these new leaders, John Augusta has been called "the most outstanding of them all."[15] He was born around 1500 in Prague to a pious Utraquist family and attended communion every Sunday. His father was a hat maker, and John followed him in his trade. He was not highly educated and indeed had little use for "ivory tower" academics. He had, however, read the works of Matthias of Janov and Hus (in Czech versions). Like Gregory and Luke before him, he had been influenced by earnest Utraquist preachers (and in his case some who were influenced by Lutheran ideas) to look for a more vibrant faith than was common in the Utraquist Church. For a time he associated with the "Weeping Nicolaitans,"* a Czech spiritualistic cult that required eccentric acts of penance and was so proud of its illiteracy that many of its priests did not know how to read. That did not satisfy Augusta either, and he was finally advised by some Prague preachers to "go to the Brethren at Boleslav." There Bishop Luke took in the 24-year-old Augusta, educated him for the priesthood, and taught him Latin. One account described him as having "an uncommonly energetic character, which did not tolerate opposition and did not give up in failure."[16]

Several observations need to be made before we proceed with our story. Events are often presented as if the Unity administration after Luke kept things exactly as they were, and that in 1532 Augusta and other "young radicals" barely out of puberty seized power and turned everything around. Though maintaining the *status quo* was certainly what Bishop Škoda and some others would have preferred, we have seen that Bishop Roh (who was in his 40s) favored change from the beginning, and that the synod of 1531 had already "turned away" from Luke and inaugurated revisions in worship, doctrine, and instructional materials. Augusta and his cohorts only thought that change needed to happen faster. In addition, though some of the "young radicals" were recently ordained,

---

* These were not related to the Nicolaitans mentioned in Revelation 2. The name "Nicolaitan" was also used by some later medieval sects, especially those that advocated a married clergy (*Oxford Dictionary of the Christian Church*, 973-94), The relation, if any, of these "Weeping Nicolaitans" to those medieval groups is not certain.

they were hardly juveniles either. Augusta himself was 32 or so, Sionský was 31,* and Martin Michalec was almost 50.

Further, members of the Augusta group are sometimes presented as scholars opposing older, less educated leaders. Luke, however, had more education than most of them. The new leaders *were* in favor of giving new clergy more education and acquaintance with classical and Reformation texts. Augusta also wanted closer relations with other churches, and throughout his life he hoped that the Unity, the Utraquists, and others might benefit from Reformation ideas and work together more closely.[17] However, he did not simply intend for members of the Unity to become Lutherans. Historian Říčan aptly observes:

> To them, Luther was a clear teacher to whose voice the Unity was obliged to pay heed and from whom they were to receive instruction. . . . Yet even in this time of intense inclination to Lutheranism, one cannot speak flatly of the Unity's Lutheranization. Even now it continued to declare its own essential existence in the mainline of dogma, especially in its concept of the church and in its stress on the obedience of faith, which must imprint a character on the whole Christian life, in private and in association with others as well.[18]

We shall see shortly that the Unity did make further revisions in its concept of the sacraments under Luther's influence, but of great importance also was its willingness to adopt an even more positive view of participation in the world and in civic functions. This in part continued the broader view of life in the world begun by Luke and the "majority party" at the close of the 15th century. Now, after the example of the Lutheran nobility, the Unity came to see participation in civic life not as a "dangerous necessity," but as a contribution to the common good. This applied not only to Unity members who were commoners, but as we have seen, to the nobles

---

* In an age when kings ruled in their teens, and many died young, that was almost "middle-aged." We also recall that the first bishop of the Unity, Matthias, was 28 when chosen.

who joined the Unity as well, and it is possible that Bishop Bavoryňský's noble origin facilitated this continued development. As an example, the Unity brought out a handbook for those who might be called up to fight the Turks, acknowledging one's duty to defend the people against invasion. This would have been unthinkable in the earliest Unity and was different in spirit even from admonitions in Luke's time to "stay in the rear" if you are forced to serve. And of all things, the booklet closes with the Hussite battle hymn.[19]

Furthermore, the Unity in these first years of the 1530s became more willing to emerge from seclusion and give a more public account of itself with the intention of influencing current events and attitudes. Sometimes the Unity's theological statements and the increased political activity of its noble members went hand in hand.

George, the margrave of Brandenburg in Germany, who was married to a sister of the former king of Bohemia, Vladislav II, had heard of the Unity. Having an interest in religious matters, he asked Lord Krajíř of Krajek for details on its history, belief, and practice. Krajíř relayed his request to the Inner Council, which in 1532 prepared for him a work called *Počet z učení* (*Account of teaching*).[20] The text was in Czech, the language the Inner Council used, which did little good for a German nobleman. So the council had it translated for him. Quite naturally it turned to its own council member and best German linguist, Michael Weisse, and in due time he produced *Rechenschaft des Glaubens* (*Account of Faith*). But upon examining the translation, the other council members found it inaccurate. Worse, they found that Weisse, as he had done with his 1531 hymnal, had inserted Zwinglian notions into the document. All that could be fixed, but to their horror the council learned that Weisse had already shown his work to some German Swiss friends, who liked what they saw and sent a copy to Zürich, the Zwinglian center. The Inner Council immediately dispatched a messenger to Zürich to retrieve the offending document, but when he reached Nürnberg he found copies of the *Rechenschaft* in print and on sale.

Several Unity synods were held at Rychnov and nearby Lhotka.
This scene shows the castle and part of the town of Rychnov.

All that could be done now was to have another translation made.* This version too did not completely reflect the Czech original, but it was closer than the first, and it was much more in line with Lutheran positions. The council sent this version to Martin Luther, thus reopening conversations that had been suspended since 1524. Luther had a few reservations about precise wording concerning the holy communion, but after discussions with Unity representatives, he pronounced himself satisfied and wrote a preface for a printed edition. This second translation of the *Rechenschaft*, together with Luther's preface, was printed in Wittenberg in 1533. At the end of the volume it specifically said that Michael Weisse's Zürich version was erroneous.

This Wittenberg edition of the *Rechenschaft* was finally delivered to Margrave George of Brandenburg, who had asked for it in the first place.

This confession gives an explanation of the Unity's history, beliefs, and practices, though it does not stress the distinctions between the essentials and ministratives as do other works by the Unity. However, it was not written for members of the Unity, but was to explain to a German nobleman the Unity's beliefs in a way he was accustomed to and could understand. In addition, it shows obvious Lutheran influence in counting only the two sacraments, baptism and holy communion, but it still lays great stress on works as the necessary fruits of faith. The Unity now had in print an account of its faith with the endorsement of the great German reformer. Moreover, after several years' interruption, personal contact of the Inner Council with Luther himself had been restored.

The Unity was not through with confusion over this confession, however. Wolfgang Musculus, a theologian with Calvinist leanings living in Augsburg, asked which version truly presented the Unity's views. Musculus admitted he favored the Zürich version, but he was assured that the Wittenberg

---

* Whether by Weisse or someone else is not known. If the former, it was assuredly with someone closely looking over his shoulder.

edition was the correct one. The entire *Rechenschaft* affair points out a drawback for the Unity. Having two versions in print* could lead some to think the Unity was two-faced, saying one thing to Zwinglians and something different to Lutherans. Since few could read the original Czech version (*Počet z učení*) to see for themselves, the Inner Council promised Musculus to publish a Latin version for whose accuracy they could vouch. That was done, but it took some years, and several events intervened.

Within the Unity itself, accommodation with other Protestant churches continued. The old seven sacraments were now generally reduced to two (though the others remained as "rites of the church"), and rebaptism of converts was officially given up in 1534.[21] On a less important level, wafers replaced plain bread for communion since this is what the Lutherans did and there was no point in being different just to be different.† Private confession to a priest was also retained but was not mandatory before every communion. On the other hand, the Unity maintained many of its own usages: pouring or sprinkling options for baptism, the parents' and sponsors' joining the priest in imposing hands in blessing infants at baptism, and singing a hymn verse in homes before and after meals "as has always been done in the Unity."[22]‡

Cordial relations with Martin Luther were now restored, and his theology and friendship were proving helpful to the Unity in several areas. The Inner Council was still worried that Wittenberg's liberal lifestyle was harming Unity students. Apparently Wenceslas Mitmánek was not the only one to come home with superior ideas and fancy clothes. At the beginning

---

* Müller in his history of the Unity distinguished between the German versions by calling one *Rechenschaft Z* (for Zürich) and the other *Rechenschaft W* (for Wittenberg). That system seems as good as any.

† Müller, 2:13, says that the decree for this asserts that they were going back to the older custom of the early Unity, which used wafers. However, one of the first things the followers of Gregory did was to substitute plain bread for Catholic and Utraquist wafers.

‡ Is this the first recorded instance of, "We've always done it that way"?

of 1535, then, John Augusta and George Izrael went to Wittenberg on behalf of the Inner Council to consult with Luther further and to see for themselves what was going on in town. Bishop Bavoryňský, whom Luther knew from his student days there, supplied the Unity visitors with letters of introduction, and the two had many conversations with Luther and with Philip Melancthon as well. On his part, Luther confessed that the Saxon churches could use a bit more discipline, but Augusta and Izrael learned that Wittenberg's morals were not as lax as had been reported. All in all, it was a good visit.[23]

Politics and religion sometimes go hand in hand. In fact, royal and imperial politics played a crucial role in causing the Unity to issue yet another confession of faith.

Bohemia's King Ferdinand, as noted above, favored absolute monarchy and ridding his realm of "heretics," but had to be careful at the beginning of his reign. Now that he had time to establish himself and the Turks were quiescent for the moment, it was time to implement his religious goals.

For Ferdinand the Unity was an irritating threat and its members "heretics" worse than the Utraquists. They thought for themselves, and that is not good for absolute monarchy. But for the moment the Unity was unassailable; it had gained powerful allies among the Czech nobility. So Ferdinand turned his attention to the Anabaptists. Inspired by Thomas Münzer (d. 1525) and others, the Anabaptists rejected infant baptism. Jacob Hutter (d. 1536), another leader who settled in Moravia, called for common ownership of property. Thus they had no noble protectors, and even the "heretics" considered them heretics. These Anabaptists, then, were a safe group for Ferdinand to begin on. As early as 1528 he made tentative moves against them, but in 1534 he launched a full-scale persecution. It was fortunate for the Unity that it just that year officially stopped rebaptizing converts, so it could not be confused with the Anabaptists as it had been in the popular mind with the Waldensians and Picards. The Unity was passed over in this persecution, but it revealed what Ferdinand would do to all dissenters when he got the chance.[24]

Ferdinand had a minor dispute in 1530 with the Unity's Lord Krajíř of Krajek over the nobleman letting the Unity use a vacant church on his domain.[25] That was a prelude.

It was 1535 when the king took his first overt step to suppress the Unity. A priest, John Pousteník, was having a very successful ministry in Domažlice, Klatovy, and Vodňany, and membership in those congregations was on the rise. When local Utraquists complained, the king banned the Unity from those towns. The Brethren asked one of their nobles to intercede. He did so, but in vain. Ferdinand then ordered the lords of Janovice (sons of mendacious Lord Suda, who had imprisoned Luke) to arrest Pousteník and turn him over. These lords of Janovice were firm friends of the Unity. As a means of making up for their father's misdeeds toward the Brethren, they offered themselves to the king instead. They ended up in prison.[26]

Once again the Inner Council called for fasting and prayer throughout the Unity. Its noble members took more concrete steps, since they saw the king's actions as an attack on the entire Czech nobility. Recalling that the German Lutheran nobles had banded together to present Emperor Charles V a confession of faith in their defense in Augsburg in 1530, the Unity's nobles in Bohemia decided to take a similar step with King Ferdinand.

The *Počet/Rechenschaft* confession was only a couple of years old, and a Latin version of it was in the works, but it was not suitable for this purpose since it contained a lengthy historical account and described services, etc., in addition to doctrine. Perhaps the confusion over this confession also inclined the Unity elders to make a fresh start. So Bishops Roh and Augusta, with assistance from young Isaiah Cepola (Izaiáš Cibulka) and possibly from Wenceslas Mitmánek,[27] were assigned to draw up a new confession containing the chief articles of the Unity's belief.

This finished document, the Confession of 1535,* draws upon the *Počet/Rechenschaft*, which was produced by the same authors only a couple of years before. Influence from the Augsburg Confession is felt, though the Unity's confession does not follow the Lutheran document verbally or in arrangement of topics. In 20 articles it sets forth basic Christian belief as taught in the Unity. Preaching the Gospel of salvation in Christ is presented as the "most important" teaching, and "Christ the Lord and faith in him" is regarded as the "sum of all Christianity and piety." Characteristically, the next article speaks of good works, "which God commands" as the fruits of faith.28

The Confession of 1535 was written as a statement by a group of Bohemia's nobles,† members of the Unity, attesting to Emperor Charles V and King Ferdinand I what their clergy regularly taught (though the nobles themselves, of course, did not write it). Twelve lords and 33 knights signed the confession, which was taken to King Ferdinand, residing in Vienna. As the leading noble member of the Unity, Kunrát Krajíř of Krajek requested and received a private audience with the king two days before the confession's formal presentation to prepare Ferdinand to receive it. His response was not encouraging. Nonetheless, on 14 November 1535 two lords‡ presented the confession in handwritten Czech to the king.29§ Ferdinand took it and said he needed a week to study it before giving a reply. He gave it to Catholic Bishop Faber of Vienna for

---

* My translation of the 1538 Latin printing of the Confession of 1535 is on the Internet as an e-book at www.MoravianArchives.org.

† Unity nobles of Moravia did not present it, since conditions there were more favorable than in Bohemia.

‡ These lords had not signed the confession, but their presenting it was formal assent to it.

§ One would think that in such a public forum the confession would have been presented in the formal language of theology and diplomacy, Latin. However, Müller says it was in Czech, though he also says on another matter that Ferdinand "understood no Czech" (2:279). Zdeněk V. David in his *Finding the Middle Way*, 465, note 153, agrees that the original was in Czech.

evaluation, who turned the typical Roman thumbs down. Since it was not politic at this moment to offend so many lords and knights of his realm, Ferdinand employed a delaying tactic. At week's end he said he had not had time to read all the confession, but they could discuss it the next time he was in Prague (which would be a long time off).

In its original intent, to win the king's approval or at least toleration, the Confession of 1535 was a failure. In political terms so was the Lutherans' Augsburg Confession. But for the rest of the Ancient Unity's existence the Confession of 1535 stood as its touchstone statement of faith. Title pages of all later editions still said it was presented before the king in 1535. Over the years a few minor revisions were introduced as the Unity moved more from Lutheran to Reformed thinking. Still, the Unity in 1535 produced a remarkable document that for centuries to come summarized its faith for members and non-members alike.[30]

The confession did not end Ferdinand's efforts to suppress the Unity. Soon after its presentation the lords of Janovice, who had offered themselves for punishment in place of the Unity's priest John Pousteník, were released from prison, but the Unity's congregation in Janovice was closed, and Unity members in Brandýs and Domažlice had to submit to Utraquist authority for a while. More was in store.

In these years, Bishop Bavorynský died in 1535, and Bishop Vít Michalec in 1536. Martin Michalec, Vít's brother, and Mach Sionský were elected to replace them in 1537. This was only a change in administrative personnel, though, not in direction for the Unity.

Contrary to the hopes of John Augusta and the Brethren, the Confession of 1535 failed to solidify new cooperation with the Utraquists, even after two printed Czech editions in 1536 entitled *Počet z viry a z učení.*[31]* The failure of the Unity's nobles to get anywhere with King Ferdinand pointed up the

---

* Not to be confused with the 1532 confession *Počet z učení* from which the German *Rechenschaft* translations were made.

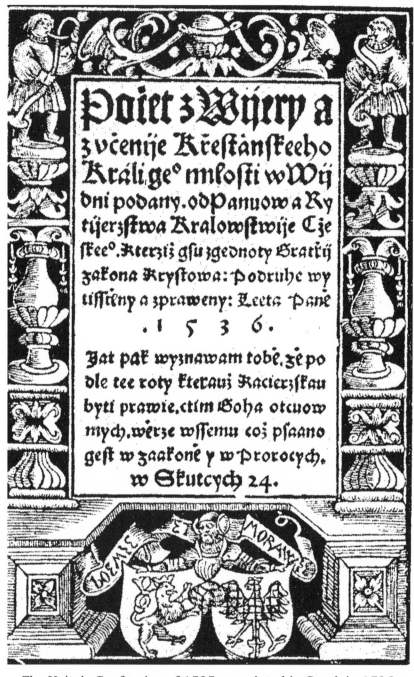

The Unity's Confession of 1535, as printed in Czech in 1536.

Unity's need for more foreign support. The Inner Council therefore turned to Wittenberg and asked Martin Luther to publish
its confession and provide a preface for it as he had done earlier
for the corrected *Rechenschaft*.[32] Luther still had questions
about the articles on "the time of grace" (*i.e.*, deathbed confessions) and celibacy, but with some conversations and a few
tweaks to the Latin text, those were worked out.

By now the Latin translation of the 1532 confession (*Počet z
učení/Rechenschaft W*), which was promised years earlier to
Musculus of Augsburg, was also ready. The Unity asked Luther
to publish this too. Luther agreed, and there matters sat.
Finally it was discovered that a lack of funds was the problem,
and when Unity lords Krajek and Kostka advanced the money,
matters rapidly proceeded.

And so in 1538, under the Latin title of *Confessio Fidei ac
Religionis*, the Confession of 1535 was published in Wittenberg
with Luther's preface. Bound with it was the Latin version of
the 1532 confession now entitled *Apologia verae doctrinae* (later
called simply the *Apologia*).[33]

Back in Bohemia the publication caused no little stir.
Utraquists were shocked, and wrote to Luther asking if he
really had written the favorable preface, or had the Unity made
it up? The papal nuncio reported to Rome that religious
matters in Bohemia had gotten worse now that the "dangerous
and loathsome sect of the Picards" had gotten the Lutherans in
Wittenberg to print their confession.[34]

Between Martin Luther and the Unity, however, relations
remained cordial, and John Augusta paid him more visits in
1540 and 1542. Luther now counted the Brethren as allies,
and told them: "You be the apostles among the Czechs, and we
among the Germans." His last letter to Augusta, when Luther
felt his own days were approaching their close, "contained an
admonition that the Brethren continue with their German
fellow believers in the fellowship of the Spirit and pure doctrine
and in the struggle against the gates of hell through word and
prayer."[35]

The abundance of Unity confessions in the early 1500s is confusing enough to need a scorecard to sort them out:

Apologia sacrae scripturae was drawn up by Luke of Prague after the 1508 Mandate of St. James and was published in 1511 in Nürnberg. A copy was sent to the humanist Erasmus in 1519. It is not directly related to later confessions, but is noted here because of possible confusion with the 1538-published *Apologia*.

Počet z učení (*Account of teaching*) was written in 1532 in response to a request of Margrave George of Brandenburg. The original was in the Czech language, which was of little use to German George. So it underwent several translations:

> *Rechenschaft des Glaubens* (*Account of Faith*) was the first German translation of *Počet z učení*, done by Michael Weisse with Zwinglian leanings. It was published without authorization in Zürich in 1532. For convenience, historian Müller labels it *Rechenschaft des Glaubens Z*.

> *Rechenschaft des Glaubens* was the second, corrected German translation of *Počet z učení*, this time with Lutheran leanings. It was officially published with a preface by Martin Luther in Wittenberg in 1533. Historian Müller labels this one *Rechenschaft des Glaubens W*.

> *Apologia verae doctrinae* was a Latin translation of *Počet z učení*. It was published by the Lutherans in Wittenberg in 1538 in the same volume with the Latin version of the Confession of 1535.

The Confession of 1535 first appeared as a handwritten Czech presentation to Bohemia's King Ferdinand. Historian Říčan (144) says a Latin and a German translation of the confession were made, but whether they were published is not known.

> *Počet z viry a z učení* is the title of two Czech editions of the Confession of 1535 that were printed in 1536.

> *Confessio Fidei ac Religionis* is the Latin version of the Confession of 1535. It was published in one volume in Wittenberg in 1538 with a preface by Martin Luther and the *Apologia verae doctrinae* (simply called *Apologia* or *Apology* for short).

Notes

1 Rudolf Říčan, *The History of the Unity of Brethren*, trans. C. Daniel Crews (Bethlehem, Pa.: Department of Publications and Communications, Moravian Church, Northern Province, 1992), 122.

2 Joseph Th. Müller, *Geschichte der Böhmischen Brüder* 3 vols. (Herrnhut: Missionsbuchhandlung, 1922, 1931), 2:1, 2.

3 Müller, 2:2-3, 5.

4 Říčan, 122.

5 Říčan, 123.

6 Müller, 2:4.

7 Říčan, 136. Müller, 2:54-55.

8 Říčan, 129-132.

9 Říčan, 123.

10 Říčan, 123. Müller, 2:4-6, 17.

11 Müller, 2:29-30.

12 Říčan, 123. Müller, 2:6-7.

13 Müller, 2:7.

14 Říčan, 124.

15 Říčan, 125-27, and Müller, 2:9-12, give basic details.

16 Říčan, 127. Müller, 2:12, says this quote is from the Unity's *Memorial Book*.

17 Müller, 2:11-12, 91-92.

18 Říčan, 124.

19 Říčan, 128-29.

20 For details of this confession and its various versions, see Říčan, 135, and Müller, 2:40-48.

21 Říčan, 137-139.

22 Müller, 2:12-13.

23 Říčan, 139. Müller, 2:54-57.

24 Říčan, 134-35. Müller, 2:52.

25 Müller, 2:60-61. Krajek backed down, but it appears that a minister of the Unity had preached there only temporarily anyway, and the paintings and statues had been stored away ready to be placed back.

26 Říčan, 141-42.

27 Müller, 2:68.

28 *The Confession of 1535*, trans. C. Daniel Crews, 2nd ed. e-book (www.MoravianArchives.org), 21, 11, 14. Both Říčan, 142-43, and Müller, 2:68-70, provide an analysis of the Confession of 1535. Jaroslav Pelikan in his *Credo: Historical and Theological Guide to Creeds and Confessions of Faith in the Christian Tradition* (New Haven: Yale University Press, 2003) makes a number of references

to it, though he lists this Unity confession as the "First Bohemian Confession."

[29] Müller, 2:71, citing the preface of the Latin edition of 1573 as authority. However, Edmund de Schweinitz, *History of the Church Known as the Unitas Fratrum*, 2nd (reprint) ed. (Bethlehem, Pa.: Moravian Publication Concern, 1901), 651-52, says Ferdinand received a Latin translation.

[30] Müller, 2:74-75, 111. Říčan, 144.

[31] Müller, 2:88-91. Říčan, 144.

[32] More information may be found in several articles by Jaroslav Pelikan: "Luther's Negotiations with the Hussites," *Concordia Theological Monthly* 20 (1949): 496-517; "Luther's Endorsement of the *Confessio Bohemica*," same journal and volume, 829-43; and "The Impact of Martin Luther upon Bohemia," *Central European History* 1 (1968): 17-130.

[33] Říčan, 148. These confessions are printed in their Latin or German texts in *Bekenntnisse der Böhmischen Brüder*, ed. Erich Beyreuter, Gerhard Meyer, and Amedeo Molnár in the series *Nikolaus Ludwig von Zinzendorf: Materialien und Dokumente* (Hildesheim and New York: Georg Olms, 1979), series 1, vol. 3. This also includes a lengthy preface by Alfred Eckert on Luther, the Unity, and the confessions. Aside from the e-book at www.MoravianArchives.org, the Confession of 1535 is available in English in Jaroslav Pelikan and Valerie Hotchkiss, eds. *Creeds and Confessions of Faith in the Christian Tradition* (New Haven: Yale University Press, 2003), 1:796-833. (Pelikan again refers to it as the "First Bohemian Confession," which can lead to confusion with the Bohemian Confession of 1575).

[34] Müller, 2:111-12.

[35] Říčan, 149.

Chapter 12

Controversies

With Utraquists, War, Prison, 1540-1548

s the 1540s opened, the Unity was thriving. Relations with Martin Luther were back on track, and friendly and promising contacts were initiated with Martin Bucer (1491-1551) and the Strasbourg reformers. Bucer held much in common with the Unity over the sacraments, order and discipline, and putting faith into practice, and like the Unity, he tended to the midpoint between extreme views. The only serious difference was Bucer's willingness to use secular power to enforce religious reform. Even here, while he did not change his mind, he traded opinions in a cordial way.[1]

The Unity learned of Bucer through his writings, and in 1540 it sent him one of its rising stars, Matthias Červenka, with a copy of its confession and other writings and a letter. Bucer received Červenka warmly, invited him into his own home, and had long discussions with him. The Unity's discipline made a particular impression on him, as did its emphasis on practical Christian living over against speculative theology.[2]

Also visiting Bucer at the time was John Calvin, whose influence on the Unity was considerable in later years. His *Institutes* had not yet made its way to Bohemia, but his other writings had, and Bishop John Augusta "liked him." For his part, Calvin had heard of the Unity as "Picards" and was surprised to learn that they were not immigrants from Picardy in France but native-born Czechs. He too praised the Unity's discipline but was concerned over its clerical celibacy.[3] Where contact with Bucer might have led is an interesting speculation, but he was soon called to Cologne to lead the reformation there, and the Unity lost touch with him.[4]* The accidental meeting with Calvin proved more important, as we shall see later.

Within the Unity, material progress was made with construction of a fine "sbor"† in Brandýs nad Labem. It was designed in the "modern" renaissance style by an Italian architect named Matteo Bogorelli. It was soon outshone by another Bogorelli edifice in Mladá Boleslav.[5] Evidently noble patrons saw such expensive projects as a means of employing their financial resources for the Unity.

A new Czech hymnal was published in 1541 (see page 207). Bishop Roh did a thorough revision of the 1519 hymnal, finishing a task that Bishop Luke did not live to complete.‡ This book, entitled *Písně chval božských* (*Songs for the praise of God*), was a large folio containing 638 pages. It had 482 hymns and 300 melodies. Almost one-fourth of its hymns were by Luke, and others were by Augusta, Martin Michalec, and Adam Šturm from among the Brethren in addition to earlier sources. Though the Unity ran printing presses, such specialized work was sometimes farmed out to outside "experts." In this case, the non-Brethren printer apparently thought the book would have a market outside the Unity, and he avoided noting on the title page that it was a "Picard" work. He even got the Utraquist

---

* Bucer eventually wended his way to England to continue reformation work there. He died in 1551. During the reign of Catholic Queen Mary, his body was exhumed and burned as a heretic.

† As with "bishops" and "pastors," which the Unity preferred to call "Seniors" and "Spiritual Administrators," it preferred not to call its worship buildings "churches" because of the bad connotations such "Roman" terms had for them. "Sbor" in this usage means "place of coming together," not unlike the German "Saal."

‡ Though the hymnal Bishop Luke was working on at the time of his death was put on hold because of the new influences coming into the Unity, "new hymns were composed and printed sporadically" (Říčan, 160).

The Unity's sbor (church) at Brandýs nad Labem, designed by Italian architect Matteo Bogorelli.

consistory to endorse it.[6] In 1544 Bishop Roh got around to revising the 1531 German hymnal in which Michael Weisse introduced Zwinglian notions. Roh's new work, entitled *Ein Gesangbuch der Brüder in Behemen und Merherrn* (*A Songbook of the Brethren in Bohemia and Moravia*), corrected Weisse's excesses.[7]*

The early 1540s also saw controversy for the Unity with outside groups. Remnants of the "Amosites" or "minority party" under John Kalenec reviled the Unity for its "betrayal" of its original ideals, though by now the Amosites themselves appear to have developed anti-Trinitarian views. This seems to have been the death rattle of the Amosites, who faded into history after Kalenec's death in the mid 1540s.[8]

Far more serious were increasing controversies between the Unity and the Utraquists. Bishop Augusta's idealistic attempts to achieve closer relations were on hold, and from 1540 differences were more acrimonious. The Utraquist administrator, Martin Klatovský, blamed the Brethren and their propaganda for this. Indeed, Zdeněk David, a modern scholar of Utraquism, says that Klatovský displayed "gentleness and civility" in the face of "vitriolic attacks" by Augusta,[9] and Říčan agrees that the Utraquist administrator wrote with "moderation."[10] True as that may be, the Utraquists' denunciations of the Unity and their cooperation with and at times instigation of royal attempts to suppress the Brethren means they were not the innocent party either.[11]

The harsher tone of these exchanges in the early 1540s might be explained by the fact that the Unity was now actively recruiting members from among the Utraquists. Members had been gained that way before, and the Utraquists were not happy about it. Now, however, Unity propaganda was not

---

* Unlike the 1505 and 1519 hymnals, the 1541 hymnal survives to await more detailed study, as do the 1531 and 1544 German hymnals. A facsimile of the 1531 Weisse hymnal and a copy of the 1544 hymnal are in the Moravian Archives in Bethlehem, Pennsylvania, and the Moravian Music Foundation in Winston-Salem, North Carolina.

only trumpeting its endorsement by Martin Luther, but also asserting that the Utraquist attempt to forge a national church with recognition from Rome was a mistake from the beginning and a failure in any case. The Unity was urging people to turn their backs on the "moribund" Utraquists and join the Unity.[12]

On their part, the Utraquists claimed that the Unity's priesthood was invalid and therefore so were its sacraments.* In fact, it was not a real church at all. In answer to this, the Unity in 1540 scheduled the public ordination of 12 priests in Mladá Boleslav, at which Bishop Augusta preached a fiery sermon defending the rightness of the Unity's separation from the Romans and Utraquists, and asserting the validity of its priesthood, for which "there was no necessity for external apostolic succession."[13]†

Augusta's sermon caused such a public hubbub that King Ferdinand heard of it and rebuked Lord Krajek, who owned Mladá Boleslav, for allowing it to happen on his estate. Krajek offered an explanation, but was told in no uncertain terms: "Don't do it again!"[14]

Bishop Augusta further fanned the flames when a 1541 work by Martin Luther entitled *Wider Hans Worst* came into his hands. He translated sections of it into Czech in such a way that Luther's criticisms of the Roman priesthood could be applied to the Utraquists as well. Augusta entitled it *Zrcadlo kněžké (The Priest's Mirror)*. This wasn't so bad, except the book contained an engraving showing a Utraquist priest looking into a mirror with the reflection of a wolf staring back. The accompanying caption urged Czech farmers to drive the wolf away from Christ's flock with a flail.[15] The Unity was now mired in the strident polemics that marred the larger Reformation.

---

* Oddly enough, Klatovský himself admitted that in case of necessity priests could be ordained by another priest (not a bishop), but that this should not be done because of the confusion it would cause. See Müller, 2:158.

† It is interesting that in this sermon Augusta made no mention of either Roman or Waldensian sources for the Unity's ministry.

With this, the king had enough and ordered the arrest of Augusta, who wisely made another quick visit to Luther's Wittenberg and so avoided the warrant.

Hopes rose for reconciliation between the two churches when Lord Kunrát Krajíř of Krajek, the leading noble member of the Unity, and John of Pernštejn, the most prominent Utraquist lord, met in 1542 to arrange a peace. But Lord Kunrát died soon into the negotiations, and his son Arnošt, also a faithful member of the Unity, had a personal falling out with Lord Pernštejn. So the nobility's effort to mediate in the religious dispute collapsed.[16]

By now the Utraquists had a familiar fellow succeeding Martin Klatovský as administrator of its consistory, Wenceslas Mitmánek.[17] Mitmánek began as a ministerial student of the Unity, which paid for his training in Wittenberg, where he liked the "freer life" and denounced the Brethren as "dismal" and "proud intolerant sectarians."[18] Switching to the Utraquists, he was ordained a priest,[19] finished his doctorate, and became pastor of the prestigious Týn Church in Prague. With the zeal of a fresh convert he attacked the Unity, and as administrator he tried to turn the recruitment tables by introducing Lutheran ideas into the Utraquist Church, such as emphasizing justification by faith and soft-pedaling intercession of the saints. He also tried to get a bishop consecrated for the Utraquists and to absorb the Unity and others into a truly national Czech church. The Unity remained unimpressed.[20]

Unfortunately for Mitmánek, he failed to take into account the mood of his own church. The Utraquist synod of 1543 was decidedly conservative over any Lutheran changes. It also reiterated that any bishop must have papal authorization plus the king's permission before being elected. Mitmánek blamed King Ferdinand and angrily told him he should stick to running the secular government and keep out of church affairs. Whereupon Ferdinand banished Mitmánek, who spent the rest of his life in exile in Poland. We shall meet up with him again, this time with the Lutherans.[21]

Showing inordinate delight, Unity historian John Černý* in his history gloated over the fall of Wenceslas Mitmánek. The Unity itself continued down the road of provocation by holding public ordinations, conducting a great funeral for the wife of the Lord of Litomyšl, and letting Augusta carry on in public.[22]

Thoroughly exasperated, King Ferdinand banished the Unity from several royal cities in 1543. This might have been the start of a general suppression of the Brethren, except yet another threatened invasion by the Turks distracted him. Then in 1544 a disastrous fire destroyed much of Prague including the records of the national assembly. During reconstruction of the documents, the infamous 1508 Mandate of St. James was included. Advocates of the Unity had for years tried to have the decree, which made the Unity illegal, omitted from the code of law, though some in the Unity said it didn't matter since the mandate outlawed "Picards" and they weren't Picards. They were whistling in the dark.[23]

In its efforts to attract members, the Unity claimed spiritual and moral superiority over the Roman and Utraquist Churches. It was the Unity's drawing card, but in these times of relative prosperity, though, the Unity itself had seen a relaxation of zeal and dedication. Several congregations were constructing fine new church buildings, but the same attention was not given to the spiritual edifice. Worse, many held the attitude of "Who can reform the world?"[24] Bishops Roh and Augusta lamented this and concluded that the "moral laxity," which Bishop Luke and others had feared would result from the Lutheran ideas of "by grace alone," had indeed come to pass. Roh and Augusta believed that turning away from the writings of Luke in their enthusiasm for new expressions was a mistake, and from 1544 Augusta began to quote Luke in his sermons.[25] The two bishops convinced the Inner Council in

---

* This is not the same John Černý who was the physician brother of Luke of Prague. "Černý" in Czech means "black," so the younger Černý sometimes used the Latin forms "Nigranus" for himself and "Niger" for his namesake of a former generation. See Říčan, 165.

1546 to turn back to Luke as a theological standard, even resurrecting Luke's *Directions for priests*, and the council admitted it had been dazzled by the eloquent (meaning Lutheran) theological writings coming in from afar.

This was not a change in doctrine. No thought was given to revising the Confession of 1535.[26] Rather, the Unity was returning to its traditional emphasis on living the faith, and it found that it had within itself sound means without having to turn to polished outside experts.

Thus the Unity was finding renewed strength within its own spiritual resources just as the Schmalkald War in Germany gave Bohemia's King Ferdinand the incentive and leverage he needed to come down upon the Unity in the harshest way. The Schmalkald League was formed in 1531 by German Lutheran princes for their mutual defense. Emperor Charles V had always wanted to crush the league, but because of the Turkish threat, war with France, business in Spain, etc., he could do little about it. Now in 1546, the year of Luther's death, he felt he had an opportunity to move against the Protestants, and he took it.[27]

Charles began his campaign by bringing charges against two leading German Lutheran nobles on "violations of order" within the empire. Everyone knew the real motivation was religious, though, and Germany's Schmalkald League rose in the nobles' defense. In Bohemia the Unity's nobles and many Utraquists saw that a Protestant victory could help their own position. King Ferdinand could see the same thing, and was determined to assist his brother Charles in every way possible. He called up Bohemian troops for defense of the realm against the Turks "or any other," meaning, of course, the German Protestants. Many lords obeyed the summons whatever their personal feelings, but others did not. The Unity's lords of the Boleslav region failed to appear, and the Utraquists' Lord Pernštejn dragged his heels. Others attended the muster but only to protest this "infringement" of their noble rights and then leave.[28]

The Czech hymnal of 1541, compiled by John Roh (Horn).
(See page 200.)

Ferdinand nevertheless set off for Germany and was a major architect of the great imperial-Catholic victory at Mühlberg in April 1547. The Protestants were utterly defeated; the Schmalkald "War" was over.[29] Returning to Bohemia flush with victory, Ferdinand determined to punish those who had joined in the "rebellion." They included several noble Unity members, who while they had not fought on the Protestant side, had not given the King the support he demanded. Besides, their sentiments were well known. By now Ferdinand had all the power he needed to do as he wished and gain absolute rule, which had been his goal all along. He appointed his son the archduke, also named Ferdinand, to oversee the retribution.[30]

The nobles in Moravia had not been directly involved in any of this, and so they were not affected by the king's revenge, but in Bohemia the estates of several lords were seized. Among these were the Brethren's Lord Arnošt Krajíř of Krajek, who lost Brandýs nad Labem entirely and was allowed to keep Mladá Boleslav only as a fief directly under the king. Lord Bohuš Kostka (the younger) lost the substantial estate of Litomyšl and was barely permitted to retain the smaller domain of Brandýs nad Orlicí.

The Unity was staring disaster in the face, for many of its noble protectors were disgraced and dispossessed, and the estates that had sheltered several of its main centers were now "under the direct over lordship of a hostile king."[31] With hindsight, Unity historians view the fire that burned the church and most of the town of Litomyšl in 1546 as a portent of greater disasters to come and as "the beginning of the suffering."[32]*

As the Schmalkald War was breaking out in early 1547 the Unity lost two of its four bishops to death. Martin Michalec died in January, and John Roh, who had been ill for a year and a half, followed him in February. The remaining two bishops,

---

* Most of the Unity archives were in Mladá Boleslav and so escaped the fire, but the originals of the letters from Luther were in Litomyšl and were lost (Müller, 2:192-93).

John Augusta and Mach Sionský, met with the Inner Council. Augusta was named president, but because of the unsettled war conditions, it was decided not to call a synod to elect more bishops.[33] That decision had dire consequences.

The Unity soon had more problems than the loss of leaders and restriction of noble protectors, for the two Ferdinands, king and son, now charged the bishops and elders of the Unity as the ones who instigated the nobles to rebel in the first place. They asserted that Augusta's visits to Germany were not to discuss theology but to join with the Lutherans in plotting rebellion. Historians Říčan and Müller indignantly deny this,[34] but there is no doubt where the Unity's sympathy lay. This was the downside of having powerful nobles as the Unity's spokesmen, and Bishop Augusta's aggressive public stand had its drawbacks too. Říčan admits: "Under his leadership the Unity no longer appeared only as a peaceful society cultivating religious life in the seclusion of its congregations."[35]

To carry out his wishes, King Ferdinand had the perfect tool: the Mandate of St. James. The 1508 decree had outlawed the Unity but was rarely enforced, though it had recently been retained in Bohemia's new code of law. Now Ferdinand determined to follow the onerous letter of the mandate. Only Catholics and Utraquists were to be tolerated, and to assure the latter's cooperation, the king promised them a bishop sanctioned by Rome as soon as the "Picards" were rooted out.* The Unity's priests petitioned for redress and asserted their loyalty, but that only brought a further order in January 1548 that their churches be nailed shut and house meetings prohibited. The severity of the measures depended on the will of the local nobles and did not apply in neighboring Moravia. Still, the nobles had lost considerable power. Even the Unity's friend Lord Kostka was afraid to risk the king's wrath; he closed the church in Brandýs nad Orlicí. Several Unity members were imprisoned, and priests went into hiding. Wives of imprisoned men, it is recorded, wrote their husbands saying

---

* He never made good on his promise.

not to worry about them and their children, but rather give a strong witness for the faith.[36]

In the Litomyšl area Bishop Augusta and his faithful assistant Jacob Bílek eluded arrest and quietly ministered to their people. Several attempts to capture them failed. Then a new sheriff, Sebastian Schöneich, arrived in town.[*] A "hard nosed" man, he was willing to lie, break oaths, do whatever it took to achieve his goals. His prime goal was to arrest John Augusta.[37]

Augusta had been finding it increasingly difficult already to get messages to his people, and his attempt to arrange a conference with the Utraquist administrator and the viceroy, Archduke Ferdinand, had been fruitless. Now Schöneich sent a message to Augusta offering him a private meeting at which he would tell him important news for the benefit of his flock. He also pledged not to arrest Augusta at the meeting, which was to be at a ruined castle near a small stream in the forest. The date was 25 April 1548.

Augusta agreed, but sent his assistant Bílek ahead to check it out. The sheriff's men jumped and seized Bílek as soon as he appeared. Hearing nothing for five hours, Augusta was worried but decided to go himself and see what had happened. His other companions tried to talk him out of such a foolhardy idea, but there was no changing Augusta once he had made up his mind. Neither would he let anyone else go with him. At least he took the precaution to disguise himself as a farmer and carry an axe over his shoulder.

As soon as Augusta came to the spot, armed men roughly seized him, but his disguise confused them, so they were about to let him go. Still not recognizing him, the men decided to hold him anyway to prevent the "farmer" from warning Augusta. The bishop later said that three men had guns, so he couldn't try to run away. Then they changed their minds again and were going to let him go. Before doing that, however, they searched

---

[*] Schöneich's exact title is not exactly clear. He is called sheriff and captain among others.

him and pulled a fine handkerchief from his breast. Humble farmers do not have fine handkerchiefs. The bishop was seized for good, and Schöneich was summoned to collect his prey. It was about 6 o'clock in the evening.

When Augusta bitterly reproached his captor for his treachery, Schöneich at first denied his pledge not to arrest him, then claimed it didn't matter, since all promises expire come nightfall.

The bishop was kept overnight in the castle at Litomyšl, then sent to Prague early in the morning. Augusta sang Unity hymns all along the way. They arrived in Prague about noon on 28 April 1548. Bílek was put in a cell under the Hradčany Castle, and Augusta confined in its infamous "White Tower."* Schöneich received his reward for capturing the long sought Augusta, a sum that historian Müller contemptuously calls his "Judaslohn," Judas pay or betrayer's money.

The jailers questioned Bílek first, trying to get him to admit that the Unity had fomented rebellion and sent assistance to the king's enemies in Germany. He denied it. Augusta was questioned for two hours on 3 May. Apparently he failed to realize how serious his plight was, for he still spoke of negotiating with the Utraquist administrator.

King Ferdinand, however, was resolved on wiping out the Unity. All he needed was a justification for public consumption, hopefully on political rather than religious grounds. A confession would be just the thing. Since simple interrogation had not worked, sterner measures were employed.

To let the bishop know what was in store for him, and presumably to encourage him to confess without further ado, on 10 May he was led in chains to a cell under the castle and forced to watch the torture of a man convicted of counterfeiting. When that did not move him, Augusta was left in chains for two days and then turned over to the executioner to be tortured.

---

* Used for political prisoners. Being sent there caused about the same chill of fear as being sent to the Tower of London.

He was first stretched out and burned with candles. Then hot pitch was applied to his body, set on fire, and ripped off with pincers, taking portions of skin with it. Later he was stretched on a rack suspended by a hook and weighed down with stones. This did not stop until he was half dead. Bílek received the same tortures.

While this was going on, Unity members heard rumors of terrible things being done to their bishop but did not know how much to believe. From the onset they tried to establish contact. One messenger sent to bring the prisoners food and clothes was himself seized and imprisoned for 10 days. Another who had a family connection in the castle tried to take Augusta's fur coat to him, but was caught and jailed. It took two years before smuggled messages started getting through.

When King Ferdinand was told torture was not working, he responded in effect: "Then use some real torture on him!" Fortunately for Augusta, before the king's orders were received,

The Křivoklát castle, where John Augusta and Jacob Bílek were imprisoned.

Augusta and Bílek had been sent to Křivoklát (Pürglitz), a former royal hunting lodge then used to house political prisoners. Nothing had been done to care for the terrible wounds caused by the burning pitch and pincers. Only two weeks later was medical attention called in, and then only because the sores were threatening to become seriously infected. The prisoners were not allowed to gain freedom through death. The wounds took seven weeks to heal.

The prisoners were confined separately in deep cells underground and not allowed to communicate with one another. Augusta's cell had only one small window high up the wall, and even that was boarded up except for a small chink approximately four by six inches (10 x 15 cm.). This hardly admitted enough light to see by, and may have been a torture in itself by showing just enough light to remind Augusta of the sunlit world that he might never see again. His bed was a couple of rough boards against the wall, with some scattered straw on the floor. Only at meals were the prisoners allowed additional light: a half candle, which was taken away as soon as the meal was done. They had nothing to do, for they were not allowed any books or writing materials, even if they could have seen to read or write in their dark cells. Twenty guards mounted constant watch in shifts day and night.

It was once thought that Augusta was kept in solitary confinement at least in the first months of his imprisonment. He would have been better off if that were true. Instead, for a while the counterfeiter whose torture he had been forced to watch was put in the cell with him. This man was described as "rough, rude, and crude." The account says that the poor bishop "had to put up with a lot from him."

In January 1549 Augusta tried to escape. He was caught and injured. The guards were ordered to keep close watch that he did not harm himself. Possibly it was feared that in his pain and despair he might try to commit suicide. Again, death was not allowed as a means of release. Later that year the prisoners were interrogated again. Again they refused to confess, and again they were tortured. In the case of Br. Bílek, the jailer's wife urged that the torture not be too severe since he was "nearly crazy." No wonder.

Bishop Augusta and Bílek continued to suffer, and we shall see that in the course of his long confinement Augusta came to be at odds with the Inner Council on how to keep the church going. Only after nearly 16 years of confinement did he emerge from prison, battered in body, strained in soul and mind, but still defiant.

Notes

1 Rudolf Říčan, *The History of the Unity of Brethren*, trans. C. Daniel Crews (Bethlehem, Pa.: Department of Publications and Communications, Moravian Church, Northern Province, 1992), 150.

2 Joseph Th. Müller, *Geschichte der Böhmischen Brüder* 3 vols. (Herrnhut: Missionsbuchhandlung, 1922, 1931), 2:116-19.

3 Říčan, 150. A convenient summary of Calvin's thought is in Hugh T. Kerr, ed., *A Compend of the Institutes of the Christian Religion by John Calvin*, 2nd ed. (Philadelphia: Westminster Press, 1964). This can also be used in conjunction with the *Compend of Luther's Theology* cited earlier to compare their positions.

4 Müller, 2:124.

5 Říčan, 179.

6 Říčan, 160. Müller, 2:25.

7 Müller, 2:31. Říčan, 161.

8 Müller, 2:100-102.

9 Zdeněk V. David, *Finding the Middle Way: The Utraquists' Liberal Challenge to Rome and Luther* (Washington, D.C.: Woodrow Wilson Center Press, 2003), 236. See also 63.

10 Říčan, 155.

11 See, *e.g.*, Müller, 2:126.

12 Müller, 2:125.

13 Říčan, 153. Müller, 2:161.

14 Müller, 2:130.

15 Říčan, 154.

16 Říčan, 155. Müller, 2:163-64.

17 Zdeněk David in his extensive study of Utraquism, *Finding the Middle Way*, makes surprisingly few references to Mitmánek, only two (11, 136).

18 Říčan, 156.

19 Říčan (156) says he was ordained in Italy, and Müller (2:166) says

he was ordained by a Greek bishop. Perhaps it was a Greek bishop residing in Italy.

[20] Müller, 2:166-68. Some have asserted that he and Augusta were both vying to become bishop of *the* Czech church.

[21] Říčan, 158, 185. Müller, 2:168-69.

[22] Říčan, 158-59. Müller, 2:178-79.

[23] Müller, 2:176-90.

[24] Říčan, 162.

[25] Müller, 2:194-96.

[26] Müller, 2:196. Říčan, 164.

[27] For a "neutral" account of the Schmalkald War (or Uprising), see Kenneth J. Dillon, *King and Estates in the Bohemian Lands, 1526-1564* (Brussels: Les Éditions de la Librairie Encyclopédique, 1976), 111-33.

[28] Říčan, 168, Müller, 2:200-202.

[29] Müller, 2:202.

[30] Říčan, 169.

[31] Říčan, 170. Müller, 2:205.

[32] Říčan, 159.

[33] Müller, 2:197-98.

[34] Říčan, 170. Müller, 2:205-6, 233.

[35] Říčan, 171.

[36] Müller, 2:207-22. Říčan, 171-72.

[37] Details of Augusta's arrest and torture are from Müller, 2:222-37, who used the first-hand accounts later set down by Augusta and Bílek themselves. Říčan, 172, simply says that Augusta and Bílek were lured out of hiding and "cunningly arrested," but says little more. Edmund de Schweinitz's account in *History of the Church Known as the Unitas Fratrum*, 2nd (reprint) ed. (Bethlehem, Pa.: Moravian Publication Concern, 1901), 270-78, sounds fanciful, but its details in almost every instance are confirmed by Müller.

Chapter 13

Exile

Prussia and the Beginnings
of the Unity in Poland, 1548-1560

Outside Augusta's prison walls the Unity as a whole was enduring hard times. King Ferdinand was not satisfied with measures taken so far for the suppression of the "Picards." Not only had he not captured all the Unity's leaders, but the nobles were not being enthusiastic enough in enforcing the Mandate of St. James, and few members had left the Unity. Some had been frightened or worn down into submission, but the Unity remained.[1]

Accordingly, at Pentecost in May 1548 King Ferdinand issued a further decree giving all members of the Unity in Bohemia six weeks to renounce their faith or emigrate from the country. Those who chose to leave were to sell their property; those who defied the edict and stayed would lose their goods and their lives as well.[2]

Since this decree did not affect Moravia, some took shelter there. Others pretended to submit, and some non-Brethren lords did not look too closely at solid and productive workers on their domains. The Inner Council tried to make things easier by saying that in case of necessity members of the Unity could allow their babies to be baptized by Utraquists. Other members tried what stratagems they could to evade the decree. For example, the Unity's printer in Litomyšl, Alexander Oujez-decký, agreed to join the Catholic Church. He thought he was safe since no Catholic priest was in the area. But rather than simply give him a certificate of conversion, the authorities insisted on seeing him adore the host and receive communion. Printer Oujezdecký quickly fled the country.[3] While there may be a grim humor in such occurrences, some congregations were lost; in others half the members gave in; and in others exile was the only option.

On estates confiscated by the king, including Litomyšl, Brandýs nad Labem, and Turnov, many resolved to emigrate, and some 800 set out in two groups in the summer of 1548. Some had to leave behind elderly relatives or children too frail to make the trip. Orphans under the care of the Unity were seized, and non-Brethren husbands refused to allow their wives to go. Although the decree expressly said that exiles could sell their property, some officials obstructed this, while others refused to pay anything like a fair price for houses, land, etc. Many left with only what they could carry.[4]

But where could they go? Fortunately for them, Duke Albrecht of Hohenzollern (reigned 1525-68) had a reputation for receiving religious exiles on his extensive domains in East Prussia. He had already given shelter to some Anabaptists and Schwenkfelders, and was still in need of solid settlers for these lands only recently received from the Teutonic Knights. In fact, Duke Albrecht had said something before about an asylum if the Unity needed one, and his chief Lutheran minister, Paul Speratus, had spoken for them.

The exiles accordingly set out to cross Poland for East Prussia even though all the details for their relocating had not been worked out. Difficulties followed them at first. The wagon drivers they hired heard of robbers waiting for them ahead and so set the people's goods off in the square in Rychnov. Providentially, other drivers from Prague had just made a delivery and were looking for cargo, so they agreed to take them on.[5]

The exiles were well received as they crossed Poland, particularly in the city of Poznań. Indeed, consideration was given to settling there, but Polish King Zikmund II Augustus refused permission. Zikmund himself had some sympathy for

Central Europe of the 16th and 17th centuries, showing Prussia and Poland with significant towns in Unitas Fratrum history.

the Reformation, but did not wish to offend Emperor Charles and King Ferdinand, especially since a treaty was in place among the three that they would not give asylum to refugees from the others' lands.[6] They headed on to Toruň, which was in royal, not East, Prussia.

The Unity provided impressive leadership for these exiles. With them went Mach Sionský, the Unity's only bishop still living and not in prison. The Inner Council wanted to get the bishop out of harm's way in Bohemia, where besides the general persecution, a printer had lodged a lawsuit against him. Sionský had placed an order for 400 hymnals, and the printer had made 400 more, planning to sell them himself. When the persecution started, the market for Unity hymnals dried up, and the printer claimed that Sionský owed him for all 800 books.[7]*

George Izrael, one of the Unity's most promising ministers, also joined the exiles. He was born in 1510 or a little earlier to a Unity family in Uherský Brod and had learned the blacksmith's trade from his father, who was reluctant to give permission for him to enter the ministry of the Unity. George persevered in his request and became an assistant to Bishop Augusta, whom he accompanied on trips to Wittenberg. Ordained in 1540, he already provided excellent pastoral leadership in Turnov.[8] He was imprisoned for a time but managed to escape,† and it was deemed prudent to get him out of Bohemia.

The exiles had to wait in Toruň until a formal agreement for their settlement could be reached. They had assumed that they could function under their own leaders, hold their own

---

* We do not know if this order was for reprints of the 1541 Czech or the 1544 German hymnal, though the former seems more likely. In any case, ordering this many books so soon after initial printing suggests that the number of Unity hymnals in circulation at this period was larger than was thought earlier.

† George Izrael was a very conscientious and scrupulous man, and Bishop Sionský had to reassure him that breaking the law by escaping from unjust imprisonment was not a sin.

services, and exercise their own discipline as a separate church, but East Prussia was officially Lutheran, and Lutherans expected uniformity. Allowing a separate church there was not that easy. In addition, the Prussians did not know who they were and circulated all sorts of stories about this "strange" Unity. Were they Anabaptists or revolutionaries? Moreover, bad penny Wenceslas Mitmánek, whom historian Müller calls the "apostate and bitter enemy of the Brethren," was claiming that their orthodoxy was suspect.9* Even Luther's endorsement of the Unity's Confession of 1535 was not enough.

Accordingly, in December 1548, the clergy of the Unity exiles were summoned to the East Prussian capital of Königsberg for a theological examination. During the grueling questioning, the Brethren were able to convince the Lutheran "church police" that they were not heretics.† The Unity leaders again asked to be allowed to have their own church, but were told they must conform to Lutheran norms if they wished to stay in East Prussia.10

So the Unity was to be given limited recognition, but conditions applied. They were to translate the Augsburg Confession into Czech, and use it rather than their own confession. Their clergy were recognized as valid ministers, but were to act only as assistants to the Lutheran ministers. As Unity ministers made their rounds, they were to be accompanied by a Lutheran to make sure everything they said conformed to the Augsburg Confession. Confession of sin could be made to a Lutheran or Unity minister, but if members of the Unity chose to confess to their own ministers, they still had to be examined by a Lutheran cleric to make sure they had a proper understanding

---

* We recall from the previous chapter that Mitmánek, a former member of the Unity who had become administrator of the Utraquist consistory, had been exiled by King Ferdinand to Poland after he told the king to keep his nose out of church business.

† This is where the Unity's Br. Hermon answered a question on the nature of the repentance required at baptism for a child not yet able to talk by saying that the Brethren had never even thought of such things. See Říčan, 186.

of the sacrament of communion. They were to attend Lutheran services, even though few of them understood German or much Polish for that matter. However, they were allowed to have a few prayer meetings of their own in the early morning hours and a Unity style communion service on Friday nights.[11]

How could Unity members submit to such indignity? Not only did the Lutheran Church leaders suspect them, but the local inhabitants did not want them there, and would not allow them into their guilds. On the other hand, where else could they go? Reluctantly the Unity agreed to these terms. Things did improve a little as the Lutherans got to know and appreciate the Unity better, but before long, most of the exiles decided if they were going to be hated and persecuted anyway, they might as well endure it at home in Bohemia. The Inner Council was informed of this by angry exiles.

A final straw was the division a few years later among the Prussian Lutherans themselves over opinions advanced by Andreas Osiander, a professor at Königsberg, over "the indwelling of the righteousness of Christ in a person." The Lutherans tried to drag the Unity into the argument, but the Brethren found the intricate nuances of the question confusing, and the acrimonious debate "scandalous."

At length, the Inner Council back in Moravia agreed that the Unity members could gradually leave East Prussia.[12] Most returned to Bohemia or went to Moravia over the next decade. Some ended up in Poland or Lithuania. By 1574 only a handful of Unity members remained in East Prussia.[13]

Though the East Prussia experiment failed, it did have one positive result. Personal contacts the Brethren made while traveling through Poland led to establishment of a Polish branch of the Unity. This development was a surprise to the Inner Council, but as Jakub Bílek wrote in his biography of Augusta, the Unity "came over to Poland as a vine from the vineyard and was planted there."[14]

The areas that concern us are the provinces of Great Poland, centered around Poznań, and Lesser Poland, centered around Cracow (Krakow). The names are misleading, since the royal capital, university, etc., were in Cracow in Lesser Poland. The political situation in Poland was similar to Bohemia and Moravia at the time, with nobles striving to maintain autonomy on their estates, the king trying to assert control but often failing, and cities advancing their own rights and identity.[15]

Since Poland was just over the mountains from the Czech lands the Poles knew of the Hussites, though they had no popular Hussite movement. Once in the 1470s a priest tried serving the chalice to the laity, but he was quickly arrested. News of the German Reformation spread into Great Poland soon after 1517, but by mid-century any movement toward a Polish Reformation was just beginning. Interest in it was at first confined to several nobles and citizens, mostly German, in Poznaň itself. In addition to religious motives, several of the nobles were ready to embrace the Reformation as a means to more power (and riches) for themselves at the expense of the Roman hierarchy. Some nobles began sending their sons to the Lutheran university at Wittenberg, though King Zikmund I had issued a decree forbidding his subjects to read the works of "a certain Augustinian monk," meaning, of course Martin Luther.[16] Even Duke Albrecht Hohenzollern, who had brought the Reformation to East Prussia and invited Unity exiles to settle there, failed to forward Reformation ideas in Poland until the first Lutheran congregations opened there in 1550.

Nevertheless, popular interest was beginning to awaken, as evidenced by the welcome Unity exiles received in Poznaň and Toruň on their way to East Prussia. In both these cities when Unity clergy conducted services local inhabitants attended. Personal friendships blossomed too. Once on one of his many journeys between Moravia and East Prussia, Bishop Sionský stopped in Poznaň in need of medical attention. The mayor himself, Andreas Lipczyński, put him up in his own house. Sionský held preaching and communion services for his new friends, and on his return trip a few weeks later found the group had increased. Among them was the powerful noble Lady Kateřina Ostroróg, whose influence later proved helpful to the Unity.[17]

Occasional visits by passing clergy were not enough for the Unity adherents in Poznań. They begged for a minister to be assigned to them on a regular basis. As yet the Unity could not station a minister there permanently, but in 1551 George Izrael was assigned to visit the city regularly while keeping his parishes in East Prussia — a 130-mile commute.

Izrael's service in Poland almost came to an abrupt close before it began. On his way at Easter for his first visit to Poznań, he found the bridge in Toruń closed by ice. Undaunted, he dismounted and ventured out on the river to see if it was frozen solidly enough to support him and his horse. The ice near the bank was thick enough, so he went farther. That too seemed stable, but as he neared midstream, there was a

George Izrael skips ice floes to safety.

sudden cracking, and solid ice splintered into many pieces. A crowd watching from the bank was horrified and expected to see the Unity minister drowned. To their amazement, Br. Izrael merely hopped from ice floe to ice floe back to the bank, singing Psalm 148, containing the words: "Praise the Lord from the earth, you sea monsters and all deeps, fire and hail, snow and frost, stormy wind fulfilling his command!" He then gathered the amazed people for a thanksgiving service, and after the ice cleared calmly went on his way. No wonder George Izrael became a legend among the people, and was called the "Apostle of Great Poland."[18]

In Poznań Izrael found "joyful and dangerous work."[19] The Catholic clergy and some Polish officials naturally opposed any Protestant incursions into their area, and a royal ban was technically in effect. Worship services had to be held secretly in private houses, the windows stuffed with pillows or other bedding to keep the sound of hymn singing from penetrating out into the street. Most services were held on market days, which came only three times a year but lasted for five days at a time when the city was overrun with boisterous crowds, and gatherings were less likely to be heard or otherwise noticed. Br. Izrael himself wore a variety of disguises, since Catholic authorities were on the lookout for him:[*] at times he was a city tradesman, a cart driver, a cook, or even a courtier.[20†]

Open proselytizing was impossible, but lay members talked with families and friends, and the congregation grew. In August 1551 Unity visitors on their way to East Prussia reported finding 30 full members and several probationary ones. Among these were several members of the nobility and prominent city dwellers. The Unity elders "began to see that there were far more opportunities in Poland than in Prussia."[21] The Poznań people's urgent request for a minister of their own began to receive more serious attention in the Inner Council. Thus in

---

[*] The Catholic bishop was reported to have hired 40 men to be on the watch for him.

[†] We can suspect Br. Izrael rather enjoyed that part of it.

1553 Br. Izrael was assigned to move to Poznań and relinquish his work in East Prussia.

In the three years since 1550 interest had been excited among the populace over Protestantism in general, and the Unity attracted a good number because it was already an organized church with contacts among the great reformers to the West. The fact that its ministers were willing to take personal risk to work among the Poles was also a point in its favor. Mayor Andreas Lipczyński joined the Unity, and Lady Kateřina Ostroróg brought in her noble lady friends Anna Kansinowska and her sister, Hedwig Sokolník.[22] Lady Kateřina did not limit her evangelistic activities to women. She soon convinced her brother-in-law to join the Unity, and together they were working on her brother Jakub.

Jakub's conversion makes an irresistible story. His wife, no doubt at Lady Kateřina's urging, invited Br. Izrael and others to hold a service in their house. Catholic friends who were visiting Jakub heard of this, and one said, "If I had a wife who brought heretics into the house, I'd set her straight with a good whipping!" Thus goaded, Jakub grabbed a whip and burst into the room where the service was being held. Br. Matthias Červenka was giving the sermon and continued as if nothing had happened. This struck Jakub dumb for a moment, but before he could recover his momentum, Br. Izrael looked at him, pointed at a vacant chair, and said in a voice of command: "Sir, you sit there." The bewildered nobleman took the seat and sat quietly for the rest of the service. By its end, he was ready to ask admission into the Unity. Whether entirely true, the tale does bear out the awe the Polish Unity had for Br. George Izrael.[23]

Not everyone was impressed. Two Reformed preachers from Lesser Poland, Felix Cruciger and Francesco Stancaro, did not like what they viewed as competition, and they tried to get Br. Izrael banned from Poznań.[24] We will soon meet them again in altered circumstances.

For the most part, however, matters were going well. The mighty Ostroróg family became protectors of the Unity in

Poland, just as the Kostkas, Krajeks, and Žerotíns were in Bohemia and Moravia. In the city of Poznaň itself, the Catholic bishop still posed a threat, but Br. Izrael was given a permanent residence on a nearby Ostroróg estate, and this became the "Mladá Boleslav of the Polish Unity."[25] Work was established also in Łobženica, Barcin, and Marszewo. By 1558, five years after the conversion of Jakub Ostroróg, the number of Unity congregations had grown to 15.[26] Other lords, such as those of Krotowski, Marszewski, Broniewski, and Lesczyński,* offered secure refuge on their estates, and many members moved from the big cities "onto the nobles' manors in rural towns and villages."[27]†

From the outset, the Unity in Poland had a different character than it did in the Czech lands. In Bohemia and Moravia the Unity began mostly among simple people, and only gradually attracted sizable numbers of the gentry and higher nobility. In Poland it was the opposite. Gentry and nobility joined first, and they then expected their subjects to follow suit. The Unity was accustomed to being a church of "personal choice," entered only after a period of soul searching and decision. Even members born into it underwent a period of personal examination and decision at confirmation. In Poland, however, nobles sometimes simply threw out the Catholic priest and replaced him with one of the Brethren's.[28]

Br. Izrael and the other Unity ministers tried to avoid becoming agents of the nobility's whims, and sought to hold on to their principle that one must not compel another in matters of conscience. George Izrael was pastor of the entire estate at Ostroróg, with a pastoral responsibility for each of its inhabitants. All those people might be considered as probationary members of the Unity. He tried, however, to instruct the people gradually before taking them to the next step of becoming

---

* This last was lord of Leszno (Lissa) where a German-speaking congregation arose that would have a critical role in Unity history.
† Gregory the Patriarch and Bishop Matthias, who distrusted cities, would have been proud!

"proficient members." In the church he first left the pictures of saints, etc., on the walls, only saying they were unnecessary for salvation. He later covered them with cloths, and only when he was sure the people truly understood did he have the pictures removed. Only those who understood and desired the Unity's teaching were to apply for full membership.29

That was the theory. But surely some simply wanted to be left alone as good Catholics, and others sought full membership to curry their lords' favor rather than for spiritual conviction.* In keeping as much as possible to the ways it had applied in its homeland, the Unity hoped to bring up an indigenous younger generation in Poland fully in accord with its precepts.30 However, historian Müller wryly observes that in Poland the Unity received a great influx of new members, but they were far less ready to stand firm in times of persecution.31

With all these new members speaking a new language, the Unity moved early on to provide devotional, worship, and instructional materials. The New Testament in Polish was a priority, but a Polish version of the Unity's Czech hymnal was a close second, since aside from worship, it was used with the catechism to instruct youth and converts. Memorizing hymns was an important part of the Unity's course of instruction. To translate their hymnal the Unity leaders in 1552 turned to a Polish Reformed (Calvinist) preacher, Valentin Brzozowski, presumably because their own Polish was not yet refined to rhyme. Remembering the Zwinglian sentiments Michael Weisse had slipped into their first German hymnal of 1531, the Unity had Brethren Izrael and Červenka carefully examine it before its publication in 1554. For the printing the Unity went first class. The job was undertaken by the Unity's former Litomyšl printer, Alexander Oujezdecký, who was now living in East Prussia's capital of Königsberg. The impressive finished product was folio size with 44 signatures, elegant borders, ornate capital letters and music notes, plus a title to match its grand

---

* Most likely even in Bohemia and Moravia Unity nobles occasionally pressured their subjects to join them in the Unity.

dimensions: *Cantional, or book of divine praise; that is, spiritual songs of the holy church according to the Gospel and the truths of Holy Scripture put into poetry. . . .*[32]*

And so although some members faced arrest for their faith, and noble protectors had to come to their aid, by the mid-1550s a sizable branch of the Unity was developing in Great Poland to the point that a Catholic clergyman lamented to his bishop, "The sect of the Waldensians grows stronger every day."[33]

Like Greater Poland, in the Cracow region of Lesser Poland opposition from the king and the University of Cracow had kept Protestant churches out, but fresh winds were blowing. The university's faculty had indeed been excited over Luther and gotten copies of his works, but when the pope condemned the writings, the faculty promptly burned them and decided the medieval church was good enough. Some nobles, though, were dissatisfied with the old-fashioned ways, and as in Greater Poland sent their sons abroad for education. On returning home, these young men formed small circles for discussion of humanistic and Reformation ideas. Their interest centered at first on Luther and Melancthon, but curiosity led them to include the writings of Calvin and Zwingli as well.[34]

As reports of reformation in Greater Poland began to filter in, many in Lesser Poland were looking for new ways and were open to new ideas. Francesco Stancaro, a professor of Hebrew at the University of Cracow, and Francesco Lismanin, the king's court preacher, were won over for the Reformation. Stancaro, we recall, had not welcomed the Brethren when he first met them in Poznań. His attitude changed as he came to see the advantages of cooperation with the Unity. Lismanin, a Greek from the island of Corfu, was first captivated by Luther,

---

* Neither Říčan nor Müller supplies the title in Polish. Note also that even at this time the Unity did not always go to outside printers for its fine hymnals. We do not know how many were printed, but when printer Oujezdecký was about to go back to Moravia a year later, he offered Duke Albrecht the remaining 200 copies for one Thaler each. Müller says he was not able to find a copy to inspect himself.

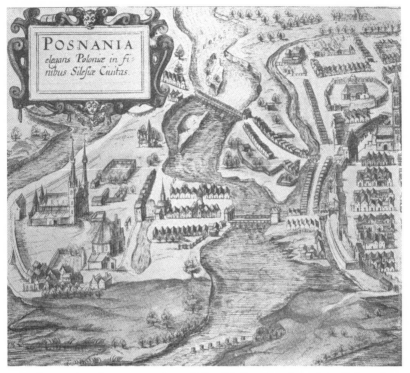

POSNANIA
*elegans Poloniæ in fi-
nibus Silesiæ Civitas.*

Poznań, where a center of the Unity developed in Poland.

but after he read Calvin's *Institutes* in 1552, he was won for
the Reformed side of the Reformation. He read Calvin's work to
Zikmund II Augustus (1548-1572), and the king was so
interested that for a time he teetered on the verge of declaring
Poland Protestant. At length the king remained Catholic and
kept the Reformation from having large success in Poland.[35]

As early as 1550 Stancaro held a first "Reformed synod" in
Lesser Poland, but this was attended by only a few clergy of
like mind. This group became more Zwinglian as time went
on, but remained the center of the growing Polish Reformed
movement. In 1553 Stancaro turned to the Unity's Inner Council in Moravia, seeking advice and assistance in organizing a
Reformed church in Lesser Poland. The council was not sure
who this Polish cleric was, and replied cautiously.

Felix Cruciger too sought assistance from the Unity in 1554 as "Superintendent of the Reformed Church in Lesser Poland." The title was grander than its reality, for the Reformed Church as yet had no congregations there. It did, however, propose a union with the Unity, since the latter already had confessions of faith, worship materials, a church administration, etc. Such a united front would strengthen the Protestant cause and give the movement a greater chance of success.[36]

For the Unity this was an opportunity, but also something of an embarrassment. On one hand, it favored churches working together. After all, a united front meant a stronger front. The Unity was also flattered that others valued its ways and wished to adopt them. On the other hand, the Unity suspected the personal character and theology of Stancaro and Cruciger, both of whom had originally opposed the Unity. Indeed, Br. George Izrael had confronted Cruciger, who claimed his opposition was based on misinformation. That did not quite convince Izrael, who also pointed out that simply setting up an administration and bureaucracy was not the same as having a church dedicated to the spiritual nurture and growth of its members. The Unity did not have the resources to care for a whole province of new members who might not value its approach in the first place.

Moreover, it was already apparent that the Protestants of Lesser Poland were moving in a Calvinist or Zwinglian direction. The Unity found much in Calvin that was worthy, but if a union church rejected Lutheran teaching, that would certainly damage Unity relations not only with Luther's Wittenberg but also with many in Great Poland. Experience in East Prussia also made Unity leaders cautious of unions that ended in others seeking to absorb the Unity without valuing its insights and traditions. Besides, how much secular force would be employed in creating and maintaining such a church?[37]

In spite of this, pressure to move ahead with a union church of Polish Protestants was considerable. Even Polish leaders in Great Poland expressed an interest in such a venture, and the Unity's Polish members of the nobility were definitely in favor of it. After considerable negotiations and assurances, the Unity sent representatives to a "union synod" in Koźminek in 1555. Though the Unity's Confession of 1535 was the basis for doctrinal discussions, it was already clear that the Polish Reformed wanted to interpret it in a thoroughly Calvinistic way. It was also clear that the Polish delegates to this synod could not guarantee their own constituents' support of what was decided.

In the final analysis, what was accomplished at Koźminek was not a union but a sort of federation of churches with the hope of working for closer ties in the future.* Izrael and other Unity delegates felt that things were moving too quickly.

The Unity's reservations proved well founded. Many of the Polish Protestant clergy in Lesser Poland resisted the Unity's confession, worship, and discipline. Some time later, Br. Izrael reported that he found little progress in the churches that were organizing. The Brethren's "drab lifestyle," as one historian puts it, did not attract the Poles.[38] Politics and religion also remained too intertwined here for the Unity, and the "union" never had the popular support its proponents expected. The union was not working.

The Poles saw this also, and following their Calvinist inclinations they wrote to the Calvinist center of Geneva to invite Francesco Lismanin back to help organize a Polish Reformed Church. More important was the return of John Łaski in 1556. He was of the Polish nobility and had assisted the Reformation in England until he had to flee Mary Tudor's Counter-Reformation in 1553. He was Reformed in theology, but also got along with the Lutherans' Philip Melancthon. All that had made Łaski a national hero, so when he arrived in Lesser Poland it was, the Brethren reported, "as if St. Peter had come down to them from heaven."[39]

Now that the Protestants of Lesser Poland had strong leaders of their own, Br. Izrael and other members of the Unity

---

* Koźminek was a precursor of the Consensus of Sandomierz 15 years later.

began to step back from efforts to forge a Polish national Protestant church, and instead concentrated on the Unity's own development. This was not a sharp parting of the ways; the Unity maintained connection with the union, but following the Unity's "centennial" synod in Sležany, Moravia, in 1557, the Polish union existed more on paper than in fact.

Back in Great Poland, the Unity remained a strong and vibrant community. The first synod of the Polish Province of the Unity was held in 1560. Reflecting the administrative differences from the "home provinces" of Bohemia and Moravia, this synod elected nine noble members as "political seniors," to represent the church in the wider world and to have responsibility for watching over the other noble members of the Unity in Poland. From its beginning, the Unity had had elders or judges to promote the spiritual growth and discipline of its members, but here in Poland, nobles and not commoners were needed to supervise the nobility. Tension remained as well between the Poles' church for all the people of a given area, meaning in effect a state church, and the Unity's original concept of a church that people joined freely out of conviction. Even among the clergy things were a little different. For instance, marriage in the Polish clergy became more frequent earlier than in the Czech lands.[40] Still, the Unity continued in a recognizable form in Poland, and its history was far from over.

Notes

1 Joseph Th. Müller, *Geschichte der Böhmischen Brüder* 3 vols. (Herrnhut: Missionsbuchhandlung, 1922, 1931), 2:236; 3:1.

2 Rudolf Říčan, *The History of the Unity of Brethren*, trans. C. Daniel Crews (Bethlehem, Pa.: Department of Publications and Communications, Moravian Church, Northern Province, 1992), 173.

3 This and the succeeding paragraph are from Říčan, 173.

4 Müller, 3:45.

5 Müller, 3:5.

6 Müller, 3:8.

7 Říčan, 184. Müller, 3:10-11.

8 Říčan, 165-66. Müller, 3:59.

9 Müller, 3:14.

10 Müller, 3:17-25, reports this examination almost word for word. See Říčan, 185, for the shorter version.

11 Říčan, 186-87. Müller, 3:26-28.

12 Říčan, 191-92.

13 Říčan, 188-90.

14 Říčan, 224.

15 Müller, 3:55.

16 Müller, 3:56.

17 Říčan, 225. Müller, 3:58.

18 Říčan, 225. Müller, 3:58-60.

19 Říčan, 226.

20 Müller, 3:60-62.

21 Müller, 3:62.

22 Müller, 3:61.

23 Müller, 3:66-67

24 Říčan, 226.

25 Říčan, 227.

26 Norman Davies, *God's Playground: A History of Poland* (New York: Columbia University Press, 1982), 1:178, provides a map showing Unity centers in Poland.

27 Říčan, 227.

28 Müller, 3:67-68.

29 Říčan, 227. Müller, 3:6-69.

30 Říčan, 228.

31 Müller, 3:69.

32 Müller, 3:69.

33 Müller, 3:72.

34 Říčan, 228. Müller, 3:63, 73-74.

35 Říčan, 229.

36 Říčan, 230.

37 Müller, 3:78-80. Říčan, 230-32.

38 Aleksander Brükner, "The Polish Reformation in the Sixteenth Century," in *Polish Civilization: Essays and Studies*, ed. Mieczysław Giergielewicz (New York: New York University Press, 1979), 79.

39 Říčan, 233. Müller, 3:89.

40 Říčan, 239, 248.

Chapter 14

Internal Tensions

Augusta in Prison and the New Bishops, 1548-1564

In Bohemia as a new decade approached, the Unity continued to know hard times. Many of its members had had to go into exile, and some congregations had been lost because of King Ferdinand's decrees following the Schmalkald War. The severity of enforcing these decrees varied from estate to estate, and sometimes from month to month. In Moravia, where the nobles had not participated in the "rebellion," conditions were much better. In East Prussia the Unity exiles continued to suffer persecution of a different sort, but new opportunities were opening up in Poland. The entire Unity suffered, however, as Bishop John Augusta continued to languish in prison, and Bishop Mach Sionský was with the East Prussian exiles and could make only occasional trips in secret to Moravia.

New and competent leaders were emerging in the Unity to meet the future with vision and guidance. We have already met Br. George Izrael, who was giving strong leadership in East Prussia and Poland.[1] There was also John Černý,* born into a Unity family c. 1508, who after some doubts remained in the Unity and at about age 20 was taken into the Brethren's House

---

* We have already noted that this John Černý was not the same John Černý who was the brother of Bishop Luke.

in Mladá Boleslav by Bishop Luke. He was ordained in 1537 and quickly gained a reputation as a fine preacher and careful administrator. He had been elected to the Inner Council in 1543, and was interested in recording the history of the Unity.

Another promising young minister was Br. Matthias (Matěj) Červenka, who was born in 1521, most probably to a Utraquist family, since a report states that he was received into the Unity at Boleslav at the age of 12. Bishop Roh was his teacher and was so impressed with his abilities that he sent him at age 15 to Wittenberg for university studies. He served as an assistant to Bishop Augusta before the latter's incarceration, and his theological knowledge and facility with languages made him a valuable representative for the Unity in many ways.

The youngest of these emerging leaders was John Blahoslav,* born at Přerov in Moravia in 1523 to a prosperous Unity family. He was educated first in Přerov by his pastor, Br. Volf, for whom he maintained a lifelong regard, and then went to study with Bishop Martin Michalec in Prostějov. He went on to attend a Latin school, where he acquired fluency and stylistic skill in that language and a liking for "Protestant humanism." He studied for a year at Wittenberg and then returned to work first as assistant to Br. Michalec and then in Mladá Boleslav.

One characteristic these new leaders shared in common was a great devotion to the Unity and its history, heritage, and continued independence from the Catholic, Utraquist, and Lutheran Churches alike. In this, they would come into conflict with the aims of John Augusta, who sought closer ties, especially with the Utraquists.[2] As for Bishop Augusta, he underwent a third bloody interrogation in 1549, but while rumors flew, no contact was allowed. A Unity account mourned it was as if the bishop and Br. Bílek "were buried alive!"[3]

---

* "Blahoslav" was not his family name. In fact his brother, also a Unity priest, was known as Martin Abdon. "Blahoslav" comes from his father's name, Blažek, which is related to the Czech word for "blessed." To add to the confusion, he sometimes used "Apteryx" as a pen name. This is a Greek translation of his mother's maiden name, Bezperová, meaning "without feather (or wing)."

Not to be outdone by Brandýs nad Labem, Mladá Boleslav also built a sbor designed by Italian architect Matteo Bogorelli. The modern-day signage says: "Former sbor of the Czech Brethren, MUSEUM."

The continued incarceration of Augusta meant a shortage of bishops for performing ordinations, etc. Since the deaths of Bishops Roh and Michalec in 1547, only Augusta and Sionský were left. Augusta was imprisoned, or dead for all the Inner Council knew, and Sionský in East Prussia suffered declining health. Therefore, at New Year's 1550 the remaining members of the Inner Council held a special meeting with Bishop Sionský, who transferred his bishop's power to four members of the council in case he should die and "if the Lord God should not return Brother Johannes [Augusta]."[4]

This does not mean that he consecrated four new bishops. Each of these four members of the council was given only a portion of a bishop's authority, to be exercised only in an emergency as determined by a synod or the rest of the Inner Council. This power was distributed as follows:

By a giving of the hand,[*] Bishop Sionský gave the power of ordination to the two oldest priests of the Unity. One was Wenceslas Vroutecký, "truly a pleasant fellow, who nevertheless worked all his life in holy deeds." He loved to tell the younger clergy about the stirring days of Gregory and Bishop Matthias. The other priest was even older. Daniel Hranický was known for his "ancient simplicity," and had accompanied the "First Exile of the Brethren" to Moldavia in 1480.[5] Both Vroutecký and Hranický had been on the Inner Council since 1516.

Administrative authority to call synods, visit the congregations, and supervise ministers was transferred to Matthias Strejc and John Černý. In addition, seven new members were chosen by the Inner Council to bring it up to strength. The Unity thus made provision to carry on as best it could, and Bishop Sionský returned to East Prussia.

---

[*] In his original history, 206, Říčan uses the Czech word "rukoudáním," which is literally "a giving by means of the hand" and which I gave in the English translation, 194, as "through the laying on of hands." But Müller, 2:292, who also had access to original documents, says it should be rendered "handshake" (*Handschlag*). This point was also discussed in chapter 8.

Just three weeks later secret communication was established with Augusta for the first time since his arrest two years earlier. At the beginning of 1550 a new warden was assigned to the prison. One of the new guards had worked in Litomyšl and knew enough about the Unity to realize that Augusta and Bílek were not criminals. The sympathetic guard agreed to leave Augusta's letters at his wife's house below the prison to be picked up by a young priest who would leave the Inner Council's replies, writing supplies, etc., for the guard to deliver to Augusta.[6]

Only then did Augusta learn of the tribulations that had afflicted the Unity in the last year and a half: forced emigration, suppression of his beloved Litomyšl congregation, and sufferings of his fellow members. In response, Augusta composed a heart-rending work called "Lament over the Flock of Christ." It is telling that in this work Augusta mourned the sufferings of the Unity, but said not one word about his own. Moreover, now that he at last had pen, paper, and candles, Augusta devoted himself to more literary work including a manual and advice for the clergy in dealing with members.[*]

This improvement in the Unity's fortunes soon received a setback. Bishop Mach Sionský died in April 1551. His health had been poor, but his death was nonetheless "unexpected." Now with no bishops outside prison, the Inner Council quickly met and asked Augusta to authorize election and consecration of additional bishops. He did not answer. Could he be set free? Friendly noblemen petitioned King Ferdinand, who rejected the idea. Others sought a general amnesty for all prisoners of the "rebellion," but the king merely promised to look into the matter. Augusta, meanwhile, with little else to do, kept up his literary output. One was *Remedy* (*Náprava*), and it stands in the line of the Unity's instruction manuals for members in various levels of society and situations of life. But still he did not reply to the Inner Council's urgent request for new bishops.

---

[*] Most interestingly, this work has a section on ministering to members in prison.

With prospects dashed for his release, the council members met in Mladá Boleslav in June 1552, ready to proceed as soon as Augusta approved. They waited several weeks before giving up and going home.

Finally in August 1552 his answer came: a resounding "No!"[7] They were to wait for his release before doing anything. The council members were disappointed, but at least they had available the two elderly priests authorized by Bishop Sionský to perform consecrations. If Augusta should be released, well and good; if not, the Unity could proceed if it had to.[8] For now, the council waited.

Also in August 1552 a new warden, Kaspar Mercerod, and six new guards arrived at Augusta's prison, and the friendly guard left. For a while, means were found to stay in contact with the bishop, but in February 1553 a linen bag of letters to Augusta fell into the wrong guard's hands. A search of Augusta's cell found nothing incriminating, for he had burned all previous letters as soon as he had read them.

In May 1553 Augusta and Bílek were chained by the feet to one another and taken to the White Tower in Prague for questioning about the letters. Both expected to be executed, but for the first time in five years the two prisoners could see and speak to one another. The interrogation over, they were sent back to Křivoklát. There they were not tortured again, but were watched more closely. Indeed, only one guard, the one who had found the letters, was allowed into their cell to give them food and drink. The result, though not as bad as it could have been, was that Augusta and the Inner Council were again out of touch.

The last word the Inner Council had from Augusta was on 10 February 1553, just before the letter smuggling was discovered. Rumor now had it that the prisoners had been executed because of these letters. The continuing life and work of the Unity was at stake. Was it time to choose more bishops and members of the Inner Council even though Augusta had not approved? Was he still alive to give approval?

The issue was even more complicated, since both priests authorized by Bishop Sionský to consecrate bishops had died by now, Br. Vroutecký in October 1552 and Br. Hranický in January 1553. Moreover, students who had finished their preparation were awaiting ordination as deacons, and several deacons needed to be ordained as priests to fill vacant pastorates. If only Augusta had agreed to the consecration of more bishops when first asked! But he had not, so now what was to be done?

Only eight members were left on the Inner Council, and these gathered 2-7 May 1553. After long deliberation, they agreed it was essential to fill vacancies on the council and to elect and consecrate new bishops. Historian Říčan observes, "Duly constituted (that is, properly elected) elders signified for the Unity the spiritual gift of God."[9] And so with a call for prayer and fasting, the Inner Council summoned a general synod of the Unity, which met in Přerov on 5 June 1553.

Duly assembling from Bohemia, Moravia, and Poland, the Unity's priests and experienced deacons reached consensus for five Brethren to fill vacancies on the Inner Council and elected John Černý and Matthias Červenka bishops.[10] Since the Unity's only bishop, Augusta, was still imprisoned or perhaps dead, the Inner Council chose its two oldest remaining members, Matthias Strejc and Paul (Pavel) Paulin, to consecrate the newly elected bishops. All the members of the Inner Council laid hands on these two consecrators to authorize this, and the next day, 8 June 1553, these two laid hands on Černý and Červenka. The Inner Council members joined in the laying on of hands, and pledged loyalty and obedience to the new bishops by a handshake.

Thus for the Unity to continue to exist, the direct succession of bishop to bishop from the time of Matthias was broken.*

---

* Müller, 2:303, here does not consider the succession to have been broken in 1500. See above. Müller also notes here that some later sources (notably Jaffet in 1599) tried to show that Strejc and Paulin were "suffragan" bishops who normally did not consecrate, but could, or even that Augusta himself had authorized them to act. Not

Theoretically, and now in practice, priests in an emergency could be authorized to consecrate validly elected bishops. In the theology of the Unity, Christ had prepared and called leaders for the church through their natural talents and the gifts of the Holy Spirit. The church, guided by this same Spirit, merely recognizes and confirms this call through a minister properly authorized to represent Christ and the church in the act of ordination/consecration. A direct passing of authority from bishop to bishop was desirable but was not essential. Moreover, the Unity considered bishops and priests to be essentially the same order of ministers, with bishops simply being priests having special functions committed to them by the church. It is important to note too that after Augusta finally left prison he was not asked to re-consecrate or otherwise validate the new bishops.[11] Nor did Augusta himself, though he resented these new bishops, reject them as invalid.

One positive outcome of Bishop Augusta's long imprisonment was the reinforcement of the Unity's conferential form of government. No one person, not even Augusta, was to make decisions, but the Unity's synods and Inner Council were to do this "collegially," and consensus rather than a simple majority of votes was the goal.

Br. Černý was named "judge" or presiding officer of the Unity* and Br. Červenka, who now returned from Poland, was given the title "Unity writer." This office was relatively recent, and seems to be a combination of writing official Unity documents and instructional materials, and reviewing what others had written.[12]†

While the Unity's future was made secure with new bishops and administration, congregation life in Bohemia revived from oppression thanks to King Ferdinand's distraction with state

---

only was this latter psychologically improbable, but it was physically impossible, since communication with Augusta was cut off at this time.

* Later he and Augusta shared this position.

† In short, the "Unity writer" functioned as a "Faith and Order Commission."

affairs. Negotiations were under way for the 1555 Peace of Augsburg, which established the principle that the religion of a region was that of its ruler. It had no validity in Bohemia, but by such means the king's attention was diverted enough that in 1554 a fine new "sbor" was constructed in Mladá Boleslav (see page 236). It was designed by Matteo Bogorelli, the same Italian architect who had earlier designed the Unity church in Brandýs nad Labem. It was a "basilica without a tower," approximately 75 feet wide and 100 feet long with a semicircular apse 16½ feet in radius.[13] The building boasted Renaissance style ornaments and could hold 1,200 worshipers.*

Lord Arnošt Krajíř of Krajek decided to have the new building consecrated on Easter Sunday 1554. On Holy Thursday, however, he heard that the king had forbidden the Easter consecration. Exercising the greater freedom enjoyed in Bohemia at the moment, Krajíř chose to obey his king's order literally by not consecrating the sbor on Easter, but on Good Friday instead.[14]

Greater freedom came to Bishop Augusta at the beginning of 1555 when communication with the outside world was restored after a two-year silence. A friendly guard set up a loom in a chamber adjoining Augusta's cell, and people coming to order cloth could talk with the prisoner and slip him letters, etc. The king's son, Archduke Ferdinand, learned of this but did nothing to forbid it. Perhaps the archduke tired of the matter, and only his father's "fanatic obstinacy" prevented the bishop's release.[15]

Augusta used the less rigorous confinement to continue to produce practical handbooks for the life of the Unity and a compendium of theology called *Summovník*, in the form of sermons based on the Apostle's Creed. He also brought out an accompanying "Register" of Scripture lessons to be used in Sunday services. This replacement of the old pericopes had been tentatively approved before Augusta's imprisonment,[16] so

---

* It still stands, after being used as a Catholic church, a car salesroom under the Communists, and a museum and civic cultural center.

he was incensed when the Inner Council made changes in it and wanted to relegate it to devotional reading and not replace the traditional Sunday and festival lessons that many knew by heart and found comforting.[17] This and similar occurrences, coupled with his earlier refusal to sanction more bishops, led to a growing hostility between Augusta and the Inner Council.

While the council continued to work for Augusta's release, it did not tell him of the new bishops. Neither would he be glad to hear that in 1557 two additional bishops were elected. The 1553 synod had elected only two bishops, Černý and Červenka, not the traditional four. Perhaps this was a compromise in case Augusta was still alive and would someday emerge from prison. In the meantime, however, Augusta was still confined, and the work in Moravia and Poland had increased to the extent that two active bishops were not enough. As fate would have it, communication with Augusta was again interrupted in 1557 by the death of his "friendly guard," so he could not be consulted.* The centennial synod in Sležany in August 1557, therefore, elected George Izrael as bishop to superintend the work in Poland, and John Blahoslav to assist Bishop Červenka in Moravia and as "Unity writer."[18]†

Communication with Augusta was not restored until 1559, and now the Inner Council wrote to tell him of developments, including the election of bishops in 1553 and 1557. Augusta replied angrily, denouncing the Inner Council's "high handedness" in taking these "unauthorized" steps. He blamed council members for not informing him of the 1553 elections when they had the chance (in 1555) and said that in any case they should have waited for his written instructions. Augusta by now seemed to think that his sufferings were "a reason for them to acknowledge his pre-eminence all the more."[19] For their part, the Inner Council members, particularly the new

---

* He almost certainly would not have approved anyway.

† We seldom remember who is "almost elected." In this case it was Br. Wenceslas Čech who came in third. He was assigned the senior position on the Inner Council after the bishops (see Müller, 2:311).

bishops, felt that Augusta was being obstructive, and that the good of the Unity, not the whim of one individual, however venerable, should determine their actions. From this point on, there was no love lost between Bishop Augusta and the new administration.[20]

Meanwhile, Archduke Ferdinand had secretly married Philippine Welser, a beautiful "commoner" whom he had met in Augsburg. Only when they had a child in 1558 did they tell King Ferdinand (who also became Holy Roman emperor that year) about the marriage. In 1560 Philippine came to live at Křivoklát, and brought with her a new captain for the castle, Ladislav Šternberk. This captain visited Augusta in his cell, was impressed by him, and promised to work for his release.

Šternberk kept his promise, but was told that Augusta's case had to be referred to a commission of Catholic clergy.* The commission decreed that Augusta must "recant" before he could be released. At this point Augusta gave up hope, but the captain reminded him that since the Brethren gave communion in both kinds, they were technically Utraquists, and Utraquists were permitted in Bohemia. If he could craft a carefully worded statement saying he was "Utraquist," perhaps he could be released without renouncing the Unity.[21]

Augusta, after so many years in prison, decided to try this. His declaration broadly defined the Utraquist Church as "the entire evangelical church, wherever the body and blood of the Lord Christ are received under both kinds."[22] He was careful not to acknowledge the Roman Church, nor did he denounce or resign from the Unity.

The Inner Council, however, took Augusta's declaration in favor of the Utraquists as if he had rejected the Unity, joined another church, and abandoned his integrity just to get out of jail. It did not accept his explanation that he did not wish to offend his new friends (Šternberk and some other Utraquists) who had urged him to do this, and since the Unity had entered

---

* Historian Müller, 2:314, says this proves Augusta's imprisonment was religious and not political as was claimed.

into fellowship with the Lutherans, etc., why could it not also do the same with its fellow Czechs in the Utraquist Church? After all, the Unity had never claimed to be the only true church. Besides, he had not resigned from the Unity, and his desire for release was not selfish but so that he could serve the Unity as a free man. The council did not buy this. It assumed Augusta had deserted the Unity because of irritation over the new administration. Moreover, he had acted arbitrarily without proper consultation with his fellow council members. So the council agreed to continue paying his physical support in prison,* but to "renounce" him until he "repented."23

About the same time, 1561, a new edition of the Unity's confession appeared. In it a sentence of previous editions hoping for eventual union with the Utraquists was dropped.24† The omission probably had less to do with Augusta than with a new Catholic archbishop in Prague, 130 years after the death of Conrad of Vechta, the previous archbishop. Catholics and Utraquists had agreed that Archbishop Antonin Brus would ordain priests of both churches,‡ and the Brethren may have feared this was the beginning of the Utraquists' submission to Rome.25 That also made Augusta's move toward the Utraquists seem more ominous to the Inner Council.

A new Czech Unity hymnal appeared in 1561 (see page 261); it was high time for a new one. The hymnal of 1541 had long been sold out, and during the persecution many new hymns had been written. The Inner Council in 1555 appointed John Černý, John Blahoslav, and Adam Šturm as the hymnal committee, and they worked for six years to get it out. They maintained tradition by including almost all the 481 texts from Bishop Roh's 1541 hymnal, but added new ones to bring the

---

* The practice in earlier times was that prisoners had to pay for their own room and board.
† Otherwise, changes in this text were mostly editorial and consisted of Blahoslav's refining the style in line with the preferred Latin of the day.
‡ He ordained Utraquists for only five years. After that the Utraquists once more had to seek ordination from bishops abroad.

total to 761.* The hymn writers' names were not printed in the hymnal but were kept in a manuscript list.† Blahoslav,‡ in addition to contributing 51 of his own hymn texts and 17 revisions to the book, soon published as a supplement to the hymnal several canticles from the Gospels and prophets, along with the Apostles' Creed to be chanted on major church festivals. Tunes for these were adapted from the Roman liturgy with a few changes required by the rhythm of the Czech texts.

The Inner Council could not find a printer in Bohemia or Moravia for the hymnal, so it turned again to the Unity's peripatetic printer, Alexander Oujezdecký, who at the moment had his print shop in Poland on the estate of Count Luke Górka in Szamotuły, or Samter in German. Thus the hymnal of 1561 is sometimes referred to as the "Szamotuły" or "Samter" hymnal. 26

The 1561 Czech hymnal was a fine achievement, a beautiful book of great significance for the life of the Unity. But not all valued it equally. John Blahoslav had more concern for rhythm and style than did others on the Inner Council, and some compromises were made. This led to further criticism, and Blahoslav said in effect that he personally would have done some things differently, but that it was the committee's

---

* Only 12 texts and four tunes are in the 1541 hymnal but not in the 1561.
† Müller, 2:361, notes that to make the list Blahoslav relied on his knowledge and memory for newer hymn writers and on the memory of older members for the rest. The list is not faultless but is generally reliable.
‡ While doing most of the work on the hymnal, John Blahoslav compiled *Musica*, the first Czech language book on music theory. He published it in 1558 to assist ministers, cantors, and others who would lead hymn singing from the new hymnal. Müller, 2:364, says *Musica* was particularly important since the Unity did not use organs to support congregational singing. A second printing was needed in 1564 and another edition in 1569, both printed in Ivančice. Müller also notes that the 1569 version contained two additional appendices: one with more tips for worship leaders, and another with advice for those who felt called to write hymns. One might consider these the forerunners of "hymn writers' workshops."

gift to the Unity, and it had done the best it could. He also observed that the sharpest criticism came not from enemies of the Unity but from its members.

And how did the Unity's senior bishop, John Augusta, still residing in prison, receive the new hymnal? He was fit to be tied. The Inner Council's hymnal committee seems to have bent over backward to please him, perhaps too much. Not only did it retain his 40 hymns from the 1541 hymnal, but it included 110 more in 1561, making about one-fifth of the book. The outrage, from Augusta's thinking, was that Blahoslav and the others had dared to revise practically all of his hymns,[27] some so extensively they were not recognizable. In a huff Augusta gathered up the hymns he had written in prison (216 of them!) and copied them into a manuscript book as his "authorized and unchanged" official version.*

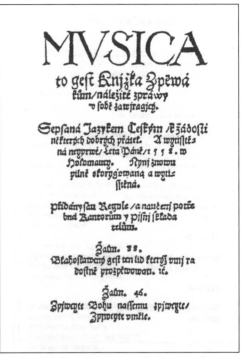

John Blahoslav's music theory book, which had several printings.

Following yet more angry exchanges, over the hymnal and other writings, over his "going over" to the Utraquists, correspondence between Augusta and the Inner Council dwindled to a halt. This time it was for personal choice, not prison guards.

---

* A copy of Augusta's manuscript at least used to be in the National Museum in Vienna.

Ironically too, all the anger and misunderstanding over his declaration for the Utraquists proved in vain, for the Catholics and Utraquists did not believe Augusta anyway.

Some things did go better in 1561 for the poor prisoners of Křivoklát. The archduke's wife, Philippine, had taken a liking to them, and she persuaded her husband to grant Augusta and Bílek's request that they be allowed to spend Easter together. Once they promised not to escape, they were given the keys to their cells and allowed free run of the castle. A guard asked Bílek how long it had been since he had seen Augusta, and he replied "eight years," not since they were taken to Prague for questioning in 1553. With tears the friends greeted one another, and Bílek had to admit he would not have recognized Augusta if he had not been told who it was the guards brought in. On the Wednesday after Easter they returned to their cells and gave back the keys.[28]

Impressed by his wife's and Captain Šternberk's favorable reports, Archduke Ferdinand again agreed to release Augusta, but his father the king (now emperor) still insisted on recantation. A chaplain suggested sending Augusta to the Jesuits in Prague in hopes they could persuade him. Augusta at first refused to go, but then agreed if he could talk to the Utraquist administrator as well.[29]

With guards but no chains, Augusta and Bílek set off for Prague on 3 May and were delivered to the Jesuits on 6 May. The prisoners were given securely locked but otherwise very nice accommodations. Perhaps the Jesuits thought good conditions would make them more compliant and less willing to return to prison. Indeed, after all those years in a dark cell, the first thing Augusta noted was that their room had seven windows! They were also given good Czech food, and from a balcony they could see the famous Charles Bridge.*

---

* The bridge was constructed in the time of King Charles (Emperor Charles IV) and stands today as a beloved Prague landmark, frequented by musicians, artists, and the local populace. In the 1620s it displayed a grim reminder of the fate of "heretics." Read on.

The Jesuits got nowhere with Augusta, who plainly told them he had agreed to meet them only so he could later have his promised conversation with the Utraquist administrator, John Mystopol. Augusta still hoped a face-to-face meeting with the Utraquist leader might result in real reconciliation between the Utraquists and the Unity. The meeting was not granted, and Augusta was told to become Catholic or Utraquist, there was no other choice. As before, he made a vague statement about belonging to the church of the Bohemian nation that serves communion in two kinds, and as before this was considered insufficient. After about a month, the Jesuits gave

John Augusta and Jacob Bílek meet after eight years apart.

up. One remarked that Augusta had "a hard head." Still denied
his meeting with the Utraquist administrator, he was returned
to Křivoklát at the end of June 1561.

Bílek wanted to accompany Augusta, but was kept in the
White Tower, though not under very terrible conditions. He was
assured that if he made a nominal profession for the Utraquist
Church and took communion he would be freed. Friends told
him they had spoken with Augusta, who said it would be all
right. They also reminded him that Luke of Prague had said
one could receive communion from a Utraquist if that was
the only choice. Further, they had found a "very Lutheran"
Utraquist priest who would give him communion without all
the vestments and ceremonial trappings. Poor Bílek was at
length worn down and agreed. He took communion, but found
to his horror that the official document certifying this declared
he had renounced "the Picards and all sects." He was assured
it was just a form document, and he need not worry about it.
Nevertheless, he insisted it be recorded that those words were
added to his statement without his knowledge.

Finally on 9 August 1561, after an imprisonment of thirteen years, four weeks, and two days, Bílek was freed. He
immediately hastened to Křivoklát and secured employment
from Captain Šternberk in the kitchen and as a weaver so as
to be close to Augusta. Bílek was officially ordered not to talk
to him, but the captain and guards looked the other way
whenever he approached Augusta's cell.

When the Inner Council heard of the conditions of Bílek's
release, and that Augusta had supposedly advised him to
accept them, it angrily condemned both Bílek and Augusta
again, and declared that they had left the Unity and could not
serve in its ministry.[30] It was not the Inner Council's finest
hour.

Šternberk and others continued to work for Augusta's
release, and the Utraquist priest who had given Bílek communion was brought to talk with him. The priest proposed the
same conditions that had led to Bílek's release, but Catholic
authorities insisted that such a prominent heretic as Augusta

should make a formal recantation. This his conscience would not let him do. All hope seemed lost, and Augusta himself asked Šternberk to cease his efforts before they so aggravated the archduke that they made things worse.[31]

In these months Augusta continued his literary activity, including a work on the holy communion. The description of its contents sounds in line with traditional Unity teaching, but the Inner Council was concerned that he was drawing closer to the Utraquists.[32]

Šternberk finally got Augusta his longed-for conversation with Utraquist administrator John Mystopol[33] in April 1563. For this, Augusta was again taken to Prague. He was confined in the White Tower but in fairly nice conditions, and was even allowed visitors.[34] Five weeks later Mystopol and Mělnický, his associate,[35] told Augusta that recanting was his last remaining hope for freedom. In the course of discussions Augusta asked what was the good of bringing up old quarrels. Would it not be better to unite against common enemies? The Utraquist administrators had to agree that "a cable of three cords" — Utraquists, Brethren, and Lutherans united against the Catholics — "is stronger,"* but they still had to deliver Augusta's answer to the archduke. Augusta promised an answer by 2 June.

Before that date Augusta was returned to Křivoklát on 25 May without giving his answer. There he remained in prison for nearly a year, though in February 1564 he was given a bright room in place of his dark cell. Then he was taken back to Prague again in March 1564. There, without explanation, he was released without recantation or posting a bond. The only condition was that he not preach in public. After 16 years Augusta was free.

He hastened to Mladá Boleslav and arrived on Palm Sunday, 26 March 1564. Bílek joined him there as soon as he could obtain release from Captain Šternberk's service.

---

* Relations between the Utraquist administration and the Catholic archbishop of Prague were strained.

But how would the Inner Council receive him? In the second half of April 1564 they met. Augusta, Bílek, and the council reconciled themselves. Bílek was allowed to return to ministerial service, and Augusta was acknowledged as senior bishop of the Unity. How was this worked out? Bílek's emotional account states: "and all the disputes which had broken out among them were laid aside." The official records say no more.

Historian Müller (2:342) observes that, given the personalities involved, it is unlikely that Augusta quietly accepted the council's earlier condemnation of his conduct. Neither is it likely that Blahoslav and the others admitted that Augusta had been right. Augusta's "unbending character," which 16 years in prison had only made stiffer, and his continued desire to have one unified Protestant church in Bohemia promised more disputes in the future between him and a council composed of likewise stubborn individuals.[36] However, that had not yet happened, and the Unity could rejoice that at long last the sufferings of Bishop Augusta in prison were over.

Notes

1 This and the following biographical notes are from Rudolf Říčan, *The History of the Unity of Brethren*, trans. C. Daniel Crews (Bethlehem, Pa.: Department of Publications and Communications, Moravian Church, Northern Province, 1992), 165-67.

2 Říčan, 167.

3 Joseph Th. Müller, *Geschichte der Böhmischen Brüder* 3 vols. (Herrnhut: Missionsbuchhandlung, 1922, 1931), 2:291.

4 Říčan, 194.

5 Říčan, 194.

6 Müller, 2:292.

7 Říčan, 195.

8 Müller, 2:296-300.

9 Říčan, 196.

10 Müller, 2:302. Sources including Müller say the synod's delegates were directed to discuss the crisis to arrive at a consensus of who should be bishop and on the Inner Council. If or how votes were cast is not clear.

11 Říčan, 196.

12 Miloš Štrupl, "John Blahoslav, Father and Charioteer of the Lord's People in the Unitas Fratrum," *Czechoslovakia Past and Present*, vol. 2, ed. M. Rechcigl (The Hague, 1968), 1232-46. A mimeographed manuscript of this is in the Moravian Archives, Winston-Salem, N.C. See typescript, 8.

13 Müller, 2:254, gives the precise dimensions as 23 by 30 meters, with an apse 5 meters in radius.

14 Müller, 2:254-56.

15 Müller, 2:305.

16 Müller, 2:365.

17 Říčan, 198-99

18 Říčan, 199.

19 Říčan, 200.

20 Müller, 2:312-13.

21 Müller, 2:314.

22 Říčan, 200.

23 Říčan, 200-201.

24 Říčan, 201.

25 Zdeněk V. David, *Finding the Middle Way: The Utraquists' Liberal Challenge to Rome and Luther* (Washington, D.C.: Woodrow Wilson Center Press, 2003), 150, 157, 160-66. Müller, 2:373.

26 Material on the 1561 hymnal is from Müller, 2:359-63.

27 See Štrupl, 9.

28 Müller, 2:321-23.

29 Details of Augusta and Bílek's 1561 stay in Prague are from Müller, 2:323-30.

30 Říčan, 202.

31 Müller, 2:334-35.

32 Müller, 2:335.

33 Opinions on Mystopol are divided. See David, 136 and 436-37, note 1.

34 Details of Augusta's last months in prison are from Müller, 2:339-42.

35 David, 10, reports that Unity writers did not think much of Mělnický. Müller, 2:339, calls Mělnický a co-administrator. David says he did not become administrator until 1568 (488, note 65).

36 Štrupl, 9-10, summarizes some of these.

Chapter 15

A Joint Confession

*From the Release of Augusta
to the Bohemian Confession,
1564-1575*

oon after the release of Augusta from prison, King Ferdinand I of Bohemia (and also Holy Roman emperor) died in July 1564. As previously agreed, his first-born son Maximilian succeeded him as Emperor Maximilian II and King Maximilian. Ferdinand's second-born son Archduke Ferdinand remained as regent until his brother Maximilian could take over in Bohemia, since Maximilian was busy with state and religious affairs in Germany.

The Unity and many Utraquists had great hopes for the new king. He had expressed inclinations toward Luther's ideas, and he was a friend of the Lutheran elector of Saxony. He favored reform in the Catholic Church and had received a personal dispensation from the pope to receive communion in both kinds. He did not like the Jesuits, the main agents of the Catholic Counter-Reformation, since he saw their aggressive methods as a threat to the peace of the empire. True, he had decided that remaining a Catholic would help his dynastic ambitions, and his father had made him promise not to leave the Roman Church as a condition to his assuming the thrones. Still, Protestants expected more favorable treatment from him than they knew under previous rulers. For the Unity, though, those hopes remained unfulfilled. As a harbinger, Maximilian sent his son and heir, Rudolf, to fiercely Catholic Spain for his education. That would haunt the Unity in the future.[1]

When Maximilian came to the throne in 1564 several Unity nobles gave him a German translation of their confession hoping he would see their beliefs were not heretical and would give the Unity better treatment. There was no response. An appeal the next year gained no better response. Maximilian left in place previous edicts against the "Picards."

Efforts to win the king's approval continued. When the Unity brought out a new edition of its German hymnal in 1566, it was dedicated to the king.[2] Some Unity nobles from Moravia gave Maximilian a copy in Vienna, asking for relief for their fellow members in Bohemia. If he looked at it, he might have admired its artistry, but he was not moved to think more kindly of the Unity.[3]*

At Bishop Augusta's suggestion, in 1566 the Unity petitioned to have its houses of worship opened for prayers for the king's success against the Turks. The request was refused, and the Unity was told Bohemia already had enough churches, Catholic and Utraquist, where the Brethren could pray.[4] The king went further, banishing the Unity from the town of Pardubice in his royal domain. Unity members there were obeying the royal decree not to have public services by meeting in their houses, but their singing was so loud the local Utraquist priest complained it could be heard over the noise of the public market.[5]

---

* This 1566 hymnal was indeed a work of art. It was quarto in size (9½ by 12 inches) with beautiful and ornate initial capitals. Its first part contained 348 Brethren's hymns, and its second part had 108 hymns from the German Evangelical tradition, mostly by Luther. It appeared in many editions for the next half century with few changes. It retained 142 hymns of Weisse's 1531 hymnal and 26 of the 32 added to Br. Roh's hymnal of 1544. It also added 180 new hymns, 90 being more or less close translations of Czech originals, and the rest by its editors, Michael Tham (the Elder), John (Jan) Jelecký, and Petrus (Petr) Herbert.

In 1567 Archduke Ferdinand resigned as regent of Bohemia. Only lately under the influence of his "commoner" wife
Philippine Welser had he thawed a bit toward the Unity.
Perhaps without him King Maximilian would be more lenient.
Instead, in 1568 Maximilian, who counted Protestants among
his friends, formally re-issued the 1508 Mandate of St. James
banning the Unity in Bohemia.[6] As before, the mandate was
not uniformly enforced, but the message from the king to the
Unity was clear.

The Utraquists also were unsure about the new king. In
1567 they asked him to rescind the old *Compacta* of Basel,
which granted them the chalice in communion. This was not a
giving up and returning to the Roman Church. Rather, many
Utraquists thought the old *Compacta* did not go far enough.
They were looking for a wider-reaching acknowledgement of
their church, and some looked to the Augsburg Confession as
the possible basis, since more and more it was becoming the
common evangelical confession, at least in German lands.
More would come of this in a few years, and the Unity would
play an important role.[7]

It was in Poland, however, where Protestants took their first
concrete steps toward a common confession. In the face of
growing Catholic opposition in Lesser Poland, the leaders of the
Reformed Church there in 1570 began looking for a means of
presenting the Protestant cause in a united front with the
Lutherans and the Unity. Preliminary discussions between
Lutheran and Reformed were held early in the year. Protestants
in Great Poland also expressed interest in the united effort.
In February representatives of the Unity and the Lutherans
gathered in the home of Lord Górka in Poznań. The Unity
acknowledged the Augsburg Confession as a valid expression
of Christian faith, and several questions on the presence of
Christ in the holy communion received answers acceptable to
both groups. In spite of this, the chief Lutheran delegate would
not extend recognition to the Unity's confession, even though
Luther himself had endorsed it. Still, the Lutherans and
Brethren did promise not to denounce one another from their

pulpits, and both Lutheran and Unity representatives accepted an invitation to a Reformed synod at Sandomierz in Lesser Poland that April. The announced purpose was to agree on a common Reformed-Lutheran-Unity confession of faith for use in Poland.[8]

As the synod began, each church put forth its own confession as the basis for unity. That was not going to happen, but remarkable harmony did prevail. Simeon Theophilus Turnovský,* speaking for the Unity, said the Unity could accept the Helvetic Confession as modified by the Polish Reformed, if the Unity could retain its own confession as well. The Lutheran delegates stopped insisting the Augsburg Confession had to be the *only* confession. They could not accept the other confessions, but they did propose the three churches write a common confession of faith that could be used by all in addition to their own confessions.

It quickly became apparent that writing such a confession would take longer than one synod. It would also have to be prepared by recognized theologians of each church, not all of whom were at Sandomierz. It was therefore resolved to reassemble after Pentecost to draft the confession. For now, a document would be issued to "convey the shared teachings of all three churches, making possible an interpretation in one direction or the other."[9] The resultant compact, or Consensus of Sandomierz, dealt mostly with the holy communion, and true to its aim it asserted the real presence of Christ in the sacrament in terms that could be interpreted by each church in its own theological direction. The true significance of the Consensus of Sandomierz was its "mutual recognition of the orthodoxy of the participating churches, especially in the doctrine of the Trinity and justification, a promise of peace and

---

* Simeon Theophilus Turnovský at this time was a deacon assigned as assistant to Bishop George Izrael. Assigning him rather than the bishop himself as a representative of the Unity may mean that the Unity was not sure just how far and how officially it wanted to be involved in whatever came out of the synod.

love, and a mutual invitation to the synods [of each church]."[10] With that, the synod adjourned on 14 April 1570.

Back in Great Poland, in May the Lutherans and Brethren got into the spirit of the new agreement. Joint worship services were held, with the Unity minister officiating in the Lutheran Church with vestments according to Lutheran usage, and the Lutheran minister officiating in the Brethren's Church while wearing a plain black robe as was usual in the Unity.

The proposed common confession of faith was never written. Reformed leaders in Heidelberg and Lutheran authorities in Wittenberg advised against preparing such a document, which they feared would be a point of discord, not unity. Yet the Consensus of Sandomierz stood as a beacon of hope in an age when churches tended to condemn differences rather than affirm what they held in common.[11] The Unity hoped that this agreement might provide a bridge between the Reformed and Lutherans elsewhere as well.

Also in 1570 an amusing if not historically significant event occurred when a Unity minister, John Rokyta, was invited to be a chaplain of a Polish delegation sent to Russia to negotiate a boundary dispute with Czar Ivan the Terrible (d. 1584). Some of the Polish Protestant nobles hoped that Ivan might be persuaded to accept the Protestant position. Br. Rokyta looked on this as a missionary opportunity, and did get admitted to the Czar's presence. He explained his beliefs to the sovereign and received a reply bound in a brocade cover decorated with pearls. The answer itself, however, was extremely negative and insulting, and Rokyta felt it was written only to show off Ivan's own theological knowledge (which was considerable). The missionary did escape with his life (which many who roused Ivan's ire did not), but the idea of a Protestant Russia was firmly rejected.[12]

Back in Bohemia, many Utraquist nobles suspected Maximilian's religious intent, and so sought a guarantee of their religious liberty. Since Maximilian recognized the religious rights of his subjects in Germany who adhered to the Augsburg Confession, these nobles thought that if they could agree on that confession and get Maximilian to recognize it in Bohemia also, their rights would be assured. Their efforts would be strengthened if they could get others to make common cause with them. Some Czech lords were Lutheran by now, and obtaining their cooperation was no problem. The Utraquists next approached the Unity nobles in 1571 as "dear brothers" in hopes of bringing them on board.[13]

They were surprised when several Unity nobles agreed and had approval of the Unity's religious leaders to do so. Closer ties with the Utraquists had long been Bishop Augusta's desire, and given the current climate, even Bishop Blahoslav was willing to talk. If a united front could be achieved without loss of integrity, it could only help the Unity, Lutherans, and Utraquists alike. Augusta arranged a meeting with the Utraquist administrator, one Henry Dvorský. Dvorský was appointed to his post by Maximilian, and like many appointees of the king, he was very anti-Protestant. Together they and the Czech Catholics managed to sidetrack union talks for now.[14]

Within the Unity new leadership had became essential. Bishop John Černý died in February 1565. He had provided valuable service in Prussia and Poland and had produced several historical works. He was buried at Carmel in Mladá Boleslav, but "secretly" because of "the danger."[15] As with Luke of Prague, who was also buried there, the Unity had good reason to fear that its enemies might dig up the grave to desecrate the body.*

Bishop Červenka died in 1569, and Bishop Augusta, suffering paralysis in his hands, stepped down, perhaps involuntarily, from the Inner Council in October 1571.[16] Only Bishops Blahoslav and Izrael remained. Not wishing to experience again the difficulties of only one or no bishops, the Inner Council immediately called a synod, which elected three new bishops: Andrew (Ondřej) Štefan (d. 1577) to work with Blahoslav in Moravia; John (Jan) Kálef (d. 1588) for Bohemia;

---

* English reformer John Wycliffe suffered that fate. Forty-four years after his death in 1384 his body was exhumed and burned.

and John Lorenc (d. 1587) to work with Bishop Izrael in Poland. They were consecrated by Blahoslav and Izrael on 11 October 1571.*

Just a month after the new leadership was in place, in November 1571, John Blahoslav died at the early age of 48. His health had been a problem throughout his life, as he suffered from stomach and liver disorders, asthma, and weak eyes.† The physical limitations did not prevent him from rendering valuable service to the Unity so that the Unity's *Memorial Book* called him "the father and charioteer of the people of the Lord." He was brought up in the Unity and studied and served with Bishops Roh and Martin Michalec. He valued its history and heritage, and he was very influential in the Unity's turning back to the theology of Luke of Prague. At the same time, he interpreted Luke according to the needs of the times, and used improved Latin and humanistic learning to explain the Unity's views more adequately to educated outsiders. His advocacy of education profoundly affected the standards for younger leaders of the Unity, and enabled them to converse more freely with scholars and theologians outside the Unity. He performed valuable service through his part in the production of the Czech hymnal of 1561, and his translation of the New Testament was a gift to generations to come. The *Memorial*

---

* De Schweinitz, 370, says Augusta participated in this consecration, and "thus the true succession was renewed" (*i.e.*, back to that of Matthias of Kunvald, "broken" when new bishops were consecrated while Augusta was in prison). De Schweinitz based his statement on part 1 of Jaffet's *Meč Goliášův* (*Schwerdt Goliaths* or *Sword of Goliath*). He did not have part 2, in which Jaffet reverses himself, stating that Augusta did not participate. See Müller, 2:424, and his *Bischoftum*, 28. If Augusta did not participate, it is possible he disapproved, or ill health (paralyzed hands) and retirement were factors. In the Unity's eyes, his participation was not necessary for the validity of the new bishops.

† We have no authentic portrait of Blahoslav, but Müller, 2:422, reports the tradition that the figure wearing glasses in the choir on the frontispiece of the 1561 hymnal is Blahoslav. He may thus be the first bishop of the Unitas Fratrum known to wear glasses.

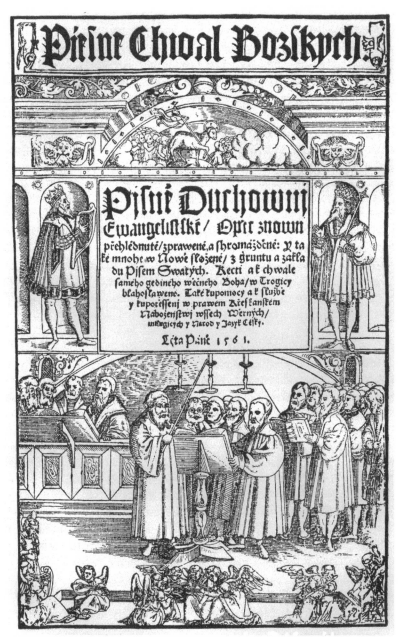

John Blahoslav was the chief compiler of the Czech hymnal of 1561. Tradition has it that Blahoslav is the bespectacled full-bearded singer behind the lectern.

Book did not exaggerate when it characterized him as a "precious treasure of the Unity."[17]

John Augusta died a few weeks later in January 1572. His contributions to the life and work of the Unity have been detailed above. His life was a tragic one, and the long years of imprisonment not only took a physical toll on him, but also meant that he and the Unity developed in separate ways. The iron-willed determination that enabled him to survive led to lasting estrangement with the new leadership. He greatly valued the Unity, but had an ecumenical vision that could see beyond its narrow confines. Ironically, as the years passed, the Unity steered more into the ecumenical path envisioned by Bishop Augusta.

Since the retirement of Augusta, Bishops Blahoslav and Izrael had shared the office of "judge," or head of the Inner Council. Izrael now continued alone as "judge," and the office of "Unity writer" was shared by Bishops Štefan and Lorenc. The new administration maintained independence from the Utraquists and Lutherans, but also perceived a decline in dedication and discipline among the Unity's members. The Unity's famous high moral standards and dedicated living had been a main ground for maintaining the Unity's continued existence and had been one of its chief attractions for converts. If the Unity became like the other churches, why should it continue to exist?

The Inner Council dealt with this problem by stressing its expectations for dedication on the part of priests and students. This was more complicated than it had been before, since in Bohemia and Moravia, as in Poland earlier, the number of married priests was increasing. Married priests did not necessarily mean a moral decline among the clergy, but "their family life gave a new character to life in the Brethren's houses."[18] The council continued to wrestle with all these issues.

Another concern was an adequate expression of the Unity's confession of faith. The 1535 confession remained in force, but the original printed editions of both the Czech (1536) and Latin (1538) texts were long sold out and hard to find. German and

Polish versions had been printed, and Blahoslav had done some work on the Czech version in 1561 and 1564. In fact, he had rewritten it so much that hardly a sentence survived without alteration. The changes were not in essential points of the confession, but rather to express ideas more clearly and "sharply."[19]

It was obvious to the Inner Council that a complete new Latin translation of the confession was badly needed. The council wanted to preserve the Unity's identity, but as we have seen, theological discussions with other churches were increasing. If the Unity was to present its confession for comparison with others, it needed a good rendition of it in Latin, which was still the language of international theological expression. That meant that the Unity had to make sure this "public" profession of faith said what the Unity intended (as interpreted by current leadership). Moreover, the style of the 1538 Latin text was admittedly "rough,"[*] and in the last quarter century readers had become accustomed to more "elegant" Latin as refined by the humanists.[20]

But who was to prepare this translation? Blahoslav had too many other responsibilities, and his health was failing.[†] The Inner Council turned to John Aeneas (Eneáš) and Isaiah Cepola (Izaiáš Cibulka), two of its students studying at Wittenberg. These tried their hand at it, but quickly admitted they needed expert assistance. With the council's approval, they approached the famous Leipzig humanist Joachim Camerarius. He said he was too old and sick to undertake such a task, but did refer them to his son-in-law Esrom Rüdinger. Rüdinger had mastered German and Latin but not Czech, so he had to work from the existing Latin version along with a newer German version provided by Br. Petrus Herbert, with Cepola answering Rüdinger's many questions. As they were completed, the sections were sent to Bishop Blahoslav for review, and he was

---

[*] Complaints uttered by the 2005 English translator verify the "rough" Latin of the 1538 printing.

[†] But he did inspect the final product.

working on these when he died. All this was a long and tedious process, but Blahoslav was pleased with the accuracy and language of what he saw. The translation was finally completed in 1572.[21]

The question then arose of how this new approved text would be made public. The Unity wanted the University of Wittenberg to print the confession, since the university often functioned as a judge of "foreign" theological documents. But negotiations proved difficult. The Lutheran professors had numerous questions over fine points, and though the Unity in exasperation reminded them that Luther himself had endorsed it, as in Poland that was not good enough. After years of discussions that began long before the final draft was finished, Wittenberg approved the text and printed the confession in 1573. It was accompanied not by an endorsement but a letter from the university theological faculty to the Inner Council affirming the validity of the Unity's ministry and ordination. The Inner Council felt the letter was little more than "pretty words" about "Christian concord and unity," and in subsequent editions of its own, the Unity reinserted Luther's endorsing preface of 1538.[22]

Historian Müller asserts that the "pickiness" of the Lutheran scholars was one reason the Brethren turned more toward Calvinism. This and continued dissatisfaction with student behavior in Lutheran Wittenberg caused the Inner Council to consider sending the Unity's theological students to Reformed universities in place of Wittenberg.[23] That would soon happen.

Opportunity or necessity for discussion with other churches soon arose again. The attempt of Bohemia's Utraquist nobles to forge a common front with the Lutherans and the Unity had failed in 1571, but the idea was not forgotten. In 1574 a sizable group of Utraquist nobles persuaded Maximilian to put the religious question on the agenda of Bohemia's national assembly. The goal was legal approval of a confession of faith that could be acknowledged by all. A common church order for Bohemia was also a possibility. The Utraquists felt these steps would strengthen their legal status as a church more than the old *Compacta* of Basel had done. Moreover, now as in 1571, these could be the first steps in forging a powerful political alliance in Bohemia among the Utraquists, Lutherans,* and the Unity.24

The assembly opened in February 1575 and with only two breaks, for Easter and in summer, met until September.25 The Utraquist nobles far outnumbered the others, but not far behind the Catholics were the nobles and knights of the Unity. Lord Karel Krajíř of Krajek had first place among the Unity lords, and Lord John Žerotín, the foremost Brethren's lord in Moravia, was also there.26†

The assembly was a swirl of political and religious pull and tug. The Utraquist nobles first considered the Augsburg Confession as a basis for agreement, but soon agreed they needed a new "Bohemian Confession" using old Czech documents and the Four Articles of Prague as its basis, thus keeping their Hussite roots intact.27 Some of the Catholic nobility saw religious cooperation as good for national unity, and "understood the need for goodwill among the estates without distinction of confession."28 As for the Unity, its leaders mistrusted the Utraquists and were uneasy about religious decisions being made by a political legislature. Bishop Kálef advised Unity members of the assembly not to rush into anything but rather to "stay in the calm."29 Ironically, the Catholics' archbishop and the Utraquist religious leaders were no happier than the Brethren about the nobles' taking the theological lead. For the Catholic clergy nothing short of a complete return to Rome would do.30

---

* These were nobles who were strictly Lutheran, not just Utraquists who had inclination or openness to Lutheran views. As yet there was little formal Lutheran church organization in Bohemia.

† This assembly was for Bohemia only, but Žerotín had estates in Bohemia and so was entitled to attend. Since the Unity was still illegal thanks to the 1508 Mandate of St. James, its lords and knights were listed in the government records as Utraquists.

Playing a double game in the assembly's proceedings was King Maximilian. He told the Utraquists and Unity he favored their interests but assured the Catholics he would not give up anything that would jeopardize Rome's position. He showed an interest in the Unity's confession, but when Unity representatives gave him a copy he used it to make the Utraquists fear the Unity was going behind its allies' back to get its own confession recognized. Unity leaders saw what was going on just in time. On their part the Utraquists were fair enough to agree that the Unity's confession would be used with other documents in preparation of the new confession.[31]

For the Unity, the question was whether it should maintain an independent existence in Bohemia. And if it became part of a "national" church, what would its relation be to the Unity in Moravia and Poland? Anything more than a sort of federation of churches, such as had been worked out in Poland, would raise severe qualms within the Unity. Although it had joined in the Consensus of Sandomierz* in Poland, there the Unity was on a more equal footing with the Lutherans and Calvinists. In Bohemia the Unity was a minority, and it feared being swallowed up by the Utraquist majority. In addition, the Unity leaders remained very uneasy about secular lords interfering in religious matters, much less drafting a confession of faith. On the other hand, to refuse to participate would benefit only the Catholic party.[32]

Proceedings in the assembly were slow and tedious, and the project threatened to fall apart more than once. Finally, though, with the help of several theologians, a document, the Bohemian Confession, was worked out that drew much of its structure and wording from the Augsburg Confession but also incorporated some phrases from the Reformed Helvetic and Heidelberg Confessions. It was far more Protestant in expression than previous documents of the Utraquist Church.[33] However, true to its Czech reform heritage, the Bohemian

---

* Indeed, the example of Sandomierz was known at the assembly, and one noble distributed 20 copies of the consensus. See Müller, 2:445.

Confession affirmed salvation by faith, but also stressed works as the fruits of faith. The Unity's confession may have had some influence here and there, but its main contribution was in the spirit of the document, which did not include condemnations of other viewpoints, as most of the other confessions did. Significantly, the section on secular authority speaks of subjects' duty to obey their superiors, but it does not deal with the lords' responsibilities to subjects and church discipline for themselves.[34*] The old Unity would have insisted on emphasizing the lords' responsibilities and discipline.

On 18 May 1575, after the Utraquists had

Předmluwa.

John Blahoslav's translation of the New Testament was a gift to the Unity and the Czech people. He signed this copy of the preface: Jan Blahoslav.

assured the Unity that it could keep its own confession and church order in addition to the new document,[35] representatives of both churches presented the Bohemian Confession to Maximilian.[36] The Utraquist religious administration, as opposed to Utraquist political leaders, was not enthusiastic about the confession, but like the Unity's Inner Council, felt it had to agree.[37] The king-emperor did not formally endorse the document, but gave only a verbal

---

* After all, the nobles were the driving force behind the confession.

promise, supposedly binding on his son and heir Rudolf also, that he would not hinder anyone's religion or allow others to do so.[38]

The Unity, the Utraquists, and the Lutheran nobles took Maximilian's comments in a favorable light. On the strength of his unspecific verbal assurances, Bohemia's national assembly agreed to accept Maximilian's son and heir as king of Bohemia.[39] The whole endeavor of the Bohemian Confession was driven by the nobility, and the king's response was conditioned by his political agenda. It was not a grass-roots movement enthusiastically supported by the common people of the Unity or of the Utraquist Church either.[40] The Bohemian Confession expanded the religious toleration worked out by the Catholics and Utraquists in their 1485 agreement to now include Lutherans and the Unity. This was also a political decision by the Utraquists, for they were closer theologically to the Catholics than they were to the Unity or the Lutherans. Many Utraquist nobles were willing to make theological adjustments for the sake of a wider political alliance,[41] particularly as the Catholic Counter-Reformation continued to develop.

If any in the Unity thought the Bohemian Confession meant official recognition and easier times for their church, they soon learned their mistake. Not only did Maximilian forbid the public printing of the confession,* but he also specifically reaffirmed the Mandate of St. James against the Unity and issued decrees forbidding its worship services. This time, the Unity's newfound allies among the Utraquist nobility lived up to their agreements with the Unity, and protested Maximilian's actions. They also afforded members of the Unity protection in several places. They reminded the king that all who held to the Bohemian Confession were "not to be hindered" in their religion. They also warned the king that if he persisted in moves against the Unity, his word could not be trusted in the

---

* To be fair, he did not allow Archbishop Brus to publish all of the decrees of the Catholic Council of Trent either. See David, *The Middle Way*, 194.

future by anyone. Maximilian, having gotten what he wanted from the national assembly (taxes and confirmation of his heir) was not unduly worried. After all, the Utraquist, Lutheran, and Unity nobles may have assumed Maximilian's agreement to their petitions for recognition and toleration, but he actually had promised very little. The Bohemian Confession was not the law of the land. Maximilian was thus a severe disappointment to Utraquists and members of the Unity alike, and when he died the next year, 1576, at only 50 years of age, "there was no lack of voices which spoke of divine punishment against the sovereign who deceived his subjects by his royal word."[42]

Notes

[1] Joseph Th. Müller, *Geschichte der Böhmischen Brüder* 3 vols. (Herrnhut: Missionsbuchhandlung, 1922, 1931), 2:371-73. Rudolf Říčan, *The History of the Unity of Brethren*, trans. C. Daniel Crews (Bethlehem, Pa.: Department of Publications and Communications, Moravian Church, Northern Province, 1992), 251.

[2] Říčan, 220.

[3] Müller, 2:381.

[4] Müller, 2:374.

[5] Müller, 2:378.

[6] See above, Chapter 7.

[7] Říčan, 251-52.

[8] Details on the Sandomierz agreement are from Müller, 2:135-43, and Říčan, 244-46.

[9] Říčan, 245.

[10] Říčan, 246.

[11] Aleksander Brükner, "The Polish Reformation in the Sixteenth Century," in *Polish Civilization: Essays and Studies*, ed. Mieczysław Giergielewicz (New York: New York University Press, 1979), 80. See also Jerzy Kłoczowski, "Some Remarks on the Social and Religious History of Sixteenth-Century Poland," in *The Polish Renaissance in its European Context*, ed. Samuel Fiszman (Bloomington: Indiana University Press, 1988), 99.

[12] Müller, 3:146-48.

[13] Říčan, 252.

[14] Müller, 2:383-85.

[15] Müller, 2:376.

[16] Müller, 2:422-23.

17 The fullest treatment of Blahoslav to date is Miloš Štrupl, "John Blahoslav: Father and Charioteer of the Lord's People in the Unitas Fratrum," *Czechoslovakia Past and Present*, vol. 2, ed. M. Rechcigl (The Hague: 1968), 1232-46. A mimeographed manuscript of this is in the Moravian Archives, Winston-Salem, N.C. See also Říčan, 208-12, 252, and Müller, 2:420-22.

18 Říčan, 253.

19 Müller, 2:408-9. Müller says the difference in the 1561 and 1564 versions is that Blahoslav used his own New Testament translation for scriptural citations in 1564.

20 Říčan, 253.

21 Müller, 2:417-18.

22 Říčan, 254. Müller, 2:425-32, has all the ins and outs of these dealings.

23 Müller, 2:433-34.

24 Zdeněk David V., "Utraquists, Lutherans, and the Bohemian Confession of 1575," *Church History* 68 (1999): 294-336.

25 Říčan, 255. Lissa Folio 14 records these events in great detail. Andrew Slaby's translation of it fills 10 notebooks. The translation is housed at the Moravian Archives, Bethlehem, Pa.

26 Říčan, 255. Müller, 2:436-37.

27 Říčan, 255-56.

28 Říčan, 255.

29 Amedeo Molnár, "The Czech Confession of 1575," *Communio Viatorum* 16 (1973): 241-47, esp. 245.

30 Zdeněk V. David, *Finding the Middle Way: The Utraquists' Liberal Challenge to Rome and Luther* (Washington, D.C.: Woodrow Wilson Center Press, 2003), 177, 188. Říčan, 255.

31 Říčan, 256-57.

32 Müller, 2:438-40. Říčan, 256.

33 David, *Finding the Middle Way*, 333, 336. David asserts it was essentially a Lutheran document. He also says, 481, where the confession deviated from the Augsburg Confession, it was to accommodate the Brethren, not the Utraquists.

34 Říčan, 258. Müller, 2:446-48.

35 Jindřich Halama, Jr., "The Doctrinal Development of the Unity of Czech Brethren in the Light of their Confessions," *Communio Viatorum* 44, special issue, (2002), 128-44. See esp. 141.

36 Molnár, 241-47.

37 David, *Finding the Middle Way*, 182.

38 David, *Finding the Middle Way*, 190-91.

39 Říčan, 259.

40 David, *Finding the Middle Way*, 168.

41 David, *Finding the Middle Way*, 196-97.

42 Říčan, 260. Müller, 2:473-79.

Chapter 16

Troublesome Times

Between a Catholic Rock and a Lutheran Hard Place:
The Unity Leans toward the Calvinists,
1576-1600

aximilian's death in 1576 brought his son, Rudolf II, to the throne of Bohemia.* This did not bode well for the Unity and other non-Catholics, for Rudolf had been brought up and educated by the Jesuits in Spain. Historian Říčan observes he was "somewhat removed from the German scene, and a total stranger to the Czech situation."[1] He had no experience with Protestants and knew them only as abominable heretics.[2] He was gifted in many ways, and devoted to the arts and sciences, but was very withdrawn personally and later had bouts of insanity. He also preferred to leave actual governing to his appointed officials, so long as they provided him the illusion of having the last word.

Most of the officials Rudolf appointed were fervent Catholics who worked for the restoration of Bohemia and Moravia to the Catholic camp. They opposed attempts by the Utraquists to carry forward the reorganization of their church as envisioned at the time of the Bohemian Confession (1575). To this end the king appointed members to the Utraquist consistory who were

---

* Rudolf had been named king in 1575, but did not begin to rule until his father's death. Rudolf also became Holy Roman emperor at this time, and had already ascended to the throne of Hungary (1572).

sympathetic to Rome. Utraquists always thought of themselves as "good Catholics," but the new consistory was thoroughly opposed to anything smacking of Protestantism.[3]

Rudolf and his counselors soon took more direct action to turn the Czech lands back to Catholicism. The Jesuits were the prime agents of the Catholic Counter-Reformation throughout Europe.[*] They had had a presence in Prague since 1556, but now the papal nuncio and the Spanish ambassador, who had great influence on Rudolf, urged that the Jesuits' activities be expanded in the Czech lands. The head of the Jesuits in 1577 devised a plan to restore a Catholic majority in Bohemia and Moravia. By planting colleges and other high quality schools throughout the land, they sought to win influence over the attending noble students and their parents.[4] The Jesuits reasoned that if they could instruct a child for a few years, that child would leave their school as a committed Roman Catholic.

These peaceful measures would be supplemented by more direct means against the "heretics" as opportunity presented itself. This was just a decade before Spanish King Philip II sent the Armada (1588) to crush English Protestants. Bohemia was not yet ripe for military measures, but it might be in the future. Meanwhile, the Unity could be a target for direct suppression since it was smaller and politically weaker than the Utraquist majority. Besides, to Catholic eyes, the Unity was the worst of heretics in Bohemia.[5] Efforts were again made to ban it from royal cities, but as before, sympathetic local officials did not carry out these decrees very harshly.[6] The 1508 Mandate of St. James was republished, but Utraquist nobles generally kept to their 1575 agreements with the Unity and spoke up for its members.[7]

The Jesuits mounted a theological attack on the Unity by appointing Wenceslas Šturm, a Czech member of their order, to study the Unity's documents in order to find the best ways to attack it. He applied himself to the task and brought out a

---

[*] Catholic writers generally prefer "Catholic Reformation" to "Counter-Reformation."

series of booklets ridiculing the Brethren's theology and denying the validity of their ministry. The Unity maintained a dignified silence to most of the charges. Then Šturm took on the Unity's hymnal of 1576. He said it was a beautifully printed book. He even liked the tunes, and admitted that Unity members sang them well and with fervor. However, he said, the book's hymn texts were full of heresy. That *did* provoke a passionate response from the Unity's elders.[8]*

In the years leading to 1600 it was educational and social pressure that the Jesuits and other Catholics brought to bear which had the most success in winning many Czechs to obedience to Rome. Their schools were a success, and many students left them with a thoroughly Roman perspective. In addition, with the ascension of Rudolf, contacts between the Czech lands and Catholic Spain and Austria increased. Many Czech nobles married Czech or Austrian Catholic wives, or arranged such marriages for their children. These included Utraquist and even a few Unity nobles. In the mid 1500s most Czech Catholic nobles had been willing to co-exist with

John Kálef, who took even the nobility to task.

the Protestants for the stability of the country. Now a more militant form of Catholicism was coming in, and these foreign spouses worked industriously to convert their husbands and to get them to further the Catholic cause. It also became apparent

---

* The 1576 edition of the Unity's Czech hymnal was identical in content to the editions of 1561 and 1564. It was even more richly decorated than those, and is considered one of the most beautiful examples of Czech books from the 16th century.

that only Catholic nobles were going to get advancement in the new administration, and this encouraged conversions as well.[9]

The most serious loss to the Unity was its major center of Mladá Boleslav. The Krajíř family had long protected the Unity on this estate. Relations with this noble family were not always smooth, as when Bishop John Kálef excommunicated the sister of Lord Adam Krajíř for immorality, and then (1577) Lord Adam himself for drunkenness and a wild party thrown at the castle.* Still, the family remained the Unity's protectors. When Lord Adam died as the last male member of his line, his widow, Marta of Veselice, became a Catholic and sold the estate to a zealous Catholic who brought in the Jesuits. The Unity Lord Peter Vok and members of the Žerotín family persuaded the new owner to sell the property to a Lutheran, who allowed the Unity to return. Just after the turn of the century, however, Mladá Boleslav was made a royal city, the Unity was expelled, and its property confiscated.[10]

In Moravia freedom of religion remained more widespread than in Bohemia, and the Unity was not encumbered with so many measures against it. Even in Moravia, though, Charles (Karel) Žerotín was ousted from his government offices because of "slanders and accusations" made against him by supporters of the Catholic Church.[11]

In Poland the Jesuits and others waged a strong campaign to win back those who had embraced Protestantism. It had never gained a real foothold among the Polish people, and many nobles now returned to the traditional fold. In their weakened state, Polish Protestants eventually bowed to pressure from their remaining nobles to have talks with the Eastern Orthodox to make a common front against Catholic expansion. The discussions had little chance of success from a theological point of view. In addition, the later Brest-Litovsk Union (1596) meant that most of the Orthodox in Poland were

---

* Lord Adam took his exclusion well and did not take measures against the Unity. Instead he stayed home on Sundays and read to his personal servants from Augusta's *Summovník* book of sermons.

again in communion with Rome. That union was short lived, and the Protestant-Orthodox dialogue in Poland came to nothing as well. In these years also, Polish Lutherans became more aggressive and less cooperative with the Unity and Polish Reformed; however, a synod in Toruň in 1595 did renew the ecumenical Consensus of Sandomierz.12

In Bohemia the increased activity of the Jesuits and royal support for them pointed up the need for greater cooperation among Protestant churches. More agreements like the Consensus of Sandomierz and the Bohemian Confession were badly needed. But just as greater cooperation was urgent, the rift between the Lutheran and Reformed Churches widened, mainly because of a growing rift within the Lutheran Church.

Hard-line Flacians, or gnesio-Lutherans as they are also called,* insisted on a "pure" Lutheranism to the exclusion of all other viewpoints. They opposed the "Philippists," followers of Philip Melancthon, an associate of Luther. This latter group was a bit more open to variety of opinion on some doctrinal points, such as the precise wording of the doctrine of Christ's real presence in the sacrament. In some ways they were closer to the Calvinists than were the gnesio-Lutherans. In fact, because he was friendly to Calvin and willing to discuss predestination and other matters with some appreciation of Calvin's views, Melancthon himself had been labeled a "Crypto-Calvinist" by the gnesio-Lutherans. The Unity generally found the Philippists more congenial, particularly since the Unity had not had an easy time with gnesio-Lutherans in Prussia and Poland.13

Lutherans were divided on which line to take, and many felt the rift could not continue. In 1577 theologians from both camps crafted the Formula of Concord, which henceforth would define positions that made one a Lutheran or not. In

---

* "Flacians" got their name from Matthias Flacius (d. 1575), who asserted the need for strict doctrinal orthodoxy among Lutherans. "Gnesio-Lutherans" means "original" or "real" Lutherans. These are two names for the same group.

1580, for the 50th anniversary of the Augsburg Confession, the formula was gathered together with the confession and other confessional documents into the Book of Concord.[14] The documents in the Book of Concord were and remain the confessional standard of Lutherans.[15] The problem for the Unity was that from this time on most Lutherans took the Book of Concord not just as *an* accurate statement of Christian doctrine, but as *the* expression of doctrine to which all should conform (and to no other). The Unity was not willing to give up its own confessions. Even the Lutherans of Great Poland, though they liked the Formula of Concord, delayed signing it because it undermined the inter-confessional Consensus of Sandomierz.[16]

These Lutheran developments offended the Utraquists.[17] The Unity too was disturbed at increasing Lutheran exclusivity, especially since the gnesio-Lutherans had already gotten the Philippist teachers excluded from the University of Wittenberg in 1574. Though many of the Unity's clergy considered Wittenberg their *alma mater*, henceforth its doors were closed to the Unity's students. The Lutheran universities at Königsberg and Tübingen were also off limits. A few students from Poland had already gone to the Reformed University of Heidelberg for their training. Now students from Bohemia and Moravia went there too, as well as to Reformed universities in Geneva and Herborn.[18]

Many in the Unity were worried by the turn of events. Bishop John Aeneas mourned: "Already the Augsburg Confession and the Reformed churches are torn apart. We will now have to declare for one or the other."* Given the circumstances, the Unity aligned more with the Calvinists from now on.

In many ways this was a natural and congenial development for the Unity. In Geneva, Theodor Beza (d. 1605), Calvin's successor, and other Calvinist theologians such as Johann

---

* Říčan, 264, who adds (though it is not clear if these are his words or a continuation of Br. Aeneas): "Neutrals come off the worst in dispute."

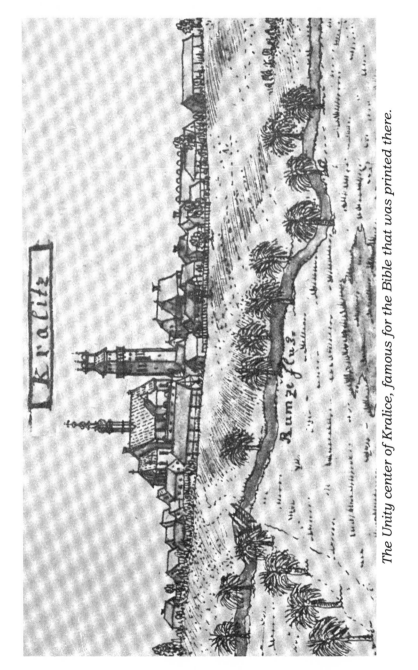

The Unity center of Kralice, famous for the Bible that was printed there.

Jacob Grynaeus (d. 1617) and Amandus Polanus (d. 1610), cultivated personal relationships with the Unity's students and future leaders. Among the Unity's lay leaders, more of its nobles began sending their sons on educational and cultural journeys to Switzerland, Holland, and England, where they made friendships among the Reformed. In addition, as they became less welcome in their own homeland, sons of the German Reformed began attending the Unity's schools in Ivančice and elsewhere. Some of these relationships resulted in lifelong friendship and correspondence, which often made up for minor doctrinal differences. Besides, the nature of Calvinism spoke more agreeably to the Unity than Lutheranism often did.[19]

Both the Unity and the Calvinists laid great stress on the Scriptures as expressing the will of God, which is to be followed in joyful surrender. Their doctrines on the holy communion were not identical, but members of the Unity could feel more comfortable with Calvinist expressions that affirmed the real but not a literal physical presence of the body and blood of Christ in the sacrament. The Unity preferred to hold simply to Christ's words of institution without elaboration, and valued the concept derived from the Taborites that Christ is present "spiritually, powerfully, and truly." That was not too far from Calvinist belief. The worship patterns of the Unity and the Calvinists were compatible, both stressing simplicity and retaining few of the medieval liturgical forms found among the Lutherans. An emphasis on Christian discipline and lay participation in congregational government was also shared by the Unity and the Reformed. Historian Müller summarizes: "In their constitution, congregational organization, discipline, and forms of worship, along with their strong biblical, earnest, moderate, rational, and world-renouncing character, the Unity was essentially related to Calvinism."[20]

The Unity and Calvinists did not agree on everything. The Brethren found the Calvinists' interest in predestination too speculative. On the descent of Christ into hell, which was a hot theological topic for a while in the latter 1500s, the Calvinists tended to spiritualize it, while the Unity (with the Lutherans this time) tended to take it more literally.[21] The Unity was also more suspicious of secular authorities' interfering in church life, and did not hold with national or regional churches to which everyone had to belong, as the Calvinists (and Lutherans) did. Still, on many topics the Unity and the Calvinists could form a true fellowship.

Closer connections with the Reformed sometimes proved too close for the Unity's comfort. In 1577 Reformed leaders invited the Unity to a meeting in Heidelberg looking toward a union agreement. It caused Unity leaders some embarrassment, since they had agreements with the Utraquists in Bohemia and with the Lutherans in Poland. But then the Reformed in Great Poland pointed out that they could not participate in the meeting because of their own agreement with the Polish Lutherans in the Consensus of Sandomierz. This saved the Unity from having to make a potentially offensive response to the German Reformed.[22]

A similar embarrassing situation arose when the Reformed in Geneva in 1581 printed a collection, called *Harmonia*, of the confessions of faith of the various Reformed churches. It included the Unity's confession as if the Unity were one of the Reformed churches. Not knowing what to do, the Unity elders did not answer Calvinist Beza's request for comments on the publication. The Reformed did not take the hint, and subsequent editions of the *Harmonia* continued to include the Unity's confession.[23]

Many in the Unity valued Reformed thought. George Strejc in 1595 made a Czech translation of Calvin's *Institutes*, and the Unity in Poland used the Reformed catechism. Several of the younger clergy were quite Calvinist in speaking of the holy communion.[24] At times they went so far that Simeon Theophilus Turnovský, one of the Unity's sharpest theologians, attempted to put the brakes on the turn to Calvinism.

Turnovský had been brought to Poland from Bohemia as a child at the time of the 1548 persecution, and had been

mentored by George Izrael, the Unity's pioneer leader there.*
Izrael sent him to Bohemia so he could get to know Bishop
Augusta. Over the years, Turnovský developed into a minister
dedicated to the "preservation of the dogmatic character of the
old Unity."25 As Blahoslav had defended Unity insights against
the Lutherans, now Turnovský defended them against the
Calvinists. It was not that he was taking a Lutheran as
opposed to a Calvinist position, but he genuinely wished for
the Unity to appreciate its own theological heritage. The Unity
valued Turnovský, and he served on the Inner Council and
later as a bishop and "judge" of the Unity. However, the rest of
the Inner Council thought some of his opinions were too anti-
Calvinist, and refused to allow their publication. As a servant
of the church, Turnovský submitted to this decision, but he
continued to champion the Unity's theological heritage. We
must remember that although many in the Unity were
becoming more Calvinist in orientation, its leaders did not
want the Unity to be absorbed by Reformed Church any more
than they wanted it to be swallowed up by the Lutherans.26

During this last quarter of the 16th century the bishops
and other members of the Inner Council tried to provide sound
and careful leadership in the midst of external threats and
theological developments within the Unity.† As a group, though
they were dedicated and certainly not without courage (as

---

* The Turnovský family felt at home in Poland, and Simeon Theo-
philus's nephew John, who also entered the Unity's ministry, used
the Polish spelling: Turnowski.
† Serving as bishops as the period opened were George Izrael
(consecrated 1557; died 1588), Andrew Štefan (consecrated 1571;
died 1577), John Kálef (consecrated 1571; died 1588), and John
Lorenc (consecrated 1571; died 1587). Following the death of
Bishop Štefan in 1577, Zacharias of Litomyšl (d. 1590) and John
Aeneas (d. 1594) were elected. In 1587 John Abdias (d. 1588) and
Simeon Theophilus Turnovský (d. 1608) were added to the bishops'
roster. John Ephraim (d. 1600) and Paul Jessen (d. 1594) were
elected in 1589. In 1594 Jacob Narcissus (d. 1611) and John
Němčanský (d. 1598) were consecrated. Finally, in 1599 Samuel
Sušický (d. 1599 after serving only six weeks) and Zacharias Ariston
(d. 1606) were chosen.

when Bishop Kálef excluded members of the powerful Krajíř family from communion), they lacked the personal charisma of a Luke of Prague, a John Augusta, or a John Blahoslav, although Simeon Theophilus Turnovský comes close.

The Unity had some solid accomplishments during this time. In Lipník, for example, a new sbor with twin towers in the Renaissance style was built. It has been called "the most beautiful Brethren's building in Moravia."27

It was in literary productions, though, that the Unity really excelled as the 16th century drew to a close. Without doubt, the greatest of these was the Kralice Bible.* It gets its name from the Unity's print shop in Kralice, which served as the Unity's main press after it was moved there from Ivančice in 1578. There had been Czech translations of the Scriptures before, but the Unity aimed to bring out a translation of the entire Bible based on the best available texts in the original languages. For this, the translators consulted the Catholic Antwerp Polyglot (1569-72), the Basel Bible (1545), as well as modern Latin versions, such as the Heidelberg text (1575-79). Pastoral as well as scholarly concerns were important also. Where older Czech translations did not accurately represent the sense of the original, the texts were altered. Where the traditional version was essentially correct, it was not changed. (Remember that Unity members, particularly those who could not afford expensive books, regularly committed large portions of Scripture to memory. There was no point in disturbing those unless necessary.)28

Bishop Andrew Štefan began and oversaw the work until his death in 1577. Bishop John Aeneas then assumed leadership in the project. The majority of the work fell to Br. Isaiah Cepola, whom we met earlier in discussing the translation of the Unity's confession. He was assisted by Nicholas Albrecht of Kamének, who knew Hebrew, and by Luke Helic, a Unity

---

* This name has been used only since the 19th century. Before that, it was known simply as the "Brethren's Bible."

The title page to volume one of the Kralice Bible.
Note the "Moravian seal," the Lamb of God, at the top.

priest of Jewish extraction who had been recalled from Poland to help in the work.

Part one (the five books of Moses) was published in 1579; part two (Joshua to Esther), in 1580; and part three (the poetical books), in 1582. The death of Br. Cepola and Lord John of Žerotín (who was the patron of the project) caused a delay until 1587, when part four (the prophetical books) appeared. Part five (the Apocrypha) was published in 1588.* With this, the Old Testament was complete.

Bishop John Blahoslav had already done a fine Czech translation of the Greek New Testament. This was published in a new edition in 1594. It contained many small changes to Blahoslav's text (but none affecting the meaning significantly). A commentary similar to those of the other volumes was also added.† Thus the Unity produced a complete translation of the Scriptures from 1579 through 1594.‡

The Kralice Bible quickly assumed among Czech Protestants the status held by the King James Bible in English. That is, it became the recognized and favorite standard translation for generations. To them it *was* the word of God. Its text was even adopted by the Lutherans in Slovakia.§ As a literary work it excels also. Historian Říčan summarizes:

---

* The early Unity had used the Catholic canon of Scripture including the apocryphal books. By now the Unity knew that these were not in the Jewish canon and did not count them as inspired in the same way as the other books of the Bible. Unity members still liked the apocryphal books, however, and Unity preachers still drew sermon illustrations from them, so they were included as a separate volume in the translation.

† As might be expected, the commentaries evidence a Calvinist viewpoint. The materials in general exhibit a copious scholarly use of religious literature of the time.

‡ Říčan, 271, notes that the title page says 1593, but the final volume came out the following year. A one-volume edition without the introductions and commentaries was published in 1596.

§ Slovakia has its own language, which is very close to Czech. Presumably the Slovak Lutherans did not also adopt the Calvinist-leaning commentaries.

As the standard of pure Czech, refined after the
example of Blahoslav, the Brethren's Bible stood for
generations as the rule of proper language and as one
of the most important sources of the Czech language's
rebirth at the beginning of the nineteenth century.[29]

Along with the Kralice Bible, the Unity's Czech hymnal of
1576 (discussed above) stands as a supreme example of
beautiful Czech 16th-century printing. Another folio edition
was printed in Kralice in 1581. Smaller (quarto) versions
appeared in 1583, 1594, and 1598. All have the same contents
as the 1561 Czech hymnal. The many printings show how
important the hymnal was for the Unity in its worship, private
devotions, and instruction of children.[30] In fact in 1579 an
octavo "shorter church hymnal" was published containing 247
of the "most important" hymns from the big hymnal. Its preface
says it was issued so "the poor can buy it more easily."[31]

The Unity did not neglect the hymnal needs of its German
members either. The 1566 German hymnal was reprinted in

*As the "King James Version" of the Bible did with the English
language, the Kralice Bible of the Brethren's Church set the
standard for the Czech language.*

1580 in Nürnberg. And in 1606 a new German hymnal for the Unity was printed in Kralice containing 377 hymns, including more from the German Lutheran tradition.[32]

In these years the Unity produced other publications to enrich its life and worship. Bishop Štefan in 1575 produced a book of sermons for the church year (*Výklad řečí Božích*). It appears that some of these sermons were copied or adapted from Luke of Prague. To these was added a sermon book (*Postila*) by Br. John Kapita in 1586. Other sample sermons circulated in manuscript. These were used to instruct ministerial students and pastors in preaching. Others also used them for personal devotions.[33] New service books (*Agenda*) for holy communion and baptism were also provided. These vary little from the versions prepared by Luke of Prague earlier in the century. The Inner Council also authorized a new Czech catechism.[34]

Interest in the Unity's history increased as outside pressures on it increased. One result of this interest was a document entitled *Historia Fratrum*, written perhaps by Bishop Kálef. George Izrael, John Lorenc, and Simeon Theophilus Turnovský produced writings on the Polish branch of the Unity. Bishop John Aeneas and several colleagues continued the work begun by Bishops Blahoslav and Černý to collect copies of documents from the early days of the Unity. These were to become the new archives of the Unity, and care was especially taken to replace (where possible) the collection lost to fire in Litomyšl in the 1540s. This collection eventually grew to 14 volumes, with records extending to 1590. It is known as *Akty Jednota* (*The Acts of the Unity*). A companion to the *Akty* is the *Dekrety* (*Decrees*), which consists of minutes of synods and the Inner Council.[35]* Work continued also on the Unity's *Memorial Book*, which provides "paragraph biographies" of many ministers and leaders of the Unity through the years.† All of these, especially

---

* Work on the *Dekrety* was not carried out until 1617. The *Akty* and *Dekrety* form the basis of the Lissa Folios, of which more later.

† Most entries were appreciative and complimentary as might be expected. Others deal honestly with the foibles of individuals. For instance, the entry about one minister who caused problems says:

the three latter works, provide valuable sources for historical research on the Unity.

A Psalter compiled by George Strejc in 1587 was also an influential Unity publication of this period. It is a Czech poetic version of the Psalms set to melodies by the French composer Claude Goudimel (d. 1572).[36] The Inner Council resisted including it in the hymnal,* but it was published as a separate volume for use in private devotions. It was so popular it went through five printings in its first seven years. By 1615 the Inner Council gave in and included the Psalter as an appendix to the hymnal.

Acta Unitatis Fratrum — *the title page of volume VII of the Lissa Folios.*

Strejc himself provides a telling example of the changes that were multiplying as the century drew to a close. His use of French melodies speaks to the Unity's widening horizons. We have mentioned above his translation of Calvin's *Institutes* into Czech. In addition to producing rhymed Czech moral books for children, he was

---

"The elders were not greatly grieved about his death." See Říčan, 276-77.

* The council's resistance may have stemmed from the fact that the Psalter was not of Unity origin but a product of Calvinist Geneva.

also a competent writer of German hymn verses, which found acceptance in Germany as well as among the Unity's members.* We have seen that marriage for the Unity's clergy became common earlier in Poland than it did in Bohemia or Moravia.† While serving in Moravia, Strejc wanted to marry a woman who was not a member of the Unity. He knew the Inner Council would forbid the marriage or advise delay, so he simply went ahead and got married, and then told the council what he had done.‡ The Unity of earlier times would have expelled him, but now, within a few years (1577), he was made a member of the Inner Council.[37] In a couple of decades marriage for the clergy, bishops included, would become the norm.

As the new century drew near, the Unity was different from the Unity of 1500. It had not abandoned the essentials of its belief, but it had refined them through contact with Catholics, Utraquists, Lutherans, and Reformed (the last two groups did not even exist in 1500). It now had a Polish branch with its own bishop. The Unity in 1600 was much more in touch with the outside world, including its political and religious elements. Indeed, the Unity's confessions of faith were not produced so much for internal use as they were to let foreign theologians and politicians know what the Unity was about. As the Unity's noble members evolved from being simply "protectors" to playing an active role in shaping church policy, the Unity itself began to look more like other churches, though it tried to balance this with a new appreciation of its own heritage. The

---

* When writing in German he called himself Georg Vetter. Georg (George) is German for his Czech first name "Jiří." "Vetter" means "male cousin" in German. There is no Czech word "Strejc" (other than the name), but there is "strýc," which means "uncle." Why he chose "Vetter" rather than "Onkel" is a mystery unless he liked the sound of "Vetter" better. After all, it is still a male relative.

† In 1577 Bishop John Lorenc got married in Poland. So far as is known, he was the first bishop of the Unity to marry. This was too much for old George Izrael, the pioneer of the Unity's work in Poland. He returned to Moravia soon after Lorenc's marriage.

‡ This may be the first recorded instance of another unofficial modern Moravian Church maxim: "It's easier to get forgiveness than permission."

ongoing challenges of the next few years would bring both unexpected triumph and tragedy.

Notes

1 Rudolf Říčan, *The History of the Unity of Brethren*, trans. C. Daniel Crews (Bethlehem, Pa.: Department of Publications and Communications, Moravian Church, Northern Province, 1992), 279.

2 Joseph Th. Müller, *Geschichte der Böhmischen Brüder* 3 vols. (Herrnhut: Missionsbuchhandlung, 1922, 1931), 3:160.

3 Müller, 3:160. Zdeněk V. David, *Finding the Middle Way: The Utraquists' Liberal Challenge to Rome and Luther* (Washington, D.C.: Woodrow Wilson Center Press, 2003), 255, 267-68, sees the Utraquist consistory as remaining more independent. Müller, 3:161, asserts that by now most Utraquist nobles saw the consistory as a "historical relic."

4 Říčan, 279.

5 Müller, 3:161.

6 Říčan, 280. Müller, 3:169.

7 Říčan, 280.

8 Müller, 3:166.

9 Říčan, 280, 284-86.

10 Říčan, 283-285.

11 Říčan, 285.

12 Říčan, 287-93.

13 Müller, 3:151, 302. Říčan, 261-63.

14 A standard English translation is *The Book of Concord: The Confessions of the Evangelical Lutheran Church*, trans. and ed. Theodore G. Tappert (in association with Jaroslav Pelikan, Robert H. Fischer, and Arthur Piepkorn) (Philadelphia: Fortress Press, 1959).

15 A study of *The Book of Concord* from a Lutheran perspective is Willard Dow Allbeck, *Studies in the Lutheran Confessions*, second printing, revised, (Philadelphia: Fortress Press, 1968).

16 Říčan, 268.

17 David, 237-38.

18 Müller, 3:302.

19 Müller, 3:302. Říčan, 264-67.

20 Müller, 3:302.

21 Müller, 3:303-4.

22 Říčan, 268.

23 Říčan, 269. Müller, 3:302.

24 Müller, 3:303.

25 Říčan, 273.

26 Říčan, 273-75. Müller, 3:153-54, 303-4.

27 Říčan, 286.

28 Details on the Kralice Bible are from Říčan, 270-72, and Müller, 3:291-94.

29 Říčan, 272. This evaluation is shared by outside scholars as well, e.g., Josef Válka, "Rudolfine Culture," in *Bohemia in History*, ed. Mikuláš Teich (Cambridge: Cambridge University Press, 1998), 129.

30 Müller, 3:288.

31 Müller, 3:288.

32 Müller, 3:290.

33 Říčan, 272.

34 Müller, 3:294-96.

35 Miloš Štrupl, "John Blahoslav, Father and Charioteer of the Lord's People in the Unitas Fratrum," *Czechoslovakia Past and Present*, vol. 2, ed. M. Rechcigl (The Hague, 1968), 1232-46. A mimeographed manuscript of this is in the Moravian Archives, Winston-Salem, N.C. See typescript, 5. Říčan, 286. Müller, 3:281-82.

36 Říčan, 269

37 Říčan, 269-70. Müller, 3:285-87.

Chapter 17

Before the Fall

Free and Legal at Long Last
1600-1618

In 1600 the Unity had about 60 congregations in Bohemia, 90 in Moravia, and 40 in Poland. In addition, an unspecified number of dependent congregations, preaching places, and scattered fellowships were cared for from the main congregations. The number of members is harder to determine. Historian Říčan estimates conservatively that the Unity had 40,000 members in Bohemia and Moravia combined, and perhaps 5,000 to 10,000 in Poland.[1]* In any event, the percentage of Unity members in comparison to the national populations was quite small.† This is not surprising given that the Unity was so often persecuted and given the strict discipline it demanded of members. Among its adherents, however, the Unity had several members of the nobility whose wealth and power gave it a religious and political significance greater than its small size implied.

The first of these was Wenceslas Budovec of Budova (1551-1621).[2] He was from a Bohemian knightly family and traveled extensively in his youth. Budova was particularly interested in Eastern Christianity, though he was disappointed that the

---

* De Schweinitz, 225, has the Unity's membership at 200,000 already at the beginning of Luther's reformation in 1517.
† The total population of Bohemia at this period has been estimated at perhaps 3 million.

Orthodox were not open to Protestant ideas. He was convinced of the need for Christian unity, not just for religious reasons, but also to make a common stand against the Turks. After his return from his travels, Budova served as a councilor on Bohemia's court of appeals and began to win a reputation as an orator. He wrote numerous works in Latin and Czech on such topics as eschatology, recent Czech history, confessional polemics, and his travels. Budova showed Calvinistic influences in his theology, but in the Unity's tradition also especially stressed that faith was to be lived out in one's actions. His calling was politician, not minister, though some of his impassioned discourses in Bohemia's national assembly at times turned into sermons. He held that differences dividing the evangelical churches were "non-essential," and in time he became the leading spokesman for the Unity, the Utraquists, and Lutherans and Calvinists alike. Budova, historian Říčan observes, was "a new type of person in the Unity."[3]

Another "new type" of member in the Unity was Peter Vok of Rožmberk. He entered the Unity in 1582, presumably because his wife, Kateřina of Ludanice, was a member. His joining the Unity greatly upset his family, which was a leading Catholic anti-Hussite power. The king was not pleased either, and the Unity assumed that the re-issuance of the Mandate of St. James in 1584 was partly in response to Vok's defection. In many ways his membership in the Unity was a mixed blessing. He was a wealthy noble, whose interests included soldiering and jousting. He found the Unity's discipline chafing and returned to the Catholic Church for a while. The majority of Vok's household remained faithful to the Unity, however, and Unity minister Matthias Cyrus had a good influence on him through personal conversations. For the Unity, Vok was "a difficult member," but his financial and political support proved invaluable. His friendship and protection did much to make up for the loss of the Krajířs of Mladá Boleslav after that noble family died out.[4]*

---

* See previous chapter.

A third influential member of the Unity among the nobility was Charles the Elder of Žerotín (1564-1636). He came from a very wealthy Unity family in Moravia, and his father John had long protected the Unity and supported its literary work. Like Budova, Charles had traveled widely, studying at least briefly in the universities at Strasbourg, Heidelberg, Basel, Geneva, and Orléans. He was a friend of Henry of Navarre (d. 1610) and had fought in Henry's army. This was while Henry was still a Protestant before he decided, "Paris is worth a Mass," and converted to Catholicism to gain the French throne. Charles of Žerotín also visited the Netherlands, and in England attended the court of Queen Elizabeth I (d. 1603). He was well known for his mastery of courtly etiquette and graces. As a true renaissance man, he knew several languages and was well read in theology. In spite of frequent illnesses, Žerotín took an active role in Moravian politics and worked for cooperation among the various religious bodies. Catholic "slanders" caused his removal from his political posts in 1602, and he temporarily retired from public life, embittered that his Evangelical "friends" had not stood up for him more. Concern for national and religious freedom induced him to emerge from seclusion in 1607, and he became a powerful statesman in the events that unfolded, but true to his Unity heritage, he worried about how much military force could legitimately be used for religious ends.[5]

The Unity needed these powerful advocates in the wider world, for King-Emperor Rudolf II was becoming increasingly erratic. He had worried the Unity, the Utraquists, and Lutherans and Calvinists for years, and now his conduct was distressing his Catholic subjects in his various domains.

Hungary was particularly troubling. The Turks occupied the center of the country, and Rudolf controlled only a narrow strip on its western border along with its dependent state of Slovakia. Transylvania passed back and forth between Christian and Islamic control. In this nervous situation, Rudolf in 1603-04 launched a program aimed at suppressing the Protestants in these areas. The Catholic nobility, however, saw this as a first step in suppressing their own rights in favor of imperial absolutism. The Hungarian nobles, led by Stephen Bocskay (d. 1606), rose in revolt. Bocskay's army entered Moravia, and at first the non-Catholics welcomed him as almost another Žižka, though they did not join in the revolt. But the Hungarian rebels devastated the land and damaged several of the Unity's buildings. Bloodshed stopped with the Peace of Vienna in 1606 when the Hungarian nobles forced Rudolf to guarantee religious and civil rights to both Protestants and Catholics.[6]*

Other members of Rudolf's Hapsburg dynasty feared that his future conduct might threaten their own thrones as well. His brother Matthias negotiated with nobles in Hungary and Austria, and persuaded them to abandon allegiance to Rudolf. With a large army, Matthias then threatened to move on Moravia and Bohemia in 1608 to force Rudolf to abdicate.[7] After receiving a verbal promise of religious freedom, the Moravian nobles acknowledged Matthias as ruler. Charles Žerotín was appointed "captain of the country." In Bohemia, however, Budova and others persuaded the nobles to remain loyal to Rudolf after they had forced a similar oral promise of religious toleration out of him as well as certain other privileges for themselves.[8]

To raise military funding for use against Matthias, Rudolf had to call a meeting of Bohemia's national assembly in 1608. Knowing Rudolf's avowed intention of bringing all Bohemians back into the Roman Church, Utraquist and Unity nobles insisted that the national religious question be placed on the agenda. Some Utraquists wanted only a guarantee for themselves and the Catholics, but others saw more was required. The Unity had strong political leaders, and many Utraquists, particularly those with Lutheran leanings, felt that only a united front could protect them all against the continuing Catholic

---

* It was actually Rudolf's brother Matthias who negotiated this treaty, as well as the companion treaty of Szitvatorok with Turkish Sultan Ahmed I.

Vok   Žerotín

Three Unity Noblemen: Peter Vok gave much financial and political support. Charles Žerotín counseled against rebellion against the king. Wenceslas Budova gave his life for his faith.

Budova

Counter-Reformation. The Unity's Budova took a leading role. To him, a common Christian faith was important, but complete agreement on ceremonies, etc., was not required. He cited the Polish Consensus of Sandomierz in this regard. For him, the Unity and Utraquists were like the various monastic orders that existed together in the one Roman Church, *i.e.*, "he saw this only as a variety but not an opposition of orders."[9] Budova insisted that recognition and legality be granted to all who subscribed to the Bohemian Confession of 1575. He drew up a list of 25 demands to accomplish this, and the majority of nobles signed it.[10]

This put Rudolf into a dilemma. The last thing he wanted was to recognize heretics, especially the noxious "Picards." On the other hand, if he did not get his requested funding from the assembly to oppose Matthias, then Rudolf would not have a throne from which to recognize anything. He agreed to place the religious question on the agenda, but said the current crisis would take up the entire session. The religious debate would have to wait until next year's session in 1609.[11] Meantime, Rudolf managed to work out a treaty with Matthias in which Matthias got Hungary, Austria, and Moravia. Rudolf kept Bohemia, and remained as Holy Roman emperor, but was much weakened politically.

When the next session of the national assembly opened in January 1609, Count Budova* spoke for the Unity, Count Henry Thurn represented the Lutheran lords, and Count Joachim Šlik represented the Utraquists. These presented their demands, which Rudolf at first rejected, claiming that Catholics and Utraquists alone were permitted in Bohemia. He said Lutherans and especially the Unity should join one of those churches. In spite of efforts by some Catholic officials to split the various churches, the nobles held firm, insisting that all of their groups should be recognized. In time a new national church order would be worked out, but for now all who acknowledged the Bohemian Confession of 1575 would

---

* By now he had been promoted from knight to count.

be legally recognized as "those who give communion in two kinds."* The Utraquists' consistory would be remade into a national consistory, and the Unity would have representation in it, but the king would surrender all rights to appoint members of the new consistory as well as officials of the University of Prague.[12]

Rudolf tried everything he could think of to avoid agreeing to these demands. During the Easter break in the sessions in April he sought assistance from Catholic princes in Germany. None was forthcoming. He considered a military option, but found he did not have enough troops loyal to him to make the attempt. When he declared that the religious situation in Bohemia would remain as it was in the past, the nobles threatened open insurrection. At last he gave in.

On 9 July 1609 the king-emperor signed the decree of religious freedom known as the "Letter of Majesty."† The decree gave legal recognition and freedom to practice their religion to all who subscribed to the Bohemian Confession of 1575. This applied not only to the nobles on their estates, but also to their peasants even if the noble was Catholic. These rights applied even to estates owned by the Catholic Church.[13] Conversely, Catholics living on Unity, Lutheran, or Utraquist estates also had guaranteed religious freedom. For the first time, inhabitants of royal cities could legally choose the church to which they wished to belong. Noble "defenders" and the new national consistory would be appointed to oversee compliance with the decree. The noble sponsors of the Letter of Majesty clearly expected the eventual formation of one Bohemian national evangelical church.

For the Unity, the decree of 1609 meant that for the first time in its history it had full legal recognition.[14] The Mandate

---

* This is exactly what "Utraquist" means, and as used here is the blanket meaning of the term which Bishop John Augusta had tried to use to prove that the Unity was "Utraquist" and therefore legal.

† In German the decree is called the "Majestätsbrief," meaning "Letter of Majesty." Some German dictionaries define the word as specifically denoting the 1609 Bohemian decree of religious freedom.

of St. James, which had plagued the Unity for a hundred years, was superseded. Written into the law of the land stood a document that granted religious rights to minorities, whether Protestant or Catholic, and the Utraquist majority voluntarily restrained itself from harming the minority. No wonder historian Říčan says: "This was one of the highest moments of Bohemian history."[15]

But Utopia had not arrived. Rudolf signed the decree only under duress, and would gladly rescind it given any excuse. Roman Catholic Church officials were not pleased, though most of the Bohemian Catholic nobility seemed willing to go along with it for the sake of stability in the land. It did have the support of most Unity and Utraquist nobles.[16]

Like the Bohemian Confession of 1575, on which it was based, the Letter of Majesty was largely hammered out by the political leaders of the respective churches. What about the religious leaders? Here there was more hesitation and suspicion. The heads of the Utraquist consistory were accustomed to opposing and sometimes persecuting the Unity. Now they were to become (at least officially) one national Bohemian church with it.* Still, Utraquist Church leaders saw that a united front was essential if the Catholic Counter-Reformation was to be thwarted. As Utraquist historian Zdeněk David observes, the Utraquists had the most to lose from a total Catholic victory in Bohemia. The Unity had settlements in Poland that could receive exiled members, and the Lutherans and Calvinists could look to Germany, Switzerland, and other places for support or sanctuary. The Utraquists had nowhere to go, unless a couple million Bohemians could somehow move to Moravia.[17]

Since the Lutherans had no church organization in Bohemia, but only a scattering of congregations on estates of a few sympathetic noblemen,[18] their perspective on the Letter of Majesty was mostly represented by "neo-Utraquists," as schol-

---

* Note again, the Letter of Majesty was made by Bohemia's national assembly. It had no legal standing in Moravia or Poland.

ars call them, though there was no separate "Neo-Utraquist Church." Perhaps because of Bohemia's long history of religious pluralism, Bohemians of Lutheran inclination tended to be less rigid on complete confessional conformity than many Lutherans in Germany (gnesio-Lutherans).[19] Though a few interpreted strictly by the Formula of Concord, the majority of Bohemian "Lutherans" took a more moderate and cooperative approach and accepted the Bohemian Confession as fundamentally agreeing with the Augsburg Confession.[20]

Calvinism was represented in Bohemia by members of the nobility who had traveled to Calvinist strongholds in the west, and by members of the Unity's clergy who liked Calvinist theological formulations, which they combined with elements of their own theological heritage. "Calvinism" remained a dirty word for many Czechs, though, as it was throughout most of Germany.

As for the Unity itself, historian Říčan admits that its bishops and other members of the Inner Council did not take as active a role as they should have in the forging of agreements that led to the Letter of Majesty of 1609.[21] In these years, the Unity's members of the nobility outshone the bishops and other spiritual leaders. Just as some Utraquists were reluctant to form one church with their former competitors in the Unity, no doubt some in the Unity feared they would now be expected to adore the host in holy communion or be swallowed up by the majority Utraquists. Moreover, while Unity members in Bohemia could accept the Bohemian Confession, they could not reject the Unity's own confessions, for these were a basis of their connection with the Unity in Moravia and Poland. Neither could they profess anything that would override the Consensus of Sandomierz with the Lutherans and Reformed in Poland.

In spite of efforts by the new Catholic archbishop of Prague, Karl Lamberg,[22] to derail the process,[23] by August 1609 a basic agreement was worked out for cooperation among the Unity, the Utraquists, and the Lutherans. A truly united Bohemian church must wait for the future, but for now the interim arrangement provided that the old Utraquist consistory would be transformed into an umbrella organization to serve all dissidents from Rome.[24] Negotiations were complicated,[25] but it was at length decided that the new consistory would have a Utraquist as its administrator.* A Unity bishop (Senior) would occupy the second spot. In addition to the presiding officer, the Utraquists were to have five representatives on the consistory, the Unity three (including the bishop), and three representatives would be appointed by the University of Prague. The previous ordinations of all priests or ministers of the churches would be recognized,† and the plan for the future was for the Utraquist administrator to participate in Unity ordinations, and for a Unity bishop to share in Utraquist ordinations. Apparently the few outright Lutherans were counted with the Utraquists for this purpose. In theory, ministers of one church could be called to serve a parish of another. In practice, that did not often happen, at least at first.[26]

As in Poland, plans for a true union of the non-Roman churches failed to go forward. The Unity insisted on retaining its own church order, rituals, and discipline, and the Utraquists continued their own liturgy as before. As in Poland, what actually resulted was a confederation not a merger of churches. Points of tension remained; for example some Utraquists continued to consider Unity members as spiritual and moral snobs because of the Unity's continued insistence on discipline. Still, the churches officially agreed not just to tolerate one another but also to try to work together. This was a puzzle to Jesuits, German Lutherans, and Swiss Reformed alike, who could not understand how there could be more than

---

* For the record, the last administrator of the old Utraquist consistory was Thomas of Soběslav. The new administrator was Elias Šúd of Semanin (1609-14). He was followed by two administrators of Lutheran inclination, Sigismund Crinitus (1614-19) and George Dykastus (1619-21). See David, *Finding the Middle Way*, 303, 316-17, 384.

† Müller, 3:197, notes that some Utraquist priests had secured Lutheran ordination in Germany.

one church sanctioned in a given territory. Given the situation in Europe at the time, the Bohemians' agreement of 1609 is remarkable.[27]

The Unity had trouble deciding who should be its chief representative on the new consistory. Bishop Bartholomew Němčanský, who was renowned for his education and erudition, would have been an obvious choice, but he died in 1609 just before the decree of toleration. Members of the Inner Council in Bohemia and Moravia wanted to call John Turnowski from Poland to assume this position. He had a doctorate in theology from Marburg,* and that would give him credibility with the non-Unity members of the consistory. He was not yet a bishop, but that could be taken care of in time.† However, he had just been called to an important position in Toruň in cooperation with the Lutherans, and Unity leaders in Poland did not want to jeopardize already delicate relations with the Lutherans by recalling him so soon. They offered Bishop Martin Gratian Gertich instead, but that suggestion did not suit the Inner Council. Finally, Matthias Cyrus, who was well known as a preacher and enjoyed the confidence of nobleman Peter Vok, was selected. He was only an assistant bishop, but that would do for now.‡ The Unity's other representatives on the consistory were John Cyril and John Korvin.[28]

The new consistory was not very effective. The confederated churches remained essentially independent, and historian Müller asserts that the Unity's having representation on it was mostly "empty form without practical significance."[29] The alliance never had grass-roots support, and its reason for being was more political than religious.[30] Still, the relative harmony was far better than the open hostility of past years.

For the Unity, legal recognition also meant there was now no external barrier to its continued progress.[31] At last it could

---

* Turnowski is apparently the first bishop of the Unity to have earned a doctorate. See Müller, 3:206-7.
† In fact he became a bishop in 1612.
‡ Cyrus was made a full bishop in 1611.

hold public services in Prague. John Korvin, one of the Unity's representatives on the new consistory, preached in German in the Church of St. Benedict and in the Chapel of the Body of God in the New Town section of Prague. More than that, the Unity was given charge of Bethlehem Chapel, the "cradle of Hussitism." Historian Říčan says this was in recognition of their being "fellow heirs of the legacy of Hus."

Since most of the congregations in Prague were using Utraquist ceremonial, the Unity's preachers were requested to wear a surplice when officiating in the city's churches.[32] Also, because some Utraquist parishioners could not get accustomed to the idea of having a "Picard" pastor, a Utraquist assistant was called to work with Br. Matthias Cyrus at Bethlehem Chapel.[33] A new church for the Unity was constructed on the site of the abandoned Catholic cloister of Saints Simon and Jude. The Unity also opened an institution of higher learning called "Nazareth" near Bethlehem Chapel. According to King Rudolf's Letter of Majesty, the theological faculty of the University of Prague was to be reconstituted. The university dragged its feet, but the Unity's John Korvin, who was an expert in Latin and Greek, began lecturing there, as did Nicholas Albrecht, who had worked on the Kralice Bible.[34]

The Unity reopened the "great sbor" in Mladá Boleslav even before Rudolf's decree of toleration. Peter Vok bought the church and other buildings and guaranteed that the Unity could use them. Vok also opened a high school in Sobieslav and put it under the Unity's care.[35]

Administratively, Bishop Jacob Narcissus (consecrated 1594) succeeded Simeon Theophilus Turnovský as head of the Inner Council in 1608. Matthias Konečný was elected a bishop in 1609 to replace Bishop Němčanský, who died that year. Matthias Cyrus led the church in Prague, and was made a bishop in 1611. After Bishop Cyrus died in 1618, John Cyril was chosen as bishop and Cyrus's successor on the consistory. John Lanetius, who had been consecrated a bishop in 1601, led the churches in northern Moravia from his seat in Přerov. When Bishop Narcissus died in 1611, Lanetius became head of the Inner Council. In Ivančice, John Cruciger (elected bishop 1606) administered the other Moravian congregations until his death in 1612. He was succeeded by George Erastus. In Poland, Bishop Simeon Theophilus Turnovský, as noted above, died in 1608, and Matthias Rybinski and Martin Gratian Gertich were elected bishops for Poland. Rybinski died in 1612, and was succeeded as bishop by John Turnowski.[36]

Now that it was legal, the Unity could continue its literary and printing work undisturbed. A new printing of the Brethren's Bible was done in Kralice in 1613. A beautiful new Czech hymnal containing George Strejc's Psalter as an appendix was produced in 1615. The print quality of the texts and tunes is outstanding, and Scripture references for each stanza are given in the margins. Many of the hymn texts are by Unity writers, and the tunes range from Gregorian chants to sprightly renaissance melodies. A favorite structure for many of the hymns is to have a series of stanzas which tell a biblical story, followed by a section which summarizes its theological significance, and ending with a series of stanzas on the implications for one's life. A pointing hand with a dainty seventeenth century ruff indicates the beginning of each section. A table in the back gives suggested hymns for the several services held on each Sunday and major festival of the church year. A slightly less luxurious edition of this hymnal came out in 1618. In its margins it has letters and numbers keyed to the sections of the 1615 edition, so that the two books can be used together.

In these years the Unity continued to print small books of extracts from the hymnals, biblical lessons, and prayer books. A favorite was the two-volume *Preachers' Prayers* (*Modlitby kazatelské*) of 1618.[37]

A new printing of the Unity's Czech confession appeared in 1607. It had some Calvinistic modifications in the section on the holy communion, and Latin and German versions printed in Herborn in 1612 conform to this version. Such modifications gave some Utraquists grounds to charge that the Unity was Calvinism in disguise, but the Unity insisted it was maintaining its own position between Luther and Calvin.[38]

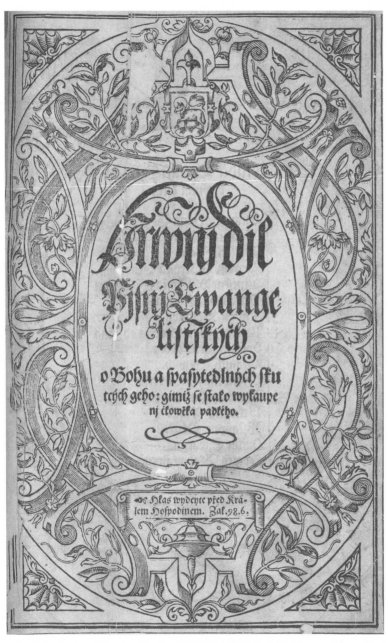

The title page of the Unity hymnal of 1615. This hymnal and the 1618 edition were the last ones printed in Czech lands until modern times.

The *Agenda* (directions for services) of 1580 was reissued with some Calvinistic modifications in 1612, and new editions of the catechism (also with Calvinist modifications) came out in 1608 and 1615. A particularly interesting use of the 1615 catechism was as a language-teaching device. It was printed in Bremen in 1615 with parallel columns in Latin, Greek, German, and Czech.[39]

Inspired by all the Lutheran and Calvinistic theological works, the Unity attempted to produce a book setting forth its own dogmatic theology. Soon after 1609 the Inner Council commissioned Matthias Konečný to undertake the work. Up to this point the Unity had been less than successful in producing a complete treatise on its theology. Bishop John Roh had seen the need for one after publication of the 1535 confession, but had not gotten around to writing it. Br. Matthias Červenka had started one, but never finished it. Now Br. Konečný, who was recognized as the best theologian of the Unity at that time, was a natural to produce a Brethren's dogmatics at long last. He began the work, called *Loci communes theologici*. But he too was distracted, and produced instead a work on the duties of a Christian in society, and another, called *The Domestic Preacher* (*Kazatel domovní*), which contained daily home devotions and suggestions for ordering the life of the home. He also produced a work on natural science from a Christian perspective. He never did finish the dogmatics.[40]*

The Unity fared no better in its historical writings in this period. John Jaffet, an assistant bishop, undertook to write historical accounts of the Unity and its reasons for separating from Rome. A prime goal was to defend the validity of the Unity's ministry against attacks from the Catholics and some Utraquists. From 1605 to 1607 Jaffet produced *The Voice of the Watcher* (*Hlas strážého*) and in 1607 *The Sword of Goliath* (*Meč*

---

* Neither did Adam Hartmann and John Joram, who were given the task after Konečný. The Unity, it seems, did not have an aptitude for scholarly dogmatics, preferring instead works on practical Christian life.

Morning and evening, parents are to instruct their household in Christian faith, as indicated in the title page of The Domestic Preacher *(Kazatel domovní).*

*Goliášův).** In the latter work particularly, Jaffet tried to show that the Unity's ministers had apostolic succession not only in keeping to the faith of the apostles, but also in a direct

---

* This rather strange title derives from 1 Sam. 21:9, where the priest Ahimelech gave Goliath's sword to David so he could defend himself against the servants of Saul. Jaffet saw his work as a sword to protect the Unity from the false charges of its enemies.

physical succession through the Waldensians back to the uncorrupted early church. In doing so, Jaffet misunderstood the
thinking of the early Unity on the ministerial office, which did
not depend on a hand-to-hand succession.[41]* Jaffet continued
in the same vein in his later work, *History of the Origin of the
Unity* (*Historia o původu jednoty*). His "uncritical historical
presentation,"[42] which mixed history with fictional apologetics,
sadly was accepted by succeeding generations (including historian Edmund de Schweinitz, so often cited in this history) as
pure fact. Historian Říčan observes:

> We know that the Brethren resorted to the thesis of
> personal apostolic succession for apologetic reasons,
> but . . . this conception does not accord with their
> actual idea of the bishop's office in the time of the
> Unity's flowering, nor does it accord with historical
> actuality.[43]

A much more helpful document of the Unity in the first
quarter of the 17th century is a comprehensive account of its
church order and life. It was first drawn up in 1609 and
entitled *Special Order among the Brethren* (*Řád zvlastní mezi
Bratřími*). The Unity synod held in Žeravice, Moravia, in 1616
expanded the document and formally adopted it as the *Church
Order of the Bohemian Brethren* (*Řád církevní Jednoty Bratří
českých*). It was translated into Latin and published in 1632 as
the *Ratio Disciplinæ*.[44] It may seem odd that the Unity was in
existence for more than 150 years before it wrote down its
constitution and church organization. But its order was set
forth in the minutes of its various synods and Inner Councils.
Tradition also played a part in that many details were passed
down by word of mouth and custom: "That's just the way we do
things." But probably most important, the Unity ever sought

---

* It is ironic that whatever "succession" Matthias of Kunvald may have
received, and whatever he passed on to Elias and Tůma, it was
Jaffet himself who recorded that John Augusta did not restore that
succession by the laying on of hands after he was released from
prison. Given Jaffet's other inaccuracies, we cannot be absolutely
sure even of this. But what reason would he have to invent facts
that contradict his own thesis of apostolic succession?

agreement through consensus of reasoned discussion and prayer, not by citing precisely drawn-up procedural regulations.* It was only at the time of the detailed negotiations concerning the 1609 Letter of Majesty that all these facts needed to be assembled in convenient form to share with the Utraquists and others.[45] The *Ratio* may not give an absolutely accurate account of the way things worked in the Unity at all times (human failings being what they are, no plan ever works perfectly). However, we get from the *Ratio* a good idea of the Unity's order and life during this time of its maturity and full "flowering." The next chapter will examine this order and life in detail.

Notes

[1] Rudolf Říčan, *The History of the Unity of Brethren*, trans. C. Daniel Crews (Bethlehem, Pa.: Department of Publications and Communications, Moravian Church, Northern Province, 1992), 299. The abridged German translation, *Geschichte der Böhmischen Brüder: Ihr Ursprung und ihre Geschichte* (Berlin: Union Verlag, 1961), 207, says that the number of congregations and members may have been somewhat higher.

[2] See F. M. Bartoš, "Wenceslas Budovec's Defense of the Brethren and of Freedom of Conscience in 1604," *Church History* 28 (1959): 229-39.

[3] Říčan, 324-27. Joseph Th. Müller, *Geschichte der Böhmischen Brüder* 3 vols. (Herrnhut: Missionsbuchhandlung, 1922, 1931), 3:195.

[4] Müller, 3:197-98. Říčan, 278-79.

[5] Říčan, 327-28.

[6] Říčan, 328-29.

[7] Müller, 3:194, 237.

[8] Říčan, 329.

[9] Říčan, 330.

[10] Müller, 3:195-96.

---

* The method for discussion at synods, going from youngest to oldest, as described by John Amos Comenius in his note 14 to the *Ratio Disciplinæ*, is common sense personified. See *Ratio Disciplinæ Ordinisque Ecclesiastici in Unitate Fratrum Bohemorum*, e-book ed. (www.MoravianArchives.org, 2007), 60-61.

11 Müller, 3:195-96.

12 Müller, 3:199-201.

13 Müller, 3:202.

14 See Zdeněk V. David, *Finding the Middle Way: The Utraquists' Liberal Challenge to Rome and Luther* (Washington, D.C.: Woodrow Wilson Center Press, 2003), 302.

15 Říčan, 330. Some have pointed out that legal recognition did not result in numerical growth for the Unity. Jindřich Halama in "The Crisis of the Union of Czech Brethren in the Years before the Thirty Years War, or On the Usefulness of Persecution," *Communio Viatorum* 44 (2002): 60, 67, goes so far (with good reason) as to say persecution was what had kept the Unity "pure and strong."

16 Říčan, 329.

17 David, 307.

18 David, 335.

19 David, 317, 339.

20 Říčan, 331.

21 Říčan, 331.

22 David, 258.

23 Müller, 3:218-19.

24 David, 311.

25 Müller, 3:203-8.

26 Říčan, 332. Müller, 3:205.

27 David, 318, 323, 330.

28 Říčan, 333.

29 Müller, 3:214.

30 David, 303-4.

31 Říčan, 333.

32 Říčan, 333.

33 Müller, 3:215.

34 Říčan, 334.

35 Müller, 3:216-17.

36 Říčan, 334. Edmund de Schweinitz, *History of the Church Known as the Unitas Fratrum*, 2nd (reprint) ed. (Bethlehem, Pa.: Moravian Publication Concern, 1901), 656-57.

37 Říčan, 334.

38 Müller, 3:311-13.

39 Říčan, 334.

40 Müller, 3:297. Říčan, 334.

41 Joseph Th. Müller, *Das Bischoftum der Brüder-Unität* (Herrnhut: 1889), 28.

42 Müller, *Geschichte der Böhmischen Brüder*, 3:222.

43 Říčan, 384-85.

44 Říčan, 332.

45 Müller, 3:209-12.

Chapter 18

The Ratio Disciplinæ

Life and Order in the Fully Developed Unity
1616

A s noted at the end of the last chapter, the Unity set forth its church order and life in the *Ratio Disciplinæ* in 1609, expanded and formally adopted it 1616, and first published it in 1632. This chapter is a summary of that document, taking into account Bishop John Amos Comenius's notes in the 1660 edition.[*] I have included needful explanations of the text in parentheses. Additional helpful, but less crucial, comments are in the footnotes.[†] Here, then, is how the Unity described itself in the opening years of the 17th century.

Introductory account

In a preface the Seniors and ministers of the Unity give a brief historical account of the rise of their church from the

---

[*] In 1866 Bishop Benjamin Seifferth published an English translation titled *Church Constitution of the Bohemian and Moravian Brethren* (London: W. Mallalieu and Co.). That translation is the basis of this chapter and the e-book edition of the *Ratio* on the Internet at www.MoravianArchives.org.

[†] A comparison of this chapter and the account of the church order of the "Old Brethren" in chapter 7 may be instructive.

"Romish" church. They also explain why the *Ratio* was written.
When religious freedom was finally gained in Bohemia in 1609,
the other churches asked the Unity's ministers "to explain
*what they had peculiar to themselves, especially with regard to
discipline and order?*" They thereupon "produced the following
statement [the *Ratio*]."1*

Doctrinal Basis

The *Ratio Disciplinæ* opens with a section on the doctrinal
foundation of the Unity. The distinction of essential, ministrative, and accidental things is explained. The *essential things*
on the part of God are the grace of God the Father, the merit
(saving work) of Christ, and the gifts of the Holy Spirit. On the
human side, the essentials are faith, love, and hope. Through
these "human essentials" one comes to share in the "divine
essentials." The *ministrative things* are the means used by
God's grace to communicate and share the essentials with
humans. These ministratives include the word of God in Scripture, the authoritative proclamation of forgiveness and new life
in Christ, and the sacraments. The church is the ministrative
context within which these essentials and the other ministratives work. (The ministratives, while they are not called
"essential," are far from unimportant or matters of indifference.
They are the means chosen by God to lead us to the essentials.
But they are not ends in themselves.) The *accidental things* are
defined as the ceremonies and external rites of the church,
which may vary according to time and place. These include
such things as the kind of bread used in communion or
specific liturgies for its celebration.

Following this brief but crucial theological foundation, the
Ratio speaks of the people and organizations that make up the
Unity.

---

* It is the habit of the Moravian Church even today to preface its
constitution with a historical account.

Classification of Members and Congregation Officials

Members of the Unity are classified as beginners, proficients, and perfect, or more precisely those going on to perfection. *Beginners* include children of Unity members and adults coming to the Unity from other denominations. These are probationary members who are receiving basic doctrinal and moral instruction. *Proficients* have received this basic instruction, have been admitted to the sacrament, and are continuing to grow in faith and life. The *perfect* have made sufficient progress to be able to instruct and guide others. (The Unity did not believe anyone can become so good as never to make mistakes. The word "perfect" is used here in its Latin sense of "having come to full maturity.") The perfect have made such progress that others may imitate them.2

Instructing the children.

It is from this last class of Unity members that the ministers and other officials are chosen. Lay officials include the *elders* of the congregations, who assist the ministers with church discipline and give advice to other members. *Female elders*, or "matrons," exercise a similar office among the women and girls of the congregation.3 *Almoners* receive contributions from the members, and after accurately recording the amounts given, distribute funds as needed to orphans, widows, the sick, those imprisoned or exiled for the faith, etc. Such distributions are made after consultation with the minister. For the maintenance of church buildings, separate contributions are received, usually quarterly, by *aediles*. These aediles (or *wardens* or *trustees* as we would say today) give the congregation a full accounting of all income and expenses once a year.

The Ordained Clergy

The clergy consists of men chosen for the ministry of word and sacrament. These *ministers* are also called *priests* and *pastors* (though the Unity was wary of the latter two terms because of their negative association in the Roman and other churches; rather than someone who offers sacrifice as in the Roman Church, the Unity saw its "priests" simply as leaders set over the people). Ministers are chosen for their faith, moral life, and gifts for teaching others. Recalling the Unity's history, the *Ratio* notes that in earlier years higher education, specifically in languages, was not required of the clergy, but now that such education is more readily available, the clergy generally take advantage of it.

Before they are ordained as priests, candidates must pass through two probationary grades of ministry.

Acoluths, or as we term them today "acolytes," are young people taken into the ministers' households to receive training for the ministry. Acoluths are expected to hold to the highest moral standards to set an example to other young people. They receive basic theological instruction from the ministers, and are expected to commit to memory the catechism, the Gospels and other portions of Scripture, and hymns. Acoluths lead household devotions as practice for future service, open the church building for services, etc., and teach the catechism to children in the schools. As they advance in their training, they may lead in evening or weekday services by reading Scripture or delivering a short memorized address. They also accompany the ministers on journeys, both to be witnesses to the ministers' proper conduct, and to learn how to behave in various situations themselves. Promising acoluths may be taken into the bishop's personal household.[4]

After a period of training and experience, acoluths who prove fit are ordained as *deacons*. Deacons continue their path to ordination as priests. Study at universities in Protestant countries may form a part of this training.* Deacons also teach in the Unity's schools and preach on occasion in church services. They can also perform baptisms if so directed by the pastor. Particularly in larger congregations, they assist in distributing the consecrated bread and wine at holy communion. Only priests can pronounce absolution and consecrate the elements, however. Deacons serve as assistant ministers until they are judged ready for ordination as priests.

A few priests are called to a special pastoral and administrative ministry. These *bishops*† are elected by the clergy to supervise the other ministers and promote order and discipline. The number of bishops may be four, five, or six as circumstances require.‡ Each bishop has a certain number of pastors and congregations assigned to him as his diocese. The *Ratio* stresses that the bishop's office is not one of honor or revenue, but of wider service. Bishops do not have a higher order of ministry than priests (or presbyters as they are also named), but are called to a special ministry of supervision. Similarly, all bishops are equal in rank, but one is elected president of the Inner Council (see below) for "the sake of order." Bishops remain in office for life unless they are removed for misconduct.§ (Though bishops may retire from administrative duties, they do not cease to be bishops.)

In addition to general administration, a bishop ordains ministers and in consultation with other bishops assigns pastors to parishes. The bishop visits each congregation, annually

---

* Some older acoluths might also be sent abroad for study before being ordained deacons.

† As noted elsewhere, the Unity preferred to call them "Seniors" or "Antistites" because of the negative connotations of "bishop" from the Catholic Church.

‡ We have seen, however, that this ideal number of bishops was not always maintained.

§ We recall that Václav Bílý was the only bishop so removed.

if possible (of which more later), and learns each church's needs and leading members. Each bishop cares for the Unity library in his area, and is expected to "increase it as much as he can with useful books." All the bishops together have charge of the Unity's printing presses, but the bishop who lives

These are they which follow the Lamb.

nearest has direct supervision. The *Ratio* says that "since it is hazardous to commit absolute power to a single individual or to a few," each bishop is to consult with his fellow bishops and other advisors. Appeal from the bishops' decisions can be made only to a general synod, *i.e.*, a meeting of all Unity ministers.

One of the bishops serves as *president* of the *Inner Council*. (The *Ratio* does not give a lengthy description of the council, which oversaw the daily operation of the Unity between synods.) The Inner Council (we could call it a Unity-wide Provincial Elders Conference today) consists of all the bishops with a variable number of ministers elected by synod. The office of *secretary of the Unity* (also called *Unity writer*) is generally held by a bishop, who records synod decisions and other official documents and inspects writings on behalf of the Unity before publication. (This office was thus a combination Archivist and Faith and Order Commission.)

Every bishop generally has two or three assistants called *conseniors* (co-seniors) chosen and consecrated to this office from among the priests. With the bishop these form a diocesan council. They bring necessary matters to their bishop's attention, and can fill in for him on occasion for visitations, etc. (Apparently in the early 1600s, the Inner Council was composed of all the bishops and conseniors. These conseniors were not "bishops" in the sense of suffragan bishops in the Roman or Anglican churches, *i.e.*, full bishops assigned not to preside over a diocese but to be assistant bishops to the diocesan bishop. Conseniors were not so much "assistant bishops," as they were "assistants *to* the bishop.")

Synods

The *Ratio* describes synods in this manner. *General synods* (Unity Synods) are usually held every three or four years in different places in Bohemia and Moravia. All bishops, priests, deacons, and older acoluths are expected to attend. "Patrons" (noblemen) of nearby churches also attend but are not voting members.[*] (Because of distance, the Unity in Poland had its own synods and sent only selected delegates to general synods.) Smaller *particular synods* (district or "diocesan" synods) may be called to deal with issues that are more local in nature.

Synods begin in the evening with devotions and a welcome from the bishops. Supper is the next order of business. The next morning, the sessions begin with a sermon from a bishop or consenior, and additional prayer services are held each afternoon and evening.

Deacons and acoluths meet in one place for instruction and encouragement.[5] The priests, who elect a chairman to preside over their sessions, meet separately to discuss the issues laid before them by the bishops. The collected body of priests can also propose to the bishops items to be added to the agenda. Every delegate is given a chance to speak briefly on each topic. When the priests reach a decision, it is reported to the bishops, and if the bishops concur, it is recorded in the minutes. If there is no consensus or concurrence, discussion continues or

---

[*] Though lacking a vote, these noble "patrons" did exert influence at synods, particularly in later years.

the matter is postponed.[6] The bishops have their own meetings to discuss ministerial appointments, etc. Synods also elect bishops and members of the Inner Council when there are vacancies in these positions. General synods always celebrate holy communion together. With business concluded, the delegates are given helpful admonitions on the needs of the times, and are sent on their way with a benediction.

Ordinations

One of the most important duties of general synods is the ordination of ministers. Following a sermon, candidates recommended for the office of acoluth by their pastor are called forward by name, asked whether they are ready to give themselves to the service of the church, and after their duties are read out to them, they are received into office by a handshake.

Acoluths recommended for advancement to the office of deacon are examined by the bishops concerning their spiritual state and knowledge. Those who pass this examination are then called before synod by name, their duties are read to them, and they vow to perform them. After prayer, the ordaining bishop lays hands on them to "confirm" them as deacons. The new deacons shake hands with the bishops and priests to promise obedience, and share a handshake with the other deacons as a sign of fellowship.

The service for the ordination of priests is similar, but more solemn. Pastors who recommend their deacon for ordination must bring a written testimonial from the congregation's elders of that deacon's fitness for advancement. Then follows a three-fold examination of the candidates. First, the names of the candidates, along with the testimonials, are placed before the priests, and each is voted on. These votes and the testimonials are sealed and delivered to the bishops. Those candidates who have passed this first scrutiny are taken before the conseniors, three or four at a time. The conseniors question them about their faith, knowledge, commitment, and general character and suitability "respecting their age and stability of judgment."

Those who pass this second scrutiny are sent individually to a bishop, who inquires further into their fitness and impresses on them the solemnity of the office they are undertaking.

The next day, after a hymn and discourse, the candidates are called forward by name. Two conseniors come forward to present them formally as qualified for ordination, and prayer is offered. The "duties of the pastoral office" are read to them, and they vow to fulfill them. As the candidates kneel, the "High Priestly Prayer" from John 17 is read.[7] The bishops ordain them with the laying on of hands as "Come, Holy Ghost, our souls inspire" is sung. After a charge from one of the bishops, they shake hands with the bishops and conseniors as a sign of obedience, and with the priests as a sign of fellowship. The deacons offer them a handshake as a symbol of respect. A hymn based on Psalm 133 is sung as this is happening. The service concludes with holy communion.

The *Ratio* notes at this point that churches or "magistrates" (nobles) are not allowed to recruit pastors for themselves, nor are ministers allowed to campaign or apply for a particular church.[8] This is the bishops' decision, and pastors have to be regularly installed by the bishop or his representative. Newly ordained priests generally serve a year or two as assistant pastors before being assigned a pastorate of their own.

The election of conseniors and seniors (bishops) is done by secret ballot of the ministers without nominations. The service for the ordination of these chief ministers is similar to that for priests, except that their previous service and election by synod are taken as proof of their fitness, and the three examinations are not necessary. After those who have been chosen accept the office to which they were elected, the bishops ordain them with the laying on of hands.

Church Services, Rites, and Sacraments

On *Sundays* throughout the year the people gather for four services, two in the morning and two after noon. The first service focuses on the prophets; the second, called the *great service*, features lessons from the Gospels; the afternoon service has readings from the "apostolic writings" (epistles); and in the evening service the entire Bible is read through in order. Beginning at Easter and throughout the summer, a fifth service is held to give children instruction in the catechism. Parents and others attend this service also (presumably to monitor the children's progress and to show their support).

The services open with a hymn, and in the *great* service

Preaching the Word.

and afternoon service, a Psalm as well.* Then the minister, after audible or silent prayer, reads and explains the text. The *Ratio* stresses that a standard lectionary (based on the traditional Catholic lectionary) is followed so that in the course of a year the main truths of the faith are covered. A table (in the back of the 1615 hymnal) lists the Sundays and festivals, with the appointed readings for each service, together with suggested hymns to accompany them. The *Ratio* says that while use of the lectionary is encouraged for "unanimity" among the congregations, the minister is free to use other readings to fit the circumstances. What is to be avoided is preaching so long that it wears the people out. (Notions of brevity vary from age to age, however.) The earlier morning and afternoon services are limited to an hour,

---

* The Unity was known for its singing. One outsider stated that hymns were a chief means among them of expressing their doctrine: "Your hymns are like homilies." (*Ratio*, 64, note 22).

including the singing. That applies to any weekday services also. The noon catechetical services and evening services are to last only half an hour. In the great service, however, a full hour is allowed for the sermon, not including the hymns and prayers. A prayer, blessing, and more singing follow the sermon. Clear explanation, not eloquence, is expected from the sermon, and where possible, Scripture is to be interpreted by Scripture. The minister and an elder (a male one for the boys and a female one for the girls) examine the young people after the noon and afternoon services to make sure they have paid attention and retain what they have heard. On Wednesdays and Fridays during Lent, additional evening services are held, especially for the younger members. These services are called *salva*, from the hymn *Salva nos Jesu* (*Save us, Jesus. . .*).*

Baptism of believers' children takes place a few days after birth. The minister reads a passage of Scripture, and the parents and sponsors make a profession of faith. Following prayer for God's grace to be given to the child, the minister baptizes the infant with plain water "in the name of the Father, the Son, and the Holy Ghost." The parents and sponsors are admonished to keep their vows to bring up these children in the church until they come to Christian maturity, and the sacrament closes with more prayer for God's blessing.

When young people are ready to make their own commitment to Christ and the church, the pastor makes sure they are properly instructed over a period of time. They then receive *confirmation.* This is usually administered by a bishop during his annual visitation of the congregation. The candidates gather in the center of the church and are asked if they are ready to confirm the covenant made for them in their baptism. After their positive answer, the main points of the Christian covenant are explained to them, based on Titus 2:11-13. They

---

* The *Ratio* also says that in former times, different talks were given at times to the different classifications of members, single men and women, married people, etc., to meet their varying needs. This sounds like the beginning of what came to be the "Choir system" of the Renewed Unity.

publicly renounce Satan, the world, and the flesh, and join in the Apostles' Creed. They then kneel and repeat a prayer for forgiveness as led by the minister. Finally, they receive absolution and the laying on of hands. Those who have received confirmation are now admitted to holy communion.

Baptized adults who wish to join the Unity meet with the congregation's elders. If they evidence a good acquaintance with sound doctrine and pledge to live according to the church's standards they are received into the Unity by shaking hands with the minister. It is noted that this handshake is not given to the minister as a person, but as a pledge to Christ Himself.

The *Ratio* describes *holy communion* as ordinarily celebrated four times a year, though special circumstances may call for additional celebrations. When the time for communion draws near, the minister meets with the elders to determine if there is any problem or scandal in the congregation, which would prevent the communion. If there is none, or after it has been dealt with, the minister publicly announces the date and time of the celebration two or three weeks beforehand. Worship services before that date include exhortations about communion and its worthy reception. In addition, every family is assigned a time to come and meet with the minister for personal evaluation and counseling.* Those found guilty of serious sin either repent and promise to do better, or they are excluded from communion.

When the appointed day arrives, the congregation prays for the forgiveness of sin and receives absolution. The minister consecrates the elements by repeating the Lord's words of institution, and breaks the bread and takes the cup as the words describe. After a short explanation of the significance of the sacrament, the minister invites the people to come forward by groups to receive it: first the ministers, then the "magistrates" (nobles), then the congregation elders, then the men and boys according to age, lastly the women and girls (in this

---

* Like the "Speaking" which preceded the communion of the Renewed Unity in the 18th century.

instance, the Unity followed the social custom of the time). The members receive communion kneeling. (In earlier years they stood to receive the elements to avoid the appearance of worshipping the physical elements, but it caused such great public offense to the Catholics and Utraquists that the Unity went back to kneeling. The *Ratio* remarks that kneeling is a properly humble posture also.) The congregation sings hymns as the elements are being distributed. The service closes with a prayer of thanksgiving, another exhortation to the people, and the benediction. In accord with the Unity's emphasis on good works as the sincerity of faith, the *Ratio* says the people "testify their gratitude" by giving alms to the poor (and other works of mercy).

Marriages are not to be done secretly, and should take place only after consultations with parents, relatives, and the ministers. The marriage service is performed in public with the congregation as witnesses. After Scripture and a statement on the nature of Christian marriage, the parties are called before the congregation and are asked if they can "freely and lawfully unite." After they make the marriage vows, the minister takes their right hands, pronounces

Marriage in the Unity.

them husband and wife, says "What God has joined together. . . ," and blesses them in the name of the Trinity.

The ceremony closes with prayer for the newly married couple and an exhortation to all present to live a sober and godly life.

Visitation of the sick is done by the minister when a member is gravely ill. The minister speaks of the need for penitence and accepting God's will, but also of God's grace in Christ and the assurance of life eternal. If the sick wish to receive communion, it is given to them. Other persons are invited to join in the communion "so that it may really be a communion of saints." At *funerals*, the minister and school children accompany the body to the grave as songs are sung. The minister then delivers a talk from Scripture on what may "serve for instruction, for consolation, or for warning."

Festival Days

Having described the usual services, sacraments, and main rites of the church, the *Ratio* devotes a section to special observances. The first of these is the weekly *Sabbath*. The *Ratio* notes that in the Old Testament this was Saturday, but the Apostles moved it to Sunday as the day of the Lord's resurrection. Not only are members to attend church and avoid physical labor, but they are also to avoid anything that might distract them from spiritual concerns, study, and meditation. Such distractions include drinking, dancing, and going to fairs. Neither should they work on their financial accounts or collect debts. Where one's employer or noble lord allows it, the quiet preparation for the Sabbath begins on Saturday afternoon.*

Festival days and seasons commemorating the main events of the life of Christ are observed. Days honoring the apostles and some of the martyrs are marked with a service to encourage people to follow their example (not to rely on them for intercession). These are not holidays, however, and if it is a weekday, one returns to one's usual employment after the service.

---

* This was the case too in the Renewed Unity of the 18th century.

Every three months, a Wednesday and Friday are kept as days of penitence and intercession. (These are similar to the "Ember Days" or "Quarter Days" observed in the Catholic, Utraquist, and Anglican Churches.) They include public services and exhortations, along with devotions in the homes.

Fasting, or abstaining from food and drink, is encouraged as a means of turning from earthly things to meditate on the things of the spirit. Giving up extra periods of sleep is included in fasting. Only those whose health can stand it are expected to fast. Fasts are called for at the quarter days mentioned above, or when there is danger from war, pestilence, or persecution, and when ministers are to be chosen and ordained at synods.

In line with the Unity's emphasis on doing positive good rather than simply abstaining from evil, *alms* for the poor are brought to the church during penitential times. These monetary gifts are distributed to the poor by the almoners, described above. Richer congregations help the poorer ones with this. However, Unity members are urged not just to give money, but to help the poor and sick and needy by "all works of mercy."

Life in the Ministers' Households

Life in the "Brethren's houses" proceeds on a tightly organized schedule. The ministers (and their families after marriage for the clergy became common), with the deacons, acoluths, and "domestics" are awakened by the bell. After washing and dressing, they spend about an hour in prayer and study. Then all assemble for devotions of prayer, Scripture, and hymns. The rest of the morning is devoted to study by the acoluths and deacons. The afternoon, "as being less suited to study" is filled with manual labor or teaching in the school. Afternoon devotions are held around 2 o'clock, and then all return to their work once more. Meal times are not spent in "trifling conversation," but during them the younger acoluths recite what they have learned so far, or discussions on a theological topic are held, or a passage from a good book may be read. The evening is spent practicing music or "psalmody." After final prayers, all go to bed. No one is allowed to sit up late or to go out in the evening. The house is locked, and the keys are delivered to whoever is responsible for waking the household and overseeing domestic operations the next day. That responsibility rotates among the pastors, deacons, and older ministerial students in turn.

Everyone takes part in the household chores of sweeping and cleaning or working in the garden. The *Ratio* makes particular mention of someone's having charge of the clock (which regulated all the other activities).

The assistant ministers, deacons, and older students are assigned to give talks at devotions and weekday services. They are also sent out to visit the sick and shut-in members of the congregation. They study the assigned lessons for the coming Sunday, and on Saturday morning they meet with the pastor. Each one, beginning with the youngest, gives his thoughts on the texts. The pastor then summarizes the most important points that should be noted concerning the texts.

The private life of the students and younger clergy is closely regulated. They are to do nothing, not even purchase something for themselves or write important letters, without the advice and permission of the pastor. Neither are they to stray far from the house without permission and an escort.

The senior ministers, of course, are subject to the same rigorous standards at home and abroad. If they must travel, they need the bishop's permission and an escort. If at all possible, they are to lodge in other Brethren's houses. This, the *Ratio* says, is in the "footsteps of the primitive [New Testament] church."

Life in the Members' Households

Regulations and schedules are not as strict in the homes of lay members as they are in those of the ministers. However, heads of household are also expected to maintain their homes and families in good order. Family devotions are to be held morning, noon, and evenings, and at mealtimes. Prayers, Scripture, and hymns form the content of these. The children and servants are to be given basic instruction in the faith, and at meals after church services the head of the house should discuss the main points of the sermon with them. Diligence in one's assigned tasks and the avoidance of idleness are to be encouraged. "Worldly diversions," such as drunkenness, dancing, and gambling are not to be permitted at home or engaged in elsewhere. That means taverns and "public houses" are off limits. "Disreputable and suspicious" means of gaining a livelihood should be avoided, and if members have a dispute with one another, they should lay the matter before the church elders and not the secular courts. In short, members should behave with decency and decorum wherever they are.

Visitations of Congregations

The annual official visitation of a congregation is a very important event. The bishop, accompanied by his conseniors, usually serves as "chief visitor," but if necessary a consenior may be assigned this responsibility. Pastors of nearby congregations usually also join the visitation party. Spring, summer, and fall are the preferred seasons for visitations, but if there is a pastor to install or a pressing problem, they may also take place in winter. If there are not enough visitors to go around because of the number of congregations or illness or infirmity (or the bishop is in prison for the faith), and if all is well in the congregation, the visitation may be put off until the next year.

Private meetings are held with the pastor, the assistant clergy, the acoluths, and the male and female elders. In each case, the bishop inquires about that individual's or group's personal state and performance, and asks about their evaluation of their colleagues and the congregation in general. The congregation's catalog of members is inspected.

The visitors look at the inventory of furniture for the Brethren's house to make sure all is present and accounted for, and that there are no deficiencies in what is provided. They also walk the buildings and grounds with the aediles (trustees) and elders to see what repairs and general maintenance are called for.

The bishop and other visitors hold special preaching services. The holy communion is also celebrated. (As noted above, confirmation of the young people was generally done during a visitation.) The purpose of the entire visitation is to encourage all in the congregation to rededicate themselves to faithful service.

Elders might be elected during a regular annual or a special visitation. The male elders are voted on by the men of the congregation before the evening service. Those who receive a plurality of votes are called forward after the service, and the chief visitor reads

Upbuilding the congregation.

them a list of their duties. The newly elected elders pledge their loyalty to the bishop, the pastor, and the congregation, and confirm this by a handshake with the bishop or other chief visitor. This inaugurates them in office. They are given special seats in the church (sbor) from which they can keep an eye on the congregation during services. (This is in a way symbolic of their role, not just during services but at all other times as well.)

Female elders are chosen in the same way, except that only the women of the congregation are present. (Such a role for women was extremely rare in other churches of the time.)

The *dedication of a new church* (sbor) is another event calling for a special visitation. When all is ready, the congregation gathers, a hymn is sung, and the chief visitor, usually the bishop, speaks on the purpose of the service and the proper use of the building. Prayer, modeled on Solomon's at the dedication of the temple in Jerusalem, 1 Kings 8, is offered. Following a charge to use the building only for the purposes for which it is intended, and an appropriate sermon, the holy communion is celebrated. The service concludes with a prayer for God's blessing on the building and all who worship there.

Discipline

Since the beginning of the Unity, says the *Ratio*, all its members have been subject to its wholesome discipline. This applies to the bishops and noble patrons as well as to the youngest member. The church needs discipline to assist and guide the spiritual growth of its members, to recall those who are going astray, and, sadly, to exclude those who will not listen, to prevent them from doing harm to the others. This is referred to as "the power of the keys," Matt. 16:19. The *Ratio* states that members of the Unity see it as a positive thing to know that there are those who are "watching their life and conversation" with authority "to warn and recall them from a perilous course."

There are three degrees of discipline in conformity with the direction of Christ, Matt. 18:15-18: Private, public, and exclusion. *Private discipline* comes first. If one sees a fault or problem with another member, that member should go and speak with the person. If this brings no positive result, the problem should be brought to the attention of the minister or an elder, who then goes and talks to the person, again in private.

If there is still no positive result, *public discipline* begins. The offender is called before the local elders and is admonished to "forsake his sin." If the person agrees, well and good. If not, the *Ratio* says: "he is suspended from the communion of the Holy Supper, until he returns to himself [Luke 15:17] and amends his conduct." (The pronouns are masculine, but church discipline included the women as well.) This is the procedure for "lighter cases."

For more serious offenses, however, the elders meet with the person several times to convince the offender to acknowledge guilt and change behavior. If the person agrees, then forgiveness is given, but with certain conditions. The person is to spend time in prayer and examination of conscience until the next communion or longer if necessary. The congregation is to pray for the person especially during this time.

Watch therefore.

The person must also make good all damages and offenses. Apology must be made to all individuals who have been justly offended. This should be done in person, but if the offender simply cannot do this (for shame or shyness, etc.) the minister may make the apology on the person's behalf. If what the person has done is not common knowledge, then apologizing before the elders is sufficient. If everybody knows what the offense was so that it is a public scandal, then a more public apology before the whole congregation is called for.

If the offense is flagrant, or the offender refuses to repent or make good the offense, then the third degree of discipline, *exclusion* from communion and the fellowship of the church, must come into play. This excommunication is publicly announced to the congregation, which replies: "Amen." Even now, this step should be taken with sorrow and tears. There is still hope for repentance through the grace of God. If this happens, after an interval to make sure the repentance is real, the person is received into the church again. This is called the "second part of the keys." That is, in the formal "exclusion," the kingdom of heaven was closed to the person. With that person's sincere repentance, the church can now unlock the kingdom to that person again.[9]

All degrees of discipline are to be administered with compassion. The aim is not to punish but to amend, to build up and not destroy.*

Conclusion

The *Ratio* concludes by saying that these are the details of the Unity's ecclesiastical order, which are derived from Scripture. Since the Unity's beginnings, its members, "in much

---

* I thank Br. Craig D. Atwood for pointing out that the section (#654) on church discipline in the 2002 edition of the *Church Order of the Unitas Fratrum* (worldwide Moravian Church) reads remarkably like this section of the *Ratio*. It says:

> The life of the congregation is nourished by the cure and care of souls and the exercise of congregation discipline.
>
> In the exercise of corrective discipline, the following aspects are recognized:
> 1. Admonition by the Minister, either alone or in fellowship with other members (Church Council, Elders, etc.) in private in a spirit of love.
> 2. Further admonition with temporary suspension from the fellowship of the Congregation as it is visibly expressed in certain privileges.
> 3. Exclusion from the membership of the Congregation.
> 4. Persons who are excluded shall be welcomed back into the membership of the Congregation after a profession of repentance on their part.

Section 654 also refers to #103, which says the same thing in more detail, including the statements:

> In Church discipline the sins and errors of the individual are considered and borne as the burden of the whole congregation. . . . Therefore the main object of Church discipline is the prevention of offenses and not the punishment of the individual.

persecution and suffering," have found these provisions to be conducive to their own edification and assurance of salvation. In the present (with the agreements with the Utraquists and Lutherans in 1609), if other churches wish to adopt this or a similar order in their churches, they are welcome to do so. "Only let the apostolic maxim be attended to: 'Let all things be done decently and in order'" (1 Cor. 14:40).

This chapter can have no better end than the *Ratio*'s itself:

> May our merciful God establish, strengthen, and perfect that sacred order of things which is pleasing to Himself, both among us and everywhere throughout Christendom, to the wholesome edification of His church, and the praise of His name! Amen.

Notes

1 *Ratio Disciplinæ Ordinisque Ecclesiastici in Unitate Fratrum Bohemorum*, e-book ed. (www.MoravianArchives.org, 2007), 8.

2 *Ratio*, 56, note 4.

3 In *Ratio*, 56, note 5, Comenius says the Unity, by following the example of the early church, was unique in its time in having female elders.

4 *Ratio*, 56, Comenius note 6.

5 *Ratio*, 59-60, note 13.

6 *Ratio*, 60-61, note 14.

7 Comenius (*Ratio*, 62, note 18) adds the detail about John 17.

8 Comenius (*Ratio*, 63, note 20) admits that there were instances of individuals, especially nobles, trying to secure clergy according to their own tastes. He says this had "no good issue."

9 See Lissa Folio 5 (film 346-348), Andrew Slaby translation, notebook 11, 147-150, in Moravian Archives, Bethlehem, Pa., for an undated letter from Unity officials expressing these sentiments to those who had been excluded.

Chapter 19

The Fall

The Bohemian Revolution and Disaster
1618-1621

here the federation of the Unity, Lutherans, and Utraquists might have led in the decades following 1609's Letter of Majesty granting religious freedom is a matter of speculation. As the churches grew more trusting of one another, a truly united Bohemian National Protestant Church might have developed. Given the remaining disparity of theological viewpoints among the partner churches, it is also possible that the union might have totally dissolved. Had the Unity lost its dedication and discipline, leaving it unable to maintain itself in the changed environment?[1] Would its larger ecclesiastical partners have absorbed the Unity? Or could spiritual renewal have led the Unity to a blossoming of life and mission? We cannot know the answers to these questions, because world politics intervened before the Bohemian church experiment of 1609 developed beyond its beginnings.

Archduke Matthias persuaded his unstable brother, King-Emperor Rudolf, to abdicate in 1611. Matthias then took full power as Bohemia's king and as Holy Roman emperor. His aim was to restore royal authority, which had eroded under Rudolf. One means of doing this was to play the various Protestant groups off against one another, exploiting their divisions for the benefit of the throne and the Catholic Church. In his German realms Matthias worked to weaken the Evangelical Union, which had been formed in 1608 under the leadership of Frederick, elector of the Palatinate. In Bohemia and Moravia, Matthias and the new Catholic archbishop of Prague, John Lohelius (1612-22), hoped to intensify the tensions that still remained among the Unity, Lutherans, and Utraquists even after the agreements of 1609. For this purpose Matthias's royal aims and those of the Catholic Counter-Reformation ran parallel.[2]*

Matthias also made provision for the future of his dynasty. In 1617 he was 60 years old and had no son. He therefore persuaded Bohemia's national assembly to accept his nephew Ferdinand as his heir. For Bohemian Protestants this was a recipe for disaster, for Ferdinand had already shown himself as an even more zealous advocate of royal and Catholic authority than Rudolf or Matthias. The Utraquist, Lutheran, and Unity nobles, who were the majority in the assembly, were reluctant to accept Ferdinand, but the emperor had caught them flat-footed, and they had no alternative candidate to suggest. After Ferdinand agreed to maintain Rudolf's Letter of Majesty for religious freedom, the nobles agreed to accept him. Moravia's national assembly also accepted him after he promised religious toleration.[3] Such promises were written on the wind.

Matters grew worse for the Protestants when Matthias moved his official residence from Prague to Vienna and left the Czech lands under a board of 10 governors or regents. The three Utraquist-Protestant governors were always outvoted by the seven Catholic governors appointed by the emperor. Greatly encouraged by this turn of events, the Catholic authorities in Bohemia and Moravia set about disrupting the agreements of 1609 at every opportunity. Where Catholic and Utraquist parties disputed properties, the decision always went to the Catholics. Religious freedom was supposed to apply even to estates owned by the Roman Church, which for this purpose

---

* Ominously, the papacy had established an official Counter-Reformation office or department.

The Defenestration of 23 May 1618.

were counted with the royal estates, but Catholic authorities increasingly disregarded that right.[4]

In response to these infringements on their freedom and rights, the official "defenders" representing Utraquist, Lutheran, and Unity nobles called for a meeting of Bohemia's national assembly in May 1618. Matthias and Ferdinand had ignored their complaints, and the nobles were out of patience not only with infringement of religious rights, but also with what they viewed as an extension of royal power at their own expense. Tempers grew hot.

The Protestant lords were so incensed at the Catholic royal governors' failure to answer their complaints that they threw two of them out of high windows of Prague's Hradčany castle — the "Second Defenestration of Prague,"* on 23 May 1618. This time the king's officials survived. They landed on a refuse heap, which broke their fall, leaving them only bruised and battered.†

---

* For the "First Defenestration" see chapter 5.
† De Schweinitz, 494, adds the colorful detail that, frustrated that the fall had not killed the officials, several nobles drew pistols and shot

The news quickly spread. The royal court in Vienna was furious. In Moravia, several nobles wanted to join their Bohemian colleagues in this "heroic defense" of their rights. Charles of Žerotín, the Unity's leading Moravian noble, counseled against this. He knew the Bohemian nobles' actions would be considered open rebellion against the king and emperor, and chances for success in such a rebellion were slim to none.[5]

For their part, the majority of nobles in Bohemia's national assembly insisted their actions were not rebellion or an effort to dethrone the king. They declared they were defending the law of the land — religious freedom — against Catholic clerics and royal officials who were breaking it. A few Catholic lords joined them in this protest. The nobles issued a series of "apologies" defending their actions, then placed the government of Bohemia in the hands of 30 "directors" along with the national assembly. William of Roupova was at their head, and the Lutheran Count Šlik and the Unity's Count Budova took leading positions in the new government. To insure the support of the people of Prague, several positions on the governing board were reserved for townspeople, who were hesitant to join in at first but were soon swept up in the heat of the moment.[6]

Rebellion may not have been the stated purpose, but it had all the markings. Bohemia's new directory raised an army for the defense of the realm against "foreign" incursions. The Jesuits were banished from the land as "inciters of unrest," and Jesuit properties were distributed to Utraquists and Protestants.[7] Royal and "national" troops skirmished. Neighboring Moravia, though still not officially involved, in May 1619 sent a regiment of foot soldiers and 600 cavalry to join the nobles' Bohemian army.[8] Nonetheless, in the months following the defenestration a peaceful solution still seemed possible as the opposing parties continued to negotiate.[9]

---

at them. They missed. No wonder some Catholics considered the regents' escape as a miracle vindicating their cause.

In Vienna most royal advisors did not want a peaceful solution. In particular, Ferdinand, the designated king of Bohemia, saw the events as a golden opportunity to rescind the 1609 Letter of Majesty and crush the pesky estates and the Reformation all at once. Murderous assault on royal officials and armed resistance to the king's troops would surely free an emperor's hand to move forcibly against the nobility. When Matthias died in March 1619, Ferdinand assumed direct rule as Ferdinand II, Holy Roman emperor. Now all hope of compromise was lost. The only question was when open warfare would burst into flame.

The spark was not long coming. Contending that Ferdinand had failed to uphold the laws of the land, Bohemia's national assembly sought a new king.* Attention went first to Johann Georg, elector of neighboring Saxony. As a Lutheran he could be expected to champion the Protestant cause. But he was not interested, and besides, his uncontrolled drinking offended some of the Unity's clergy.10 The obvious remaining choice was Frederick V, elector of the Palatinate. He was the leader of the Protestant League in Germany, which could be expected to rise to his and Bohemia's defense. Many Czech nobles had studied at Heidelberg and had friends at the elector's court there. His wife Elizabeth was daughter of King James I of England, so surely that Protestant power would send troops to aid the Czech Protestants. To top it all, Frederick was the only elector of the Holy Roman Empire who was a member of the Reformed Church; this made him especially appealing to the Unity.11

So on 26 August 1619 Bohemia's national assembly, thinking it was finally finished with Ferdinand, duly elected Frederick of the Palatinate as king of Bohemia.12

Trouble arose almost at once. Elector Johann Georg of Saxony, while he had not wanted the Bohemian throne, was offended when it was not offered to him. In addition, his

---

* The Bohemian throne was elective, so the nobles could claim that if they had the right to elect a king, they also had the right to "un-elect" one, in this case Ferdinand II.

Lutheran court preacher, Matthias Hoë, was a violent opponent of Calvinism in any form. He urged the elector to join with the Holy Roman emperor (Ferdinand, who still firmly gripped this title) to stamp out Calvinism in Bohemia. Perhaps Hoë thought the emperor, thoroughly Catholic and unsympathetic to any Protestant notion, would allow Lutherans to remain undisturbed in Bohemia after the Calvinists were eliminated. In any event, Saxony declared in favor of the emperor, and one ally for the new Bohemian administration was lost.[13] Other German Lutheran princes also moved to distance themselves from this spread of Reformed power within the Empire.

In spite of this, the newly reorganized national religious consistory in Prague made preparations to welcome the new king. The Unity's representative, Bishop Matthias Cyrus, had died in 1618, and had been succeeded by Bishop John Cyril. John Korvin remained on the consistory, and Paul Fabricius had been named to fill the Unity's third spot. Utraquist leadership changed too. Administrator Sigismund Crinitus died in June 1619, and his place was taken by George Dykastus.[14]

"King" Frederick and his wife Elizabeth received a festal welcome as they arrived in Prague at the end of October 1619. On 4 November he was crowned king of Bohemia in St. Vitus Cathedral by the Utraquist administrator Dykastus and the Unity Bishop John Cyril.* The Reformation had "reached its climax in Bohemia."[15]

The rapturous enthusiasm with which Bohemia's Protestants (and some Catholics as well) welcomed Frederick was soon dampened by his foolish and high-handed actions. Indeed, many wondered if they had exchanged a Catholic tyrant for a Reformed one. He knew and understood little about Bohemia,[16] and he had brought his court preacher, Abraham Scuttetus, with him. Scuttetus was a fanatical Calvinist who was determined to bring about a "fundamental Reformation" in the Czech lands. He did not bother with the Unity, which he

---

* So far as I know, this is the only coronation ever performed by a bishop of the Unity.

considered mostly Reformed, and the Lutherans could be dealt with later. The Utraquists were another matter. Scuttetus called them "idolatrous quasi-papists," and moved to make them mend their ways. For Scuttetus and Frederick this was natural, for under the terms of the Peace of Augsburg, a land's religion should be that of its ruler who had a duty to "reform" his people's religious beliefs to match his own, in this case Calvinist. Neither man could grasp the Czechs' acceptance of different ways and traditions in the Czech church, which included toleration even for the minority Catholics.[17]

The king's "reform" began in Prague's St. Vitus Cathedral, a Utraquist church. Anything having the least hint of Catholicism was "cleansed" or destroyed. Pictures, statues, and the high altar itself were torn down. Aside from their religious significance, some of the statues and paintings were national treasures of art that fell to this act of "pure vandalism."[18] Moreover, by the king's command, the orders of service of his Reformed Church of the Palatinate were introduced on all royal estates, thus forcing Utraquists to lay aside their beloved Catholic liturgy, which had been practiced in the archdiocese of Prague since the 1300s.[19]* The Utraquists were scandalized. The Lutherans, who also kept more medieval usages, were unhappy as well, for they had no more use than the Catholics and Utraquists for the austere Reformed services.

As for the Unity, Utraquist scholar Zdeněk David asserts that the Brethren cooperated in the desecration of St. Vitus.[20] Doubtless, some Unity members wholeheartedly approved, though the Inner Council did not agree with such rapid "Calvinization."[21] In Poland when formerly Catholic parishes were given to the Unity, its ministers gradually removed pictures, etc., and they prepared the people for the change. Neither did they destroy such statues and pictures, but care-

---

* The Roman Church had introduced revisions in its liturgy at the Council of Trent in the mid-1500s. This Tridentine liturgy remained in use until the mid 20th century. The Utraquists had maintained the older forms.

fully stored them.* Besides, the Unity had its own customs and orders of service, and it was not ready to abandon them for forms imported from the Palatinate. Indeed, in 1620 Bishop Cyril had brought out a new *Agenda* (*Orders of Service*) for use in former Utraquist churches now served by the Unity. These kept the essential form of the Unity's traditional services, but used terms familiar to the Utraquists (priest, altar, hosts, etc.) to make them more palatable for the people. Theologically, these services were not extremely Lutheran or Reformed. They might even have provided a beginning point for a united liturgy in the future.[22] But that was not what Frederick and the radical Reformed had in mind. He demanded uniformity in worship, and he wanted it now. In general, though, the Unity maintained its belief that the forms of worship were non-essential and should not be imposed by the state.

Some of the new Czech government's leaders embraced Frederick's changes with enthusiasm. Count Šlik, formerly the leading Czech Lutheran noble, waxed so enthusiastic he wished the whole country would become Reformed. At Christmas 1619, the Unity's Count Budova happily took part in a Reformed communion in the "cleansed" St. Vitus Cathedral. At Easter 1620 Budova wanted Bishop Cyril to put aside the Unity's Easter service and use the Reformed's. Bishop Cyril replied he would rather leave Prague than do so.[23]

While Budova and other Bohemian revolutionaries may have enjoyed the breath of Reformed "freedom" sweeping their country, they were disappointed that the nobility of Moravia did not join them. At least in part, Moravia's reluctance to rise in revolt was a result of the continued efforts of the Unity's Lord Charles of Žerotín and his efforts to keep Moravia loyal to the emperor. Not that he was fond of Ferdinand. Rather, he believed revolution could not succeed, and he foresaw disaster for those who got mixed up in it.[24]

---

* See chapter 13. Unity ministers did, however, at times paint over frescoes on the walls.

When Ferdinand II received word of his ouster as king of Bohemia, he fell into a long period of depression. Meanwhile, he reasserted his authority in Austria, and solidified his claim as Holy Roman emperor on the death of his uncle Matthias in March 1619. Boosted by his renewed position and power, he rallied and laid plans to take back the Bohemian throne. With the resources of the empire and his widespread Hapsburg family, he began to assemble a mighty army. He received money and troops from Spain, the papacy, the Catholic League in Germany, and some from the disgruntled Protestant elector of Saxony. This was in addition to his personal Austrian forces. Because of its powerful Protestant nobles, Catholic Poland did not respond as had been hoped, but Ferdinand now had a huge and powerful force to put down the Bohemian revolt.

No doubt the rebellious Bohemians thought of the glorious days of John Žižka, when the Hussite heroes had repelled the mighty invading armies one after the other. Not only did the leaders in Prague envision the Bohemian nation turning out for the defense of its freedom, but they still confidently expected help from abroad. Frederick was head of the Protestant League in Germany, and troops from there would surely arrive shortly. They counted heavily on armies from England, assuming that King James would come to his daughter and son-in-law's defense.

Help failed to materialize. German Protestants had other matters to think of, including a brewing war of their own with Catholic Ferdinand. Besides, many Lutherans had no interest in assisting a Reformed ruler far away. Hungarian Protestants joined the rebellion, but were slow to organize and failed to arrive in time. The only sizable foreign troops who rallied to Frederick's cause came from Reformed Holland, but they proved undisciplined and spent most of their time plundering Czech farmsteads. Instead of fighting Catholic invaders, Czech peasants had to defend themselves against the Dutch.[25]

But what of the aid that was sure to come from England? Frederick and the Bohemian revolutionaries forgot that King James I of England was as much an advocate of the divine right of kings and royal absolutism as any Hapsburg. He considered that Frederick had accepted the Bohemian throne illegally from a bunch of rebels. James was also facing growing opposition from the Puritans at home. The Bohemians would look in vain for armies bearing England's red cross of St. George to come marching to their aid.

When Ferdinand's armies crossed the frontier into Bohemia in November 1620, the Czech defense was grossly unprepared. The leaders of the revolution failed to understand the gravity of their plight. Not only did they vainly hope for help from abroad, but they failed to equip and train their own forces. Bohemia's revolutionary army rushed toward Prague to meet Ferdinand's army, which had advanced toward White Mountain (Bílá Hora), about three miles to the west of the city.

Bohemia's defense force reached Prague on 7 November and deployed at White Mountain.[26] Frederick was with them, but decided to spend the night in the greater comfort of the city. The next morning the commander of the army sent Frederick word that the imperial forces were about to attack and urgently begged the king come rally his troops. Frederick, however, discounted the news, went to a prayer service at the cathedral, and met with the English ambassadors. He then sat down for a leisurely midday meal. It was then that news arrived that the battle was on. Now Frederick finally summoned the 500 men detached to guard the castle, and at their head started for the battlefield. He got no farther than the city gate, when his generals met him as they fled from the field. The battle had lasted only an hour, and the Czech national forces had been completely defeated. Frederick turned and ran. The Battle of White Mountain on 8 November 1620 remains one of the critical events of Czech history.[27]*

---

* Over the years the story of these events has been passed down and perhaps embellished from generation to generation. In 1977 Bishop Adolf Ulrich took me to the battle site and led me to the spot where by tradition the last Czech officer made the final stand with his company. After the soldiers were cut down one by one, the officer alone was left standing, surrounded by the enemy. He was given a

A few Bohemian and Hungarian troops had not yet reached the battlefield, but with the flight of Frederick,* any further fighting was hopeless. Bohemia and Moravia surrendered. True to its old militant reputation, Tábor held out the longest of the cities, and in the Vlašsko region of far eastern Moravia some resistance continued for years.[28] For all intents and purposes, however, the revolution was finished.

Prague was immediately occupied and plundered by the imperial troops. Most of the revolutionary leaders who had not already fled with Frederick went into hiding. So did the Unity's ministers stationed in Prague. They remained in the area to give what spiritual care they could, but danger of capture was constant.[29]

Fear of what might come was general. Unity historian Říčan views it this way: "Bohemia and Moravia surrendered themselves to the mercy, or lack of it, of their conquerors."[30] Utraquist scholar Zdeněk David gives a more lengthy, poignant assessment:

> During the restored reign of King Ferdinand II, Bohemia witnessed an abrupt and drastic imposition of the Counter-Reformation, which proceeded in an unrestrained way due to the simultaneous introduction of royal absolutism by the victorious Habsburg. Gone was the remarkable state of relative tolerance, respect for human rights, unfettered learning, and economic prosperity that hitherto had characterized the Kingdom of Bohemia. The era of Camelot was over.[31]

Bohemia was placed under the direct supervision of Karl of Liechtenstein. He was a wealthy Moravian noble and a former student of the Brethren's school at Ivančice who had changed his allegiance to Rome. Moravia was under Cardinal Franz von

---

chance to surrender, but with a loud cry he hurled his battle axe at the imperial soldiers and threw himself upon their spears and swords.

* Frederick of the Palatinate has been given the rather contemptuous title of the "Winter King" because of the shortness of his reign, which lasted only a year. He disappeared like melting snow when the heat was on.

Dietrichstein, bishop of Olomouc. Both had worked together for years to suppress all non-Roman churches. Now they had their chance.[32]

Many Bohemian and Moravian nobles fled the countries. Budova, however, remained behind. He said his conscience was clear, that he and the other leaders had done nothing wrong and therefore had nothing to fear. For three months it appeared that Budova might be right, and that Ferdinand would take no further action against them. The rebel leaders came out of hiding. In February 1621 the nobles who had led the revolution were summoned to appear before Karl of Liechtenstein to hear a pronouncement from the emperor. Leaders who were not of the nobility were summoned to appear before the Prague city council. In spite of warnings to run, these men obeyed the summons. All 43 of them, nobles and commoners alike, were taken into custody.[33]

A royal command required any revolutionary leaders who had fled to return for trial within six weeks. None did. Count Šlik, however, was apprehended in Saxony and brought back to Prague to join his compatriots in prison. Their trial, which began on 29 March, was only a formality. Each prisoner was arraigned and interrogated separately, which stretched the process well into June, but the question was not guilt or innocence, only how severe the sentence would be. Recommended verdicts were passed on to Ferdinand, who reduced a few death sentences to life in prison or confiscation of all property, but otherwise let the judges' verdicts stand.

The prisoners were assembled in the Hradčany castle on Saturday, 19 June 1621, to hear the formal sentences read. Twenty-seven were condemned to death. Among these were Counts Šlik and Budova. Seven members of the Unity, counting Budova, were among those sentenced to die. One Catholic, Dionys Černin, was among the condemned. His only crime appears to have been opening the castle gates to the rebel leaders on the day of the "defenestration." Sixteen other

Sunrise on the Týn Church, 21 June 1621 — the Day of Blood.

"rebels" were condemned to life in prison. Monday, 21 June, was set for the executions.

That Saturday night and Sunday, 20 June, the prisoners prepared for death. Ferdinand at first intended to allow only Catholic priests to counsel the condemned. He was prevailed upon to permit a few Lutheran clergy to speak with the men. One of these clergymen, John Rosacius, wrote a compelling eyewitness account of the executions titled *The Unfading Crown (Koruna neuvadlá)*, which provides the grim details.[34] Members of the Unity were not allowed to have their own clergy minister to them. A final service of holy communion was held for them, but Count Budova and Otto of Los declined to partake since their own Unity ministers were not allowed to give them the sacrament.[35]

Several Jesuits also visited the prisoners, hoping to get last-minute confessions and acceptance of the Catholic Church. Count Budova in particular took delight in arguing with the Jesuits, displaying a great knowledge of the Scriptures in refuting their arguments.[36]

The day of execution, 21 June 1621, arrived. It is known in Czech history as the "Day of Blood." No one can set the scene better than historian de Schweinitz:

> Toward dawn they prepared for their execution as though it were a marriage feast. They bathed and put on their finest linen. . . . When they were ready they gathered at the windows and looked out.
>
> A spectacle presented itself that might well have sent a thrill into their hearts. Fronting the *Grosse Ring* [the Old Town Square in Prague; see page 97] there had been built a scaffold, covered with black cloth and connected with the balcony of the Council House by a short flight of steps. The executioner was at his post. Near by lay four two-edged swords. Around the scaffold were drawn up in closed ranks squadrons of horse and companies of infantry. On the *Ring* itself surged a great multitude of spectators; others thronged the windows and even the roofs of the surrounding houses. Beyond, on the eastern side, was seen the venerable Thein [Týn] Church, with its two quaint towers; and on the peaked façade between

them appeared the colossal cup set up by the Hussites, the symbol of that heroic struggle for religious liberty which had endured for two centuries, but was now about to end in blood, oppression and woe. As the doomed men gazed upon this spectacle the sun rose in all his glory.[37]

At five in the morning a cannon fired from the castle signaled the beginning of the executions. They continued for five hours. The first to die was Count Šlik. On the scaffold he looked toward the sun and said: "O Christ, Thou Sun of Righteousness, grant that I may, through the shadow of death, come to Thy light." He paced and prayed for a few moments, then knelt on the black cloth in front of the executioner. "One swift blow and his head fell."[38] Six men wearing black masks carried his body away, and a clean black cloth was spread.

Budova came next. On his way to the scaffold he said: "Now I go in the garment of righteousness; thus arrayed I will appear before God in whom I have hoped." At the place of execution he ran his fingers through his hair and beard and said: "Thou old gray head of mine,* thou art highly honored; thou wilt be decorated with the martyr-crown."[39] After prayer he knelt before the executioner and was beheaded.

The other condemned prisoners followed one by one. Some expressed noble sentiments like Šlik and Budova; others met death with quiet stoicism. One, John Theodore Sixtus, was pardoned as he reached the scaffold. Most of the others were

---

* He was 74 years old but was not the oldest victim. Kaspar of Sulevič was 86.

beheaded, though three were hanged. Around 10 o'clock the executions were completed.*

The heads of 12 of the most prominent of them were put into iron baskets and placed on the towers of Prague's famous Charles Bridge, six at one end, six at the other.[40] There for the next 10 years, as a grim warning to all who would dispute the emperor's power, they kept their ghastly vigil over the city.

Notes

1 Joseph Th. Müller, *Geschichte der Böhmischen Brüder* 3 vols. (Herrnhut: Missionsbuchhandlung, 1922, 1931), 3:229.

2 Rudolf Říčan, *The History of the Unity of Brethren*, trans. C. Daniel Crews (Bethlehem, Pa.: Department of Publications and Communications, Moravian Church, Northern Province, 1992), 340. Müller, 3:223.

3 Říčan, 340.

4 Říčan, 341.

5 Müller, 3:272.

6 Zdeněk V. David, *Finding the Middle Way: The Utraquists' Liberal Challenge to Rome and Luther* (Washington, D.C.: Woodrow Wilson Center Press, 2003), 346-47.

7 Říčan, 341.

8 Müller, 3:273.

9 Müller, 3:224.

10 Říčan, 342.

11 Müller, 3:224.

12 David, 347.

13 Říčan, 342.

14 Müller, 3:225.

15 Říčan, 342.

16 Müller, 3:225.

17 Říčan, 342.

18 Říčan, 342. Müller, 3:225.

19 David, 144, 344.

20 David, 348-49.

21 Říčan, 342.

22 Müller, 3:226-27.

---

* A mosaic spelling out the date 21 June 1621 is set into the square to mark where the scaffold stood.

23 Müller, 3:226.

24 This and the next paragraphs are from Říčan, 343.

25 See also, David, 348.

26 This account is based on Edmund de Schweinitz, *History of the Church Known as the Unitas Fratrum*, 2nd (reprint) ed. (Bethlehem, Pa.: Moravian Publication Concern, 1901), 501-2. Říčan, 343, and Müller, 3:227, mention the battle, but omit the colorful details.

27 See Josef Petráň and Lydia Petraňová, "The White Mountain as a symbol in Modern Czech History," in *Bohemia in History*, ed. Mikuláš Teich (Cambridge: Cambridge University Press, 1998), 143-63.

28 Říčan, 346.

29 Müller, 3:317.

30 Říčan, 343-44.

31 David, 349.

32 Říčan, 344, 284-85.

33 Říčan, 345, supplemented by details from de Schweinitz, 505-6.

34 Říčan, 345. De Schweinitz, 509-31, uses sources based on this account to detail the execution of each prisoner, last words, etc.

35 Müller, 3:318.

36 Říčan, 345.

37 De Schweinitz, 509-10.

38 De Schweinitz, 512.

39 De Schweinitz, 516.

40 Müller, 3:318. Říčan, 345. Identification of Charles Bridge is an engraving of the first half of the 17th century published in *Unitas Fratrum Moravian Church in Pictures* (Prague: 1957), 74, also picture caption #2, 146.

Chapter 20

Exile and Shattered Hopes

To the Peace of Westphalia
1621-1648

$\mathfrak{F}$ollowing the Day of Blood, 21 June 1621, agents of the Roman hierarchy, accompanied by imperial soldiers and mercenaries, fanned out from Prague to begin the re-establishment of Catholicism as the only church in the land. In July 1621 they reached Fulnek in northeastern Moravia, home of the Unity's leading German-speaking congregation.

The Unity's minister there was a 29-year-old named John Amos Comenius (Komenský).[1] He was born on 28 March 1592 into a well-to-do Unity family in the region of Uherský Brod[2] in eastern Moravia. He was orphaned at the age of 12, and the Hungarian invasions under Bocskay in 1603-06* resulted in the ruin of much of the family property. He received his elementary education in the Unity's school at Strážnice, and at age 15 he advanced to its high school in Přerov. He impressed Bishop John Lanetius with his academic abilities, and upon the bishop's recommendation, Charles of Žerotín agreed to fund his further education abroad, first at the academy of Herborn in Nassau, and then at the university in Heidelberg. When he returned home in 1614 Comenius was ordained a deacon and was assigned to teach in the Unity's school in Přerov. There he took to the academic life, and published a

---

* See chapter 17.

Latin grammar in Prague in 1616. He began work on a Czech dictionary and encyclopedia. He married Magdaline Vízovská, the daughter of another well-to-do Unity family, was ordained a Unity priest in 1616, and in 1618 was assigned to the Fulnek congregation. There he combined pastoral duties and writing additional instructional works. Comenius was settled down for a fruitful, peaceful career.

All that changed in July 1621 when imperial Spanish troops rode into Fulnek. Warning of their coming had been given, so Comenius had already taken his personal library to the town hall for safe-keeping, and he and his family fled into hiding. That did not spare the town, for in the coming months the soldiers herded the inhabitants into the Unity's sbor (church building) and made them listen to sermons by Capuchin monks. After two years of indoctrination in the schools, the children

John Amos Comenius.

were sent home to look for "heretical" books and bring them to the town square. There in May 1623 they were instructed to throw the offending volumes on the fire. Comenius's library had been discovered in the town hall, and it too was burned. Unity ministers still in hiding in the area continued to hold secret services for their members, but with a Spanish garrison stationed in Fulnek, it was too dangerous there, so services were held in nearby Suchdol (Zauchtenthal in German). [3]

Ferdinand II had banned non-Catholic ministers from the country at the end of 1621. In deference to the Lutheran elector of Saxony, who had allied himself with the emperor during the revolution, Lutheran clergy were spared at first, but these were also banned in 1622.[4]

The Unity's Lord Charles of Žerotín had not participated in the rebellion, and indeed had argued against it. He therefore was not subject to the retribution that befell many other Unity nobles. He was even able to arrange an audience with Ferdinand to plead for cessation of the forcible re-Catholicization of the Czech lands. He was told, however, that "the leading of people into the Roman Church was not a punishment for the revolt — rather, it was an expression of the sovereign's obligatory care for the salvation of his subjects."[5]

For a time Žerotín could offer shelter to Unity ministers on his estates of Přerov, Náměšť, Kralice, and Brandýs nad Orlicí.* It was to Brandýs that Comenius came at the end of 1622. He must have been near the depths of despair, not only because of the national tragedy but also because of the loss of his own home, books, and writings. In addition, after more than a year of hiding, he had left his wife and child with her mother in Přerov. Magdaline was expecting another child, and so could not undertake a rigorous journey. Soon after giving birth, mother and both children died of the pestilence.[6] Nevertheless, in Brandýs Comenius devoted himself to writing "comforting works" to encourage his Brothers and Sisters in the Unity. The best known of these is *The Labyrinth of the World* (*Labyrint světa*), a Czech *Pilgrim's Progress* in which the pilgrim on his travels experiences all the ills and injustices of the world until he finds the only true rest in Christ in "the paradise of the heart."[7]

The fate of Unity congregations not on Žerotín's estates was similar to Fulnek. As the long-time headquarters of the Unity, Mladá Boleslav received particular attention. Bishop Matthias Konečný left there for his own safety around the time of the

---

* In such perilous times, the shelter offered at Brandýs made it seem a "promised land." The refugees referred to it as "Canaan."

Eliminating all trace — burning Unity books.

Day of Blood.* He died in Brandýs nad Orlicí, where Bishop George Erastus had also taken shelter, in 1622. Imperial authorities occupied Mladá Boleslav in 1623 and declared the congregation closed. The pastor was thrown out of the congregation house and given until sunset to leave town. With contemptuous irony, the Unity members were then told that since they did not have a minister, they must attend the Catholic Church. The Brethren's school was closed as well, and the children were sent to the now Catholic city school. A Catholic Mass, with communion for the people in one kind only, was said in the old city church for the first time in 200 years. The next year, 1624, the Unity's fine sbor was also turned into a Catholic church. Since the sbor had no "proper" altar, a Catholic bishop sent a special altar stone on which

---

* A cache of Unity books and documents belonging to Konečný, hidden after White Mountain, was discovered in 2006 in Mladá Boleslav. See *Moravian Messenger* (British Province), Jan. 2007, 4.

Mass could be celebrated. To add insult to injury, the non-Catholic inhabitants of the city were assessed a hefty sum for the stone. The sbor was re-consecrated as the Church of St. Wenceslas, and the Brethren's Scripture verses painted on the walls were whitewashed over. For a time, Unity ministers held secret services in the area, but heavy fines were levied on anyone caught going to them. An imperial garrison patrolled to enforce compliance with imperial decrees. Some Unity members slipped into exile, but that was costly and dangerous. Most eventually became nominal Catholics.[8]

The Unity center of Ivančice in Moravia was also lost. The local lord, Berthold of Lupa, had joined in the revolution. All his lands were confiscated, and he was sentenced to three years in prison. Upon the completion of his sentence, he was banished from the country; he died in poverty in Hungary.[9] As in Mladá Boleslav, Unity members in Ivančice were forcibly converted and their children indoctrinated.

In 1624 a new proclamation of banishment was issued. This time there were no exceptions. Nobles, including those who had been loyal to the emperor, were forbidden to protect Protestants, even on their own estates. Žerotín found churches on his land closed or given to the Catholics. In anger he ripped the emperor's seal off one of the closed churches, but was warned that no "heretic" clergy would be tolerated anywhere in the country. This stricter banishment applied to both Moravia and Bohemia, and placed the lives of approximately 200 Unity ministers at even greater risk.[10]

In cities and villages throughout the two countries forced mass conversions continued apace. Unity churches were shuttered, and historian Říčan writes of "enforced administration of the sacrament under one kind."[11]* Tears and pleading did

---

* This is ironic from the perspective of the Roman Catholic Church today. The official *Daily Roman Missal*, ed. James Socías (Chicago: Midwest Theological Forum, 2004), 799, quotes the Catholic Church's *General Instruction of the Roman Missal, 2003*, 281: "The sign of communion is more complete when given under both kinds, since the sign of the Eucharist meal appears more clearly. The

no good. Those who begged for mercy were told: "It must be so!"[12] In places, the country people tried to resist, but contingents of imperial troops from throughout the Hapsburg empire kept ironclad order. Nobles could provide no protection. Indeed, most of the friendly nobles had had their properties confiscated, and their estates were given to Czech Catholics or unsympathetic foreigners.[13]

Utraquism was suppressed by Ferdinand and his agents as well. Utraquist priests who had secured Lutheran ordination in Germany were counted as Protestants and banned.* Utraquist priests with Roman ordination were allowed to continue their ministries if they would swear complete obedience to Rome and the decrees of the Council of Trent. Henceforth, they were to administer communion in one kind only and use Latin alone in services.† A separate Utraquist consistory was prohibited. As a symbol of the complete integration of the Utraquists into the Roman Church, the large chalice of the Hussites was removed from the front of the Týn Church in Prague in 1623. The statue of George Poděbrady, the "heretic king," was also removed. Followers of the Counter-Reformation were determined to stamp out anything remotely Hussite. Even John Rokycana, the 15th-century Utraquist leader, fell prey. His tombstone, which portrayed him in archbishop's vestments, was removed from the Týn Church, and his body was exhumed and burned in the churchyard. He had died a century and a half before.[14]

In the meantime, Ferdinand II turned his attention to the total defeat of Frederick of the Palatinate in that unlucky ruler's home territory. After some initial successes, Frederick's

---

intention of Christ that the new and eternal covenant be ratified in his blood is better expressed, as is the relation of the eucharistic banquet to the heavenly banquet."

* The great majority of Utraquist clergy had Roman ordination. Müller, 3:206, notes that a few (in the later years after some Utraquists inclined more to Lutheranism) had obtained ordination in Lutheran Germany. Traditional Catholic-leaning Utraquists would not recognize such an ordination.

† The Utraquists had made limited use of Czech in prayers, hymns, etc.

troops were roundly defeated, and the Palatinate fell firmly into Ferdinand's hands by the end of 1624. The German Protestants had not worried over the fall of Bohemia, but the loss of the Palatinate did alarm them. They feared Ferdinand would use it as a springboard to attack them, Reformed and Lutheran alike. England and France were also alarmed,* but were entangled in various alliances with Hapsburg Spain and so did not intervene directly. King Christian IV of Denmark and Norway, however, entered the war in 1625 on the Protestant side. His motives had more to do with gaining control of the Duchy of Holstein than defending Protestantism. Still, the Bohemians and others took hope from his intervention, though Catholic forces under Count John Tilly and Albrecht von Wallenstein soon won victories that strengthened Ferdinand's power in the empire. Now well under way, the Thirty Years War would drag on for decades, sapping the economic resources and spirits of all who fought in it.

Despite continued hope that Protestant victory in Germany might revive Czech fortunes, the Unity's leaders decided that preparations must be made in case mass exile became necessary. Unity members in Moravia could move to Slovakia, which at the time was Hungarian territory and so for the moment was spared the fate of the Unity in Bohemia and Moravia. The Czech and Slovak languages were similar, and they were all Slavs, so Moravians could fit in there with relative ease. Exile from Bohemia was not so easy. Refugees would have to traverse all of Moravia to get to Slovakia. Besides, Slovakia did not have the room for Bohemian as well as Moravian Unity exiles. And so in 1625 the Inner Council sent John Amos Comenius to Poland to search out a sanctuary where a sizable group of refugees might settle alongside the Unity congregations already there. He reported back in 1626

* France's concern was political, not religious. Catholic or not, King Louis XIII of France and his prime minister, Cardinal Richelieu, did not want the Holy Roman emperor to become too powerful.

that Count Lesczyński had offered them a place on his estates around Lissa (Leszno).[15]

About this time, Comenius came into contact with one Christoph Kotter, the first of several self-proclaimed mystic prophets who predicted the fall of the Hapsburgs. He later fell under the spell of other such charlatans, notably Christina Poniatovská and Nicholas Drabík.[16] Like many at the time, Comenius was so eager for the restoration of his native land that he believed Kotter's prophecies, much to his later regret. The predictions of all these "prophets" proved false, and the character of their lives indicates a less than heavenly origin for their visions.

The Unity was fortunate it was preparing for hard times ahead rather than trusting in prophecies for the fall of the Hapsburgs and King Frederick's return. On 31 July 1627 a new constitution was proclaimed for Bohemia. The date alone was ominous — the feast day of Ignatius Loyola (d. 1556), founder of the Jesuits, who were leading the Catholic Counter-Reformation. In this constitution, Hapsburg supremacy was affirmed. It was also declared that henceforth only Roman Catholics would be allowed in Bohemia. Everyone who would not convert was given six months to leave the country. This applied not only to commoners, but to all the nobility as well. A similar constitution was proclaimed for Moravia in 1628.[17] Now even such an opponent of the revolution as Charles of Žerotín had to become Catholic or leave his ancestral lands.

The order was strictly carried out. Žerotín left Moravia. For safekeeping, he took with him the official library of the Unity bishops, and he settled in Bratislava in Slovakia. From there he assisted Unity priests and other exiles. He also had the Unity's printing press moved from Kralice to Lissa. As a reward for his previous loyalty to the emperor, he was allowed to retain ownership of most of his estates and was permitted to return to them for brief periods.[18]*

---

* On one such visit he died in Přerov in 1636. He was buried in Brandýs nad Orlicí without any religious service.

Other nobles, townspeople, and farmers were not so fortunate. They could either become Catholic or leave. Selling their homes and other real properties was difficult, for there was a glut of these on the market, and prices were correspondingly low. Renting out property was impractical, for collecting the rent from abroad depended on the honesty of the renter. On the other hand, even if renters were honest and willing to pay, imperial officials might take a dim view of people who were sending money out of the country to "heretics" abroad. In effect, most of the Unity's exiles lost their property.

The Utraquists were included in this ban as well, but there were too many of them to emigrate *en masse*. Protestants in Germany and elsewhere offered assistance but were not prepared to cope with crowds of Bohemians showing up on their doorsteps. Groups of Utraquists, nevertheless, did cross into Saxony. They were told they could stay and have Czech congregations, but only under Lutheran control and order.[19] No wonder most Czechs chose to remain at home and become nominal Catholics.

The Unity was now thoroughly uprooted in Bohemia and Moravia. Many members from Moravia did slip over the border into Hungarian-controlled Slovakia, where they formed Unity congregations as they could. In Bohemia, Bishop George Erastus and John Amos Comenius prepared to journey into Poland with groups of refugees. On 1 February 1628 Comenius crossed the Riesen Mountains, never to set foot in his earthly homeland again. Tradition records that the band of exiles knelt at the crest of the mountains, while Comenius offered a heartfelt prayer that God would again bless the Czech lands and leave a "hidden seed" there which would someday burst forth into a renewed faith and church.[20] "The year 1628," historian Müller observes, "marks the end of the Brethren's Church as an independent church in Bohemia and Moravia."[21]

For a time, though, the heritage of the Unity still flickered in its homelands. The majority of it members did not flee, but stayed home in Bohemia and Moravia. Within a generation or two, many became Catholic. Others pretended conversion but

Comenius leads his congregation into exile: "Blessed be the day when I must roam."

secretly continued to hold on to their Unity faith. Congregation elders or heads of households conducted services in homes when they could. Their Bibles, New Testaments, hymnals, catechisms, and prayer books nurtured their souls and trained the children. At least for a time, Unity clergy made secret trips into Bohemia and Moravia to hold services and to smuggle in new publications.[22]

The number of Unity members who went into foreign countries was between 5,000 and 6,000. Exile was easiest for the nobility and gentry, who could find service in foreign courts. Other Unity members became teachers, doctors, and writers abroad.* Many went to Holland, where Frederick of the Palatinate had taken refuge, and most of them eventually joined the Reformed Church.

A Unity congregation was formed in Brieg in Silesia,[23] which was near the Czech border, so the exiles could return home quickly if the Protestant forces from Germany succeeded in overthrowing the Hapsburgs. That never happened. Many Unity members from Moravia settled in the regions of Skalica and Považí in Slovakia. They too hoped for a speedy return home. Unity congregations persisted there for a few decades but were eventually absorbed by the Reformed Church.[24]

In Poland the Unity's exiles from Bohemia settled in and around Lissa and on the estates of friendly nobles, principally in Skoki, Ostroróg, and Włodawa. There, as formerly in Bohemia, the nobility protected them. The exiles did not merge with Polish Unity congregations, but tried to keep together as Czechs, since they still expected to return home in the near future. Comenius wrote works to prepare the Unity for its renewal in that ever-elusive new day. For now, Bishop Erastus settled alongside Bishop Martin Gratian Gertich in Lissa,† and Bishop John Cyril went to Brieg. The Unity maintained a

---

* From this time, the word "Bohemian" came to refer to intellectuals and artists who roamed Europe outside conventional society.

† Martin Gratian Gertich died in Lissa in 1629. His cousin, also named Martin Gertich, became a bishop in 1644. The similarity of names has led to confusion of the two.

separate administration for the six or so Bohemian exile congregations, and the Bohemian bishops also looked after the three or four congregations that had gathered in Hungarian-controlled Slovakia.[25]

In Lissa, Comenius began to rise to prominence. In 1624, before the final decrees of exile, he had married Dorothy (Dorota), daughter of Bishop John Cyril, and thus he had a close relationship to the Unity's leadership. Now he engaged in extensive literary activity on behalf of the Unity, which gained him respect on his own. Historian Říčan characterizes his piety as "lively, witty, and full of personal feeling," though thoroughly "biblical." He says Comenius's tone is "appreciably different from the sober and less personally absorbed view of faith of the old Brethren towards God revealed in Christ."[26] He was influenced by neo-platonic philosophy and by writers such as the German mystic Jacob Böhme (d. 1624) to see God as the center of all. All wisdom and goodness flow from God, so science and knowledge of the physical world are good, and there is no sharp distinction of secular and religious learning.[27] And all knowledge must be seen in conjunction with God as revealed in Christ. Rather than "total depravity," Comenius believed humans had a "good 'root'" inside that is cultivated through the grace of Christ.[28] He was therefore a humanist, though not a "secular" humanist, for without Christ, the best human achievements are perverted and oppressive.

Comenius expressed his views on learning in *Didactica,** which he intended for the guidance of Czech teachers once the fortunes of the nation were restored. In 1631 he wrote *Janua linguarum reserata* (*The Gate of Languages Unlocked*) for the school children of Lissa. It proved so effective it was widely used all over Europe and made Comenius a name recognized in educational circles, though he himself never forgot his first calling as a minister of the Unity.[29] He later became famous for his use of pictures in textbooks. Medieval cathedrals had for centuries used statues, paintings, and stained glass windows

---

* This was not published until later in a reworked form.

as teaching tools. Books also had had illustrations. It was Comenius who introduced illustrations into books as part of a graded curriculum. In his later *Orbis sensualium pictus* (*The Visible World in Pictures*) he presented domestic scenes keyed to a vocabulary. Later editions used this device to teach several languages at once, with parallel columns in Latin, Czech, German, and even Turkish, all keyed to the picture on the page.[30]*

Meanwhile, the Thirty Years War staggered on in fits and starts and shifting alliances, with neither side able to crush the other. It entered a new phase in 1630 when King Gustavus Adolphus of Sweden invaded northeastern Germany. Sweden was Protestant, but here too the motives were more territorial than religious. Fortunes of the war wavered back and forth from battle to battle. Saxony now joined the Protestant side and invaded Bohemia. By the end of 1631 Prague itself was in Saxon hands, and the victory so longed for by the Bohemian exiles seemed at hand. Many who had fled to Silesia returned, and several Protestant nobles came to reclaim their estates. The Lutherans in Bohemia formed a consistory, and much of the Catholic Counter-Reformation was undone. At last the heads severed on the Day of Blood 10 years earlier were taken down from the Charles Bridge in Prague.[31]

The Unity waited to see what happened before returning, but its leaders began making plans for reconstituting the church in its homeland. They weighed the advantages of complete independence against benefits of a federation of Protestants like that of 1609. Comenius wrote a work called *Haggai Brought Back to Life* (*Haggaeus redivivus*), in which he gave advice for the restoration of public life in Bohemia, as the biblical prophet Haggai had written instructions for the Jewish exiles returning from Babylon.[32]

---

* Among his many works on education is one he wrote for the first and best teachers of children, their mothers. *The School of Infancy* (*Informatorium školy mateřské*) (Chapel Hill, N.C.: University of North Carolina Press, 1956) is a homily of wise advice on educating children in their earliest years.

The blossoming of Protestantism in Prague lasted less than a year. In 1632 Albrecht of Wallenstein drove out the Saxons and reoccupied Bohemia for the emperor. Protestant hopes were dashed once more, the Jesuits returned, and the Catholic Counter-Reformation was on again.

In this changed situation the Unity held its first general synod since the exile. It met in Lissa in October 1632. Bishop Cyril had died five months before, and Bishop George Erastus, the only remaining bishop of the Bohemian-Moravian Unity, was growing frail. In spite of all previous disappointments, the synod delegates still hoped for a return home. They therefore elected new bishops to have the traditional full complement of four for the Czech lands: Matthias Prokop for Bohemia and its exiles, Paul Fabricius for the Bohemian exiles in Saxony, Laurentius Justinus for the Moravians at home or exiled in Slovakia or Silesia, and John Amos Comenius of Moravia as Unity "writer" and to guide the education of the Unity's youth.[*] Bishop Erastus performed the consecrations of three of these new bishops at the Lissa synod. Br. Fabricius's consecration had to be done later since dangerous travel conditions in Saxony prevented his attending the synod.[33]

In further anticipation of returning to the Unity's home-lands, the 1632 synod called for a reprinting of the Kralice Bible and the first printing of the *Church Order of the Unity*, the *Ratio Disciplinæ* of 1616. Plans were also made to bring out a biblical concordance, a revised edition of Jaffet's pseudo-history, and books of sample sermons. Only the *Ratio* and a smaller collection of historical tales were printed.[34]

Protestant hopes received a major setback just a month after the Lissa synod when King Gustavus Adolphus was killed at the battle of Lützen in November 1632. However, the Protestants were not completely defeated, and the Peace of

---

[*] The Polish Unity already had Bishops Daniel Mikołajewski and Paul Paliurus. The new ones were to take care of the exiles until the "return" to Bohemia and Moravia. De Schweinitz, 568, says Fabricius was for Poland, presumably since he never returned to Bohemia. He died in Lissa in 1649.

Prague, which ended "the Swedish Phase" of the Thirty Years War in 1635, gave some concessions to the Saxon Lutherans. No concessions were given for Bohemia and Moravia.

The Polish Unity and the weakened Polish Reformed Church in Lesser Poland and Lithuania entered into a union at Włodawa. The church order of the Unity was taken as a pattern, and a joint hymnal was called for. Unity and Reformed members did not live in the same areas, so this was not a merging of congregations. Each church maintained its own administration. The Unity congregations retained their traditions and services, but Unity bishops (Seniors) and Reformed superintendents were to meet together at stated intervals. Again this was a federation rather than a merger. The two churches together, however, could present a stronger front toward continuing Catholic pressure in Poland.[35]

The Unity in Poland took a more pronounced Reformed orientation in these years, which led to estrangement between Unity and Utraquist exiles from Bohemia who had settled in Saxony, Silesia, and Slovakia. These Utraquists were more Lutheran in their sympathies, and in exile had affiliated with the Lutheran state churches. A sore point arose about collections raised elsewhere in Europe for the relief of Bohemian refugees. Squabbles broke out over what share the Unity and the former Utraquists should get from the funds.[36]

In response to such theological and mercenary debates, Comenius in 1637 wrote *Way of Peace* (*Cesta pokoje; Via pacis*) calling for understanding and cooperation among the various Christian churches. Few were willing to listen.

Comenius also continued to work on his "pansophia" project, by which he hoped to spark a movement of scholars to collect and classify all human knowledge for the betterment of all. An English scientific and scholarly enthusiast, Samuel Hartlib, had one of Comenius's preliminary works on this project published,[37] and it attracted the notice of several members of the English Parliament. In 1641 they invited Comenius to come to England to discuss his ideas further. He hesitated to go, and indeed some members of the Unity had complained in 1639 that Comenius was neglecting his pastoral duties by becoming too involved in educational projects.[38] Since he misunderstood the invitation as an official one from the English government, he felt he had to go. Not only did he hope to further his pansophia project, but he also wanted to secure additional assistance for suffering Bohemian exiles. Upon his arrival in England in September 1641, he was disappointed to learn that his invitation was not as official as he had thought. Moreover, the outbreak of the English Civil War between royalists and Puritans a few months later put an end to all such lofty idealistic schemes. While in England he did write *The Way of Light* (*Via lucis*), in which he outlined his vision for a golden age when the light of God's truth would illuminate and reform human society.

Comenius did not accomplish his aims in England, but his visit made him widely known there and apparently in England's American colonies. In his *Magnalia Christi Americana*, Cotton Mather wrote that Comenius was offered the presidency of the fledgling Harvard College in Massachusetts.* Details of the event are contradictory. If an offer was made, Comenius could not leave his responsibilities in Europe to make such a move. That alone would have made such a venture nearly impossible. Besides, his wife had not wanted to accompany him for a lengthy stay in London, where she did not know the language or the customs. How could he ask her to move to the wilds of America?[39] Still, we may wonder what might have been the results if he had accepted such an offer and arranged for an American home for Unity exiles.

After his return from England, Comenius set about revamping the school system of Sweden. He was suggested for the task by the Dutch industrialist Louis de Geer, who had huge holdings in Sweden. Comenius was received by Queen Christina, who declared she had learned Latin from his textbooks. His reasons for doing educational work for the Swedes

---

* Cotton Mather's comment has become a literary byword: "That incomparable *Moravian* became not an *American*."

had as much to do with securing help for Bohemian exiles as it did with education. The chancellor of Sweden, Axel Oxenstern, had often promised that Sweden would some day liberate Bohemia. Based on this, many Bohemians had joined the Swedish army.* It was Comenius's hope that by doing a favor for Sweden, Oxenstern would see to Sweden's promise to free Comenius's homeland.[40]

Comenius was able to rework Sweden's educational curriculum from Elbing, Prussia, which was under Swedish jurisdiction at the time. This kept him close enough to Poland to take part in the administration and life of the Unity. He arrived in Elbing with his family at the end of 1642, and he remained there (with occasional trips to Poland) for six years. Then developments in the Unity demanded his more permanent return to Lissa.

Bishop Laurentius Justinus, who had been president of the Inner Council of the Unity since the death of Bishop Erastus in 1643, died in April 1648. Comenius was chosen as the new president of the council, and thus had to leave Elbing to assume his new duties. At this point world events complicated the life of Comenius and the Unity.

The Thirty Years War had straggled on with shifting alliances, advances, and defeats all around. France's entry on the "Protestant" side did nothing to resolve the conflict. In the mid-1640s the balance of power at last turned against the Hapsburgs, but Emperor Ferdinand III would not concede. By now both sides were like boxers in a drawn-out match too worn out to keep punching. So on 24 October 1648 the Peace of Westphalia was signed. Besides recognizing Switzerland and the Netherlands as independent states, the treaty greatly reduced the power and significance of the Holy Roman emperor in Germany. France became the leading power of western Europe.

Bohemia's exiles watched with eager anticipation as negotiations progressed for the end of the war. Surely the Swedes

---

* A Swedish army did indeed besiege Prague briefly in 1648.

With the settlement of exiles from Bohemia and Moravia in 1628, Lissa (Leszno) in Poland became the administrative center for the Unity. But Lissa's days too were numbered.

FAITH, LOVE, HOPE: A HISTORY OF THE UNITAS FRATRUM

 FAITH, LOVE, HOPE: A HISTORY OF THE UNITAS FRATRUM

and others would make good their promises to gain freedom for Bohemia. But the Hapsburgs remained immovable on that point, and the Protestant states were unwilling to keep the war going over one smallish country in central Europe. Religious boundaries would remain as they were in 1624.[41] Bohemia and Moravia not only remained under Hapsburg rule, but were officially recognized as Catholic countries. Comenius's piteous and angry reproaches failed to move Sweden's Oxenstern. Bohemian and Moravian Brethren were now utterly homeless, and this was now recognized by a treaty among the major European states.

"The Peace of Westphalia (1648)," historian Říčan writes, "sealed the catastrophe of White Mountain, the subjugation of the Czech nation, and the destruction of the organized church life of the Czech Evangelical church and the Unity in their homeland."[42]

Comenius was now administrative head of the Unity, but what was left to administer?

Notes

[1] The most recent biography of Comenius is Jaroslav Pánek, *Comenius: Teacher of Nations* (Prague: Orbis, 1992). A long-time standard is Matthew Spinka, *John Amos Comenius, That Incomparable Moravian* (Chicago: University of Chicago Press, 1943; reissue New York: Russell & Lowell, 1967).

[2] Earlier accounts say he was born in Nivnice near Uherský Brod. In the foreword to the 1967 reissue of his biography, Spinka says he now favors Uherský Brod.

[3] Joseph Th. Müller, *Geschichte der Böhmischen Brüder* 3 vols. (Herrnhut: Missionsbuchhandlung, 1922, 1931), 3:326-27.

[4] Rudolf Říčan, *The History of the Unity of Brethren*, trans. C. Daniel Crews (Bethlehem, Pa.: Department of Publications and Communications, Moravian Church, Northern Province, 1992), 345.

[5] Říčan, 346.

[6] Müller, 3:322. Spinka, 37.

[7] For the text see Howard Louthan and Andrea Sterk, trans., *The Labyrinth of the World and the Paradise of the Heart* (New York: Paulist Press, 1998). Still good is Matthew Spinka, trans. and ed., *The Labyrinth of the World and the Paradise of the Heart* (Chicago:

National Union of Czechoslovak Protestants in America, 1942). For a study of the *Labyrinth* see C. Daniel Crews, "Through the Labyrinth: A Prelude to the Comenius Anniversary of 1992," in *Transactions of the Moravian Historical Society* 27 (1992), 27-52.

[8] Müller, 3:319-20.

[9] Müller, 3:326.

[10] Müller, 3:323. Říčan, 346.

[11] Říčan, 346.

[12] Müller, 3:330.

[13] Říčan, 346.

[14] Zdeněk V. David, *Finding the Middle Way: The Utraquists' Liberal Challenge to Rome and Luther* (Washington, D.C.: Woodrow Wilson Center Press, 2003), 349-61, esp. 357.

[15] Říčan, 347. Müller, 3:324.

[16] Müller, 3:324-25, 337.

[17] Říčan, 347.

[18] Říčan, 347.

[19] Müller, 3:333.

[20] Müller, 3:325.

[21] Müller, 3:333.

[22] Říčan, 348.

[23] Müller, 3:333-34.

[24] Říčan, 349.

[25] Müller, 3:335-37.

[26] Říčan, 351.

[27] See Sook Jong Lee, "The Relationship of John Amos Comenius' Theology to His Educational Ideas," Ph.D. diss. (Rutgers University, 1987).

[28] Říčan, 353. John Sadler, *John Amos Comenius and the Concept of Universal Education* (New York: Barnes and Noble, 1966), 57.

[29] Říčan, 353. See Josef Smolík, "Comenius on Justification and Sanctification," *Communio Viatorum* 40 (1998): 137-44, esp. 137.

[30] For more on Comenius as an educator, see C. H. Dobinson, ed., *Comenius and Contemporary Education* (Hamburg: UNESCO Institute for Education, 1970), and John Sadler's *John Amos Comenius and the Concept of Universal Education*, cited above. More recent works include Daniel Murphy, *Comenius: A Critical Reassessment of his Life and Work* (Dublin and Portland, Ore.: Irish Academic Press, 1995), and Jean-Antoine Caravolas, "Comenius (Komenský) and the Theory of Language Teaching," *Acta Comeniana* 10 (1993): 141-62.

[31] Müller, 3:337. Říčan, 354-55.

[32] Říčan, 354-55.

[33] Müller, 3:338.

[34] Říčan, 356. Müller, 3:339.

[35] Říčan, 358.

36 Říčan, 358-59.
37 Spinka, *John Amos Comenius*, 72-74.
38 Říčan, 378.
39 Spinka, 84-86.
40 Říčan, 361-62. Spinka, 93-94, 98-99.
41 Müller, 3:347.
42 Říčan, 362.

Chapter 21

The Gathering Darkness

A Church of Hope

1648-1670. . .

After the Peace of Westphalia in 1648 the Bohemian and Moravian Unity members lost heart. With the rest of their suffering nation, they had received no recognition or legal status, and their persecution could continue unopposed. Even Czech Catholics saw their once proud land relegated to a backwater of the Hapsburg empire. Everyone else seemed to have forgotten them. Czechs who had fought with honor for the Swedes in the war were not paid the wages that country owed them, and widows of fallen soldiers were left penniless.[1]

John Amos Comenius continued his efforts on behalf of the Unity and Czech Protestants. He raised considerable funds from England and elsewhere, but hope for a return home was lost. He continued his literary work as well. In 1650 he brought out *The Bequest of the Dying Mother, the Unity of Brethren* (*Kšaft umírající matky Jednoty bratrské*). In this he depicts the Unity on her deathbed (like the patriarch Jacob in the closing chapters of Genesis) calling her children (the other churches) around her for a final blessing and bequest. The mother cannot give her children earthly goods, for all have been taken from her. Instead she gives them blessing and admonition to live a better life. To the Lutherans, she wishes "a better ordered discipline, and a better understanding of the article of justification." To the Reformed, who share her love of discipline, she advises "more simplicity and less speculation," and avoidance of divisiveness. She commends a desire for reconciliation to all Christians, and to her own Czechs she gives assurance that "after the passing of the storm," God will give them freedom again.* To the Catholics she can leave only a bad conscience.2

Comenius continued to labor in hope against hope, but when the death of Bishop Paul Fabricius in 1649 left Comenius as the only bishop for the Bohemian and Moravian portion of the Unity, additional bishops were not chosen. They were not needed, since so few members were left.† Comenius was very concerned that the legacy of the Unity should live on, and in his writings urged renewed faithfulness and dedication. He was convinced that a moral decline of the exiles and their children was the reason God was not allowing their return home.3

Bequest of the Dying Mother
— the Unitas Fratrum.

---

* Spinka, *John Amos Comenius*, 118, writes that Comenius's prediction was recalled 270 years later when Czechoslovakia finally gained its independence following World War I.
† Bishops were still being elected for the Polish branch of the Unity, however.

The Polish Unity was facing challenges as well. Bohuslav Lesczyński, whose family had protected the Unity on its estates in Poland, had become a Catholic in 1642 for political advancement. He promised the Unity he would continue to protect it. But a few years later in Lissa the city church was taken from the Unity and given to the Catholics. The Unity built a new, larger church for itself, but portents for the future were not good.[4]

In Slovakia Unity exiles from Moravia had benefited from the protection of the Calvinist prince of Transylvania, George I Rákóczy, who had won some concessions for Hungarian Protestants[*] near the close of the Thirty Years War. Unity members in Slovakia had affiliated themselves with the Reformed Church there, and thus had some legal status. They did not live in the same area as the Slovak Reformed Church, so they could maintain their own congregations and many of their Unity customs. These Unity members had also hoped to return to Moravia, but at the end of the war they began to consider Slovakia as their permanent home. They built a new church for themselves in Skalica. They were mindful of their heritage, however, and called for an official visitation from the Unity administration in Lissa. Comenius came to hold services for them at Easter 1650, and many members slipped over from Moravia for the celebrations. Comenius consecrated the new church, and introduced to them their new "Senior," John Chodníček. He was, however, a Reformed official and not a Unity bishop. Still, the members hoped that the Unity could live on in Slovakia in some way, even as part of the Reformed Church. Comenius approved this arrangement.[5]

During his visit to Slovakia Comenius met again a former Unity priest named Nicholas Drabík.[†] This "prophet" had been expelled from the Unity and was known for drunkenness and greedy behavior. After initial hesitation, Comenius came to

---

[*] Slovakia, Hungary, and Transylvania were part of the same realm at the time.
[†] See previous chapter.

believe Drabík's prediction that the Rákóczy family of Transylvania would win the Hungarian throne and then would lead an army for the liberation of Bohemia and Moravia. By this time, Comenius was so desperate for any voice of hope that his judgment was clouded.[6]

To encourage the Rákóczys to assume their role as deliverers, Comenius sought to do them a favor by reforming the schools in their town of Sárospatak in Transylvanian Hungary. Perhaps too he could prepare the next generation for their noble calling.[7] With his genuine interest in educational reform, Comenius hoped to establish a whole system of schools employing his belief that students should be treated as people and not animals. By kindly explaining concepts, and beginning from the simple and moving on to the more complex, teachers could cultivate the good that was in their students. Schools could become places of joy rather than "slaughterhouses of the mind."[8]

Comenius labored from 1650 to 1654 in Sárospatak, and his school had initial success, though it was short-lived. The prophecies of Drabík proved false when George Rákóczy nearly lost his throne in an abortive invasion of Hungary. And yet Comenius made good use of his years there.* He expanded his *Janua linguarum* and composed his *Orbis pictus* as an effective means of teaching languages, particularly to children.[9] This work became widely popular. In England it went through at least a dozen editions well into the 18th century. The expanded *Janua* also saw wide use. Based on the many copies left by alumni to libraries, it seems to have been a standard Latin text at Harvard for many years.[10]

Just as Comenius finished his sojourn in Transylvania, catastrophe befell Poland and the Unity members there. The king, John Kazimierz (1648-88), a fervent Catholic, went to war in 1655 with Protestant King Charles X Gustavus (1654-60) of Sweden over claims to the Swedish throne. The war is known

---

* Sárospatak cherishes the brief residence of its renowned educator, for its branch of the University of Miskolc is named for Comenius.

in Polish history as "the Deluge." For a time almost all of Poland was under Swedish control.[11]

Protestants in Poland tended to sympathize with the Swedish invaders. In Lissa, Unity members welcomed a Swedish garrison with open arms, believing the whole country would soon become Protestant.[12] The Swedes, however, behaved so badly in the rest of the country that Polish pride and resistance stiffened, and Catholic Poles united to drive the invaders from their territory. The small Swedish garrison in Lissa was attacked and routed. The Swedes quickly fled with all the wagons they could commandeer.* The Unity residents of Lissa were left to the mercy of vengeful Poles. Mercy was not to be found.[13]

On 27 April 1656 Lissa was sacked and burned by Polish troops. Comenius may have been in Lissa or on a visitation to exiles in Silesia,[14] but like the townspeople, he lost his home and possessions. Worse, his library and many unpublished manuscripts were burned. Among these was the Czech-Latin dictionary he had been working on for 46 years. Many of his pansophia writings perished also. Gone as well were the official libraries of the Bohemian and Moravian provinces of the Unity. Historian Müller marks 27 April 1656 as the real end of the Bohemian and Moravian branches of the Unity.[15]†

From that point on, the few remaining exiles from the Czech lands scattered. Most, like Comenius, escaped with only the clothes on their backs. A few joined remaining Polish Unity congregations, but most were simply lost to the Unity.

Lissa itself was rebuilt in 1658 and again became the center of the Polish Unity. The handful of congregations maintained the succession of bishops, and the Unity's heritage was not forgotten. Indeed, a Czech sermon was preached in Lissa as late as 1700. In reality, though, these congregations were part of the Polish Reformed Church. Their bishops (Seniors) were consecrated in the line of the old Unity mostly in hope

---

* Three hundred is the number given in contemporary sources.

† That opinion has merit, but it was the Peace of Westphalia that ended the hope for the Unity's return to its homelands.

against hope, and they generally held positions in noble courts elsewhere. The Unity itself was more memory than reality.

As for Comenius, he made his way across Europe and found refuge in August 1656 in Amsterdam through the generosity of Lawrence de Geer, son of his former patron. City officials welcomed him as a distinguished educator and scientist. In 1657 he found the strength to bring out his *Complete Didactic Works* (*Opera didactica omnia*) as the culmination of his educational efforts. In 1659 he published a final Czech hymnal for the Unity, though there were no Czech congregations left. This *Kancionál* was not a reprint of the 1615 edition. It was based on that hymnal, but was essentially a new work containing traditional Unity hymns, Strejc's psalter, some other canticles, and translations of German and Polish hymns as well. In addition, Comenius included several of his own hymns.* In 1660 he arranged for the printing of a Polish Bible. This was intended particularly for use in training ministers for the Polish Unity.[16]

A most important publication, also in 1660, was the *Church Order*, the *Ratio Disciplinæ*, of the Bohemian and Moravian branches of the Unity. Oliver Cromwell, the Puritan lord protector of England, had remarked that the English Church might profit from combining the good parts of its ministry of bishops with a generally Presbyterian organization, and he cited the Unity as a model.[17] The suggestion got nowhere in England, but it inspired Comenius to reprint the *Ratio Disciplinæ*, which has left for us a description of the Unity in its mature development as it wished to be. Comenius added a brief historical introduction and comments of his own as notes to his publication, which is based on the 1632 edition.†

Lawrence de Geer provided funds for these publications, as Comenius continued to labor for the benefit of the Unity's

---

* It was a small book. Comenius said a hymnal should be small enough to be carried easily. Given the number of times he had to flee for his life, that sentiment is very understandable.
† See chapter 18 for a full description of the *Ratio Disciplinæ*.

John Amos Comenius in the twilight of life.

exiles. When the Unity's printing press arrived in Amsterdam in 1661 Comenius used it as a personal press to publish materials for and about the Unity. This press had escaped the fires of Lissa, and had been taken to Brieg by Daniel Strejc (of the George Strejc family) and other exiles seeking shelter in Silesia. They arranged for its shipment from there to Comenius in Amsterdam.[18]

Comenius's publications included the Unity's Czech confession of faith. For this 1662 edition, Comenius remarked that even as a bishop of the Unity he had trouble laying his hands on an older copy of the confession. He used the 1564 version for this, not the more Calvinistic 1607-12 version.[19] He also reprinted the Unity's Czech catechism, as well as a catechism in German and a German hymnal, though this hymnal is more ecumenical and less specifically for the Unity alone.

Comenius took steps to ensure that a revived Unity, whenever that day came, would have bishops. In 1662 he sent written concurrence for the only other remaining bishop, John Bythner, to consecrate Comenius's son-in-law, Peter Figulus Jablonský, as bishop for the Bohemian-Moravian branch of the Unity. At the same time, Nicholas Gertich was consecrated for the Polish branch. But Peter Figulus died in January 1670, and this dying out of the Bohemian-Moravian line of bishops was a bitter pill for the elderly Comenius to swallow. The remaining Bohemian and Moravian members of the Unity now considered the Polish line of bishops as their own as well.[20]

In 1665 Comenius once again turned to unfounded political prophecies with *Light out of the Shadows* (*Lux e tenebris*), an expanded edition of an earlier work. He was now frantic to find aid anywhere for his suffering nation, and he did not care if it was the French under Louis XIV or the Turks who brought relief: anyone who would put down the Hapsburgs was welcome. He even wrote to the Ottoman Sultan, looking for his conversion to Christianity.[21] His appeal went unanswered.

Comenius published *Angel of Peace* (*Angelus pacis*) in 1667. He was grieved that two Protestant nations, England and Holland, were at war with one another. By this time in

European politics, control of sea lanes counted for more than religion. Comenius urged these nations to stop fighting one another and to join together in missionary endeavors to bring the light of Christ to all the world.[22] As for arguments among Christian churches, historian Říčan summarizes Comenius's belief:

> The Word of God is higher than any opinion of the human word, even any church dogma, and human laws, even church laws. The answer to God's Word must not be any other than the faith of an obedient life. The **Reformation**, with which Komenský is in agreement on basic principles, **cannot be considered as completed** if it remains stuck in dogmatic formulas without love towards God, and in intolerant confessional strife without the love of Christian towards Christian. Only nurturing of the three Christian essentials, faith, love, and hope, can build a full, real, and true Christianity.[23]

Seeing that his own earthly end was approaching, Comenius in 1668 wrote *The One Thing Needful* (*Unum Necessarium*). Here he urges people to concentrate on things that truly matter, and let the rest go. In this work some writers have found echoes of what came to be pietism. He says his form of prayer is the Lord's Prayer, and his rule of life the Ten Commandments. As for theology and all the rest, he does not profess to know much. "I have found Christ. . . . Christ is all to me." In reflecting on his own life, Comenius again assumes the role of a pilgrim, and says he can see his heavenly fatherland, "to whose borders my leader, my light, my Christ has led me, all the way."[24]*

To the end, Comenius labored for the betterment of his country and his church. Now, however, "his powers were exhausted."[25] He died on 15 November 1670 in Amsterdam, and was buried in the Walloon church in Naarden. At the time it was customary for residents of expensive larger cities to be

---

* It is in *Unum Necessarium* that Comenius, borrowing a phrase, wrote: "The prime law of Christian concord is threefold: in absolutely necessary things to maintain unity, in less necessary things (which they call adiaphora) liberty, in all things, toward all, love."

buried in smaller, less costly towns nearby.[26] There his earthly
pilgrimage found its quiet end.[*]

Epilogue

Except for the small and shrinking number of congregations in Poland, the Unity had ceased to exist as an
ecclesiastical institution. Was it a failure? In worldly terms,
yes. It had never had many more than 100,000 members in its
homelands, less than three percent of the population. Now
those were gone. In spiritual terms, however, the Unity had for
more than 200 years provided positive assurance and
disciplined guidance for generations, and that is far from a
failure. It had developed a rich theological expression as well,
especially in its hymns. If the Unity had disappeared without a
trace, the good it had done would still be meaningful.

Yet the heritage of the Unity did not vanish. In spite of
concerted efforts to destroy them, copies of its publications
remained to speak to future generations in distant places.
Among those impressed by the Unity's church order and piety
were Philipp Jakob Spener and August Hermann Francke,
leaders of 18-century pietism in Germany.[27]

Miraculously too, when Lissa was reduced to ashes in
1556, the 14 volumes of minutes of the synods and Inner
Council and other official writings of the Unity (the *Akty* and
Dekrety) were not burned. Somehow they ended up in the
vestry of the Church of St. John in Lissa.[†] The discovery of

---

[*] When Czechoslovakia was created after the end of World War I in
1918, the Dutch government, in tribute to Comenius, deeded his
grave plot to the new nation and declared it to be part of Czechoslovakia, so that Comenius, even hundreds of miles away, could
finally rest in his "native soil."

[†] Thirteen of them were discovered in 1836, and were purchased for
the Unity Archives in Herrnhut. The 14th turned up later in the
Bohemian Museum in Prague (de Schweinitz, xii). Joseph Th. Müller
made great use of these materials in writing his history. As noted in

these "Lissa Folios" centuries later gave historians an intimate portrait of the ancient Unity.

In Bohemia and Moravia the Unity's principles were passed down, and in places lay persons kept the old faith alive by holding secret services. These people had to conform outwardly to the Catholic Church, but in some of them the Unity's spirit of independence lingered. A case in point is Samuel Schneider, whose family had kept the Unity's teachings in Suchdol (Zauchtenthal) near Fulnek. In 1710, when Schneider was on his deathbed, the local Catholic priest came to give him the sacrament of the last anointing. Schneider refused, saying that he had already been anointed for eternal life and did not need the priest's oil to get him into heaven. When the priest asked him if he was sure of this, Schneider pointed to the sky and said: "As surely as your honor sees the sun shining in heaven, so assured am I of my salvation."[28] And this was more than 80 years after the Unity congregations were closed in the Czech lands.

Schneider may be an extreme case, but later in the 18th century when religious toleration was at last granted to Lutherans and Reformed in Bohemia and Moravia, 10,000 to 15,000 persons proclaimed themselves Protestants.[29] By no means were all of these direct descendents of the Unity, but in later years as Czech Protestant churches, such as the Evangelical Bohemian Brethren's Church (*Českobratrská církev evangelicská*) came to be formed, most of these claimed a part of the Unity's spiritual heritage.

In these ways the soul of the Unity lived on.

The Unity too would rise again, though in a different form and in a different place, when a former Catholic now Lutheran itinerant carpenter named Christian David met a Lutheran Saxon count of the Holy Roman Empire named Nicholas Ludwig von Zinzendorf. The count allowed David to lead Unity and other Czech Protestant descendants to his estate and

---

our preface, these documents remain the property of the Unity, but are housed in Prague.

settle a village called Herrnhut. The Polish Unity bishop Daniel Ernst Jablonský* consecrated a bishop for them, and from there they spread the Renewed Unity in settlements and missions throughout the world.

But that is a story for another volume.

For now, in the closing years of the 17th century, most members of the Unity could only express their loss through the words of the Czech exiles' hymn:

> Nothing have we taken with us,
> Nothing throughout the whole world —
> But our Bible of Kralice
> And our "Labyrinth of the World."

> Nevzali jsme ssebou
> Nic, po všem věta
> Jen bibli Kralickou
> Labyrint světa.[30†]

> Amen.

---

* Son of Peter Figulus Jablonský and thus grandson of John Amos Comenius.

† A portion of this hymn, but not this verse, appears in the 1995 *Moravian Book of Worship*, 794, as "Blessed Be the Day When I Must Roam."

Notes

1 Rudolf Říčan, *The History of the Unity of Brethren*, trans. C. Daniel Crews (Bethlehem, Pa.: Department of Publications and Communications, Moravian Church, Northern Province, 1992), 363.

2 John Amos Comenius, *The Bequest of the Unity of Brethren*, trans. and ed. Matthew Spinka (Chicago: National Union of Czechoclovak Protestants in America, 1940), 26, 28, 29, 31, 23. See also Říčan, 363-64; Joseph Th. Müller, *Geschichte der Böhmischen Brüder* 3 vols. (Herrnhut: Missionsbuchhandlung, 1922, 1931), 3:347.

3 Říčan, 365.

4 Müller, 3:348-49.

5 Říčan, 366.

6 Müller, 3:348.

7 Říčan, 367.

8 John S. Laurie, *John Amos Comenius, Bishop of the Moravians: His Life and Educational Works* (Syracuse, C. W. Barker, 1892), 30. John Sadler, *John Amos Comenius and the Concept of Universal Education* (New York: Barnes and Noble, 1966), 57. More recent sources for Comenius's educational theory and work include Daniel Murphy, *Comenius: A Critical Reassessment of His Life and Work* (Dublin and Portland, Ore.: Irish Academic Press, 1995), and Jean-Antoine Caravolas, "Comenius (Komenský) and the Theory of Language Teaching," *Acta Comeniana* 10 (1993): 141-62.

9 An edition of this is *Orbis Pictus* (Syracuse: C. W. Bardeen, 1887). (Reissued Detroit: Singing Tree Press, 1968). This is from the Charles Hoole English translation issued in London in 1658.

10 Otakar Odložilík, *Jan Amos Komenský* (Chicago: Czechoslovak National Council of America, 1942), 19, 22.

11 Müller, 3:349-50.

12 Müller, 3:349-50.

13 Říčan, 368. Müller, 3:350.

14 Matthew Spinka, *John Amos Comenius, That Incomparable Moravian* (Chicago: University of Chicago Press, 1943. reissue New York: Russell & Lowell, 1967), 137 (but see 136). Müller, 3:351.

15 Müller, 3:350-51.

16 Říčan, 369. Müller, 3:352-53.

17 Říčan, 370.

18 Müller, 3:351.

19 Říčan, 369.

20 Müller, 3:354. Říčan, 374.

21 Říčan, 372.

22 Říčan, 372.

23 Říčan, 376.

24 John Amos Comenius, *Unum Necessarium: The One Thing Necessary*, tr. Vernon H. Nelson, e-book ed. (www.MoravianArchives.org, 2008). See also Müller, 3:357-59.

25 Řičan, 375.

26 Řičan, 375.

27 Řičan, 382.

28 Ernst W. Cröger, *Geschichte der erneuerten Brüderkirche* (Gnadau: Verlag der Buchhandlung der evangelischen Brüder-Unität, 1852), 10-11.

29 Řičan, 386.

30 This Czech verse, with a more florid English translation, is on the frontispiece of Count Lützow's *The Labyrinth of the World and the Paradise of the Heart* (New York: Arno Press and the New York Times, 1971; reprint of the E. P. Dutton edition, 1901).

APPENDICES

Bishops of the Unitas Fratrum

#	Name / Notes	Consecrated	Died
1.	Matthias of Kunvald (president[1] 1467-1500)	1467	1500, Jan. 22
2.	Tůma Přeloučský (president 1500-1517)	1499	1517,[2] Feb. 23
3.	Elias of Chřenovice	1499	1503, Sept. 5
4.	Luke of Prague (president 1517-1528)	1500, Apr. 19	1528, Dec. 11
5.	Ambrose of Skuteč	1500, Apr. 19	1520
6.	Martin Škoda (president 1528-1532)	1517,[2] Aug. 15	1532
7.	Wenceslas Bílý Removed from office, date unknown.	1529 Sept. 21	1533
8.	Andrew Ciklovský	1529, Sept. 21	1529, Oct. 28
9.	John Roh (president 1532-1547)	1529, Sept. 21	1547, Feb. 11
10.	John Augusta (president 1547-1571)	1532, Apr. 14	1572, Jan. 13
11.	Benedict Bavoryňský	1532, Apr. 14	1535, Aug. 25
12.	Vít Michalec	1532, Apr. 14	1536, Mar. 3
13.	Martin Michalec	1537, Dec. 2	1547, Jan. 23
14.	Mach Sionský	1537, Dec. 2	1551, Apr. 16
15.	John Černý	1553, June 8	1565, Feb. 5
16.	Matthias Červenka	1553, June 8	1569, Dec. 13

As no bishop was available to consecrate Černý and Červenka, by order of Inner Council they were consecrated by council members Matthias Strejc and Paul Paulin.

---

[1] The Unity frequently interchanged the terms "president" and "judge."

[2] De Schweinitz, 228-29, gives 1517 as the year of Tůma's death and Škoda's consecration. Müller, 1:389, n. 273, 390, gives 1516 as the year of Škoda's consecration and 1518 as the year of Tůma's death.

#	Name	Notes	Consecrated	Died
17.	George Izrael (Poland) (president 1571-1588)		1557, Aug. 26	1588, July 15
18.	John Blahoslav		1557, Aug. 26	1571, Nov. 24
19.	Andrew Štefan		1571, Oct. 11	1577, June 21
20.	John Kálef (president 1588)		1571, Oct. 11	1588, Dec. 12
21.	John Lorenc (Poland)		1571, Oct. 11	1587, July 9

It appears that Bishop Augusta did not participate in the consecration of Stefan, Kálef, and Lorenc, and so the "old succession" from Matthias of Kunvald lapsed.

#	Name	Notes	Consecrated	Died
22.	Zachariáš of Litomyšl (president 1588-1590)		1577, Aug. 30	1590, Apr. 4
23.	John Aeneas (president 1590-1594)		1577, Aug. 30	1594, Feb. 5
24.	John Abdias		1587	1588, June 24
25.	Simeon Theophilus Turnovský (Poland) (president 1594-1608)		1587	1608, Mar. 22
26.	John Ephraim		1589, June 5	1600, Oct. 22
27.	Paul Jessen		1589, June 5	1594, May 24
28.	Jacob Narcissus (president 1608-1611)		1594, July 14	1611, Feb. 27
29.	John Němčanský		1594, July 14	1598, Sept. 9
30.	Samuel Sušický		1599, July 6	1599, Aug. 6
31.	Zacharias Ariston		1599, July 6	1606, Feb. 8
32.	John Lanetius (president 1611-1626)		1601, May 9	1626, Nov. 17
33.	Bartholomew Němčanský		1601, May 9	1609, June 1
34.	John Cruciger		1606, Apr. 28	1612
35.	Matthias Rybinski (Poland)		1608	1612, May 20
36.	Martin Gratian Gertich (Poland) (president 1626-1629)		1608	1629, Mar. 7
37.	Matthias Konečný		1609	1622, Feb. 8
38.	Matthias Cyrus		1611	1618, Mar. 14

#	Name	Notes	Consecrated	Died
39.	John Turnowski	(president 1629)	1612	1629
40.	George Erastus	(president 1629-1643)	1612?	1643, May 8

Erastus was made a bishop sometime after the death of Cruciger in 1612 and before the synod in April 1616.

41.	John Cyril		1618	1632, May 30
42.	Daniel Mikołajewski (Poland)		1627, Dec.	1633, Apr. 4
43.	Paul Paliurus (Poland)		1629, July 6	1632, Nov. 27
44.	Laurentius Justinus	(president 1643-1648)	1632, Oct. 6	1648, Apr. 18
45.	Matthias Prokop		1632, Oct. 6	1636, Feb. 16
46.	John Amos Comenius	(president 1648-1670)	1632, Oct. 6	1670, Nov. 15
47.	Paul Fabricius		1632 or 1633	1649, Jan. 3

Fabricius could not attend the 1632 synod, because travel was too dangerous. He was consecrated later.

With the exception of Peter Figulus, the remaining bishops were consecrated for the Unity's Polish branch.

48.	Martin Orminius		1633, Apr. 17	1643, Dec. 31
49.	John Rybinski		1633, Apr. 17	1638, Sept. 13
50.	Martin Gertich		1644, Apr. 15	1657, Dec. 10
51.	John Bythner		1644, Apr. 15	1675, Feb. 2
51a.	Wenceslas Lochar		1649	1656, Jan. 8

Lochar may have been only an assistant bishop (Müller, 1:346, n. 62).

52.	Nicholas Gertich		1662, Nov. 5	1671, May 24
53.	Peter Figulus Jablonský		1662, Nov. 5	1670, Jan. 1
54.	Adam Samuel Hartmann		1673, Oct. 28	1691, May 29
55.	John Zugehör		1676, Aug. 13	1698, Nov. 29
56.	Joachim Jülich		1692, June 26	1703, Nov. 14
57.	Daniel Ernst Jablonski		1699, Mar. 10	1741, May 25
58.	John Jacobides		1699, Mar. 10	1709

#	Name	Notes	Consecrated	Died
59.	Salomon Opitz		1712, July 11	1716
60.	David Cassius		1712, Nov. 4	1734
61.	Samuel William Kasur		1719	1732
	or			
	Paul Cassius		1729, Feb. 26	
62.	Christian Sitkovius		1734	1746

Daniel Ernst Jablonský, with Christian Sitkovius concurring by letter, consecrated David Nitschmann in 1735 and Nicholas Ludwig von Zinzendorf in 1737 in Berlin for the Renewed Unity. Other bishops continued to be consecrated for the remnant of the old Unity in Poland's Reformed Church until the last one there, Samuel David Hanke, died in 1841 without having consecrated a successor. The "Moravian" bishops of Herrnhut consecrated bishops for the Polish "Reformed" Unity in 1844, 1858, and 1883, and the line continued for some years after that.

Rulers of Bohemia

Dates of Reign	Name	Relationships
		Dukes and kings of the Přemyslid line
c. 870-894	Bořivoj I	Baptized with wife Ludmilla c. 880
c. 894-915	Spytihněv I	Son of Bořivoj I
915-921	Vratrislav	Brother of Spytihněv I
921-935 (or d. 929)	Václav I	Duke; "Good King Wenceslas"; patron saint of Czech lands; assassinated by friends of his younger brother
935-972	Boleslav I	Younger brother of Václav I
		Several dukes of the Přemyslid line
1198-1230	Ottocar I	Duke, 1197-1198; first to hold title of king
1230-1253	Wenceslas I	Son of Ottocar I
1253-1278	Ottocar II	Son of Wenceslas I; killed in battle
1278-1305	Wenceslas II	Son of Ottocar II
1305-1306	Wenceslas III	Son of Wenceslas II; assassinated; last of the Přemyslid line
1306-1310	Interregnum	
		Luxembourg line
1310-1346	John of Luxembourg	Son of Holy Roman Emperor Henry VII; son-in-law of Wenceslas II; killed at Crécy
1346-1378	Charles IV	Son of John of Luxembourg; Holy Roman emperor, 1346-1378 (crowned 1355); opened the university in Prague and built the bridge in Prague, both named for him
1378-1419	Wenceslas IV	Son of Charles IV; Holy Roman emperor, 1378-1400 (elected but never crowned); died of apoplexy over First Defenestration of Prague
1419-1437	Sigismund	Brother of Wenceslas IV; Holy Roman emperor, 1410-1437 (crowned in 1433); not accepted as king in Bohemia until 1436; last of the Luxembourg line

Dates of Reign	Name	Relationships
1421-___	Sigismund Korybut	Rival king elected by Bohemia's national assembly
1438-1439	Albrecht II	Son-in-law of Sigismund; Hapsburg line
1444-1458	regency	George Poděbrady, regent
1440-1457	Ladislas	Posthumous son of Albrecht II; crowned in 1453; Hapsburg line; died of disease
1458-1471	George Poděbrady	Non-dynastic
1471-1516	Vladislav II	Jagellonský line; son of king of Poland; nephew of Ladislas; husband of Anna de Foix-Candale
1516-1526	Ludvík	Jagellonský line; son of Vladislav II; died at Battle of Moháč at age 20

Hapsburg line

Dates of Reign	Name	Relationships
1526-1564	Ferdinand I	Brother-in-law of Ludvík; brother of Holy Roman Emperor Charles V; Holy Roman emperor, 1556-1564
1547-1567	regency	Archduke Ferdinand, regent; second son of Ferdinand I; brother of Maximilian; married "commoner" Philippine Welser
1564-1576	Maximilian	First son of Ferdinand I; Holy Roman Emperor Maximilian II, 1564-1576
1576-1611	Rudolf II	Son of Maximilian; Holy Roman emperor, 1576-1612
1611-1619	Matthias	Brother of Rudolf II; Holy Roman emperor, 1612-1619
1619-1637	Ferdinand II	Nephew of Matthias; Holy Roman emperor, 1619-1637
1619-1620	Frederick of the Palatinate	Elected by Bohemia's nation assembly; defeated and deposed at the Battle of White Mountain; the "Winter King"
1627-1657	Ferdinand III	Son of Ferdinand II; Holy Roman emperor, 1637-1657
1657-1705	Leopold I	Brother of Ferdinand III; Holy Roman emperor, 1658-1705

A Chronology of Events

A.D. 33:   Pentecost: Fifty days after Easter the church begins its mission of proclaiming the word of the resurrected Christ. (Page 1.)

c. 50:   The Council of Jerusalem accepts Paul's view that the gospel of Christ is for all peoples, not just those observing Jewish law. (Pages 1-2.)

70:   Jerusalem falls to Roman soldiers and the temple is destroyed for a second time.

200:   An authoritative canon of Scripture is being established, and the language increasingly preferred by the Western Church is Latin. In addition, the Roman Church's practice of observing Easter on a movable Sunday gains acceptance, as does its baptismal creed, soon to be called the Apostles' Creed. (Page 3.)

312:   28 October: Constantine's victory under the "Chi Rho" sign of Christ at the battle of Milvian Bridge assures legitimacy for Christianity in the restored Roman Empire. (Pages 4-5.)

325:   The Council of Nicea, the first "General Council" of the Church after the Council of Jerusalem, declares that the Son was "begotten, not made," and was "of one substance" with the Father. (Page 6.)

405:   Jerome has provided a translation of Old and New Testaments into Latin, which becomes known as the Vulgate, the standard translation of Scripture for the Roman Catholic Church well into the 20th century. (Page 7.)

410:   Rome, the "master of the world," falls to the barbarians. (Pages 7-8.)

451:   The Council of Chalcedon, the fourth General Council of the Church, further defines the Council of Nicea by declaring Christ as fully divine and fully human in one person, the understanding generally accepted by Christianity into the 21st century. (Page 9.)

732:   October: At the battle of Tours, Charles Martel turns back the Islamic tide, which had swept across northern Africa and through Spain into France. (Page 11.)

756:   Pepin, son of Charles Martel, grants the territory around Ravena to the pope, creating the Papal States in Italy and making the Roman Catholic Church a temporal sovereign, which will last until 1870. (Page 11.)

800:   Christmas Day: Charlemagne, son of Pepin, is crowned emperor of the newly established Holy Roman Empire by Pope Leo III. The empire will remain part of European history until 1806. (Pages 11-12.)

863:   Two priests, Cyril and his brother Methodius, enter Moravia to spread the Gospel. They use a simple tool: the language of the people, Czech. (Pages 25-26.)

1054: Eastern (Orthodox) and Western (Catholic) Churches complete their split over doctrine and authority. (Page 11.)

1096: The First Crusade sets out to liberate the Holy Land from Moslem control. Other Crusades follow until they peter out in 1270. Later crusades will also be conducted in Europe against such heretics as Cathars and Hussites.

1170s: Followers of Peter Waldo seek to live a simple live of extreme poverty and piety. These Waldensians are condemned by the Roman Church and are driven into remote regions. (Pages 14-15.)

1179: The Third Lateran Council, the 11th General Council of the Church, declares clerical marriages invalid. It is reiterated by the Council of Trent, 1545-63, and it remains the general rule of the Roman Catholic Church for priests in the 21st century. (Page 10 n.)

1215: The Fourth Lateran Council proclaims transubstantiation, the doctrine that the bread and wine of holy communion are replaced by the true body and blood of Christ at the time of consecration. For fear of spilling the blood of Christ when taking communion, the laity ask the chalice be withheld from them. The priests comply. (Pages 15-16.)

1229: The synod of Toulouse systematizes the Inquisition as a means of rooting out heresy. (Page 17.)

1309: The papal residence is transferred from Rome to Avignon, beginning the 70-year "Babylonian Captivity." (Page 18.)

1346-78: During his 32-year reign of Bohemia, Charles IV elevates Prague to an archbishopric (1344), establishes the University of Prague (1348), and builds the Charles Bridge across the Vltava (Moldau) River. (pages 30, 31.)

1347: The "Black Death" sweeps through Europe. Up to one-third of the population is carried away, leaving survivors to question such a "punishment from God." (Page 18.)

1370s: John Wycliffe challenges Church authority and doctrine. Since all "dominion" derives from God, the church, when not acting "in a state of grace," may be deprived of its property. Rather than transubstantiation, though the body and blood of Christ are present in the elements of holy communion, there is a "remanence" of the bread and wine. (Pages 18, 41.)

1377: Pope Gregory XI returns from Avignon to Rome, ending the 70-year "Babylonian Captivity." (Page 18.)

1378: The College of Cardinals deposes its newly elected Pope Urban VI and elects Clement VII instead. The Church now has two popes. The Great Western Schism has begun. (Page 19.)

1391: Bethlehem Chapel is constructed in Prague for the free preaching of the Gospel in the language of the people. (Page 33.)

1402: March: John Hus is installed at Bethlehem Chapel, and he preaches in the language of the people, Czech. (Page 40.)

1403: May: The University of Prague condemns all 45 articles of John Wycliffe. They had been brought from England by John Hus's friend Jerome. (Pages 40-42.)

1409: A council held at Pisa tries to solve the Great Western Schism by unseating the two popes and electing a third. Result: three popes. (Pages 45, 47.)

1414-18: The Council of Constance, the 16th General Council of the Church, brings an end to the Great Western Schism by deposing the rivals and electing its own pope, Martin V. This time the election gains widespread support. (Pages 53-54, 77.)

1415: The Council of Constance condemns serving the chalice of wine — the blood of Christ — to the laity in holy communion. The Roman Catholic Church will withhold the cup until the 1960s when the Second Vatican Council returns it to the laity. (Page 69.)

1415: 6 July: Condemned by the Council of Constance for holding Wycliffite ideas, John Hus is burned at the stake and his ashes are thrown into the Rhine River. The Council also condemns John Wycliffe, and later his body is disinterred and burned. (Pages 70-72, 65, 259 n.)

1416: 30 May: John Hus's friend, Jerome of Prague, is burned at the stake after the Council of Constance also condemns him of Wycliffite heresies. (Pages 76-77.)

1419: 30 July: the "First Defenestration of Prague" opens the Hussite war of Catholics against followers of Hus who champion serving holy communion "in both kinds," the bread *and* wine — the body *and* blood of Christ. (Pages 79-80.)

1420: The "Four Articles of Prague" are agreed upon by the various Hussite factions: (1) The Word of God is freely preached. (2) Holy communion is ministered in both kinds. (3) Clergy abandon all secular office and live pious lives. (4) All mortal sins are prohibited and punished in each estate. (Page 82.)

1420s: Peter of Chelčický writes against use of any force in religious persuasion and sees a Christian's main duty is a life according to the Law of God. Preferring the simple statements of Scripture itself, Chelčický acknowledges Christ's real presence in the holy communion, but how that presence is constituted remains a mystery of God in Scripture. (Pages 84-85.)

1424: 11 October: After leading his peasant troops to victory over numerous Catholic "crusades" against them, the Hussites' superb blind commander, John Žižka, dies. (Page 86.)

1433: Exhausted by war, Catholics and Hussites agree upon the *Compacta* of Basel, a watered-down version of the Four Articles of Prague. The Hussites gain holy communion in both kinds, but only in Czech lands, not in the Church as a whole. (Pages 87-89.)

1434: 30 May: The radical Taborite and Orebite armies are utterly defeated at Lipany, effectively ending the Hussite war. The only gain has been holy communion in both kinds, which Prague's ancient Týn Church proclaims with a massive chalice mounted atop the peak of its roof. (Page 89-90.)

1452: The last Taborite stronghold, Tábor itself, surrenders, leaving followers of John Hus's reforms asking where can they turn. (Page 92.)

1453: 29 May: Constantinople, the seat of the Eastern (Greek) Orthodox Church, falls to Sultan Mohammed II and Islam. (Page 107.)

1454: Johann Guttenberg produces the first book using movable type — the Bible. Printing, rather than copying by hand, will make the flow of ideas a flood.

1457: 1 March: Gregory, later called "the Patriarch," and his followers meet in Kunvald, a remote community on the Litice estate of Bohemia's regent, George Poděbrady. Their aim is a truly apostolic society grounded in Scripture, the Four Articles of Prague, moral living, and peacefulness, with holy communion "in both kinds." This is traditionally considered the birth of the Brethren and Sisters of the Law of Christ — the Unitas Fratrum, the Unity. (Pages 98-102.)

1461:   Revival of an old law of Bohemia bans heresy, and that includes the Unity. Several members including Gregory the Patriarch suffer imprisonment. (Page 105.)

1464:   A synod meeting in the mountains of Rychnov (Reichenau) draws up a series of "Statutes," the oldest existing expression of the Unity's faith and order. (Pages 106-7.)

1467:   Jacob (Jakub) Chulava of Vyškov is burned at the stake. He is the first member of the Unity to die a martyr's death. (Page 108.)

1467:   26 March: The synod of Lhotka takes steps to establish a ministry independent of the Roman Catholic Church or the conservative Hussite Utraquist Church. Three are selected, Matthias of Kunvald, Tůma Přeloučský, and Elias of Chřenovice, with Matthias accorded first place. It will be Matthias who is consecrated by Michael Bradacius, a Utraquist priest of Roman ordination who has received consecration from the "oldest" Waldensian priest of Bohemia. With these steps the Unity has established its own independent priesthood and is now a church in its own right. (Pages 109-12.)

1478:   The Unity adopts the practice of infant baptism. Adults entering the Unity are still rebaptized. (Pages 121, 127.)

1481:   All members of the Unity are ordered to leave Moravia — the "First Exile of the Brethren." The exiles flee to Moldavia but return to Moravia when persecution eases, thus assuring that future members of the Unity would be called "Moravians" and not "Moldavians." (Page 122.)

1485:   To avoid civil war, Roman Catholics and Utraquists agree to recognize each other's church as legal in Bohemia. Left out of this accord is the Unity. (Page 124.)

1494:   Through the art of ambiguity, a synod at Rychnov allows for progressive membership in the Unity while honoring the simple life championed by Gregory the Patriarch. Two priests break away, claiming the Unity has lost its purity. But the ambiguous decision opens the door for members of the nobility to join and for Luke of Prague to refine and enrich the liturgical life of the Unity. (Pages 139-41.)

1503:   Dr. Henry Institoris, the Dominican monk who wrote *Malleus Maleficarum*, undertakes to convert members of the Unity. He meets little success. In addition, Bohemia's King Vladislav declares, "Heretics are more noxious than Turks," and bans the Unity. But his decree is effective only in the territories under his direct control. (Page 149-50.)

1505:   The Unity publishes its first hymnal, *Hymns for the praise of God* (*Písně chval božských*). It contains many old Latin hymns translated into Czech and others by Luke of Prague and other Unity members. This first "official" Protestant hymnal follows the "first Protestant hymnal," which was printed in Prague in 1501 by private sources. (Pages 147-48, 153.)

1508:   25 July: Bohemia's national assembly enacts the Mandate of St. James, making King Vladislav's 1503 decree the law of the land. For the next hundred years the mandate will outlaw the Unity in Bohemia. Many sympathetic nobles, however, will chose to ignore the mandate on their own estates. (Page 155.)

1511:   The Unity publishes its first confession of faith. It is entitled *Apologia sacrae scripturae*, and Luke of Prague wrote it. Among those to receive a copy is Desiderius Erasmus, but nothing comes from this brief contact in 1520 with the famous Dutch Catholic humanist. (Pages 157, 162-63.)

1517:   31 October: Martin Luther, a young German monk in search of salvation for his soul, nails his "Ninety-Five Theses" on the cathedral door at Wittenberg. The Protestant Reformation has begun in earnest. (Pages 163-64.)

1526:   Following the death of young King Ludvík fighting the Turks at the battle of Moháč, Bohemia's national assembly turns to Ferdinand, a Hapsburg, as king. Hapsburg family rule of Czech lands will not end until World War I of the 20th century. (Pages 172-73.)

1528:   11 December: Luke of Prague, the "theologian of the Unity," dies. (Page 174.)

1530:   The Unity begins sending ministerial students to the Lutherans' university at Wittenberg, not always with satisfactory results. (Page 179.)

          Twelve powerful nobles join the Unity in a public ceremony at Mladá Boleslav. (Page 179.)

1531:   A synod quietly lays aside many of the writings of Luke of Prague and authorizes a new catechism and ritual. In addition it is no longer necessary to observe saints' days, as had been done, but the major festivals of Christ's life and doctrines are sufficient.

1531:   The Unity publishes its first German-language hymnal, *Ein new Gesengbuchlen* (*A New Little Songbook*). Michael Weisse is its editor and gives it Zwinglian tendencies. It will be the oldest hymnal of the Unity to survive into the 21st century. (Page 180-82.)

1534:   Influenced by the thinking of other Protestant churches, the Unity ends its practice of rebaptizing adults entering its membership. (Page 189.)

1535:   11 November: Following the Lutherans' example of presenting their Augsburg Confession to Emperor Charles V in 1530, the Unity presents its Confession of 1535 to Bohemia's King Ferdinand I. Martin Luther writes a preface for the Unity's Confession, which is published in Wittenberg in 1538 in Latin with the title *Confessio Fidei ac Religionis*. All future Unity confessions will be based on this Confession of 1535. (Pages 192-95.)

1541-42: The Unity builds a fine sbor, or church, in Brandýs nad Labem. It will be followed in a few years by a more impressive sbor in Mladá Boleslav. (Pages 200, 242.)

1544:   To guard against moral laxity in the face of Lutheran ideas of "by grace alone," Bishop John Augusta and other leaders of the Unity revive the works of Luke of Prague in a return to the Unity's traditional emphasis on living the faith. (Pages 205-6.)

1546:   The church and much of the town of Litomyšl — with original letters of Martin Luther to the Unity — are destroyed by fire. (Page 208.)

1547-48: Fresh from the Hapsburg-Catholic victory over the German Lutherans in the short-lived Schmalkald War, Ferdinand I takes reprisal against Unity nobles who had not supported him, and he
makes use of the 1508 Mandate of St. James to shutter churches
and imprison Unity members. (Pages 206-9.)

1548:   25 April: Among Unity members arrested is Bishop John Augusta
with his assistant Jacob Bílek. Augusta will spend 16 years, with
occasional torture, in prison. (Pages 210-14.)

1548:   May: In a further decree, King Ferdinand I gives Unity members six
weeks to renounce their faith or leave the country. Some 800 set
out in two groups to cross Poland and settle in Lutheran East
Prussia. The venture fails when the resident Lutherans insist on
conformity to Lutheran practices. By 1574 only a handful of
Unity members remain in East Prussia. (Pages 216-21.)

1551:   While trekking between Czech lands and East Prussia, Unity members make a discovery: the Poles along the way like them.
Especially after George Izrael skips over ice floes at Toruň and is
called the "Apostle of Great Poland." Br. Izrael makes visitations
at first, then in 1553 is assigned as resident minister in Poznań.
The Unity's popularity in Poland is with the nobles, whose ten-
dency is to impose it upon their estates. This differs from the
Czech lands, where joining the Unity is a matter of "personal
choice." A Polish-language hymnal is published in 1544, and the
first "Polish Province" synod is held in 1560. (Pages 222-25, 226,
227, 232.)

1553:   5-8 June: With the Unity's only remaining bishop, John Augusta, still
imprisoned, a synod meeting in Přerov, Moravia, elects two new
bishops, John Černý and Matthias Červenka. (Page 240.)

1555:   The Peace of Augsburg establishes the principle that the religion of a
region is that of its ruler. It has no effect in Bohemia and Moravia
for now, but the precedent has been set. (Page 242.)

1564:   March: After 16 years of prison and torture, Bishop John Augusta is
given his freedom. (Page 251.)

1570:   April: The Unity attends a Reformed synod at Sandomierz, Poland.
The announced purpose is a common Reformed-Lutheran-Unity
confession of faith, but the practical result, the Consensus of
Sandomierz, is a mutual recognition of each other's churches —
a confederation of churches in the same territory, Poland. Such a
unique agreement has Lutheran and Unity ministers holding
joint services in Poland. (Pages 257-58.)

1575:   Seeing the wisdom of a united Utraquist-Lutheran-Unity front against
the Catholic Counter-Reformation, Bohemia's national assembly
draws up a common confession of faith, whereby all who accept
it would not be hindered in their religion. This "Bohemian Confession of 1575" is presented to King Maximilian on 18 May. In
response, Maximilian reaffirms the 1508 Mandate of St. James
banning the Unity. (Pages 265-69.)

1577-80: Rifts within the Lutheran Church lead to the unifying Formula of
Concord in 1577 and the confessional Book of Concord in 1580,
the 50th anniversary of the Augsburg Confession. Many
Lutherans view this as the *only* acceptable statement of Christian
faith. In response, the Unity leans more toward Reformed views

and sends more of its ministerial students to Reformed universities. (Pages 275-79.)

1579-94: Over a 15-year span the Unity produces a Czech translation of the entire Bible from the best available texts of the original languages. This "Brethren's Bible," or Kralice Bible after the town where it is printed, quickly rises to the status among Czech Protestants equal to the King James Version among the English. (Pages 281-84.)

1609: 9 July: King Rudolf II signs the "Letter of Majesty," granting freedom to practice their religion to all who accept the Bohemian Confession of 1575. For the first time in its history, the Unity has full legal recognition in Bohemia. (Pages 296-97.)

1610s: The Lutherans have their Book of Concord. The Reformed have John Calvin's *Institutes of the Christian Religion*. What the Unity needs is a complete work setting forth the Unity's own dogmatic theology. So, say Unity leaders. Several bishops attempt it with no success. One is specifically assigned the task. The result: *The Domestic Preacher*, containing devotionals and practical advice for ordering home life. The Unity: A practical faith for practical people. (Pages 304-5.)

1615: The Unity publishes a beautiful new Czech hymnal. It and its 1618 edition are the last Unity hymnals printed in Czech lands until modern times. (Pages 301-2.)

1618: 23 May: Frustrated by Catholics' disregarding the religious freedoms granted by the 1609 Letter of Majesty, Protestant nobles throw two Catholic royal governors out the windows of Prague's Hradčany castle — the "Second Defenestration of Prague." It begins the Thirty Years War. (Page 333.)

1619: 26 August: Contending that kingship is an elective office, Bohemia's national assembly elects Frederick V of the Palatinate as king of Bohemia, supplanting Holy Roman Emperor Ferdinand II, a Hapsburg. (Page 335.)

1620: 8 November: Holy Roman Emperor Ferdinand II utterly defeats the Bohemian forces at the Battle of White Mountain, regaining his title as king of Bohemia. Hapsburgs will hold the Czech lands for the next 300 years. "King" Frederick of the Palatinate earns the title "Winter King," for he disappears like the melting snow when the heat is on.

1621: 21 June: Czech nobles who participated in the uprising face the consequences. Twenty-seven have been condemned to death including seven members of the Unity. The executions take place in Prague's Old Town square before the ancient Týn Church. They begin at five in the morning and end five hours later. It is the first day of summer, the longest day of the year. In Czech history it is known as the "Day of Blood." (Pages 342-46.)

1620s: One by one, Unity centers fall. Fulnek is occupied in 1621, and a book burning is held in 1623. Mladá Boleslav is occupied in 1623 and a Catholic Mass with communion in only one kind for the people is held in the old city church for the first time in 200 years. The Unity's sbor is made into a Catholic church in 1624 (Pages 349, 351.)

1623: The Catholics remove the large Hussite chalice from the peak of the roof of the Týn Church in Prague. (Page 353.)

1627-28: New constitutions are issued for Bohemia and Moravia banning all churches but Roman Catholic. All others must convert or leave the country. Among Unity members choosing exile is the young priest John Amos Comenius, who on 1 February 1628 leaves his native Moravia never to return. He and other exiles find a new home at Lissa in Poland. (Pages 355-56.)

1632:   Now that it no longer exists in Bohemia and Moravia, the Unity publishes its church constitution, which was first drawn up in 1609 and formally adopted by the synod of 1616. The 1632 publication is in Latin, with the title *Ratio Disciplinæ Ordinisque Ecclesiastici in Unitate Fratrum Bohemorum*. It outlines the life and work of the Unity in its full maturity. (Pages 306-30.)

1641:   Having gained renown in Europe as an educator, the Unity's Bishop John Amos Comenius visits England. This will lead Cotton Mather to write that Comenius was offered the presidency of the fledgling Harvard College in Massachusetts, but "that incomparable *Moravian* became not an *American.*" (Pages 362-63.)

1648:   24 October: The Thirty Years War ends. The Peace of Westphalia sets religious boundaries as they were in 1624 with Bohemia and Moravia under Catholic Hapsburg rule. The Unity is ignored in the negotiations. (Pages 364-66.)

1656:   27 April: In war between Sweden and Poland, the Unity center of Lissa is sacked and burned by Polish troops. Once again John Amos Comenius must seek refuge, this time in Amsterdam, where he labors for his dying Unity. (Page 373-74.)

1670:   15 November: John Amos Comenius, last native Moravian bishop of the Unity, dies. But his son-in-law Daniel Ernst Jablonský, also a bishop of the Unity, in future years will consecrate two bishops of the renewed Unitas Fratrum, David Nitschmann and Nicholas Ludwig von Zinzendorf. (Pages 377, 380, 388.)

1836:   In Lissa, the last center of the ancient Unity, there are discovered 13 large manuscript volumes of church documents. With a later-discovered 14th volume they comprise the "Lissa Folios," which centuries later give historians and readers an intimate portrait of the pioneer church of the Protestant Reformation. (Pages 378-79.)

Bibliography

Agnew, Hugh LeCaine. *The Czechs and the Lands of the Bohemian Crown.* Stanford: Hoover Institution Press of Stanford University, 2004.

Allbeck, Willard Dow. *Studies in the Lutheran Confessions.* 2nd printing, revised. Philadelphia: Fortress Press, 1968.

"Die anglicanische Kirche und der brüderische Bischofsweihe," *Zeitschrift für Brüder Geschichte* 2, no. 1 (1908): 89-101.

Atwood, Craig. *Always Reforming: A History of Christianity since 1300.* Macon, Ga.: Mercer University Press, 2001.

Bainton, Roland. *Here I Stand: A Life of Martin Luther.* Rev. ed. Nashville: Abingdon Press, 1978.

Bartoš, F. M. *The Hussite Revolution 1424-1437.* English ed. prepared by John M. Klassen. New York: Columbia University Press, 1986.

_____. "L'Unité des Frères Tschèques." *Communio Viatorum* 21 (1978): 29-48, 139-55.

_____. "Wenceslas Budovec's Defense of the Brethren and of Freedom of Conscience in 1604." *Church History* 28 (1959): 229-39.

Bekenntnisse der Böhmischen Brüder. Edited by Erich Beyreuter, Gerhard Meyer, and Amedeo Molnár. Series 1, vol. 3, *Nikolaus Ludwig von Zinzendorf: Materialien und Dokumente.* Hildesheim and New York: Georg Olms, 1979.

Bibliographie zur Religions- und Kirchengeschichte der böhmischen Länder. Part 1: *Literatur in westlichen Sprachen und in polischer Sprache: Zeitspanne 1380-1620.* www.collegium-carolinum.de/doku/lit/kig/bibl-kig-3.

Book of Concord: The Confessions of the Evangelical Lutheran Church. Translated and edited by Theodore G. Tappert (in association with Jaroslav Pelikan, Robert H. Fischer, and Arthur Piepkorn). Philadelphia: Fortress Press, 1959.

Brock, Peter. *The Political and Social Doctrines of the Unity of Czech Brethren in the Fifteenth and Early Sixteenth Centuries.* The Hague: Mouton and Co., 1957.

Brükner, Aleksander. "The Polish Reformation in the Sixteenth Century." In *Polish Civilization: Essays and Studies.* Edited by Mieczysław Giergielewicz. New York: New York University Press, 1979.

Caravolas, Jean-Antoine. "Comenius (Komenský) and the Theory of Language Teaching." *Acta Comeniana* 10 (1993): 141-62.

Catholic Encyclopedia. New York: Robert Appleton Co., 1907-14. E-book ed.: www.newadvent.org.

Church Constitution of the Bohemian and Moravian Brethren. Translated by Benjamin Seifferth. London: W. Mallalieu and Co., 1866. Revised and reissued as *Ratio Disciplinæ Ordinisque Ecclesiastici in Unitate Fratrum Bohemorum* (see below).

Comenius, John Amos. *The Bequest of the Unity of Brethren.* Translated and edited by Matthew Spinka. Chicago: National Union of Czechoclovak Protestants in America, 1940.

_____. *Orbis Pictus.* Translated 1658 by Charles Hoole. Syracuse: C. W. Bardeen, 1887. Reissued Detroit: Singing Tree Press, 1968.

_____. *The Labyrinth of the World and the Paradise of the Heart.* Translated by Howard Louthan and Andrea Sterk. New York: Paulist Press, 1998.

_____. *The Labyrinth of the World and the Paradise of the Heart.* Translated and edited by Matthew Spinka. Chicago: National Union of Czechoslovak Protestants in America, 1942. Rev. ed., Ann Arbor: University of Michigan, Department of Slavic Languages and Literatures, 1972.

_____. *Unum Necessarium: The One Thing Necessary.* Translated by Vernon H. Nelson. E-book: www.MoravianArchives.org, 2008.

The Confession of 1535. Translated by C. Daniel Crews. 2nd ed. e-book: www.MoravianArchives.org, 2007.

The Confession of Holy Christian Faith of All Three Estates (Bohemian Confession of 1575). Translated by Andrew Slaby. E-book: www. MoravianArchives.org, 2008.

Coulton, G. G. *Inquisition and Liberty.* Boston: Beacon Press, 1938.

Crews, C. Daniel. "Luke of Prague: Theologian of the Unity." *The Hinge* 13, no. 3 (Autumn 2005): 21-54.

_____. "The Theology of John Hus." Ph.D. diss., University of Manchester, 1975.

_____. "Through the Labyrinth: A Prelude to the Comenius Anniversary of 1992." *Transactions of the Moravian Historical Society* 27 (1992): 27-52.

Cröger, Ernst W. *Geschichte der erneuerten Brüderkirche.* Gnadau: Verlag der Buchhandlung der evangelischen Brüder-Unität, 1852.

David, Zdeněk V. "Utraquists, Lutherans, and the Bohemian Confession of 1575." *Church History* 68 (1999): 294-336.

_____. *Finding the Middle Way: The Utraquists' Liberal Challenge to Rome and Luther.* Washington, D.C.: Woodrow Wilson Center Press, 2003.

Davies, Norman. *God's Playground: A History of Poland.* Vol. 1. New York: Columbia University Press, 1982.

Dekan, Ján. *Moravia Magna: The Great Moravian Empire, Its Art and Times*. Translated by Heather Trebatická. Minneapolis: Control Data Publishing, 1981.

De Vooght, Paul. "Huss a-t-il enseigné la remanentia substantia panis post consecrationem?" *Hussiana*. Louvain: Publications Universitaires de Louvain, 1960.

_____. *L'hérésie de Jean Huss*. 2 vols. (Louvain: Publications Universitaires de Louvain, 1960.

Dillon, Kenneth J. *King and Estates in the Bohemian Lands, 1526-1564*. Brussels: Les Éditions de la Librairie Encyclopédique, 1976.

Dobinson, C. H., ed. *Comenius and Contemporary Education*. Hamburg: UNESCO Institute for Education, 1970.

Evans, M. J., trans. *Wiclif and Hus*. London: Hodder and Stoughton, 1884. Translation of Johann Loserth. *Huss und Wiclif: Zur Genesis der husitischem Lehre*. Prague, 1884.

Ferguson, Thomas. "The Moravian Episcopate and the Episcopal Church." *Anglican and Episcopal History* 71, no. 4 (2002): 498-518.

_____. "A Reply to Colin Podmore." *Anglican and Episcopal History* 72, no. 3 (2003): 385-90.

Foušek, Marianka. "The Perfectionism of the Early Unitas Fratrum." *Church History* 30 (1961): 396-413.

Fudge, Thomas. "Ancellus Dei and Bethlehem Chapel." *Communio Viatorum* 35 (1993): 127-61.

_____. *The Magnificent Ride: The First Reformation in Hussite Bohemia*. Aldershot and Brookfield: Ashgate, 1998.

Gonnet, Jean, and Amedeo Molnár. *Les Vaudois au Moyen Age*. Turin: Claudiana Press, 1974.

González, Justo L. *The Story of Christianity*. 2 vols. San Francisco: HarperSanFrancisco, 1984.

Halama, Jindřich, Jr. "The Crisis of the Union of Czech Brethren in the Years before the Thirty Years War, or On the Usefulness of Persecution." *Communio Viatorum* 44 (2002): 51-68.

_____. "The Doctrinal Development of the Unity of Czech Brethren in the Light of their Confessions." *Communio Viatorum* 44, special issue (2002): 128-44.

Herold, Vilém. "Jan Hus — a Heretic, a Saint, or a Reformer." *Communio Viatorum* 45 (2003): 5-25.

Heymann, Frederick G. "John Rokycana: Church Reformer between Hus and Luther." *Church History* 28 (1959): 240-80.

_____. *John Žižka and the Hussite Revolution* Princeton: Princeton University Press, 1955. Reissue. New York: Russell and Russell, 1969.

Irvin, Dale T., and Scott W. Sunquist. *History of the World Christian Movement*. Maryknoll, N.Y.: Orbis Books, 2001.

Jirásek, Alois. *Old Czech Legends*. Translated by Marie K. Holoček. Boston: Forest Books, 1992.

Kaminsky, Howard. *A History of the Hussite Revolution*. Berkeley: University of California Press, 1967.

Kantor, Marvin. *The Origins of Christianity in Bohemia: Sources and Commentary*. Evanston: Northwestern University Press, 1990.

Kerr, Hugh T., ed. *A Compend of Luther's Theology*. 2nd ed. Philadelphia: Westminster Press, 1966.

_____. *A Compend of the Institutes of the Christian Religion by John Calvin*. 2nd ed. Philadelphia: Westminster Press, 1964.

Klassen, John M. *Warring Maidens, Captive Wives, and Hussite Queens: Women and Men at War and Peace in Fifteenth Century Bohemia*. New York: Columbia University Press, 1999.

Kłoczowski, Jerzy. "Some Remarks on the Social and Religious History of Sixteenth-Century Poland." In *The Polish Renaissance in its European Context*, edited by Samuel Fiszman. Bloomington: Indiana University Press, 1988.

Knowles, David. *The Evolution of Medieval Thought*. London: Longmans, Green, and Co., 1962.

Krmíčková, Helena. "The Janovite Theory and the Renewal of the Lay Chalice." *The Bohemian Reformation and Religious Practice* 3 (2000): 63-68.

Laurie, John S. *John Amos Comenius, Bishop of the Moravians: His Life and Educational Works*. (Syracuse, C. W. Barker, 1892).

Lea, Henry Charles. *A History of the Inquisition of the Middle Ages*. 3 vols. New York: Macmillan Co., 1887. Reprint, 1922.

Lee, Sook Jong. "The Relationship of John Amos Comenius' Theology to His Educational Ideas," Ph.D. diss., Rutgers University, 1987.

Leff, Gordon. *Heresy in the Later Middle Ages: The Relation of Heterodoxy to Dissent c. 1215- c. 1450*. 2 vols. Manchester: Manchester University Press, 1967.

Lissa Folios 5, 6, and 14. Microfilms 31-33, 331-66. Translated by Andrew Slaby, notebooks 11-14. In Moravian Archives, Bethlehem, Pa.

Loomis, Louise R., trans., *The Council of Constance: The Unification of the Church*. Edited by John H. Mundy and Kennerly M. Woody. New York: Columbia University Press, 1961.

Loserth, Johann. *Huss und Wiclif: Zur Genesis der husitischem Lehre*. 2nd ed. Munich: R. Oldenbourg, 1925. First edition (Prague, 1884) translated by M. J. Evans as *Wiclif and Hus*. London: Hodder and Stoughton, 1884.

Lützow, [Francis] Count. *The Hussite Wars*. New York: E. P. Dutton and Co., 1913.

Lützow, [Francis] Count. *The Labyrinth of the World and the Paradise of the Heart.* New York: Arno Press and *The New York Times,* 1971; reprint of the E. P. Dutton edition, 1901.

_____. *The Life and Times of Master John Hus.* London: J. M. Dent and Co., 1909.

Macek, Josef. *The Hussite Movement in Bohemia.* 2nd ed. Prague: Orbis, 1958.

Molnár, Amedeo. *Bratr Lukáš: Bohoslovec Jednoty.* Prague: Husová Fakulta, 1948.

_____. "Bratrský Synod u Rychova." In *Bratrský sborník.* Prague: Komenského evangelické fakulta bohoslovecká, 1967. Translated by Molnár(?) as "The Synod of the Unity of Brethren at Lhotka near Rychnov, 1467-1967," a copy of which is at Moravian Archives, Winston-Salem, N.C.

_____. "The Brethren's Theology." In Rudolf Říčan. *The History of the Unity of Brethren.* Translated by C. Daniel Crews. Bethlehem, Pa.: Department of Publications and Communications, Moravian Church, Northern Province, 1992: 390-420.

_____. "The Czech Confession of 1575." *Communio Viatorum* 16 (1973): 241-47.

_____. "L'Évolution de la théologie Hussite." *Revue d'Histoire et de Philosophie Religieuses* 43 (1963).

_____. "Études et conversion de Luc de Prague." *Communio Viatorum* 3 (1960): 255-57.

_____. "Hus et son appel à Jésus Christ." *Communio Viatorum* 8 (1965): 95-104.

_____. "Luc de Prague devant la crise de l'Unité des années 1490." *Communio Viatorum* 4 (1961): 316-24.

_____. "Pasteur dans le tormente." *Communio Viatorum* 6 (1963): 282-83.

_____. "Recent Literature on Wiclif's Theology." *Communio Viatorum* 8 (1964): 186-92.

Müller, Joseph Th. *Das Bischoftum der Brüder-Unität.* Herrnhut: 1889.

_____. *Geschichte der Böhmischen Brüder* 3 vols. Herrnhut: Missionsbuchhandlung, 1922, 1931.

Murphy, Daniel. *Comenius: A Critical Reassessment of his Life and Work.* Dublin and Portland, Ore.: Irish Academic Press, 1995.

Novotny, V., ed. *M. Jana Husi Korespondence a dokumenty.* Prague: Komise pro vydávání pramenu náboženského hnutí českého, 1920.

Oakley, Francis. *The Western Church in the Later Middle Ages.* Ithaca and London: Cornell University Press, 1979.

Oberman, Heiko. *Luther: Man Between God and the Devil.* Translated by Eileen Walliser-Schwarzbart. New Haven: Yale University Press, 1989.

Odložilík, Otakar. *Jan Amos Komenský*. Chicago: Czechoslovak National Council of America, 1942.

_____. *The Hussite King: Bohemia in European Affairs, 1440-1471*. New Brunswick: Rutgers University Press, 1965.

Oxford Dictionary of the Christian Church. Edited by F. L. Cross and E. A. Livingstone. 2nd ed. with revisions. Oxford: Oxford University Press, 1983.

Palacky, F., ed. *Documenta Mag. Joannis Hus*. Prague: F. Tempsky, 1869.

Pánek, Jaroslav. *Comenius: Teacher of Nations*. Prague: Orbis, 1992.

_____. "Luther's Endorsement of the *Confessio Bohemica*." *Concordia Theological Monthly* 20 (1949): 829-43.

_____. "Luther's Negotiations with the Hussites." *Concordia Theological Monthly* 20 (1949): 496-517.

_____. "The Impact of Martin Luther upon Bohemia." *Central European History* 1 (1968): 17-130.

Pelikan, Jaroslav, and Valerie Hotchkiss, eds. *Creeds and Confessions of Faith in the Christian Tradition*. 3 vols. New Haven: Yale University Press, 2003.

_____. *Credo: Historical and Theological Guide to Creeds and Confessions of Faith in the Christian Tradition*. New Haven: Yale University Press, 2003.

Peschke, Erhard. *Die Theologie der Böhmischen Brüder in ihrer Frühzeit. Vol 1: Das Abendmahl, Untersuchungen*. Stuttgart, 1935.

Podmore, Colin. "The Moravian Episcopate and the Episcopal Church: A Personal Response." *Anglican and Episcopal History* 72, no. 3 (2003): 351-84.

Rashdall, Hastings. *The Universities of Europe in the Middle Ages*. Edited by F. M. Powicke and A. B. Emden. 2 vols. Oxford: Clarendon Press, 1936.

Ratio Disciplinæ Ordinisque Ecclesiastici in Unitate Fratrum Bohemorum. E-book: www.MoravianArchives.org, 2007. Revision and reissue of *Church Constitution of the Bohemian and Moravian Brethren* (see above).

Říčan, Rudolf. *The History of the Unity of Brethren*. Translated by C. Daniel Crews. Bethlehem, Pa.: Department of Publications and Communications, Moravian Church, Northern Province, 1992. First published as *Dějiny Jednoty bratrská*. Prague: Kalich, 1957. Published in abridged edition as *Geschichte der Böhmischen Brüder: Ihr Ursprung und ihre Geschichte*. Berlin: Union Verlag, 1961.

Sadler, John. *John Amos Comenius and the Concept of Universal Education*. New York: Barnes and Noble, 1966.

Sawyer, Edwin. "The Waldensian Influence on the Moravian Church." *Transactions of the Moravian Historical Society* 25 (1988): 47-61.

Sayer, Derek. *The Coasts of Bohemia: a Czech History.* Princeton: Princeton University Press, 1998.

Schaff, David. *John Hus: His Life, Teachings, and Death after Five Hundred Years.* New York: Charles Scribner's Sons, 1915.

Schweinitz, Edmund de. *History of the Church Known as the Unitas Fratrum.* 2nd (reprint) ed. Bethlehem, Pa.: Moravian Publication Concern, 1901.

Smith, John Holland. *The Great Schism, 1378.* New York: Weybright and Talley, 1970.

Smolík, Josef. "Comenius on Justification and Sanctification." *Communio Viatorum* 40 (1998): 137-44.

_____. "Martin Luther and Luke of Prague." *Communio Viatorum* 27 (1984): 243-51.

Spinka, Matthew. *John Amos Comenius, That Incomparable Moravian.* Chicago: University of Chicago Press, 1943; reissue New York: Russell & Lowell, 1967.

_____. *John Hus: A Biography.* Princeton: Princeton University Press, 1968.

_____. *John Hus at the Council of Constance.* New York: Columbia University Press, 1965.

_____. *John Hus' Concept of the Church.* Princeton: Princeton University Press, 1966.

_____. "Peter of Chelčický, the Spiritual Father of the Unitas Fratrum." *Church History* (1943), 271-91.

Spinka, Matthew, trans. and ed., *The Letters of John Hus.* Manchester: Manchester University Press, 1972.

Štrupl, Miloš. "The Confessional Theology of the Unitas Fratrum." *Church History* 33 (1964): 279-93.

_____. "John Blahoslav, Father and Charioteer of the Lord's People in the Unitas Fratrum." In *Czechoslovakia Past and Present.* Vol. 2, edited by M. Rechcigl. The Hague, 1968.

Teich, Mikuláš, ed. *Bohemia in History.* Cambridge: Cambridge University Press, 1998.

Thompson, S. Harrison. *Czechoslovakia in European History.* 2nd. ed. Princeton: Princeton University Press, 1953.

Unitas Fratrum Moravian Church in Pictures. Arranged by Radim Klafus. Prague: 1957.

Unity Statutes of 1464. E-book: www.MoravianArchives.org, 2008.

Wagner, Murray L. "Petr Chelčický: A Free Church Separatist," *Transactions of the Moravian Historical Society* 24 (1986): 63-70.

_____. *Petr Chelčický: A Radical Separatist in Hussite Bohemia.* Scottdale, Pa.: Herald Press, 1983.

Walker, Williston. *A History of the Christian Church.* 3rd ed. revised by Cyril C. Richardson, Wilhelm Pauck, and Robert T. Handy. New York: Charles Scribner's Sons, 1959.

_____. *A History of the Christian Church.* 4th ed. revised by Richard A. Norris, David W. Lotz, and Robert T. Handy. New York: Charles Scribner's Sons, 1985.

Workman, Herbert B. *John Wyclif: A Study of the English Medieval Church.* 2 vols. Oxford: Clarendon Press, 1926. Reprint. Hamden, Conn.: Archon Books, 1966.

Wrastislaw, S. H. *John Hus.* London: Society for Promoting Christian Knowledge, 1882.

Zeman, Jarold Knox. *The Anabaptists and the Czech Moravian Brethren in Moravia, 1526-1628.* The Hague: Mouton, 1969.

Index

(Page numbers in *italics* indicate picture.)

(n. = note.)